ROMANS

NEW INTERNATIONAL BIBLICAL COMMENTARY

ROMANS

JAMES R. EDWARDS

Based on the New International Version

© 1992 Hendrickson Publishers, Inc.
P. O. Box 3473
Peabody, Massachusetts 01961–3473
U.S.A.

Original Hendrickson Publishers edition 1992

First published jointly 1995, in the United States by Hendrickson
Publishers, and in the United Kingdom by the Paternoster Press,
P. O. Box 300, Carlisle, Cumbria CA3 0QS
All rights reserved.

Printed in the United States of America

Library of Congress Cataloging-in-Publication Data

Edwards, James R.
     Romans / James R. Edwards
          p. cm. — (New International biblical commentary: 6)
     Includes bibliographical references and indexes.
     1. Bible. N.T. Romans—Commentaries. I. Bible N.T.
     Romans. English. New International. 1991 II. Title.
     III. Series.
BS2665.3.E39 1991
227'.1077—dc20   91–37200
                                                                             CIP

ISBN 0–943575–34–6

British Library Cataloguing in Publication Data

Edwards, James R.
     Romans. – (New International Biblical Commmentary Series;
     Vol. 6)
     I. Title   II. Series
227.107

ISBN 0–85364–660–0

To Harold Strandness
colleague, mentor, friend

Table of Contents

Foreword
New International Biblical Commentary

Although it does not appear on the standard best-seller lists, the Bible continues to outsell all other books. And in spite of growing secularism in the West, there are no signs that interest in its message is abating. Quite to the contrary, more and more men and women are turning to its pages for insight and guidance in the midst of the ever-increasing complexity of modern life.

This renewed interest in Scripture is found both outside and inside the church. It is found among people in Asia and Africa as well as in Europe and North America; indeed, as one moves outside of the traditionally Christian countries, interest in the Bible seems to quicken. Believers associated with the traditional Catholic and Protestant churches manifest the same eagerness for the Word that is found in the newer evangelical churches and fellowships.

We wish to encourage and, indeed, strengthen this world-wide movement of lay Bible study by offering this new commentary series. Although we hope that pastors and teachers will find these volumes helpful in both understanding and communicating the Word of God, we do not write primarily for them. Our aim is to provide for the benefit of every Bible reader reliable guides to the books of the Bible—representing the best of contemporary scholarship presented in a form that does not require formal theological education to understand.

The conviction of editor and authors alike is that the Bible belongs to the people and not merely to the academy. The message of the Bible is too important to be locked up in erudite and esoteric essays and monographs written only for the eyes of theological specialists. Although exact scholarship has its place in the service of Christ, those who share in the teaching office of the church have a responsibility to make the results of their research accessible to the Christian community at large. Thus, the Bible scholars who join in the presentation of this series write with these broader concerns in view.

A wide range of modern translations is available to the contemporary Bible student. Most of them are very good and much to be preferred—for understanding, if not always for beauty—to the older King James Version (the so-called Authorized Version of the Bible). The Revised Standard Version has become the standard English translation in many seminaries and colleges and represents the best of modern Protestant scholarship. It is also available in a slightly altered "common Bible" edition with the Catholic imprimatur, and a third revised edition is due out shortly. In addition, the New American Bible is a fresh translation that represents the best of post–Vatican II Roman Catholic biblical scholarship and is in a more contemporary idiom than that of the RSV.

The New Jerusalem Bible, based on the work of French Catholic scholars but vividly rendered into English by a team of British translators, is perhaps the most literary of the recent translations, while the New English Bible is a monument to modern British Protestant research. The Good News Bible is probably the most accessible translation for the person who has little exposure to the Christian tradition or who speaks and reads English as a second language. Each of these is, in its own way, excellent and will be consulted with profit by the serious student of Scripture. Perhaps most will wish to have several versions to read, both for variety and for clarity of understanding—though it should be pointed out that no one of them is by any means flawless or to be received as the last word on any given point. Otherwise, there would be no need for a commentary series like this one!

We have chosen to use the New International Version as the basis for this series, not because it is necessarily the best translation available but because it is becoming increasingly used by lay Bible students and pastors. It is the product of an international team of "evangelical" Bible scholars who have sought to translate the Hebrew and Greek documents of the original into "clear and natural English . . . idiomatic [and] . . . contemporary but not dated," suitable for "young and old, highly educated and less well educated, ministers and laymen [*sic*]." As the translators themselves confess in their preface, this version is not perfect. However, it is as good as any of the others mentioned above and more popular than most of them.

Each volume will contain an introductory chapter detailing the background of the book and its author, important themes, and other helpful information. Then, each section of the book will be expounded as a whole, accompanied by a series of notes on items in the text that need further clarification or more detailed explanation. Appended to the end of each volume will be a bibliographical guide for further study.

Our new series is offered with the prayer that it may be an instrument of authentic renewal and advancement in the worldwide Christian community and a means of commending the faith of the people who lived in biblical times and of those who seek to live by the Bible today.

W. WARD GASQUE

Preface

This commentary began with a telephone call from Eileen Triplett in the spring of 1983, asking if I would write the Romans commentary for Community Bible Study. At the time that the call came, Jamestown College, where I am Professor of Religion, was undergoing a series of difficult passages, and the invitation presented in a very unexpected way a *kairos* for me personally, an "opportune moment," as the Greeks would say. The ensuing labor of exegesis on this towering epistle became an immensely edifying and unforgettable experience. The kernel of the first commentary is still present in this one, but after nearly a decade of studying, teaching, and reflecting on Romans, I think the present effort, which is the result of a gracious invitation from Ward Gasque to join the New International Biblical Commentary project, is a much expanded and, I trust, more mature work.

The interpreter who tackles Romans is ushered into a pantheon of commentators, both past and present, which no other book of the Bible can begin to claim. One can literally go through the alphabet and supply the names of Romans' commentators beginning with nearly every letter, from Achtemeier to Zeisler. There are even commentators for the hard letters—*J* for Jülicher, *O* for Origen, *V* for Vaughan. If there remain three or four blank letters, they are richly compensated for by the *B*'s, for instance, where no less than a dozen names wait in line. Of the few blank letters even the *E* is now claimed by the author of this commentary!

If my teaching schedule has not permitted me to read every commentator on Romans, I have nevertheless read many of the great ones. Anyone who snoops in the Additional Notes will quickly learn the names of those who have contributed the most to my understanding of Paul. It is a privilege to acknowledge them; indeed, given my indebtedness to them, it would be an injustice not to mention, in particular, the names of Luther, Calvin, Bengel, Sanday and Headlam, Barth, Dodd, Schlatter, Gaugler, Leenhardt, Nygren, Michel, Barrett, Käsemann, Cranfield, Achtemeier, and Dunn. I hope that the insights and quotations which I include from these and other scholars, and particularly from the Germans who have not been translated into English, will give my readers a taste of the feast of erudition which has been mine to share in writing this commentary. These and other scholars have ever remained authorities in my eyes, but, like the person to whom this book is dedicated, they have become mentors and friends as well. With some of them I have been in frequent agreement, with others less so, but from all of them I have learned much. No one who has yet to enter their company can know how humbling and yet how gratifying it has been both to sit at their feet and to stand on their shoulders.

The list of persons to whom I am indebted in this commentary must also include, though for very different reasons, the names of my parents, whose prayers and support have been a constant encouragement. Even more so must be added the names of my wife, Janie, and our children, Corrie and Mark. The children have become teenagers in the course of the writing of this commentary, and I credit them with a generous spirit not to have accused their father of overdosing on Romans. I should also like to add the name of my student assistant, Priscilla Larson, whose exacting and tireless labors, especially on the index, have helped to make a big project more manageable.

If this preface reads somewhat like the final chapter of Romans—both of which consist largely of names—that cannot be entirely coincidental. I have not intentionally designed it so, although it is perhaps inevitable that it has turned out this way, for any labor in service of the gospel—and I have written this commentary in that service—brings one ineluctably into a rich and diverse company of believers. I can say only that my sense of indebtedness and affection for the names listed herein is no less heartfelt than was Paul's for the names he lists in chapter 16.

I should note two unrelated, though not unimportant, matters in closing. The first concerns the use of Greek. J. B. Phillips said that translating the Greek New Testament was like rewiring an old house with the current on! Another, and equally graphic, metaphor was offered by the great Hellenist A. T. Robertson, who said that the difference between reading the New Testament in Greek and in English is like the difference between eating fresh and frozen strawberries! The reader of this commentary will readily discover my undisguised love for the Greek New Testament. If I have made liberal references to Greek words and phrases, I trust the reader will accept them in the spirit I intend them, as bridges, and not as barriers, to the text.

Second, the greater part of this commentary has been written during the momentous changing of the guard of Eastern Europe during 1989–90. To be engaged with the redeeming and liberating message of Romans at the same time that such historic change has taken place from East Germany to Romania and from there eastward—due in no small measure to the faithful witness of the churches in those countries—has been yet a second *kairos* in my study of Romans!

Jamestown, North Dakota
James R. Edwards

Abbreviations

Complete references can be found at the end of the commentary in "For Further Reading."

'Abot	Tractate of Mishnah and Talmud
Ann.	Tacitus, *Annals*
Ant.	Josephus, *Antiquities of the Jews*, LCL, 6 vols.
2, 3 *Apoc. Bar.*	Syriac, Greek *Apocalypse of Baruch*
arr.	arranged
Confessions	Augustine. *Confessions*. Trans. R. S. Pine-Coffin. Baltimore: Penguin, 1961.
b.	born; prefaced to rabbinic tractate = Babylonian Talmud
BAGD	W. Bauer, W. F. Arndt, F. W. Gingrich, and F. Danker. *A Greek-English Lexicon of the New Testament and Other Early Christian Literature*. 2d ed. Chicago: University of Chicago Press, 1979.
BAR	*Biblical Archaeology Review*
BibRev	*Bible Review*
bk.	book
Bonhoeffer	*The Cost of Discipleship*. Trans. R. H. Fuller. New York: Macmillan, 1963.
ca.	*circa*, about
cf.	compare
ch(s).	chapter(s)
CT	*Christianity Today*
d.	died
Did.	Didache (Apostolic Fathers)
DSS	Dead Sea Scrolls
ed(s).	editor(s)
EDNT	*Exegetical Dictionary of the New Testament*. Ed. H. Balz and G. Schneider. Grand Rapids: Eerdmans, 1990.
e.g.	for example
1, 2, 3 Enoch	Ethiopic, Slavonic, Hebrew Enoch

esp.	especially
Exod. Rab.	Exodus Rabbah, rabbinic midrash
4 Ezra	4 Ezra
Gk.	Greek
HBNT	Handbuch zum Neuen Testament
HBT	*Horizons in Biblical Theology*
HNTC	Harper's New Testament Commentaries
ibid.	ibidem, in the same place
IDB	*Interpreter's Dictionary of the Bible.* Ed. G. Buttrick. 4 vols. Nashville: Abingdon, 1962.
IDBSup	*Interpreter's Dictionary of the Bible Supplementary Volume.* Ed. K. Crim. Nashville: Abingdon, 1976.
ICC	International Critical Commentary
i.e.	that is
Int.	*Interpretation*
JBL	*Journal of Biblical Literature*
Jos. As.	*Joseph and Aseneth*
JRE	*Journal of Religion and Ethics*
Jub.	Jubilees
Lat.	Latin
LCC	Library of Christian Classics
LCL	Loeb Classical Library (Harvard/Heinemann)
Lewis, *Preface*	Lewis, *A Preface to Paradise Lost.* New York: Oxford, 1961.
lit.	literally
LXX	Septuagint, Greek translation of Hebrew OT
1, 2, 3, 4 Macc.	1, 2, 3, 4 Maccabees
Merton	*Life and Holiness,* Garden City: Doubleday, 1963
MeyerK	Meyer, H. A. W., Kritisch-exegetischer Kommentar über das Neue Testament
Metzger	*The New Testament. Its Background, Growth, and Content,* New York: Abingdon, 1965
Metzger, *TCGNT*	B. Metzger, *A Textual Commentary on the Greek New Testament.* New York: UBS, 1971.
Milton, *PL*	*Paradise Lost*
MNTC	Moffatt New Testament Commentary
mod.	modern

NBD	*New Bible Dictionary.* Ed. J. Douglas. Grand Rapids: Eerdmans, 1962.
n.d.	no date
NCBC	New Century Bible Commentary
NIBD	*Nelson's Illustrated Bible Dictionary.* Ed. H. Lockyer, Sr. Thomas Nelson, 1986.
NIV	New International Version of the Bible
NT	New Testament
NTTS	New Testament Tools and Studies
Num. Rab.	Numbers Rabbah, rabbinic midrash
OCD	*Oxford Classical Dictionary.* 2d ed. Oxford, 1978.
OT	Old Testament
OTA	Old Testament Apocrypha
OTP	*Old Testament Pseudepigrapha.* Ed. J. Charlesworth. 2 vols. Garden City: Doubleday, 1983, 1985.
p.	prefaced to rabbinic tractate = Palestinian Talmud
PCB	*Peake's Commentary on the Bible.* Ed. M. Black and H. H. Rowley. Nashville: Thomas Nelson, 1962.
Pesiq. Rab.	Pesiqta Rabbati, rabbinic midrash
1QH	Thanksgiving Hymn, DSS
1QS	Manual of Discipline, DSS
rev.	revised
RSV	Revised Standard Version of the Bible
Sanh.	Tractate of Mishnah and Talmud
sec.	section
Sib. Or.	Sibylline Oracles
Sir.	Sirach, also known as Ecclesiasticus, or the Wisdom of Jesus the Son of Sirach
SNTW	Studies of the New Testament and Its World
Spec. Leg.	Philo, *On the Special Laws*
Str-B	Strack, H. and P. Billerbeck, *Kommentar zum Neuen Testament aus Talmud und Midrasch,* 5 vols. Beck, 1926–56.
TAPS	Transactions of the American Philosophical Society
T. Benj.	Testament of Benjamin, Testaments of the Twelve Patriarchs

TDNT	*Theological Dictionary of the New Testament.* Ed. G. Kittel and G. Friedrich, 10 vols. Grand Rapids: Eerdmans, 1964–74.
T. Gad.	Testament of Gad, Testaments of the Twelve Patriarchs
Tg. Neof.	Targum Neofiti I
Tib.	Suetonius, *Tiberius*
T. Jud.	Testament of Judah, Testaments of the Twelve Patriarchs
T. Levi	Testament of Levi, Testaments of the Twelve Patriarchs
Tob.	Tobit
trans.	translated
War	Josephus, *The Jewish War*, LCL, 2 vols.
WBC	Word Biblical Commentary
Wisd. of Sol.	Wisdom of Solomon
ZNW	*Zeitschrift für die neutestamentliche Wissenschaft*
ZTK	*Zeitschrift für Theologie und Kirche*

Introduction

It would be difficult to overestimate the influence of Romans on Christianity. Of all the books of the Bible, none has left its mark on the theology and language of the Christian faith like this magisterial epistle. "All have sinned and fall short of the glory of God, and are justified freely by his grace through the redemption that came by Christ Jesus" (3:23–24)—here is the heart of the gospel, salvation by grace through the sacrifice of Christ. "For we maintain that a man is justified by faith apart from observing the law" (3:28)—here is the doctrine of reconciliation, accomplished not by human achievement, but by faith alone. "I urge you, in view of God's mercy, to offer your bodies as living sacrifices, holy and pleasing to God—which is your spiritual worship" (12:1, paraphrase)—here is the rock of Christian ethics, the sublime understanding that morality is ultimately a sacrifice of gratitude for God's unmerited favor.

Whenever the church has experienced the winds of reform, the Bible has been the source of renewal, and more often than not, Paul's letter to Rome has played a crucial role. In the fourth century a young professor of rhetoric in Milan, after years of struggling with lust and pride, sensed a divine command to open the Bible and read the first passage he came to. His eyes fell upon the following passage from Romans:

> Not in orgies and drunkenness, not in sexual immorality and debauchery, not in dissension and jealousy. Rather, clothe yourselves with the Lord Jesus Christ, and do not think about how to gratify the desires of the sinful nature (13:13–14).

"In an instant," writes St. Augustine, "the light of confidence flooded into my heart and all the darkness of doubt was dispelled."

More than a millennium later a young German—a monk of the Augustinian order in fact—wrestled in the depths of his soul with his sense of sin and God's wrath. Out of compassion the vicar of the monastery in Erfurt sent him to the newly established University of Wittenberg to lecture on the Epistle to the Romans.

The discovery that "The righteous will live by faith" (Rom. 1:17) propelled the monk, Martin Luther, to launch the greatest reform the church has ever known.

Luther's commentary on Romans played in turn a decisive role in the great Methodist revival in England in the eighteenth century. Although John Wesley had been raised in a devout home and had even traveled as a missionary to Georgia in the New World, the twenty-one-year old Oxford graduate could find within himself no assurance of salvation. "In the evening [of May 24, 1738] I went very unwillingly to a society in Aldersgate Street," writes Wesley, "where one was reading Luther's preface to the *Epistle to the Romans*. About a quarter before nine, while he was describing the change which God works in the heart through faith in Christ, I felt my heart strangely warmed. I felt I did trust in Christ, Christ alone for salvation; and an assurance was given me that He has taken away *my* sins, even *mine*, and saved *me* from the law of sin and death."

In the twentieth century, in the shattering aftermath of World War I, a young pastor in Safenwil, Switzerland, found in Romans an affirmation of the *unique* revelation of God in Jesus Christ, a revelation which surpasses all ideas of religion as an expression of feelings, or trust in human capabilities, reason, or culture. Karl Barth's *Römerbrief* fell, in the words of Karl Adam, "like a bombshell on the playground of the theologians." Describing the role which his commentary played in recalling Protestantism away from its alliance with culture and back to a biblical basis, Barth spoke of himself as a man

> ascending a dark staircase of a church tower and trying to steady himself, reached for the bannister, but got hold of the bell rope instead. To his horror, he had then to listen to what the great bell had sounded over him and not over him alone.[1]

What is said of the word of God in Hebrews 4:12 is true of Romans: it is "alive, powerful, and effective," to paraphrase the Greek. Romans has a proven record in the history of Christianity—and it will again awaken faith whenever people discover in it the transforming message of the gospel.

An Outline of Romans

In the NT Paul's epistles are arranged according to length, the longest coming first and the shortest last. Romans stands at the head of the list because it is the longest, but it is also Paul's most important epistle. It contains the most formal and systematic development of the apostle's understanding of the gospel. The driving concern throughout is *salvation*—that righteousness comes as a free gift of God and is received by faith alone.

The epistle can be divided into two parts, a longer, predominantly doctrinal section in chapters 1–8, and a section of more practical application in chapters 12–16. In between, in chapters 9–11, is an excursus, a special consideration in which Paul struggles to understand why the gospel, which was intended for the Jews, has on the whole been rejected by them.

In the opening chapter Paul scales to the height of his argument that the gospel is the power of salvation for everyone who believes (1:16–17). He sets this theme temporarily aside, however, in order to demonstrate the *need* of all humanity for salvation. In the case of Gentiles the need is apparent, for they have transgressed the law of conscience, and "the wrath of God is being revealed . . . against all the godlessness and wickedness of men" (1:18–32). But Jews, even though they pride themselves on their righteousness, are equally guilty before God for failing to live by the law of Moses (2:1–3:20). Once Paul demonstrates that both Gentiles and Jews are guilty before God, deserving God's wrath and judgment, he then returns to the opening theme of salvation. In a passage loaded with theological ammunition (3:21–31), Paul lets loose a volley of high caliber terminology—righteousness, faith, law, grace, redemption, atonement, sin—to attest that humanity is made right with God not by its supposed merits, but by squarely facing its faults and appealing to God's grace in the saving work of Jesus Christ. Paul substantiates this in chapter 4 by citing the example of Abraham to show that the promise of God is realized by faith, not by law. The consequence of justification by faith is a life of peace and confidence before God (5:1–11). If in chapter 4 Abraham exemplifies the life of faith, in the latter half of chapter 5 Adam exemplifies life held hostage to sin (5:12–21). But Jesus Christ overcomes Adam's sin. To paraphrase John Calvin, Christ's ability to save is greater than Adam's ability to corrupt.

Paul then turns to the problem of sin in the Christian life. Some may assert that since salvation comes by grace rather than works, believers are free to do as they please. Paul vigorously denies this. Grace can never be regarded as a stimulus to sin;

rather, it draws believers into a loyal union with Christ (6:1–14). Christ has freed believers from slavery to sin so that they may become, so to speak, slaves to righteousness (6:15–23). But if justification comes through faith, what is the role of the law? Using an analogy from marriage in 7:1–6, Paul declares that the cross has transferred believers from the principle of law to the person of Christ. Paul concedes that one (although not the only) function of the law is to convict Christians of sin by bringing it to light. The straightedge of the law graphically convinces humanity of its need for a savior (7:7–25). Paul concludes the first part of the epistle by one of the most triumphant chapters in the Bible. Believers are not condemned by God because of the poverty of their moral and spiritual lives, but are raised by the power of the Holy Spirit to face all adversity through the costly and redeeming love of God in Jesus Christ (8:1–39).

In chapters 9–11 Paul devotes a lengthy and ardent excursus to a theme he introduced as early as 1:16–17, i.e., the relationship of Israel to the gospel. Along with many early Christians, Paul was deeply perplexed concerning why the gospel had fared worse among Jews for whom it was intended than among Gentiles for whom it was not. In broad outline, Paul's discussion of the problem falls into three parts. First, he vindicates the faithfulness and justice of God in chapter 9. He then shows in chapter 10 that although Israel knew the gospel, Israel rejected it. Finally, in chapter 11, Paul testifies that the remnant of Jews who had accepted Jesus as Messiah, along with the more numerous Gentiles, were a foreshadowing that "all Israel will be saved" (11:26).

Chapters 12–16 comprise the second major division of the epistle and introduce several practical ramifications of the gospel which Paul developed in the first eight chapters. There can be only one proper response to the liberating love of God in Jesus Christ, and that is to present oneself as a living sacrifice to God (12:1–2). In addition to bestowing life to believers, God's grace bestows gifts for living. The gifts of the Spirit are given not to compete with others, nor to conform to others, but to complement the gifts of others in the church (12:3–8). This is followed by a series of instructions for Christian behavior in society (12:9–21). Chapter 13 broaches the question of Christian attitudes toward government (1–7), neighbors (8–10), and the second coming (11–14). This is followed by the problem of judging others (14:1–12) and cooperation (14:13–15:13). Paul concludes the epistle with his travel plans to Spain (15:14–33) and a surprisingly long list of warm and personal greetings (16:1–27).

Introductory Considerations

Readers of a document are usually curious about the circumstances which brought it into existence. This is no less true of an ancient document like Romans, although it may be more difficult to supply the information. Who wrote it, and what do we know of its author? When was it written and from where? Who were its recipients and what problems did they face which occasioned the letter?

Such questions are called introductory matters. They are not matters of concern only to ministers and scholars. The first minutes of a conversation between two strangers will invariably take up such things. Job applications, résumés, and personnel files are filled with all kinds of information that individuals deem relevant to a proper understanding of themselves. Such information is not a substitute for the individual, nor is it a complete biography, but it offers a background or context in which to become acquainted with someone's character.

The problem with Romans—indeed with all the books of the Bible—is that much of the information we are curious about is missing—or it takes some detective work to uncover it. Our discussion of the historical background of Romans will, therefore, necessitate some pick and shovel work in matters of authorship, place and date, and the purpose of the epistle. In the former matters a few turns of the spade will uncover relatively certain information; but much digging on the purpose and occasion of Romans has yielded less certain results, and our conclusions there remain more tentative.

Authorship

The author of Romans is named in the first word of the epistle, "Paul." Although it has been fashionable in the last century and a half to challenge the traditional authorship of many books of the Bible, there has never been any serious doubt about the authorship of this epistle. Hence, the Pauline authenticity of Romans remains a matter of virtual certainty. There are, to be sure, only two autobiographical sections of the letter (1:8–15;

15:22–33), but that is understandable in light of the fact that Romans is Paul's most reasoned, consistent, and systematic presentation of the gospel. The historical circumstances behind Romans accord well with what we know of Paul from Acts, and in style and theology Romans is unassailably Pauline. Justification, grace, faith and law, Jew and Gentile, sin as slavery, the Holy Spirit, the church as the body of Christ, the sovereignty of God, the return of Christ—these are vintage Paul, and all are present in Romans.

Place and Date of Composition

Where and when the epistle was written are also reasonably certain. The circumstances of writing in Romans 15:22–32 correspond favorably with what Luke reports in Acts 19:21–20:6. Paul has completed his third missionary journey to Asia Minor and Greece (ca. A.D. 54–58, see Acts 18:23–21:15). At the end of his three-year stay in Ephesus he made a brief trip overland to Corinth, where he stayed three months (Acts 20:2–3). This must have been in late winter or spring since Paul left Corinth after Passover, hoping to make it to Jerusalem for Pentecost (late May–early June). Paul planned to go to Jerusalem to deliver a collection for the needy Jewish Christians there, after which he hoped to travel to Rome, and from there to Spain. Exactly what year it was we cannot say. We know that Paul was in Corinth on the second missionary journey when Gallio was proconsul of Achaia from the spring of A.D. 51 to the spring of 52 (Acts 18:12–17). Our best reckoning indicates Paul was again in Corinth some six years later. Thus, with Rome on his mind, it appears that Paul wrote Romans from Corinth in the spring of perhaps A.D. 57 in preparation for his anticipated visit to the capital.[2]

Most scholars agree more or less with these data, and there is no serious evidence to challenge them. But when we venture beyond the beaten path of the above conclusions and inquire into the beginnings of Christianity in Rome, or the nature and problems of the church there, or the reasons why Paul wrote this particular letter to the Roman Christians, the way is much less clear. The remaining discussion, therefore, requires that we think of ourselves more as explorers with crude maps than as tourists to familiar sites.

Historical Situation

First, a word about Rome in Paul's day. Unlike modern empires which are named after nations, the Roman Empire took its name from a single city. Rome was the capital of an empire equal in geographical size to the United States of America, and the population of the empire was about the same as that of America in 1880—some 50 million people. Rome's dimensions were as majestic as its imperial status. Its streets were paved, there were bridges over the Tiber River, temples and market-places abounded, and there were at least some sections where population densities forced high rise apartments up several floors. Both Juvenal and Martial, complaining of narrow stairways leading to fourth floor apartments and streets choked with noise and commotion, offer a glimpse into the seamier side of inner-city Rome.[3] Rome's water supply was sluiced along aqueducts from the Sabine hills nearly fifty miles away. The city could boast of a municipal sewer system the equal of any modern Western metropolis. The Roman Forum, suggestive even today of Rome's impressive grandeur, was only one of four different Forums in the history of the city. Dio Cassius reports that at the end of the first century the Emperor Trajan rebuilt and enlarged the imperial race course, the Circus Maximus, to a seating capacity of some 100,000 people—an arena that would rival the Rose Bowl today.[4]

Rome's visitors were more eloquent of its grandeur, however, than factual about its population. Augustus and Claudius took the last censuses of Roman *citizens* (as distinct from the total number of people under Roman occupation) and found between four and six million people.[5] There are no exact figures on the population of the city of Rome itself, and estimates vary depending on the criteria used to determine them. Writing about A.D. 75, Pliny the Elder gave as the circumference of Rome the exact distance of the Aurelian walls some two centuries later, an area just shy of 1000 hectares of living space.[6] If one multiplies this figure by 200 persons per hectare—a relatively high figure by medieval standards—Rome's *urban population (not including suburbs)* would total some 200,000 persons. It is likely, however, that Rome's population exceeded that. In the *Monumentum Ancyranum* Augustus states that he paid a gratuity to 320,000 of the urban *plebs* in 5 B.C., and this figure seems to be corroborated by estimates derived from

Rome's grain supplies and bakery capacities.[7] We do not know, of course, the number and sizes of Rome's suburbs, but the common estimate that Rome's population in the first century A.D. was around a million seems somewhat inflated.[8] The above data (if they are at all accurate) suggest a population of perhaps a half-million people.[9]

The Beginnings of Christianity in Rome. Romans was written to a church which Paul had neither founded nor visited. In introducing the epistle, Paul writes, "I pray that now at last by God's will the way may be opened for me to come to you" (1:10). Who did found the church we do not know. Some four centuries after Paul, Ambrosiaster wrote in his commentary on Romans, "The Romans had embraced the faith of Christ, albeit according to the Jewish rite, although they saw no sign of mighty works nor any of the apostles."[10] Traditionally, Peter is thought to have brought Christianity to Rome, but it is reasonably certain that he did not reach Rome before the 50s at the earliest, and the church had already existed there some time before that. It is highly likely that Christianity grew out of the Jewish synagogues in Rome. Acts 2:10–11 records that there were at Pentecost in Jerusalem "visitors from Rome (both Jews and converts to Judaism)." It is not improbable that such converts, returning to Rome, brought the gospel to the imperial city shortly after the resurrection of Jesus sometime in the early 30s.

There are indications of an impressive Jewish community in Rome as early as 62 B.C. when Pompey, after subjugating Judea under the Roman eagle, brought Jewish captives back to the capital. These Jews were subsequently freed and increased in number. Already in 59 B.C. Cicero mentions a large crowd of Jews at the trial of Flaccus. "You know," said Cicero to the jury, "how numerous they are and how clannish, and how they can make their influence felt."[11] In 4 B.C. a delegation of 50 Jews traveled from Judea to Rome to plead for the recall of the tyrant Archelaus. Josephus tells us that the Jewish deputies "were joined by more than 8,000 of the Jews in Rome."[12] The numerical growth of Jews in Rome was evidently matched by proselytizing efforts. When Fulvia, a woman of high rank, was converted to Judaism in A.D. 19, Tiberius, the Roman Emperor, "ordered the whole Jewish community to leave Rome," according to Josephus. The Romans then conscripted some 4,000 Jewish youth for military service.[13] How long Tiberius's expulsion lasted we cannot say, but the Jews returned in greater numbers, thus provoking a second expulsion under Claudius some 30 years later—an event which doubtlessly bears on our epistle.

Before turning to the edict of Claudius, we may say three things of the Jewish community in ancient Rome: it was large, it was diverse, and it was influential. We must think of the Jewish minority divided among many synagogues in Rome, some guarding their Jewishness zealously, others adopting Roman names for their children and adapting in varying degrees to Roman norms. Some ten to fifteen different synagogues have been identified from the walls of the catacombs, and there were doubtlessly many more. Commentators estimate that perhaps as many as 50,000 Jews lived in Rome in Paul's day, and from them we may rightly expect Christianity to have been introduced to the capital.[14]

The Edict of Claudius. Claudius, who ruled Rome from A.D. 41 to 54, found the *Pax Romana* threatened by Jewish disturbances from Rome to distant Egypt. In his first year of office he imposed a restraining order on the Jews, "forbidding them to meet together in accordance with their ancestral way of life."[15] Eight years later, in A.D. 49, he cracked down on foreigners in general. The Roman historian Suetonius says, "Since the Jews constantly made disturbances at the instigation of Chrestus, [Claudius] expelled them from Rome."[16] It is virtually certain that this is the same event referred to in Acts 18:2 when Paul teamed up in Corinth with Aquila "who had recently come from Italy with his wife Priscilla, because Claudius had ordered all the Jews to leave Rome." Moreover, it is likely that Aquila and Priscilla had brought their Christianity with them from Rome, since in reviewing his converts and baptisms in Corinth Paul nowhere mentions their names (1 Cor. 1:14ff.; 16:15).

Although "Chrestus" was a common enough slave name, we may assume that Suetonius, writing 70 years after the event and himself a less reputable historian than his contemporary Tacitus in matters pertaining to Christianity, confused "Chrestus" for "Christus," the Latin name for "Christ." Behind the reference to "persistent rioting of the Jews in Rome" we have a momentous social history which likely bears on the writing of Romans. A plausible reconstruction of the events before and after the edict of Claudius is offered in the following.

In the first three decades or so of the Christian movement evangelism followed a definite pattern: Christian missionaries and evangelists began in the Jewish synagogues and later branched

out (or were forced out because of Jewish antagonism) to the
Gentiles. This was the natural course for a movement which regarded itself, as did the earliest church, as a form of Judaism. The
Book of Acts records this pattern beginning in Jerusalem (Acts
3–10), continuing in the Pauline missionary expansion (Acts 13–
14; 17–18), and ending in Rome (Acts 28:17–31). Whoever the first
Christian missionaries to Rome were, they undoubtedly began
their witness in Jewish synagogues. But Rome's Jewish scene was
larger and more diverse than the smaller, more homogeneous
situations which Paul, for instance, had encountered in Philippi,
Thessalonica, or Galatia. Some of Rome's synagogues may have
incorporated the Christian message readily, but others—the majority, we suspect—surely followed the pattern we see in Acts, in
which the newly proclaimed gospel first caused a period of strife,
after which it was rejected. Into an already diverse and perhaps
divided Jewish minority in Rome the introduction of Christianity
injected another destabilizing force, resulting in disturbances and
rioting among Roman Jews. Claudius responded by expelling the
Jews from Rome, Aquila and Priscilla among them.

The expulsion of Jews from Rome dramatically changed
the constituency of the fledgling Christian communities there. A
movement that from its inception had identified more or less
with Judaism was now confronted with a predominantly, if not
exclusively, Gentile Christian membership. Freed from the influence of scrupulous Jewish Christians, particularly in dietary
matters, the Gentile Christian communities would have grown
numerically stronger. But more importantly, they more than likely
developed a distinctly antinomian consciousness during the
absence of their Jewish Christian counterparts. How long this
situation lasted we cannot say, but the five years between the
proclamation of the edict in A.D. 49 and Claudius' death in A.D. 54
is a reasonable guess.

This changed when Claudius died and the edict lapsed. It
is not difficult to imagine the difficulties which must have ensued
when Jewish Christians returning from exile tried to reestablish
themselves in Christian communities that had since matured in
Gentile character, especially regarding laxness toward the Torah.
Paul's greetings at the end of Romans seem directed to several
different (house) churches (see 16:5, 14, 15), the existence of
which may be evidence of tensions between Jewish and Gentile
Christians. If our dating of Romans is correct—and the date can-

not have been more than a year or two away from A.D. 57—then Romans was written only a few years after the onset of this social and religious maelstrom.[17]

The Debate Over the Purpose of Romans

In the wake of Luther's and Calvin's commentaries in the post-Reformation period, Romans was regarded, in the words of Luther's protégé, Philip Melanchthon, as "a compendium of the Christian religion." Whatever social or historical concerns lay behind the epistle were unknown or unimportant. In Melanchthon's judgment, Romans was a crystalline formulation of the gospel, universal in scope and timeless in extent. This remained the dominant understanding of Romans until the dawn of the historical-critical method under Ferdinand Christian Baur in the mid-nineteenth century. Many commentators, however, still belong to this school of interpretation.[18]

More recently there has been a growing interest among NT scholars to relate Romans either to the life of Paul or to circumstances at Rome. A surprising number of propositions has been advanced, many of them speculative and experimental. The various views can be assigned to three general categories. First, some propose that Romans is a summary or recapitulation of Paul's theology, which was then employed for various purposes. This may be termed the theological purpose of Romans. Another view is that Romans was directed to specific problems at Rome, especially the friction between Jews and Gentiles, and that its intent, like that of other Pauline letters, was to address the gospel to pressing concerns of a real congregation, albeit one Paul had not visited. This may be called the pastoral interpretation of Romans. A third view is to regard Romans primarily as an advance emissary to Rome in preparation for Paul's impending visit there on his way to Spain. We may call this the missionary purpose of Romans.[19] Each of these positions deserves further discussion.

The Theological Purpose. The main contention of the theological theory is that "the topic of the letter is . . . [the] gospel, not the person of the apostle," to quote Helmut Koester.[20] This is corroborated by the fact that only at the beginning (1:8–15) and end (15:22–33) does Paul break into the letter in the first person. Otherwise Romans can be read as a sustained theological treatise, developing the themes of sin, justification, faith and sanctification, and the practical application of these to everyday life. In this respect the theological interpretation of Romans agrees with the traditional view of Melanchthon, that Romans is "a compendium of the Christian religion."

Modern scholars have attempted to associate this theory with Paul's missionary career. Noting that a few manuscripts omit "Rome" in 1:7 and 1:15, and that some ancient versions of Romans circulated without the final chapter (16), T. W. Manson argued that Romans was actually a manifesto of Paul's deepest convictions in search of the widest publicity. Hence, Paul sent it not only to Rome, but to Syria and Palestine, and above all to Ephesus, for which chapter 16 served as a cover letter.[21]

In a similar vein, Jacob Jervell argues that we know virtually nothing about problems at Rome (and Paul knew little more). In his opinion Romans is rather a summary of Paul's theology, written as a defense for his upcoming appearance in Jerusalem. Aware that he would be opposed in Jerusalem by legalistic Jewish Christians on the one hand and by libertarian Gentile Christians on the other, Paul wrote Romans in hope that it would enable believers in Jerusalem to accept him as well as his financial collection for the mother church (see 15:25–28).[22]

Another exponent of the theological purpose is Günther Bornkamm. Like Manson, Jervell, and others, Bornkamm concedes that we know precious little about conditions in Rome which might have occasioned the epistle, but unlike them he refrains from positing a non-Roman destination for it. He argues that Romans owes its existence not to a church still *before* Paul, but to the congregations now *behind* him. That is, Romans is a summary or restatement of Paul's theology which had been hammered out on the anvil of the Gentile mission—a last will or final testament, to use Bornkamm's words.[23]

The strength of the theological position is that it recognizes the thoroughgoing theological nature of Romans. This position, however, and others like it, implies that Paul is writing less to Rome than to himself.[24] Correctly admitting that we know *little* for certain about the Roman situation, the above position concludes that we know *nothing* about it and neglects what certain information Paul does provide (e.g., 1:8–15; 15:22–33), as well as additional clues behind Paul's arguments. Moreover, arguments that Romans was actually written for another destination raise questions about Paul's integrity, suggesting that he wrote with ulterior motives and at some variance from his stated purpose.

The Pastoral Purpose. Until recently Romans scholarship has been characterized by the assumption that little, if anything, can be known of the conditions in Rome which occasioned Paul's letter. Consequently, unlike Paul's other letters which were addressed to specific situations, Romans has been regarded as the *magnum opus* of Paul's theological expression. In other words, it was believed to owe its existence to circumstances in Paul's experience, not to conditions at Rome.

We have already considered the likelihood that the edict of Claudius may have been evoked by the friction between Jews and Gentiles, which was caused, in part at least, by the preaching of Christianity in Roman synagogues. Moreover, although it is true that Paul had not visited Rome, he can hardly have been ignorant of affairs there. It was his day, after all, that coined the expression, "all roads lead to Rome." Aquila and Priscilla had traveled those roads after their expulsion from Rome, and they would have informed Paul of the latest events as the threesome practiced tent-making together. If, as we argue in our commentary on Romans 16, the final chapter originally belonged to the epistle, it would be odd for Paul to know some thirty individuals in Rome by name and yet know nothing of their circumstances. Paul expressly acknowledges that "your faith is being reported all over the world" (1:8) and congratulates the Romans on their goodness, knowledge, and instruction (15:14). These are rather hollow eulogies if Paul did not know what was happening in Rome.

Moreover, Romans is not devoid of clues regarding its provenance. The sustained discussion concerning Jews and Gentiles (chs. 1–4; 7; 9–11) makes sense, of course, when read in light of Paul's missionary experiences described in Acts. But it makes better sense when read against the background of friction between Jewish and Gentile Christians in Rome after the edict of Claudius. The discussion of the "strong" and "weak" in chapters 14 and 15 is surely a tactful and charitable way of addressing the judgments traded between libertarian Gentile believers and more legalistic Jewish believers. The reference to paying taxes in 13:6–7 may be more than a striking coincidence in light of Tacitus' note about complaints in Rome over payment of taxes (ca. A.D. 58).[25] Moreover, Paul's greetings in chapter 16 include at least three different house-churches.

In short, Paul was far from ignorant about events in Rome.[26]
Like other Pauline letters, Romans was drafted with an awareness
of certain basic needs of the Christian congregations addressed.
It thus owes at least some of its form and content to conditions in
Rome and is scarcely the pure summary of Paul's theology, divorced from the pains and joys of real congregations, that scholars once thought it was.

Nevertheless, a degree of caution is in order. Our hypoth-
esis of conditions between Gentile Christians and Jewish Christians, plausible as it is from the sources at our disposal, remains
but a tentative reconstruction. Supposing we are right about events
in general, we have no way of knowing if, or to what degree, such
events affected the particular congregations to which Paul wrote.
The pastoral motive surely influenced the writing of Romans to
some extent, but it was scarcely the only motive for the epistle.
Paul's own testimony about the purpose of Romans makes this
apparent.

The Missionary Purpose. Twice in Romans Paul declares his
intention in writing. "I long to see you so that I may impart to you
some spiritual gift to make you strong" (1:11), he says at the
outset. He expands this statement at the end of Romans where he
labors to bring in "the full number of the Gentiles" (11:25–26)
while the Jews delay in embracing the gospel. This ministry he
has conducted "from Jerusalem all the way around to Illyricum"
(15:19)—roughly from Israel to the Balkans today. But sensing
that there "is no more place for me to work in these regions"
(15:23), Paul set his sights on Spain. Rome, of course, was the
logical stop on the way to Spain. "For many years" (1:13; 15:22–
23) Paul had desired to visit the capital and establish there a base
camp for his proposed westward expansion (15:24).

In the meantime Paul desired the prayers and support of
the Roman Christians as he delivered the collection to Jerusalem.
The collection weighed heavily on his mind (15:25–29; also 1 Cor.
16:1–4; 2 Cor. 8:1; 9:2, 12). It was far more than a charitable contribution for the financially depressed Jerusalem church. The gift
of the Gentile churches was a symbolic test of the unity of the
church, for the acceptance of the collection in Jerusalem would
signal an endorsement of Paul's missionary outreach and show
solidarity with the Gentile churches. But, of course, there was no
assurance of this. Paul's language graphically betrays the urgency
of the situation: "I urge you . . . to join me in my struggle by

praying . . . that I may be rescued from the unbelievers in Judea
. . . so that by God's will I may come to you" (15:30–32, NIV).[27]

The Purpose of Romans

It should be obvious from the foregoing that Romans owes
its existence to more than one impulse of the apostle. The theological, pastoral, and missionary hypotheses each claim support,
though none claims total support. In what follows let us attempt
a plausible reconstruction of our own.

According to Paul's own testimony, Romans is anchored in
his missionary consciousness. This is consonant with the picture
of Paul from Acts as well as from his epistles. Having concluded
a phase of missionary work in what is now Turkey and Greece,
Paul planned to visit Jerusalem and deliver the collection to the
impoverished Jewish Christians, after which he would turn west
to Rome, and from there to Spain. His plan was buttressed by two
resolves. First, as his "literary ambassador" Romans would provide an account of himself before his appearance in the capital
(1:10; 15:23–24).[28] Second, conscious of the sensitive task of deliv-
ering the collection to Jerusalem, Paul would enlist the Romans
in prayer support for his visit to the Holy City (15:30–32). Both
resolves were designed to involve the Romans in Paul's ministry.

These are Paul's stated purposes, and we take them seriously. There is at least one other rationale, however, about which
Paul, for reasons which will become obvious, was advisably reti-
cent. When he hopes to "impart some spiritual gift to make you
strong" (1:11), or to "have a harvest among you" (1:13), Paul hints
at a deeper impulse in the letter. The theme of Jews and Gentiles
ebbs and flows throughout the epistle. It is clear that Romans is
addressed to predominantly Gentile congregations (1:5; 13–15;
11:13), though one in which a significant Jewish element was
present (1:16–17; 9:11; 14:15). If our reconstruction of the background of the epistle is anywhere near accurate, then Romans is
addressed to the problems which inevitably resulted when Jewish Christians began returning to Rome following the edict of
Claudius. We can imagine their trials of readjusting to churches
which had become increasingly Gentile in their absence. Would
Gentile believers who had established their supremacy during
the Jewish absence, and for whom the law was now largely irrelevant, continue to find a place within their fellowship for a Jewish

Christian minority which still embraced the law? Paul cannot
have been unaware of such concerns.

Paul was a veteran of two decades of Gentile-Jewish tug-
of-war. If there was a champion in early Christianity to address
the situation in Rome it was he. Naturally he would (and did)
draw upon doctrines which had proved their mettle in previous
combat. In no other Pauline letter do we hear so many echoes
from earlier letters. From Galatia, where Paul had labored in a
situation similar to Rome, he reintroduces justification by faith
(Gal. 3–4; Rom. 1–4; 9:30–10:4), Abraham as the father of faith and
nations (Gal. 3; Rom. 4), and the sending of the Son as the redeemer for sin (Gal. 4:4ff.; Rom. 8). From Corinth he repeats his
analogy of the first and last Adam (1 Cor. 15:22ff.; Rom. 5:12ff.),
the languishing of natural humanity under law, sin, and death
(1 Cor. 15:56f.; Rom. 7:7–25), the church as the body of Christ
(1 Cor. 12; Rom. 12:4ff.), and the reconciliation of dissensions
between Jews and Gentiles over ethnic customs (1 Cor. 8–10;
Rom. 14–15). These and other ideas from his arsenal of experience
proved invaluable at Rome.

There were, of course, strategic interests at Rome about
which Paul had been less concerned when he wrote to Galatia
and Corinth. Those churches he had founded, and his jealous
labors on their behalf allowed him, when necessary, to confront
them head-on when his gospel was jeopardized. Paul was a man
of profound territorial instincts, but such instincts had to be
tempered when he wrote to Rome, for he had not founded the
church there, and he was ever mindful not to build on someone
else's foundation (15:20). In Romans Paul must assume a lower
profile and avoid airs of presumption. His task was to present an
answer he was confident of to a situation he was familiar with,
but without the benefit of a firsthand relationship. Consequently,
he relies on the content of the gospel rather than on the personal
influence he otherwise might have enjoyed.

To conclude our discussion: the theological, pastoral, and
missionary motifs all played a role in the purpose of Romans. We
may be confident of this quite apart from whatever merits our
historical reconstruction possesses, for the three purposes were,
always and everywhere, inextricably a part of the man Paul. Paul
was an impassioned mind. He believed that the gospel of Jesus
Christ held the ultimate solution to the problems of the world
because it had provided the solution to the problems in his own

life. The gospel was for him an objective and compelling truth. The knowledge of Christ dwarfed everything else in his life and propelled him to hazard all for regions that had not heard the name of Christ. Paul was, however, more than an impassioned mind with a profound missionary call. He was possessed by a pastor's heart. A man with an immense capacity for human relationships, he labored, contended, and wept for his flocks scattered around the shores of the Mediterranean world, indefatigably confident that the gospel would transform them as it had him.

Paul and the Law

One point at which the Pauline landscape has seen upheaval in the past decade is in Paul's relationship to Judaism and the law. Protestant interpreters especially have tended to place Paul's thesis of justification by faith in antithesis to justification by works. According to this understanding, justification by faith is a gift of grace available to Jews and Gentiles, in contrast to a mistaken pursuit of justification by merit and works of law in Judaism. Faith and works are here pitted against each other as two competing means of salvation, the right one Christian, the wrong one Jewish.

In the post-Bultmannian era (beginning roughly in the mid 1970s), interest shifted away from the Hellenistic roots of Christianity to a reinvestigation of its Judaic background. Several major studies have reopened the question of Paul's relationship to Judaism and the law.[29] Two refrains have emerged from the ensuing conversation. One is that Pauline interpreters, particularly in their reading of Paul from the perspective of Luther's opposition to indulgences and works in medieval Catholicism, have wrongly characterized ancient Judaism as a religion of works-righteousness, merit, and legalism. Some scholars would say that Paul himself was guilty of this misunderstanding, and that he misjudged the place of law in Judaism. Sanders posits a corrective in the term "covenantal nomism," by which he argues that the fundamental premise of Judaism was (and is) not law but covenant.

This leads to a second point on which many recent commentators agree, namely, that covenant precedes Torah, rather than the reverse. Sanders distinguishes between "getting in" and "staying in," i.e., Jews enter the covenant by grace (e.g., Deut. 7:6–11), but they maintain their position within it by observance

of the law. It might be likened to receiving a piece of property as
a gift (= covenant of grace), but then being obliged to pay the
property taxes on it for oneself (= Torah observance).

What is the position of this commentary on the issue? First,
as for the possibility that Paul misunderstood Judaism, the strongest reservation must be registered. It is extremely improbable that
one who understood Christianity better than his contemporaries
did so on the basis of a misunderstanding of Judaism. It will be
recalled that Paul was a Pharisee (Phil. 3:5; Acts 23:6), a pupil of
Rabbi Gamaliel (Acts 22:3), who boasted of "advancing in Judaism beyond many Jews of my own age, [being] extremely zealous
for the traditions of my fathers" (Gal. 1:14). We may as well suspect Shakespeare of misunderstanding drama as suspect Paul of
getting his wires crossed on Judaism. The truth is that following
his conversion to Christianity Paul saw Judaism in a radically new
light. Should it be countered that many other Jews were converted
who did not arrive at such drastic conclusions, it need only be
recalled that no other Jew underwent such a momentous conversion as did Paul near Damascus. The Christophany there revolutionized his perspective on Judaism. In 2 Corinthians 3:13–18 Paul
speaks of having a veil removed from his understanding of the old
covenant, the result of which is evident in Galatians and Romans.

Exactly how was his perspective revolutionized? In Romans Paul makes six pronouncements about the law, the first
being that it *reveals* sin: "through the law we become conscious of
sin" (3:20). The law does not cause sin, but it does make it known.
It fulfills a diagnostic function of revealing transgression against
God's will. Second, the law *incites* sin (5:20; 7:8). The prohibition
not to do something awakens a desire for it. Paul speaks of sin
seizing the occasion of the commandment and "springing to life,"
thereby "increasing transgressions." As a consequence, thirdly,
the "law brings *wrath*" (4:15). Apart from the straightedge of the
law, sin, although present in the world, was not reckoned as sin
(5:13), and humanity lived in relative ignorance. The advent of
law, however, revealed sin for what it is and disclosed God's
wrath and curse on it (Gal. 3:10), and on those who do it (1:18ff.).
Fourth, the law is *provisional* and not eternal, as is evinced by
Paul's marriage analogy (Rom. 7:1–3; 1 Cor. 7:39). All four of these
purposes are presented concisely and compellingly in 7:1–12.

It might be inferred from this that the law *is* sin. That is an
inevitable though mistaken conclusion which Paul energetically

denies (7:7). On the contrary, the law is "holy, righteous, and good" (7:12). Paul's fifth point thus is that "the law is spiritual" (7:14) and of *divine origin*. Spiritual though the law is, humanity is not spiritual but sinful, and herein lies the rub. The law reflects God's will, but the miserable infection of sin (8:3), as "another law at work in the members of my body, waging war against the law" (7:23), prevents humanity from even approximating the ideal.

Finally, the *intent of the law is fulfilled by the indwelling of the Spirit in believers* (8:4; Gal. 5:16). Paul's radical critique of the law does not lead to antinomianism and moral anarchy. As Romans 12:9–21 demonstrates, his ethics, like those of Jesus (e.g., the Sermon on the Mount, Matt. 5–7), conformed to the moral standards in the Torah, although neither he nor Jesus grounded them in the "letter" (i.e., in the requirement), but in the inner transformation of the Spirit which recovers the original intent of the law. That intent is summed up and fulfilled in love (13:8–10).

Two questions implicit in our discussion might help to complete Paul's perspective on Judaism and the law. Most importantly, what is the relationship of the law to Christ? The new perspective on Paul is correct in denying that Paul attacks the law as a means of salvation. Nowhere in Romans does Paul imply that Torah observance was the gateway of salvation. Righteousness, as he argues from the case of Abraham (ch. 4), was from the beginning a gift of grace received through faith. Abraham's response of faith in Yahweh (Gen. 15:6) is the archetype of the believer's response of faith in Jesus Christ for salvation. The law was not given until some 430 years later, and it could not therefore be a second or competing means of righteousness. Rather, in the inimitable expression of Galatians 3:24, the law was a *paidagōgos*, an escort or school bus perhaps, which was "put in charge to lead us to Christ," the schoolmaster. If it did so by making humanity inescapably aware of its need for a savior, it did so nonetheless. This illustrates the provisional nature of the law, and it is surely the meaning of the much debated passage in Romans 10:4 that "Christ is the end of the law." Christ is not the end of the law in the sense of nullifying it, but in the sense of being its proper goal and fulfillment. Other occurrences of the word "end" (Gk. *telos*) in Romans 2:27 and 6:21–22 concur. Christ does not put an end to the law, but is the law's rightful end, the omega point to which God had been moving the chosen people from Abraham onward. The metaphor of the olive tree in 11:17ff. illustrates and completes this idea. Both Jews and Gentiles must be engrafted by grace onto the "root," which culminates in Christ.

This brings us to a second and final question. If Paul does not attack the law as a means of salvation, what does he attack? Some suggest that his argument is not with the moral law, but with the cultic law, especially questions of sabbath observance, dietary regulations, circumcision, and marriage, all of which were prominent in first-century Judaism. But this is not borne out by an examination of law (Gk. *nomos*) in Romans, nor, for the most part, in Paul's other letters. The guilt of humanity in 1:18–2:24, the failure of moral righteousness in 3:9ff., the discussion of law in chapter 4, and the preoccupation with law (20 times) in chapter 7 all reflect the moral covenant at Sinai, not the cultic law. The discussion of circumcision in 2:25ff. and 4:1ff. is no exception, since the problem is that of taking the sign more seriously than the reality it represents. The single reference to the cultic law in Romans is the discussion of dietary practices in 14:1–15:13, about which Paul is benignly flexible—although not about the judgments which result from such practices. Paul's heroic (though futile) struggle in Romans 7 would be a farce had he been thinking of food laws, fat offerings, and firstfruits—and this goes for his enormous preoccupation with the law as a whole.

The law under discussion, then, was the moral law, which, in itself, was good. What was not good was the sense of *pride* which developed in those who held it. It was this problem which engaged Paul so vigorously. The law became for Jews a mark of distinction and superiority over against Gentiles. The conviction of being chosen by God and favored with Torah inspired in Israel a sense of privilege, which in the early days evoked both wonder and gratitude (Deut. 7). But following the exile it hardened into attitudes—and laws—of separation. Ezra's reforms, to be sure, heightened Judah's identity and ensured its survival amidst alien cultures. But those same reforms ran a danger of making the *signs* of election—Torah, circumcision, and marriage, for example— seem like the thing itself. Following the Maccabean revolt, when true believers felt compelled to separate themselves further from Gentiles and from less observant Jews, pride in Torah became a veritable trait of Judaism.

The result was an inordinate concern for distinctions which led invariably to value judgments and feelings of superiority. It would be unfair to conclude that all Jews were this way; that is a

bias with a long and ugly history in Christian exegesis, and the
new perspective on Paul is right in trying to uproot it. But it
cannot be denied that the tendency was inherent in first-century
Judaism. Paul himself had been given to it before his conversion
(Gal. 1:14; Phil. 3:5), and Jesus challenged it on more than one
occasion (Matt. 23; Mark 7:1–22). Paul summed up the dangers of
the moral law and its signs by the word "boasting," which occurs
some 50 times in his letters (and only four times elsewhere in the
NT). Boasting and pride pit themselves against grace, and grace,
which can only be received by humility and faith, sums up the
gospel. The essential conflict for Paul is between boasting and
grace, not law and grace. Grace teaches that there are no distinctions, for all have sinned and fallen short of the glory of God.
Where then is boasting? It is excluded on the sole basis of justification by faith (3:21–28).

Notes

1. For St. Augustine's conversion, see *Confessions*, bk. 8, sec. 12; for
Luther, see R. Bainton, *Here I Stand. A Life of Martin Luther* (Nashville:
Abingdon, 1950), ch. 3; for Wesley, see C. Nehemiah, ed., *The Journal of
John Wesley* (New York: Eaton & Matins, 1909), vol. 1, pp. 465–78; for Barth,
see Karl Barth, *How I Changed My Mind*, ed. J. Godsey (Richmond: John
Knox, 1966), pp. 24–25.
2. That Paul wrote Romans from Corinth was reinforced by an
archaeological discovery in Corinth in 1929. In limestone paving blocks
just east of the theater a Latin inscription was unearthed which reads:

ERASTVS PRO AEDILIT[AT]E S[UA] P[ECUNIA] STRAVIT

"Erastus in return for his aedileship laid [the pavement] at his
own expense." An *aedile* was a commissioner of public works. Paul sends
greetings to the Roman church from "Erastus, who is the city's director
of public works" in 16:23. Since Erastus is a rather uncommon name, and
no other Erastus is known to have been an official at Corinth, it is likely
that the Erastus of the inscription is the same person named in Romans
16:23, who was the traveling companion of Paul mentioned in Acts 19:22
and 2 Timothy 4:20. See V. P. Furnish, "Corinth in Paul's Time," *BAR* 15 (3,
1988), p. 20.

On the Gallio inscription and its dating, see C. K. Barrett, *The New Testament Background: Selected Documents* (New York: Harper Torchbooks, 1961), pp. 48–49.

3. Juvenal, 3.188–202; Martial, 1.117; 7.95; 8.23; 12.57.

4. Dio Cassius, *History* 68.7.

5. Augustus, *Monumentum Ancyranum* 8.

6. Pliny the Elder, *Natural History* 3.5.66. A hectare is about two and one-half acres.

7. Rome had some 250 bakeries, with a total daily capacity of perhaps 450,000 loaves.

8. So R. M. Grant, "Rome," *IDB*, vol. 4, p. 104.

9. On the question of Rome's population, see J. C. Russell, *The Control of Late Ancient and Medieval Population* (Philadelphia: The American Philosophical Society, 1985), pp. 8–40; idem, *Late Ancient and Medieval Population*, TAPS, New Series—volume 48, part 3 (Philadelphia: The American Philosophical Society, 1958), pp. 63–66. T. H. Hollingsworth (*Historical Demography* [Ithaca: Cornell University Press, 1969], p. 281) suggests a maximum population of between 500,000 and 750,000.

10. Quoted in F. F. Bruce, *Paul: Apostle of the Heart Set Free* (Grand Rapids: Eerdmans, 1977), p. 379.

11. *Pro Flacco* 28.66.

12. *War* 2.80–83; *Ant.* 17.299–303.

13. *Ant.* 18.81–84. This expulsion is mentioned by the Roman historians Tacitus (*Ann.* 2.85.4), Dio Cassius (*History* 57.18.5a) and Suetonius (*Tib.* 36). Describing the severity of Tiberius' decree, Suetonius writes, "he suppressed and compelled those who were engaged in that superstition (= Judaism) to burn their religious vestments with all their apparatus. . . . the rest of that race, and those who adopted similar opinions, he expelled from the city, on pain of perpetual slavery if they did not obey."

14. See H. J. Leon, *The Jews of Ancient Rome* (Philadelphia: Jewish Publication Society, 1960), pp. 135ff.; and Bruce, *Paul: Apostle of the Heart Set Free*, pp. 379–92.

15. Dio Cassius, *History* 60.6.

16. *Claudius* 25; see Barrett, *New Testament Background*, pp. 13–14. The dating of these events is not altogether certain. Dio Cassius (*History* 60.6) places Claudius' restraining order in A.D. 41, whereas Orosius (*History* 7.6.15f.) places it in A.D. 49. Many scholars, assuming that Dio Cassius and Orosius refer to the same event, are forced to decide which of the two competing dates is (more?) correct. Suetonius, however, says that the Jews "constantly made disturbances," and I am inclined to regard Dio Cassius and Orosius as referring to separate actions of Claudius necessitated by unresolved Jewish agitation in the capital. In this I follow A. J. M. Wedderburn, *The Reasons for Romans*, SNTW, ed. J. Riches (Edinburgh:

T. & T. Clark, 1988), pp. 57–58; Dunn, *Romans 1–8*, WBC 38A (Dallas: Word Books, 1988), p. xlix; and Bruce, *Paul: Apostle of the Heart Set Free*, p. 381.

17. For fuller treatments of this reconstruction, see J. Drane, "Why Did Paul Write Romans?" in *Pauline Studies. Essays Presented to F. F. Bruce on His 70th Birthday*, ed. D. Hagner and M. Harris (Grand Rapids: Eerdmans, 1980), pp. 217–19; and Wedderburn, *Reasons for Romans*, pp. 58–65.

18. Bishop Anders Nygren (*Commentary on Romans*, trans. C. Rasmussen [Philadelphia: Muhlenberg Press, 1949], pp. 1–9) calls Romans "The clearest gospel of all." Karl Barth's commentary belongs to this category, although with an existential emphasis. See especially his preface to the second edition.

19. Dunn (*Romans 1–8*, pp. lv–lviii) also adopts this threefold division, although he labels the purposes as apologetic, pastoral, and missionary.

20. *Introduction to the New Testament* (Philadelphia: Fortress, 1982), vol. 2, p. 140.

21. T. W. Manson, "St. Paul's Letter to the Romans—And Others," in *The Romans Debate—Revised and Expanded Edition*, ed. K. Donfried (Peabody, Mass.: Hendrickson, 1991), pp. 3–15.

22. Jacob Jervell, "The Letter to Jerusalem," in *Romans Debate—Revised*, pp. 53–64.

23. G. Bornkamm, "The Letter to the Romans as Paul's Last Will and Testament," in *Romans Debate—Revised*, pp. 16–28; idem, *Paulus* (Stuttgart: Kohlhammer, 1969), pp. 103–11.

24. Note John Drane's summary: "What we have in [Romans, Paul's] *magnum opus*, is therefore a conscious effort to convince himself as well as his opponents that it is possible to articulate a theology which is at once antilegalistic without also being intrinsically antinomian" ("Why Did Paul Write Romans?" pp. 223–24).

25. *Ann.* 13.

26. Wedderburn (*Reasons for Romans*, pp. 54–65) discusses this matter in detail and concludes: "We can argue that Paul knew a great deal about what was going on in Rome, and that his advice to them was written in light of that knowledge, and is to be interpreted by us in the light of that situation" (p. 63). So too, Dunn, *Romans 1–8*, pp. lvi–lviii. Wolfgang Wiefel offers a helpful reconstruction of events in Rome in "The Jewish Community in Ancient Rome and the Origins of Roman Christianity," in *Romans Debate—Revised*, pp. 85–101.

27. Günter Klein interprets 1:11 and 15:20 to mean that Paul desired to visit Rome to lay a proper apostolic foundation for a church which had not been founded by an apostle ("Paul's Purpose in Writing the Epistle to the Romans," in *Romans Debate—Revised*, pp. 29–43). Klein's argument is ingenious but weak. Paul registers no dissatisfaction with the foundation of the Roman church; in 15:14, in fact, he praises the founda-

tion. In Philippians 1:15–18 Paul even concedes that the gospel preached from the wrong motives is still the gospel.

28. See Robert Jewett, "Romans as an Ambassadorial Letter," *Int,* 36 (1982), pp. 5–20.

29. The debate was launched by E. P Sanders in *Paul and Palestinian Judaism* (London: SCM Press, 1977), and followed by *Paul, the Law, and the Jewish People* (Philadelphia: Fortress, 1983). Subsequent voices in the debate include L. Gaston, "Paul and Torah," in *Antisemitism and the Foundations of Christianity,* ed. A. T. Davies (New York: Paulist Press, 1979); J. Gager, *The Origins of Anti-Semitism. Attitudes Toward Judaism in Pagan and Christian Antiquity* (New York: Oxford, 1985); H. Räisänen, *Paul and the Law* (Philadelphia: Fortress, 1986); Dunn, *Romans 1–8,* lxiii–lxxii, and further, *Jesus, Paul and the Law. Studies in Mark and Galatians* (Louisville: Westminster/John Knox, 1990); and Stephen Westerholm, *Israel's Law and the Church's Faith* (Grand Rapids: Eerdmans, 1989).

§1 The Salutation (Rom. 1:1–7)

The first seventeen verses of Romans serve as an introduction to the epistle and fall into three parts. The first part,
verses 1–7, is Paul's salutation. In the second part, verses 8–15,
Paul introduces himself and speaks of his desire to visit Rome.
The third and final part is verses 16–17, in which Paul broaches
the seminal theme of his gospel, justification by faith for both
Jew and Gentile.

First, the salutation. Letters in Hellenistic times followed a
standard literary pattern. Unlike the modern convention of beginning letters with an address to the recipient, salutations in the
Greco-Roman world normally included three pieces of information: the name of the sender, the name of the recipient, and a brief
greeting. Two letters recorded in the book of Acts (15:23 and
23:26) follow this pattern quite closely, as do 1 Thessalonians and
James.

In writing to Rome Paul expands the salutation considerably. After introducing himself as one commissioned for the gospel of God (v. 1), he plunges into a description of the gospel and
his apostleship. Not until verse 7 does he complete the salutation
with mention of the recipients and a greeting. In Greek the first
seven verses are a single sentence of some ninety words! This is
the longest and most formal introduction of a Pauline epistle,
containing a mixture of conventional formulae and innovation.
This is probably due to the fact that Paul is writing to a church
which he neither founded nor visited. He expands the salutation
into a brief *credo* of the faith which he holds in common with the
Romans in order to establish credibility with a church to which
he is personally unknown. Moreover, if Paul has any apprehen-
sions that his subsequent message might raise eyebrows among
his Roman readers, he endeavors from the outset to make the most
favorable impression possible. Finally, Paul normally mentions
his fellow missionaries as co-senders of his epistles (Sosthenes,

Timothy, or Silvanus). In Romans, however, he writes alone. One gets the impression from this and from the overall salutation that the apostle intends to take special responsibility for the contents of this epistle.

1:1–2 / The first verse of Romans is an extraordinary testimony to the God who breaks into the world of humanity. **Paul, a servant of Christ Jesus, called to be an apostle and set apart for the gospel of God.** Here are two planes of reality. There is Paul, a human being who belongs to the same world we do; and there is God, who is beyond our world and yet intersects it with the gospel of Jesus Christ. God and humanity, heaven and earth, the eternal and temporal, the invisible and visible. Paul's message is not about a closed universe in which human beings are laboratory rats conditioned by their environment. The first stroke of his pen heralds an open universe, a world much larger than our empirical experience of it, a world, to be sure, which begins at our human level but which is not limited to it. There is a God who breaks into this world and enlarges its possibilities. Above and yet within the dirge of human history can be heard a single pure note of divine music, penetrating and transforming the entire orchestration. God has spoken in the gospel, and the words of this world can never again be the same.

Paul's role in this divine-human encounter is characterized by the words **servant, apostle,** and **set apart**. Each term is packed with meaning. The word *doulos*, which in Greek means a slave, is in the NIV rendered **servant**. In ancient Greece and Rome there were basically two social classes, the upper-class, known as *makarioi*, and the lower-class, *douloi*. Slavery is the ownership of one person by another; a slave was hence the possession, property, or commodity of someone else. Slavery in the ancient world was not based on theories of racial inferiority, as it was in the antebellum South, for instance. In this respect ancient slavery was a more humane institution. Nevertheless, if slaves were not regarded as chattel, they were regarded as inferior beings, destined for a variety of roles of servitude, constituting perhaps one-fourth of the population.

In referring to himself as a **servant of Christ Jesus,** Paul does not desire to conjure up abject associations of subjugation, drudgery, and cruelty. His intention rather is to assert his exclusive allegiance to God's absolute sovereignty. As a slave, Paul belongs to God. It is not Paul who determines what he will say and do; God's sovereign decision determines who he is and what he must do. In this respect Paul's use of *doulos* agrees with its usage in the OT. Moses (Josh. 14:7), Joshua (Josh. 24:29), David (Ps. 89:3), the prophets, and Israel are called "servants of the Lord." Israel had been chosen by God and was his peculiar people and "treasured possession" (Exod. 19:5), uniquely set apart by God and hence singularly committed to God. Similarly, God's claim on Paul is total; Paul's loyalty to God is final.

James Dunn (*Romans 1–8*, p. 8) suggests that Paul employs *doulos* with specific reference to the Servant of the Lord hymns in Isaiah (42:1–4; 49:1–6; 50:4–11a; 52:13–53:12). The second hymn declares, "You are my servant" (Isa. 49:3), and adds, "I will also make you a light for the Gentiles, that you may bring my salvation to the ends of the earth" (v. 6). Paul's life was a commentary on this verse. He considered himself the apostle to the Gentiles (Acts 22:21; Gal. 2:9), and he aspired to preach to Jews and Gentiles, not only in Rome but to "the limits of the West," as Clement of Rome would later say (1 Clem. 5:7).

Paul also refers to himself as an **apostle.** The Greek noun *apostolos*, from which the English word "apostle" is derived, comes from the verb *apostellein*, "to send someone with a commission." It was at his conversion on the road to Damascus and his subsequent reflection on that event (Acts 9:1–22) that Paul became aware that he was God's "chosen instrument to carry [God's] name before the Gentiles" (Acts 9:15). By prefixing **called** to **apostle** Paul denotes that he is no self-appointed ambassador, but divinely appointed and commissioned. He stands in the tradition of Abraham (Gen. 12:1–2), Moses (Exod. 3:10ff.), Isaiah (6:8–9), and Jeremiah (1:4–5), all of whom were called by God. **Apostle** speaks not only the language of election but also the language of grace, for "it is not the godly who are called, but precisely the ungodly whom God has justified and made his own people" (Kaylor, *Covenant Community*, p. 21). "For I am the least of the apostles and do not even deserve to be called an apostle, because I persecuted the church of God. But by the grace of God I am what I am, and his grace to me was not without effect" (1 Cor. 15:9–10).

The consciousness of being God's chosen instrument is further established by **set apart.** Paul's election was understood not as a general truism (e.g., that all people are loved by God), nor in a sense of national pride (e.g., that most peoples consider their nations to play a unique role in history). Like every Jew, Paul knew that God had chosen men and women in the history of Israel to do his particular will (e.g., Jer. 1:4–5). **Set apart** expressed Paul's personal destiny; he was gripped by the conviction that *he* was chosen for a unique vocation, for "God set me apart from birth and called me by his grace" (Gal. 1:15; see also Acts 13:2). The Greek word for **set apart**, *aphorismenos*, is the normal Greek rendering of the Hebrew word for "Pharisee," which probably means "to separate." If Paul is indulging in a word play he seems to indicate that he now is a different kind of Pharisee from what he had been. Previously he had been a Pharisee separated *from* Gentiles; now he is separated *for* them!

Verse 1 is unambiguous about Paul's self-understanding. He does not fancy himself a religious genius, nor does he trumpet his creative ability. His message is not from himself but from God, and whatever honor is ascribed to Paul must be attributed not to any greatness in him but to a power above him, to God who has radically intersected his life. The preeminence of that encounter forever changed his orientation, and at a deeper level his self-understanding. Only one response could be appropriate to the overwhelming favor of God, and that was to allow Christ absolute claim over his life, and to surrender himself to a truth and to a task which alone were worthy of his existence.

That truth was **the gospel of God. Gospel** in Greek comes from a compound word meaning "good report," or as we say, "good news." In saying that he was **set apart for the gospel of God** Paul does not mean, generally speaking, that he now believes the gospel whereas he formerly did not. He means that he has been specifically commissioned to proclaim the gospel, to make it known. For Paul the gospel was not something a person possesses, but rather something which possesses him. The gospel was more than a state of affairs or a truth which could be exhausted in a propositional statement. Rather, it is the ceaseless energy of God's love to illuminate the darkness, whose purpose it is to bring salvation to the lost. The gospel is really not a thing, but a person, Jesus Christ!

God **promised** the gospel **beforehand through his prophets in the Holy Scripture** regarding his Son (vv. 2–3; see Titus 1:2). This connects Paul's experience as a Christian with his history as a Jew. It establishes that Jesus Christ is not an afterthought of God, a scissors-and-paste remedy when the human experiment failed. Rather, Jesus Christ had long been foreseen in Israel, and apart from him all that had gone before was incomplete. Jesus Christ was the goal in a long history of salvation, the anchor runner, so to speak, in the divine relay from Abraham to the day of salvation. God's work in Israel had not been an impersonal force, randomly groping toward a higher state of perfection. Paul is rather proclaiming the one, personal God who before all ages created the world, called a people in Abraham, and throughout their history purposefully and patiently increased their knowledge of him. Then, in Paul's own time, God spoke his last word. The awesome finality that Jesus Christ was the fulfillment of God's eternal purpose stamped Paul's consciousness with an indelible sense of duty and obligation. Paul is a **servant, called, apostle,** and **set apart**.

1:3–4 / Verses 1–2 introduce the gospel, but verses 3–4 explore its meaning. The gospel **regards** God's **Son**, which means that Jesus Christ is the content of it. Paul names Jesus Christ four times in the first seven verses (vv. 1, 4, 6, 7). This leaves no doubt that God's Son is not merely the founder of the gospel, he *is* the gospel!

Verses 3–4 contain a brief credal statement, the parallelism of which is clearer in Greek than in the NIV: **As to his human nature** he **was a descendant of David, and who through the Spirit of holiness was declared with power to be the Son of God by his resurrection from the dead**. It is likely that Paul is citing a christological formula with which the Romans were already familiar, not unlike 2 Timothy 2:8. This is a much debated passage, but a straightforward reading of it offers the most credible understanding. The subject is God's Son who was revealed in two stages or is known in two time periods: according to the flesh he was born of Davidic descent, according to the Spirit he was declared Son of God in power. The Greek word for "flesh" (NIV, **human nature**) is often in Paul used pejoratively to imply human weakness, fallibility, and sin. But there are instances where Paul uses the term to mean "human existence" without any negative reference, and this appears to be one of them. In referring to Jesus as a descendant of David, Paul is speaking of his earthly, pre-resurrection life. Jesus is thus the Messiah promised to David (see 2 Sam. 7:11–14), indeed more than the Messiah, the Son of God, but the Son of God in humility, incognito. The revelation and minis-

try of God's Son thus stands in continuity with the OT, the "gospel
[which God] promised beforehand through his prophets" (v. 2).

The resurrection, however, separates the two stages or time
periods. It is a dividing line not in Jesus' status as Son of God, but
in his function as Son of God. As seed of David Jesus was the Son
in humility; as Son of God in power he enters his role as exalted
Lord. The NIV rendering of verse 4 (he **was declared with power
to be the Son of God**) might suggest that Jesus *became* the Son of
God at the resurrection, although he had not been so beforehand.
That is scarcely Paul's thought. At the resurrection Jesus was
constituted Son of God *in power*, whereas before the resurrection
he had been Son of God in suffering. Thus, verses 3–4 are not
about Jesus' promotion or adoption as God's Son. Both parts of
the formula are **regarding** God's **Son** (v. 3), but God's Son in two
manifestations: as servant and Lord, in humiliation and exaltation, in earthly ministry and heavenly reign.

1:5 / Paul now moves from the content of the gospel to
the commission of the gospel. **Through him and for his name's
sake, we received grace and apostleship**. Grace is not a vague
force of benevolence in the universe, nor merely the good intentions of the Almighty. Grace is absolutely personal, for it is
focused in and channeled through the person of Jesus Christ—
Through him . . . we received grace. Grace is an *act*, not a feeling
or disposition. It is something which God did at a particular point
in space and time when Pontius Pilate was governor from A.D. 26
to 36 of an imperial province on the eastern fringe of the Roman
Empire. Grace is the incomprehensible fact that God loves the
world in spite of its rebelliousness. It is the master plan of God's
love, the wonderful and awesome surprise that where the world
deserved *nothing* from God it could hope for *everything* from God.

Grace was the origin of Paul's apostleship. The NT makes
two seemingly contradictory statements about Paul. By his own
admission he was "the chief of sinners" (1 Tim. 1:12–17), but he
was also a "chosen instrument" of God (Acts 9:15–16). These two
statements reveal the paradox of grace. Grace is the intersection
where unconditional love meets human unworthiness.

Paul's commission is to lead the Gentiles to **the obedience
that comes from faith**. This passage, along with verses 13–15 and
11:13–21, indicates that Paul is writing to Gentiles and that his
commission is to bring them to "the obedience of faith," to trans-

late the Greek literally. This phrase both commences (1:5) and
concludes the epistle (16:26), and everything which Paul says in
between serves this goal. There is no separation in Paul's mind
between faith and obedience, between believing and doing. "Only
he who believes is obedient," said Dietrich Bonhoeffer, "and only
he who is obedient believes" (*Cost of Discipleship*, p. 69). The Book
of James is particularly aware of the problem of saying one thing
and doing another (James 2:14–26). Jesus himself taught that a
tree is known by the fruit it bears (Matt. 7:15–20; see also 21:28–
32). His call to "Follow me" demands an *act* which embodies a
belief.

1:6–7 / Paul concludes the salutation in verses 6–7. He
has been commissioned as apostle to the Gentiles, and hence he
writes to the Gentiles in Rome, who, like himself, are **called to
belong to Jesus Christ**. Paul's reputation had preceded him to
Rome. He makes no mention of his conversion or his years on the
mission field; surely these have long been identified with his
name. But less desirable reports have also been associated with
his name. Shortly after writing Romans Paul traveled to Jerusalem
where James reported to him, "Many thousands of Jews . . . have
been informed that you teach all the Jews who live among the
Gentiles to turn away from Moses" (Acts 21:20–21). Aware of such
reports, Paul does not fail at the beginning of Romans to point
out his divine commission as well as his orthodoxy and his common faith to the Romans, and to appeal to the unity of all who
are **called to belong to Jesus Christ**.

The Romans are **loved by God and called to be saints**.
Luther notes that God's love precedes his call. God does not
demand that humanity do certain things to earn his love; rather,
he loves humanity and enables it to do things according to his
will (*Epistle to the Romans*, p. 21). The word **saints** comes from
Hebrew and Greek roots meaning "to be set apart" or "holy." A
saint is a saint not because of any personal merit but because of
God's love and call.

The salutation concludes with Paul's characteristic ascrip-
tion of **grace and peace**. Grace (*charis*) is a Greek concept which
summarizes the gospel in a single word; peace (*šālôm*) is a Hebrew
concept which means wholeness and well-being. Both come only
from God our father and the Lord Jesus Christ. Thus, the chief
blessings of the old and new covenants find their fulfillment in

Jesus Christ. The essence of the gospel, as T. W. Manson rightly concludes, is to know God as Father (8:15; Gal. 4:6) and to acknowledge Jesus as Lord (10:9–10; 1 Cor. 12:3; Phil. 2:11; see *Romans*, p. 941).

Additional Notes §1

For a recent study of epistolary forms in the NT, see F. Schnider and W. Stenger, *Studien zum Neutestamentlichen Briefformular*, NTTS 11 (Leiden: Brill, 1987).

1:1–2 / Especially noteworthy is Karl Barth's powerful beginning to Romans and his emphasis on the gospel as God's distinct pronouncement in human history. See *Epistle to the Romans*, pp. 27–28.

There is an informative discussion of slavery in the ancient world in *A History of Private Life I: From Pagan Rome to Byzantium*, ed. P. Aries and G. Duby, trans. A. Goldhammer (Cambridge, Mass., and London: Belknap Press, 1987), pp. 51–93.

For discussions of slavery in both the OT and NT, see I. Mendelsohn, "Slavery in the Old Testament," *IDB*, vol. 4, pp. 383–91, and W. G. Rollins, "Slavery in the New Testament," *IDBSup*, pp. 830–32.

1:3–4 / Regarding the christological formula in vv. 3–4, several elements are strange to Paul, including "the seed of David," "a Spirit of holiness," the Greek word for "declare" (*horizein*), and the two participial constructions *genomenou* and *horisthentos* (neither of which is recognizable in the NIV). Failure to mention the death of Christ is also somewhat unPauline. None of these observations alone is proof of a pre-Pauline formula, but their combined effect, especially when condensed within two verses, argues for the probability of an early Christian creed.

On Paul's use of "flesh" with regard to Jesus, see 9:5; 2 Cor. 5:16; 7:5; 10:3; Gal. 2:20; Phil. 1:22, 24. Nevertheless, a merely human understanding of Jesus is a misunderstanding of Jesus. George Ladd rightly says, "For Paul, only the Holy Spirit could enable a man to understand correctly what had really happened in [Jesus'] history." In other words, the witness of the Holy Spirit is necessary to convince a person that Jesus is God's Son. See George E. Ladd, *A Theology of the New Testament* (Grand Rapids: Eerdmans, 1974), pp. 414–15.

The discussion on vv. 3–4 is summarized from a section of my doctoral dissertation, "The Son of God. Its Antecedents in Judaism and Hellenism and its Use in the Earliest Gospel," Ph.D. diss., Fuller Theological Seminary, 1978, pp. 105–6.

1:5 / Two brief and helpful discussions of grace can be found in H. Conzelmann, "*charis*," *TDNT*, vol. 9, pp. 373–76, and A. Richardson,

An Introduction to the Theology of the New Testament (New York: Harper & Row, 1958), pp. 281–84.

On the issue of discipleship Bonhoeffer avers that the call to faith is a call to discipleship, and that discipleship is a concrete form of adherence to Christ which can only be undertaken by following Jesus. "Unless he obeys, a man cannot believe" (*Cost of Discipleship*, p. 72).

1:6–7 / T. W. Manson ("St. Paul's Letter to the Romans—and Others," in *Romans Debate, Revised*, pp. 4–5) argues that the absence of "Rome" (vv. 7, 15) in some ancient manuscripts (G 1739[mg] 1908[mg] it[g] Origen) indicates that Romans may have circulated in alternate forms as an open letter. See the discussion of Manson's position in the Introduction. Textual evidence for Manson's thesis is considerably limited by the fact that the manuscripts omitting **Rome** are few and late. The evidence for including **Rome**, both in terms of number and age of manuscripts, is vastly superior. See B. Metzger, *TCGNT*, p. 505.

§2 Paul: The Man and His Message
(Rom. 1:8–15)

In the second part of the introduction (vv. 8–15) the apostle scales down from lofty theological heights to news of himself
and the occasion for writing. His focus changes from the gospel
to himself, and he signifies this by casting most of his verbs and
pronouns in the first person. Paul expresses his thankfulness for
the believers in Rome and assures them of his repeated desire
to visit them. There is a tension in this passage, however, which
demands a resolution. On the one hand, Paul is constrained to
preach the gospel to the Gentiles; on the other hand, outward
circumstances have prevented him from preaching at the heart
of the Gentile world, Rome. Beneath Paul's testimony one perceives an inexorable hope that at last his commission to preach
to the Gentiles will open a way to Rome.

1:8 / Paul customarily begins his epistles with thanksgiving to God for his churches. It was not his custom to write
timeless theological essays; rather, Paul penned letters to church
communities and individuals whom he knew and cared for. His
letters, in other words, are spawned from pastoral concern, and
Romans is no exception.
**First, I thank my God through Jesus Christ for all of you,
because your faith is being reported all over the world** (see also
1 Thess. 1:8). Thanksgiving is Paul's first word. The use of **First**
leads us to expect a "second," but Paul's train of thought gets
carried afield and he fails to continue the sequence. He is grateful
because their **faith is being reported all over the world**. His
gratitude is neither a vague sense of euphoria nor an unaccount-
able sense of well-being, but gratitude for specific acts of God.
Whether the Romans' faith was more noteworthy than the faith
of other churches, or whether Paul was giving thanks simply
because the Christian faith had taken root in Rome, is difficult to

say. Whatever the reason, Paul celebrates that the flag of the gospel has been planted in the capital of the ancient world.

Although we are not told who planted it or how it came about, it is clear that Paul takes no credit for establishing the beachhead. The church in Rome existed before the apostle ever reached the imperial city, and long before he penned this epistle. The Book of Acts records that when Paul finally reached Rome "the brothers there traveled to meet us" (Acts 28:15). It is highly likely that Roman Christianity grew out of the large Jewish population there, and it is not unlikely that the church owed its existence to believers returning from the outpouring of the Holy Spirit at Pentecost (see Acts 2:10). If so, there were Christian churches in Rome more than two decades before Paul wrote this epistle.

1:9–10 / This section and chapter 15:14–33 are the only clearly autobiographical parts of Romans. Paul recounts the history of his longing to visit Rome, a history of expectant hopes and frustrated desires. The God whom he worships is witness to his constant prayers for Rome (v. 9) and longstanding desire to visit the city (v. 11). **God, whom I serve with my whole heart** has the ring of an oath, which is not uncommon in Paul. It should not be overlooked that "the gospel of God" in verse 1 is "the gospel of his Son" here in verse 9. The exact relationship between Jesus and God would require several centuries before the definition of Nicea (A.D. 325) determined that the Son was "true God from true God, begotten not created, of the same essence (Gk. *homoousion*) as the Father." Early Jewish Christians, for whom monotheism was a zealous article of faith (Deut. 6:4), must have been reluctant to equate Jesus with God, but Paul comes extremely close to doing so here.

In verse 10 Paul gives the impression that at last he sees daylight in his plans to visit Rome. If and when he comes, however, the success of his venture will depend on God's design, a design shaped and influenced by his prayers.

1:11–12 / One reason for visiting Rome was to establish something of a base camp for Paul's missionary outreach to Spain (15:22–38). But here there is no mention of Spain. Paul may want to avoid giving the impression that his epistle is written from ulterior motives, specifically that the chief reason for writing is to strike up a relationship that will be serviceable for subsequent missionary work. On the contrary, the roots of Paul's desire to visit Rome go deeper than his plans to visit Spain.

Here and in verse 13 Paul gives his reason for desiring to visit Rome. **I long to . . . impart to you some spiritual gift to make you strong.** What is the **spiritual gift** Paul hopes to impart to the Romans? The Greek word *charisma*, commonly translated "gift," practically owes its existence to the apostle. It occurs in Romans 12 and 1 Corinthians 12 with reference to special gifts or endowments of the Holy Spirit for the purposes of ministry. Here the **spiritual gift** seems to be related to Paul's preaching of the gospel, for he closes this section by repeating that he desires "to preach the gospel also to you who are at Rome" (v. 15). In verse 13 he expresses the hope to "have a harvest among you." The Greek word for **harvest,** *karpos,* appears again in 15:28 with reference to the collection for the poor believers in Jerusalem. It is, of course, possible that Paul uses these two expressions generally of "blessing," or perhaps with reference to his missionary labors, i.e., that in Rome he may see new converts and deeper conviction in faith.

Another possibility is worth considering, however, especially since *charisma* and *karpos* normally refer to specific phenomena. It is not to be discounted that the **spiritual gift** which Paul hopes to give and the harvest which he hopes to reap are subtle references to the need for reconciliation between Gentile and Jew in Rome. We have noted that following the repeal of the edict of Claudius when Jewish Christians returned to the capital, they likely discovered a Christianity which had become increasingly Gentile in their absence (see Introduction). Without presuming to know more than he does about the situation, and without presuming to be able to achieve more than he can, Paul may have chosen these two expressions to signal the reconciliation which he hopes his exposition of the gospel will effect in Rome.

The difficult grammar of verse 12 is indicated in the NIV by a dash. The awkward construction may be due to the fact that Paul must tread delicately and forestall any suspicions that he is intruding in Roman affairs. Lest he antagonize his readers by an attitude of condescension, Paul meets them as an equal, **that you and I may be mutually encouraged by each other's faith.** The Greek word *symparakalesthai,* here translated **mutually encouraged,** occurs nowhere else in all the Bible. If Paul's faith can strengthen theirs, so can theirs strengthen his. This sense of bonding is reinforced in verse 14 where Paul says, "I am **obligated.**" A debtor is someone who owes something to another, and in Paul's case it was the debt of love (13:8). No Christian, not even the apostle Paul, stands *above* or *outside* the church. It is only *within* the church that apostles or believers have any authority and their message any credibility.

1:13 / Paul assures the Romans that his failure to visit them is not due to lack of desire on his part. Rather, he has been **prevented from doing so until now**. In 1 Thessalonians 2:18 he writes similarly that he was prevented by Satan from visiting the Thessalonians. There is no mention here, however, of Satan's blocking his course; indeed, Jewish writers often employed the passive voice (as Paul does here) with reference to God. Especially in light of verse 10, it is preferable to conclude that Paul's delay in reaching Rome was due to God's will.

1:14–15 / Paul testifies that **I am obligated both to Greeks and non-Greeks, both to the wise and the foolish.** The word translated **non-Greeks** is literally "barbarians." There have been attempts to understand **non-Greeks** as an allusion to Spain or perhaps to peoples of unintelligible language. It seems more likely, however, that Paul is thinking of the greater Gentile world of all non-Israelites. By **the wise and the foolish** he probably means "the cultured and the uncultured." One thing is for certain: **to preach the gospel** to **Greeks and non-Greeks** was the center and sum of Paul's apostolic calling.

Additional Notes §2

1:9–10 / On Pauline oaths, see 9:1; 2 Cor. 1:23; 2:17; 11:31; 12:19; Gal. 1:20; Phil. 1:8; 1 Thess. 2:5, 10.

Like Jesus, Paul came from a people who knew how to pray. At no point did Jews differ more drastically from Gentiles than in the matter of prayer. The late Hellenistic world-view was characterized by grave uncertainty and anxiety. The proliferation of mystery religions and the thousands of magical papyri with their countless names and epithets bear clear if sorry testimony to the loss of confidence in prayer in the Greco-Roman world. Jews, on the contrary, remained steadfast in their conviction that God is both personal and sovereign, and they preserved this conviction in the ritual of praying three times daily, at morning, noon, and evening. "Commit your way to the Lord; trust in him and he will do this," said the Psalmist (37:5). Passages such as these were the ground of Paul's faith and ministry, as they had been for Jesus and other pious Jews before him. For a discussion of daily prayer in ancient Judaism, see J. Jeremias, *The Prayers of Jesus* (Philadelphia: Fortress, 1978), pp. 66–81.

For a discussion of the christological formulation of Nicea, see J. Pelikan, *The Emergence of the Catholic Tradition (100–600)* (Chicago: University of Chicago, 1971), pp. 200–204.

1:13 / For Paul's understanding of **harvest**, see F. Hauck, "*karpos*," *TDNT*, vol. 3, p. 615, and Barrett, *Romans*, p. 26.

1:14 / Paul Achtemeier says, "Good preaching is never a one-way street. Only those who listen are able to preach and teach" (*Romans*, p. 31). One is also reminded of Dietrich Bonhoeffer's enduring little book, *Life Together* (trans. J. Doberstein [San Francisco: Harper & Row, 1954]). Among the many valuable thoughts therein is Bonhoeffer's idea that Jesus Christ is the mediator not only between God and the believer, but also between believer and believer. Christ thus mediates *all* relationships. Karl Barth (*Romans*, pp. 33–34) expands this idea with reference to **obligated** (v. 14). Barth says Christians are of value to each other not so much because of what they *are*, but because of what they are *not*! As long as someone is aware of his or her own importance (e.g., 12:3) the work of the Spirit is throttled. But where believers realize that in themselves they have nothing to offer to others, there they can offer Christ. Only where one offers up one's inner emptiness to God can God fill one with the Spirit. Similarly, Paul conceives of his entire life "through Jesus Christ" (v. 8). He was forever a debtor to Christ and others.

§3 The Gospel: The Power of Salvation (Rom. 1:16–17)

These verses rise like a majestic summit of Paul's gospel. This is not simply a high plateau of thought reflecting the terrain of what lies below, but a massif of bold and powerful words and ideas, each one like a shimmering peak. We must consider each aspect of this daring formulation, for, as all interpreters of Romans agree, these verses contain the heart of Paul's understanding of salvation.

1:16–17 / **I am not ashamed of the gospel,** writes Paul (v. 16). The apostle had to be aware that a carpenter from Galilee posed problems as the savior of the world. In an earlier letter to Corinth he wrote, "we preach Christ crucified: a stumbling block to Jews and foolishness to Gentiles. . . . But God chose the foolish things of the world to shame the wise; God chose the weak things of the world to shame the strong. He chose the lowly things of this world and the despised things—and the things that are not— to nullify the things that are" (1 Cor. 1:23, 27–28). Verse 16 is the only place in the Pauline corpus (with the exception of 2 Tim. 1:12, 16) which mentions shame in connection with the gospel. In a place like Rome it took courage not to be ashamed of what must have seemed like an absurdity: that an unknown Jew who suffered a disgraceful death on the eastern fringe of the Roman Empire was being proclaimed as God in human flesh!

But in a daring counteroffensive Paul calls the gospel **the power of God.** The epistle to Rome was written to a people who, like modern Americans, were conscious of their power. Ancient Rome needed no lessons in the meaning of power; indeed, Rome defined power. The Roman army controlled the better part of the Western world, the Roman navy plied and pacified the Mediterranean Sea, and Roman roads laced the patchwork of nations surrounding the Mediterranean and extending northward into Europe together into a united fabric of life. The Latin tongue would increasingly replace Greek as the mode of communication in the ancient world, and Rome's currency measured the scale of values. Roman justice was the arbiter of what was right and wrong, who would live and die. The genius which made it possible was the Roman faculty for administration, symbolized by the raised eagle of the Roman standard.

In comparison with Rome's self-evident power, the gospel of Jesus Christ must have been dismissed as something of little consequence. But the power of which Paul speaks is a different power. It is not the power of state, ideas, movements, technology, progress, or whatever. It is the power of God, and God's power is a combination of his freedom and sovereignty to do what he wills to do. The power of God is expressed supremely in God's way of dealing with the world, which is summed up in the gospel. The gospel, as we noted, is not a thing, but a person, Jesus Christ. The power of God does not compete with other powers in this world, nor can it be compared to them. The ways of God are not the ways of this world (Isa. 55:8–9).

This power in Greek is called *dynamis*, from which the English word "dynamite" is derived. But unlike the powers which so mesmerize our age—wealth, beauty, status, weaponry, winning, control—the power of God in Jesus Christ is a supernatural power. The power of God does not grow from the soil of worldly power, and thus it confronts the powers and values of this world as a paradox, indeed as an offense. It is a power whose instruments are not the great things of this world, but the weak things. It is strength in weakness (2 Cor. 12:9), wealth in poverty (2 Cor. 8:9), life in death (Gal. 2:19–20), the Son of God being crucified as a common criminal (Phil. 2:6ff.). That which the world rejects God elects for his sovereign purposes (1 Cor. 1:18–31), so that what God ordains is solely indebted to God and not to this world. God's power is thus the opposite of naked power. Power for its own sake is the sign of satanic power, power as brute force in and of itself, with no purpose other than unleashing itself and destroying everything around it—and finally itself—in its maddened heat.

God's power, on the contrary, is power with a purpose, power *for* salvation. The noun *sōtēria* in Greek comes from the verb *sōzein*, which means to rescue or save. Jews, of course, were acquainted with God as savior. God had been their deliverer from Egypt, the superpower of the ancient Near East, and had rescued them from the threatening waters of the Red Sea. God had saved them from the hand of their enemies and delivered them from exile under Babylon. This much was clear to every Jew. But Paul never uses the word *sōtēria* with reference to rescue from temporal danger. Human oppressors and dangers must have seemed to him only symptoms of the ultimate forces of enslavement—sin, death, and Satan. It is for these, and especially for the human relationship with God, that Paul reserves the term **salvation**, for these are the final realities which either destroy or perfect the human soul.

Salvation for Paul has both a negative and a positive side. Negatively he understands it as a saving *from* the wrath and judgment of God (5:9). But salvation is more than the absence of inimical or menacing circumstances. Positively Paul understands salvation as a saving *for* the glory for which the entire created order longs (8:18–19, 30). The positive side of salvation is the more important, for it entails the restoration of the goodness and harmony which God originally created, apart from the rupture of sin. Salvation is thus a saving from sin and death, and a saving for eternal life (4:25). It is the only successful rescue operation which the fallen creation has ever been offered.

Two things always characterize salvation in Scripture: it is God's saving initiative, and it is offered to sinners. The radical news about salvation is not only *who* performed it—God alone— but also *to whom* it is available. Paul's answer, as startling as it is terse, is that salvation is for **everyone who believes: first for the Jew, then for the Gentile** (v. 16). The power of God in Jesus Christ is not for some and against others; salvation is not a matter of maneuvering oneself via nationality or good works or intentions into a favorable position with the deity. God's power is not an arbitrary power but a creative power, constituted and executed **for everyone who believes**.

The universality of salvation is accentuated in three ways in verse 16. First, Paul inserts the pronoun **everyone**, which includes Jews as well as non-Jews (Gentiles). Second, **to the Jew first** emphasizes Jewish priority regarding salvation, although not Jewish jurisdiction over it. Salvation began with the Jews because they were chosen first, but it was not limited to them, and hence their priority in the scheme of salvation can not be understood as exclusiveness. Finally, the untranslatable Greek particle *te* implies a fundamental equality between Jews and Greeks. Paul will shortly remind his readers that *all* have sinned (3:23; 10:12), that there is no distinction between Jews and Greeks with regard to the need for salvation, and hence faith remains the only access to it.

The lifeline between God the rescuer and humanity the foundering victim is faith. Faith is often the object of misunderstanding. Some regard faith as a formula or creed, as a set of words (indeed, very true words) sufficient to save them. Others see faith as *faithfulness*, i.e., as something which human beings possess independently of the gospel, thus shifting the emphasis from what is believed or the act of believing to the believer. In an extreme form this results in the preposterous assertion that "It doesn't matter what you believe as long as you believe it."

For Paul, faith is distinct from all such ideas. Faith is always and only the human response to the gospel. Apart from the work of the cross there can be no faith. Faith is the response which God's unmerited grace evokes from an individual, and it can best be defined as trust, belief, and commitment. Trust is a relational term. One does not trust in some*thing* but in some*one*, and in the NT the some*one* is Jesus Christ. Paul will discuss this posture of total dependence on God in the case of Abraham (ch. 4). But faith is more than active response. It is also a content of belief which depends on the character of God. Were it only response it would evaporate into subjectivism. But God has done something in the cross of Jesus Christ which is objectively true, apart from human participation and in spite of any response of it. This truth determines the destiny of individuals, nations, and the cosmos itself. Finally, faith is commitment. Commitment is the decision to live in the present according to the promises of the future. Commitment is the radical choice to entrust one's destiny to God despite circumstances to the contrary. Faith is the corresponding human response to the divine initiative of righteousness. Righteousness and faith thus belong together. Where Paul broaches the subject of righteousness in Romans he turns to the vocabulary of faith; but where righteousness is absent (e.g., chs. 6–8), so too is the language of faith.

Thus, **righteousness . . . is by faith from first to last** (v. 17). The expression, **faith from first to last**, is an agreeable rendering of the Greek, which literally reads, "from faith to faith." The saving activity of God occurs prior to human response and finds its correlative in faith. God's righteousness both awakens faith and produces faith. Paul's use of the present participle, **everyone who believes** (rather than an aorist participle which denotes completed action), denotes faith as an ongoing activity. Faith is less a quantum of something possessed than an orientation in which one participates actively and freely.

The Greek word *dikaiosynē* can be rendered by either "righteousness" or "justification." The former word usually refers to the character and activity of God, whereas the latter usually refers to the justified condition of the believer. Context alone determines how it should be understood. In classical Greek, *dikaiosynē* usually meant ethical rightness or goodness. In the OT righteousness refers above all to God's faithfulness to the covenant with Israel, an understanding reflected several times in Romans (3:3–5, 25; 9:6; 10:3; 15:8). But Paul's typical usage of **righteousness** carries the sense of acquitting, or conferring a righteous status on someone. It contains the idea of transference or conversion, the essence of which is that God considers believers right with himself even though they are not yet morally good. The Christian life might be said to begin in a fiction, for when God declares a believer righteous the person is at the moment no better than he or she was before. But the fiction appears different from the divine perspective, for God's declaring believers righteous through the death of Christ is grounded in a truth deeper than the human perspective can penetrate. God deals with humanity not by what it is, but by what it can be, indeed, what it will be through the work of Christ. Moreover, Paul says that God's righteousness **is revealed**. The Greek construction (imperfect active indicative) means that righteousness is *being* revealed or unfolded in the gospel, thus underscoring its dynamic impact. Righteousness is therefore a new condition established by God, which bears fruit in new life, which is known as sanctification.

The concluding quotation, taken from Habakkuk 2:4, is better rendered, "The one who is justified by faith will live" (rather than the NIV, "The righteous will live by faith"). The idea is that God grants life to the person who first is made right with him by faith. Not works, but faith—defined as trust in God, commitment to God, and belief in God—is the only proper fulfillment of the law of God. This is the nucleus of Romans. The pattern of righteousness-faith-life in the Habakkuk quotation provides Paul with an overall thematic development of the epistle, in fact. In chapters 1–3 Paul will discuss the righteousness of God; in chapters 4–8 the meaning of faith, particularly in relation to sin (6:1–14), law (6:15–7:25), the Holy Spirit (8:1–39), and the salvation of Jews and Gentiles (9–11); and in chapters 12–16 the consequences of the new life for the church (12), government (13), and reconciliation between Jews and Gentiles (14–15).

Additional Notes §3

1:16–17 / See Karl Barth's vigorous exposé of the difference between divine and worldly power in *Dogmatics in Outline*, trans. G. Thomson (New York: Harper & Row, 1959), chs. 7 and 13.

For a clear and helpful discussion of the biblical understanding of salvation, see A. Richardson, "Salvation, Savior," *IDB*, vol. 4, pp. 168–81.

Wolfgang Wiefel ventures that **first for the Jew** ought to be understood against the sociological and ethnic divisions which existed in Rome when Paul wrote. Paul resists the trend of siding with the Gentile majority, a trend which Wiefel maintains gained momentum during Jewish absence from Rome under the edict of Claudius. Refusing to adopt an anti-Jewish position, Paul affirms the historic mandate of salvation from Israel to the nations (e.g., Isa. 49:6). Wiefel concludes: "the message about the universality of God's salvation is directed especially towards those who have closed themselves off decisively and whose rejection appears most incomprehensible" ("Jewish Community in Rome," in *Romans Debate— Revised*, p. 101). Wiefel's insight seems corroborated not only by the fact that Paul raises this issue in Romans 9–11, but also by the remark at the end of Acts that when he reached Rome, Paul visited the disbelieving Jewish synagogues and not the Christian congregations (Acts 28:17–28).

For a discussion of faith as trust, belief, and commitment, see J. Edwards, "Faith as Noun and Verb," *CT*, August 9, 1985, pp. 21–23.

A good excursus on "The Righteousness of God" is offered in Sanday and Headlam, *Romans*, pp. 34–39. We cannot fail to mention the seminal role which Rom. 1:17 has played in the history of Christianity. It was this passage above all which caused Luther to see that righteousness is not something which a wrathful God requires of humanity, but something which a merciful God bestows on humanity through faith in Jesus Christ. The righteousness which God demands is that which he graciously gives. The position of humanity before God was thus vastly changed for Luther: the sinner was no longer the object of God's wrath but the object of his mercy. Luther said that when he grasped the essence of the righteousness of God, he felt as if he were born anew and transferred to paradise. See M. Brecht, *Martin Luther. Sein Weg zur Reformation, 1483–1521* (Stuttgart: Calwer Verlag, 1981), vol. 1, pp. 219–22.

On the role of Hab. 2:4 in Judaism, Simlai, a third-century A.D. Palestinian rabbi, attempted to argue that all 613 laws traditionally given by Moses found their completion in Hab. 2:4, the same verse quoted by the former rabbi Paul. But unlike Paul, for whom faith assumed center stage in the religious and moral life, Simlai relegated it to the wings. Habakkuk 2:4 plays a unique role in the history of both Christianity and Judaism, therefore, but with a different emphasis. The former elevates faith to the central principle of religion, the latter relegates it to a status of lesser importance. See Str-B, vol. 3, pp. 542–44.

§4 *Truth and Tragedy (Rom. 1:18–32)*

Paul now launches into the body of the epistle with an indictment against humanity. He will maintain the charge until 3:21, at which point he will return to righteousness by faith which he introduced in 1:16–17. Romans 1:18–3:20 is a sobering exposé of the dark side of human nature. Throughout the attack Paul labors to demonstrate that there is no distinction between Gentile and Jew in the matter of sin and guilt, a point reasserted in 3:10–12, 3:23, and 11:32. Gentile and Jew are equally guilty before God, but they are not guilty in the same way. In 1:18–32 Paul focuses primarily on the Gentile sins of idolatry and immorality. His accusations, which are generally typical of Jewish allegations of Gentiles, are remarkably similar to those found in Wisdom of Solomon 12–15. In 2:1–3:20 Paul then turns to Jews and their problems of pride, judgment, and disobedience. But despite the particular sins of Gentiles and Jews, both represent the larger fundamental problem of humanity. "There is no difference, for all have sinned and fall short of the glory of God" (3:22–23).

Paul's negative assessment of the human condition will no doubt offend many Westerners who have been raised to believe in the basic goodness of human nature. It may appear that Paul has left the "good news" in verse 17 and embarked on a depressing, and for many, degrading, rehearsal of everything bad in life. But Paul has not left the gospel. This section too begins with the *revelation* of God, the same idea with which he concluded in 1:17. There it was the revelation of the righteousness of God, here the revelation of the wrath of God against the wickedness of humanity. Romans 1:18ff. is not a tirade by a religionist bent on dredging up human faults. The wrath of God against human corruption is also the revelation of God, and therefore an element of the gospel. Love and wrath are not opposites. They are, in the words of Ernst Gaugler, "the same living energy of the divine holiness which expresses itself in the gospel, on the one hand in God's opposition to sin, and on the other in his love which draws us homeward. Where one knows nothing of God's wrath, there one knows nothing of his love" (*Der Römerbrief*, vol. 1, p. 46 [my translation]). Elsewhere Paul recalls "the kindness and sternness of God" (11:22). If the message of wrath is less welcome, it is no less necessary for salvation. Necessary as wrath may be, it is not God's first word or his last. The *first* word is grace, that the gospel is powerful to save (1:16–17). Only the one who first knows the love and acceptance of God can hear the grim truth about oneself. It is the physician who holds some hope of a cure who can reveal to a patient the severity of the diagnosis.

There are many ways to think of the ignoble side of human nature. Drama and literature speak of a "tragic flaw" which frustrates a hero's fulfilling his or her potential. Psychology speaks of "the human predicament" which arises from imperfect choices. Sociology conceives of persons as victims of social, environmental, or hereditary circumstances. Paul, however, attributes to humanity a more active role in its misfortune. Verses 18–32 stress the deliberate nature of human rebellion against God and its ineluctable guilt. Paul speaks of a knowing suppression of the truth (vv. 18, 25). Three times he says that God has made known that which otherwise could not be known (vv. 19, 20). Thrice again he asserts that humanity *can* know God and does in fact experience God (vv. 19, 21, 32), but tragically—and this he repeats four times—humanity "exchanged" such knowledge for a counterfeit (vv. 23, 25, 26, 27). In fifteen verses Paul makes twelve references to the manifestation or knowableness of God's power and divine nature. In spite of this, humanity has chosen neither to glorify nor to give thanks to God (v. 21), and as a consequence, it has, in the words of Luther, fallen into ingratitude, hollowness, blindness, and total departure from God. "The sin of omitting that which is good leads to the sin of committing that which is positively evil" (*Epistle to the Romans*, pp. 28–30).

Thus, the human predicament results neither from ignorance nor from a malevolent fate. The problem is not lack of knowledge, but failure to *acknowledge* God and render proper worship and obedience. There is nothing essentially new in Paul's exposé of human nature; indeed we should be wary if there were, for the human problem has been diagnosed much the same by others. As we noted, a reading of Wisdom of Solomon 12–15 will

reveal how closely Paul echoes contemporary Jewish accusations
of Gentiles—though with one important difference. Whereas the
author of the Wisdom of Solomon commends the faithfulness of
Israel (15:1–19) in contrast to the faithlessness of the Gentiles (chs.
12–14), Paul charges *both* with unrighteousness. Paul's argument
is more radical and universal. Instead of accepting itself as made
in God's image (Gen. 1:26–27), humanity feverishly tries to reverse the order of creation and remake God in its own image.
Humanity has not been denied the fair winds of fate; rather, its
willful denial of God has shipwrecked it on the reefs of a world
centered in self.

Although God made humanity free to refuse him, he did
not make it free from the consequences of its refusal. "For Paul no
[one] is ever really without a master or on his own," says Ernst
Käsemann. "He who evades the Creator runs into his Judge"
(*Romans*, p. 43). Rebellion against God disrupts not only humanity's relationship with God, but *all* relationships, including those
with self, nature, and others. The perversion of the relationship
between humanity and God results in *idolatry* (vv. 19–23). Humanity's gaze falls from the glory of God to itself, and even below
itself to the animals (v. 23). The second disruption results in *immorality* (vv. 24–27). Exchanging rightful sexual relationships for
abnormal ones results in homosexuality, in which the natural
desire for one's sexual opposite is inverted upon the self. The
third and final disruption is that human relationships become
characterized by *strife and greed* (vv. 28–32). One's neighbor becomes one's adversary, and harmony among persons sours into
the cacophony of vices listed in verses 29–31. In the primary
relationships of self, nature, others, and God, human failure to
acknowledge God leads not to an evolution of something better,
but to a devolution of something worse. In each case God's response to human refusal is the same: three times Paul says, "God
gave them over to" the wretchedness they desired (vv. 24, 26, 28).
This refrain falls like so many blows of the ax, severing the ropes
by which humanity could pull itself back to God.

1:18 / The **wickedness of men** is now contrasted with
the "righteousness of God" in 1:17. The Greek word translated
wickedness, *adikia*, is the negative of the "righteousness" (*dikaiosynē*) of God in verse 17. Thus, the Greek draws an unmistakable
parallelism between the revelation of God's righteousness (v. 17)

and the revelation of God's wrath against human *unrighteousness* (v. 18). The object of God's wrath is the suppression of **the truth**. The truth Paul has in mind is probably not truth in general (although suppressing truth in any form is bad enough), but *the* truth of God. "Sin is always an assault upon the truth," says Cranfield (*Romans*, vol. 1, p. 112). God's wrath burns against perverting the truth, for once people stop believing in the truth, as G. K. Chesterton once said, they do not believe in nothing, they believe in anything! Sacrificing the truth of God leads to the denial of reality (v. 20), a lie (v. 25), a depraved mind (v. 28), and the approval of unrighteousness (v. 32).

Wickedness, appearing twice in verse 18 and again in 1:29, 2:8, and 3:5, dominates Paul's treatment of the guilt of humanity. In the Greek text verse 18 is introduced with the conjunction "for" (*gar*, omitted in NIV), which links verses 18ff. with verses 16–17. "For" adds a necessary corollary to what Paul has already said about salvation, namely, that one cannot be made right with God other than "by faith from first to last" (v. 17). Paul is thus not getting sidetracked on the sorry state of the world, but is demonstrating that apart from faith there can be no receiving of grace.

The wrath of God (v. 18) is revealed along with the righteousness of God (v. 17) and is inseparable from it. Although they may seem like opposites, both righteousness and wrath comprise the gospel. God's anger appears to contradict what we know of his love and forgiveness. Wrath, at least in human experience, connotes vengeance and retaliation fueled with self-interest, which erupts in irrational and injurious excess. But God's wrath is different. It is not an arbitrary nightmare of raw power. It is guided by God's covenant relationship with his people. God's wrath is divine indignation against the corruption of his good creation. When understood in this way, God's anger does not jeopardize his goodness; rather, it is a corollary of it, for if God were not angered by unrighteousness he would not be thoroughly righteous (see Eph. 2:3–5). God's wrath is thus not an aberration of his divine nature, but the result of holy love encountering evil and unrighteousness.

God's wrath is not always apparent in the course of history. Bad consequences do not necessarily follow bad actions; good things sometimes befall them, and conversely, bad things sometimes befall good actions. We cannot say that the **wrath of God** is simply a nemesis, the inevitable process of cause and effect in a moral universe, as does C. H. Dodd (*Romans*, pp. 21–24). Nor must we try, as did ancient Jewish rabbis, to divorce wrath from God by ascribing it to angelic intermediaries. God's wrath is rather a judgment **from heaven**. It is grounded in God's righteous perspective on evil and his power over it. God's wrath is not synonymous with historical catastrophes, as Hegel, for example, regarded it, but it is divine judgment *in* history. God's wrath is witnessed supremely in Gethsemane and Golgotha, where, in the forsakenness of his Son, God took the extreme penalty for sin on himself!

Wrath and righteousness, therefore, are equally expressions of God's grace. If in what follows we hear the gavel of condemnation, it is only to hush all human protestations and self-justifications so that the acquittal of grace may be heard. The Judge condemns *in order to* save. Only those who know that they are lost will look for help. The good news of free salvation can be heard only by those who have first been briefed on the hopelessness of their case.

As an expression of holy love in the face of human evil, God's wrath is directed not against persons, but against their **godlessness and wickedness**. Its object is that which specifically opposes the divine goodness and will. The adjective **all** may suggest that Paul understands **godlessness and wickedness** rather synonymously, but the words carry different nuances. The Greek *asebeia* entails the denial of the holy or *unrighteousness*, here rendered **godlessness**. Paul may be thinking of those offenses against the majesty of God which are found in the first four commandments (Exod. 20:1–8). *Adikia* (NIV, **wickedness**), on the other hand, means immorality or *self-righteousness* and is an offense against the just ordering of human relationships as required in the final six commandments (Exod. 20:12–17). God's wrath is directed against whatever fractures divine and human relationships, whether in motive or in deed.

1:19–21 / Verses 19–21 are critical for the argument because they assert that the problem of human guilt is not God's hiddenness and therefore humanity's ignorance, but rather God's self-disclosure and humanity's rejection of it. The Greek conjunction *dioti* (NIV, **since**) at the beginning of verse 19 carries a causal force. Thus, **men are without excuse**. Twice (vv. 19, 21) Paul says that God can be **known**. Several commentators translate the

Greek word *gnōston* (NIV, **known**) as "knowable," thus suggesting that even if humanity did not know God, it could have known God. "Knowable," of course, also lessens humanity's guilt. Paul, however, indicates that humanity did know at least something of God (see v. 21: **they knew God**), and his argument depends on its having known him. Moreover, in the Greek NT, *gnōston* normally means "known" as opposed to "knowable"; its root, in fact, means not knowledge *about* something, but knowledge *of* it by experience. Paul is therefore saying that all persons have experienced God . . . and could have experienced more. Creation bears God's fingerprints, and through it humanity has experienced something of God's wisdom, power, and generosity. The idea here echoes Paul's Areopagus speech (Acts 17:27–28) that God is not far from his creatures.

A word may be in order at this point about natural theology. Is Paul saying that it was possible for humanity to know God apart from revelation in Jesus Christ? Again in 2:14 he seems to hint of a natural morality among the Gentiles who had never been taught the Mosaic law. These passages have been the subject of confusion, due in part to lack of definition of terms. As it was developed during the Enlightenment of the seventeenth and eighteenth centuries, "natural religion" meant the ability of unaided human reason to perceive and know God. But Paul is not exactly speaking of unaided human reason. His starting point is not humanity (as epitomized by natural theology), but God *who makes himself known through creation*. His topic is thus *revelation*, although revelation through nature and morality rather than through Jesus Christ, or revelation via creation as opposed to revelation via salvation history. Ultimately Paul is less interested in *how* the world knows God than *that* it has experienced God and is hence **without excuse**.

The guilt of humanity, then, is due not to want of truth, but to the suppression of **the truth** (v. 18). If guilt were due to ignorance it would be an intellectual problem, but in reality it is a problem of the will, which is sin. The fundamental problem of humanity was not, as the Greeks thought, a problem of reason, but a problem of the will (v. 27). The proper response would have been to glorify **God** and give **thanks to him**. But when humanity rejected what God had declared of himself in creation it **became futile and their foolish hearts were darkened** (see also Eph. 4:17–18). Having denied God they denied themselves and nature. This became the first step in substituting a counterfeit for God, which is idolatry.

Loss of touch with reality leads to confusion, from which terrible ironies arise. The mystery of revelation consisted in a paradox: **God's invisible qualities . . . have been clearly seen.** This sounds like an oxymoron, for how can something invisible be seen? Nevertheless, God has continued to make known his invisible attributes, both his power and deity, through the created order, and no one can claim ignorance of them. A conception of humanity groping to a higher understanding of God seems foreign to Paul. Knowledge of God begins with God: **God has made it plain to them.**

Again in verse 21 Paul employs the causal *dioti* (NIV, **for although**) to summarize verses 19–20. Humanity's knowledge and experience of God did not lead people, as it should have, to glorify **God** or give **thanks to him,** but to "futility," "foolishness," and "darkness" (v. 21). Paul broaches the idea that he will develop below, namely, that humanity substitutes a false god for the true God. According to the prophets this was the reason for the fall of both the Northern (2 Kings 17:15) and Southern (Jer. 2:5) Kingdoms. In an earlier epistle Paul spoke of the Gentiles as "slaves to those who by nature are not gods" (Gal. 4:8). Luther rightly spoke of the problem of imaginary gods. "How many there are even today who worship him not as if he were God but as if he were as they themselves imagine him for themselves!" (*Lectures on Romans,* p. 25). In a withering criticism of religious aspirations Feuerbach asserted that "god" is simply a projection of the human imagination. This is supremely illustrated by Milton's Satan, who, seeing the Son of God at the Father's right hand, suffered a "sense of injur'd merit," and "thought himself impaired" (*PL* 1.98; 5.662). Plotting to usurp the Son's position, Satan commits the folly of a creature revolting against its creator and becomes, in the words of C. S. Lewis, himself more a "Lie than a Liar, a personified self-contradiction" (*Preface,* ch. 13).

1:22–23 / The demotion of God and the exaltation of self give birth to bitter irony: **although they claimed to be wise, they became fools.** How often this script has been replayed in history! Wisdom is one of the few self-evident virtues, and yet its pathway is littered with irony and tragedy: irony because those who consider themselves wise deny their wisdom by their behavior; tragedy because they do not even recognize their failure. Eve took the fruit which would make her wise and seeing, but she saw only her nakedness (Gen. 3:6–8). The ancients desired to erect a tower to heaven and make a name for themselves throughout the earth, but they were dispersed like so many bricks (Gen. 11:4–8). The most obvious allusion of Paul's thought, however, is to the golden calf in Sinai, where Israel rejected the glory and might of Yahweh for a dumb calf (cf. Exod. 32; Deut. 4:15–19; and Ps. 106:20).

Throughout 1:18–32 Paul employs a number of clever word plays, one of which occurs here. The **futility** (*mataioun*) of giving up God led to **foolishness** (*morainein*). In all this there is a paradox, for the ways of the Creator differ radically from the ways of his creatures. Jesus said the kingdom of God belongs to the *poor in spirit* (Matt. 5:3), and Paul said the wisdom of God could be seen only in the foolishness of the gospel (1 Cor. 1:21). But when people **exchanged the glory of the immortal God for images made to look like mortal man**—and for lesser images—they fell into idolatry. Idolatry is devotion to the made rather than the Maker. Seeking to rid themselves of the mystery of God and creation, they became utterly "sophomoric" (literally, "wise fools," v. 22) and a riddle to themselves.

The Greek word for **glory** (*doxa*, v. 23) often renders the Hebrew *kābôd* in the LXX and means "splendor," "majesty," or "glory." The root meaning carries the idea of "honor," "riches," or even "heaviness." God's glory, especially in the OT, is his "weight," his solidness or substantiality, symbolized by clouds, lightning, storm, and fire, before which the mountains melt like wax (Ps. 97:1–5). His glory is a consuming fire (Exod. 24:15ff.), his presence earth-shattering (Judg. 5:4; Ezek. 1:1ff.). But in substituting **images** for **glory**, humanity opts for shadow over substance, likeness over reality. The root sin in verses 18–23, and the reason for God's wrath, is the sin of *idolatry*.

1:24–25 / There is a theological Gresham's law at work here: as bad money drives good money out of circulation, so false gods render the true God unbelievable. When this happens God gives people **over in the sinful desires of their hearts** (v. 24). Four times Paul says humanity **exchanged** the authentic for the counterfeit (vv. 23, 25, 26, 27) and that as a consequence God **gave them over** to what they desired (vv. 24, 26, 28). We note a shift from human guilt to human fate, from the reasons for God's wrath to the consequences of it. The Greek word translated **gave them over**, *paradidōmi*, means "to give over" or to hand something down intentionally. It is more than an anthropomorphism for the passive judgment of God, i.e., that the withdrawal of God's gracious aid leads to the inevitable consequences of human corruption. Paul ascribes a more active role to God's judgment, as does the OT at those terrible places where human actors are bent on resisting the divine will. Pharaoh hardens his heart against God (Exod. 7:22), but God hardens Pharaoh's heart also (Exod. 4:21ff.); Ahab insists on going to war against God's will, and God drives him to disaster (1 Kings 22:22–23; see also 2 Sam. 16:10). If people persist in believing lies about God, God will obscure the truth from them. At first a lie is simply more important than the truth, but it ends up becoming the truth.

Here too there is a surprising paradox in God's wrath against idolatry. We would expect a list of terrible punishments of humanity's rebellion and immorality, but no list appears. Rather, "had Paul not told us they were signs of wrath, we could easily have mistaken them for signs of grace! When God visits his wrath in the way described in this passage there is no divine cataclysm, no fire from on high sent to consume sinful society. Rather, the wrath which God visits on sinful humanity consists in simply letting humanity have its own way. The punishment of sin is there simply—sin!" (Achtemeier, *Romans*, p. 40). Their wish becomes their punishment.

It is awesome to consider that God hands people over to the evils they desire. How can a good God deliver people to evil purposes contrary to his will? This passage suggests that God hands sinners over to their wretchedness *so that* they will recognize its horrid face and turn to God's merciful countenance. A similar idea governs the teaching of Alcoholics Anonymous that an alcoholic will recover from addictive drinking only by being allowed to experience the unmitigated consequences of it. There is in verses 24ff. no mention of finality. A parallel passage in Ephesians 2:1–4 says that it was precisely on those who "were by nature objects of wrath" that God's rich mercy was shown. Isaiah said that God struck Egypt in order to heal it! (19:22). "God has bound all men over to disobedience so that he may have mercy on them all" (11:32).

Verse 25 repeats the thought of verse 23, that exchanging the truth for a lie is the root of idolatry. Idolatry paves the way for persons to destroy themselves and society. It turns creation into chaos. The idea that they **worshiped** and **served created things** rather than the Creator (another word play), i.e., giving spiritual reverence as well as physical obedience to something other than God, evidently so horrified Paul that, according to the custom of Jewish rabbis, he sanctified God's name with a doxology (so Käsemann, *Romans*, p. 48).

1:26–27 / Paul illustrates the consequences of idolatry by turning to the errors of lesbianism and homosexuality. The problem of "sexual impurity" was mentioned in verse 24; now he turns to one of its ramifications. It must be recognized that Paul does not condemn homosexuality primarily as a moral aberration (although he regarded it as such); had that been his concern he would have included it among the list of immoralities in verses 29–31. Rather, homosexuality illustrates the theological error he has been expounding since verse 18, namely, the exchanging of something authentic for something counterfeit. Paul cites homosexuality ("homo" comes from the Greek word meaning "same," not the Latin *homo*, "man") not because it is a worse sin but because it exemplifies better than other sins the very nature of sin, which is the perversion of an original good, and hence idolatry. His choice of terminology, **natural . . . unnatural relations**, is instructive. Homosexuality is a forsaking of a natural relationship instituted according to the purpose of the Creator, i.e., heterosexuality, for an unnatural relationship which reverses the Creator's purpose. Homosexuality changes something originally oriented to the opposite sex as a complement and inverts it to itself, thus perverting the created order. Like all sin, it is a disorientation which leads to confusion. Thus, the dishonoring of God results in the disordering of human life.

Paul's attitude towards homosexuality was unambiguous; these verses cannot be construed to argue that Paul regarded homosexuality as an alternative lifestyle acceptable to God. It is common today to hear that Paul's pronouncements on this subject were historically and culturally conditioned and are therefore no longer morally valid. We have observed, however, that Paul condemns homosexuality not primarily on moral but on theological grounds. Moreover, although Paul stood within Judaism, which strictly condemned homosexuality, he was writing to a primarily Gentile audience which held a vastly different atti-

tude towards it. Studies of primitive and ancient societies reveal
that fully two-thirds of them affirmed homosexuality as an
acceptable lifestyle (see Additional Notes on 1:26–27). The Greco-
Roman world belonged to this number, sometimes viewing homosexuality and pederasty as a higher form of sexuality (see
Plato's *Symposium*).

In his teaching on homosexuality Paul was swimming
against the moral current of much of his audience. This undercuts
the claim that his teaching on this subject simply reflected the
beliefs of his time. Paul regarded homosexuality as a mirror of sin.
It was for him a "wandering from the truth" (the literal meaning
of *planē*, translated **perversion**, v. 27) of God's intended purpose
for human sexuality, a wandering which eventually would be
assessed its **due penalty**.

1:28 / In verse 28 the apostle shifts from the consequences of idolatry for self (vv 24–27) to its consequences for
society. Again there is a word play, which might be paraphrased,
"Since humanity did not think it fit (*edokimasan*) to acknowledge
God, God handed them over to an unfit (*adokimon*) mind." The
word for "unfit" (NIV, **depraved**) means "failing the test," or "dis-
qualified." For most people sin probably conjures up images of
immoral behavior as something one *does*. But John Calvin (among
others) drew attention to its noetic or intellectual effects. Before
sin affects behavior it affects *thinking*. This idea is presented here.
When humanity gave up honoring the one whom it ought to
have honored, God gave it over **to do what ought not be done**.
This expression, like several others in the latter half of this chapter, appears to be indebted more to Stoicism than to Hebrew
thought. It implies a self-evident duty in accordance with nature,
or natural law.

1:29–31 / These verses contain a list of twenty-one terms
(in Greek) of things which "ought not be done" (v. 28). They are
consequences, not causes, of exchanging the truth of God for a
lie. As the consequences of God's wrath they are thus their own
punishment. The list is arranged in three distinct groups. The first
group consists of four abstract nouns qualified by **filled**: **wickedness, evil, greed and depravity**. **Wickedness** is in Greek *adikia*,
which is twice mentioned in verse 18 as the reason for God's
wrath. As the root of other sins, these four terms poison the well
of human behavior. They are followed by a second group of five

nouns all qualified by **full: envy, murder, strife, deceit and malice.** The final group is a series of twelve terms which (all in the accusative case) describe various acts of wickedness. Again in Greek there are several word plays, especially **envy** (*phthonou*) and **murder** (*phonou*), and **senseless** (*asynetous*) and **faithless** (*asynthetous*).

Most of the terms in the list are self-explanatory. Each term, of course, has its particular meaning, but Paul's intent seems to be in the composite effect of all of them. It is a salvo of terms describing how people in general act when they have a "depraved mind" (v. 28). We need not suppose the list to be tailored specifically for Rome; such catalogs of vices were well known in the ancient world, particularly among Jews and Stoics. By appealing to a conventional morality Paul condemns a series of vices which nearly all the ancients would have condemned. Acknowledgment of God would have cultivated behavior agreeable and edifying both to God and others, but when humanity cast its verdict against God, it banished all constraints, thus prodding a nest of pinfeather sins to wing their way as grotesque birds of prey.

1:32 / This verse repeats the thought of verse 20 and concludes Paul's indictment of Gentile humanity. But there is a new and startling thought here which prepares the way for what will follow in chapters 2–3. Paul says that *approval* of the behavior described above is as bad as—or worse than—the actual behavior. In modern law an accomplice to a crime is less guilty than the perpetrator of a crime. But Paul might not agree. The consenting bystander is normally more premeditative than the impassioned aggressor, and worse yet, consent (or silence!) in the face of wrongdoing lends subtle support to make something fashionable which deserves to be condemned. Modern media and advertising barons have made this truth painfully clear. Bengel's word is perhaps more appropriate today than it was when he wrote it two centuries ago: "He is a worse man, who destroys both himself and others, than he who destroys himself alone" (*Gnomon*, vol. 3, p. 25). Paul himself was once a consenting bystander to a man's murder (Acts 7:58–8:1; 22:20). One wonders if his reflection on that event might have influenced the wording of this verse.

With good reason modern readers may come to the end of this section feeling rather assaulted, particularly those who think themselves good persons. No one is guilty of all the sins Paul accuses humanity of in these verses. Even Stalin was kind to his daughter and Goebbels to his dogs, we are told. Is not Paul's assessment of human nature excessively bleak and unfair?

Every age has its forbidden subjects. For the Victorians it was sex, for the modern West it is sin. One of the ironies of the twentieth century is that it has experienced greater evil than perhaps any previous century, and yet it has no category for sin. The nineteenth century taught that nature has evolved and progressed from primitive life-forms to more advanced ones. This idea has so permeated the modern bloodstream that it is axiomatic to speak of development, progress, and fulfillment in all disciplines, including history and religion. "Earlier" means primitive, "later" means more advanced and sophisticated.

Such thinking would have left Paul blinking in incredulity. The apostle was too penetrating a thinker not to reflect on the tragic flaw or "frustration" in creation (8:20). Nor does he think that humanity is evolving to something higher and better. To the contrary. When people leave the true knowledge and worship of God there is a "devolution" to that which is low and bestial. When God is replaced with a lie the general conditions described in this section prevail.

Paul's intent in 1:18–32 is not to describe anyone's life in particular. He is, rather, like a physician showing a transparency of various maladies on a screen before a group of patients. No one patient has all the disorders, but somewhere there is a malady (or more than one) that describes everyone's condition and that, if left to its own course, will prove fatal.

Romans 1:18–32 asks if we do not recognize our own *predisposition* to immorality and idolatry. Our individual sins (whatever they are) are like spokes connected to a single hub, all stemming from and leading to the same thing—the demotion of God and the promotion of self. Jesus hinted at such complicity when he said, "Let the one without sin throw the first stone" (John 8:7). No one is guilty of all these sins, nor is anyone innocent of them all. Romans 1:18ff. may not be a personal letter to any of us (but then again, it may), but it is an open letter to the human race of which we all are part.

Additional Notes   §4

1:18 / For the influence of Gen. 3 on 1:18ff., see Dunn, *Romans 1–8*, pp. 53ff. Adolf Schlatter's discussion of God's wrath is particularly insightful. "It is precisely because Romans was written to testify to the grace of God (5:12–21) that it belongs to those parts of the NT which witness powerfully to the wrath of God. We understand nothing of grace if we do not sense the depths of divine indignation with which God opposes all evil. The degree to which we measure the truth and seriousness of divine wrath is the same degree to which we measure the truth and greatness of divine grace. It is pure nonsense to say that God's wrath makes faith all the more difficult. The reverse is true: no one would dare trust in God unless we all were quite convinced that God is the relentless enemy of our wickedness. We despise anyone who fails to show indignation in the face of evil" (*Der Brief an die Römer*, p. 20; my translation).

Dodd approaches the wrath of God from the perspective of psychology, considering it an "irrational passion of anger." "The idea of an angry God is a first attempt to rationalize the shuddering awe which men feel before the incalculable possibilities of appalling disaster inherent in life, but it is an attempt which breaks down as the rational element in religion advances" (*Romans*, p. 24).

For rabbinic attempts to link evil to fallen angels, see Str-B, vol. 3, pp. 30ff.

Franz Leenhardt's discussion of wrath and salvation has helped shape the discussion of this verse. See *Romans*, p. 60.

On the meaning of **godlessness** and **wickedness**, see Schlatter, *Gottes Gerechtigkeit*, p. 49, and Str-B, vol. 3, p. 31.

1:19–21 / The hallmark of the Enlightenment was free inquiry through unimpeded reason, which included a rejection of all forms of revelation or church authority, belief in the essential goodness of humanity, and an understanding of nature as a perfect machine with God as its manufacturer. Thus, reason and nature became the (only) two avenues of knowledge about God, thus reducing religion generally to a code of ethics. Such ideas are reflected in Benjamin Franklin's "Articles of Belief and Acts of Religion" (*Autobiography and Other Writings*, ed. R. Nye [Boston: Houghton Mifflin, Riverside Editions, 1958], pp. 163–65). Both Nygren, *Romans*, pp. 102–5, and Gaugler, *Der Römerbrief*, vol. 1, p. 54, offer balanced discussions of natural theology in 1:18ff.

Paul's concept of God in 1:18ff. differs somewhat from the rabbinic concept. The rabbis elevated God's invisible nature so greatly that they questioned whether the angels themselves could see God. That humanity could see God was as impossible as looking at the sun. Gentiles were not thereby exonerated, however, for the rabbis taught that God had revealed himself to them not through the created order (so Paul), but through an inner moral law. See Str-B, vol. 3, pp. 31–43. Paul, of course, does not say humanity can see God directly, but that God's witness to himself in creation is sufficient to reveal his power and deity. His thinking here seems to be indebted to certain Stoic words and concepts. See Dunn, *Romans 1–8*, pp. 57–58.

1:24–25 / The "theological Gresham's law" is the theme of C. S. Lewis' *The Last Battle*, in which a lion's skin thrown over a hapless donkey causes Narnians to stop believing in the true lion, Aslan. "Tirian had never dreamed that one of the results of an Ape's setting up a false Aslan would be to stop people from believing in the real one" (*The Last Battle* [New York: Collier Books, 1970], p. 74).

1:26–27 / It should be noted that homophobia (fear or hatred of homosexuals) is itself a sin as bad as the sin it condemns, combining both arrogance and malice listed in 1:29–31.

For biblical and extrabiblical references to homosexuality, see Gen. 19:1–28; Lev. 18:22; 20:13; Deut. 23:17f.; 1 Kings 14:24; 2 Kings 23:7; Isa. 1:9; 3:9; Lam. 4:6; Wisd. of Sol. 14:26; T. Levi 17.1; Sib. Or. 2.73; 3.596ff.; Philo, *Spec. Leg.* 3.39; NT: Matt. 10:14f.; 11:23f.; 1 Cor. 6:9; 1 Tim. 1:10; 2 Pet. 2:6ff.; Jude 7.

For studies of homosexuality in the Gentile world, see *Encyclopaedia Britannica* (1964), vol. 11, p. 648. For a discussion of homosexuality in the biblical world, see M. Pope, *IDBSup*, 415–17, and V. Furnish, *The Moral Teaching of Paul*, 2d ed. (Nashville: Abingdon, 1985), pp. 52–82. For a discussion of this passage, see R. B. Hays, "Relations Natural and Unnatural: A Response to John Boswell's Exegesis of Romans 1," *JRE* 14 (1, 1986), pp. 184–215; also D. F. Wright, "Homosexuals or Prostitutes?" *VC* 38 (1984), pp. 125–53. Romans 1:26 is the only place in the Bible where lesbianism is mentioned. Why Paul mentions it before male homosexuality is uncertain. Was he following Gen. 3 where Eve sinned first? Or is it a prelude to male homosexuality, which he describes in more aggressive terms (**inflamed with lust**)?

1:29–31 / For a helpful discussion of the terms in vv. 29–31 and the meaning of each, see Cranfield, *Romans*, vol. 1, pp. 129–33.

§5 The Responsibility of Privilege (Rom. 2:1–16)

The discussion of the guilt of humanity in 1:18ff. presupposes the Gentile world, that is, humanity without special revelation from God. The prominence given to homosexuality in 1:26–27 and the list of vices in 1:29–31 typify Jewish prejudice against "Gentile sinners," as Paul once referred to them (Gal. 2:15). We noted how clearly 1:18–32 echoes the Jewish indictment of Gentiles from the Wisdom of Solomon (chs. 11–15). Gentiles could have known God from creation. "They live among his works," says Wisdom of Solomon 13:7, yet they "did not recognize the craftsman while paying heed to his works" (13:1). Therefore, they "are [not] to be excused," for "they had the power to know so much," yet "[failed] to find sooner the Lord of these things" (13:8–9). For these reasons they became "hateful to God" (14:9) because of their "confusion over what is good [and] forgetfulness of [God's] favors" (14:26). Their idolatry led to sexual perversion (14:12), and they were forced to "learn that one is punished by the very things by which he sins" (11:16). These quotations and ideas from the Wisdom of Solomon find a striking parallel in Paul's exposé of Gentile guilt in 1:18–32.

Jewish readers and perhaps even moral Gentiles such as Stoics would have found little discomfort and much to applaud in Paul's castigation of Gentile humanity. The morally upright have a sharp eye for the faults of the wicked. There were, we may be sure, no fewer Caligulas or Neros then than there are Stalins and Hitlers today.

The judgment which Paul hurled at unrighteous Gentiles in chapter 1 comes whirling back like a boomerang on heads held high in moral satisfaction in chapter 2. True, Jews are not named until 2:17, and it is possible to regard 2:1–16 as directed to moral humanity in general. This would include Jews as well as Stoics, for example, who were renowned for their moral philosophy. Nevertheless, although Paul does not mention Jews by name in this section, it is fairly certain that he is speaking to them, for when he mentions Jews in 2:17 he does not appear to introduce a new subject, but to identify a subject already under consideration. Moreover, just as 1:18–32 echoed many of the ideas from Wisdom of Solomon 11–14, chapter 2 echoes Wisdom of Solomon 15, which asserts the moral superiority of Jews over unrighteous Gentiles: "But thou, our God, art kind and true, patient, and ruling all things in mercy. For even if we (= Jews) sin we are thine, knowing thy power; but we will not sin, because we know that we are accounted thine. For to know thee is complete righteousness" (Wisd. of Sol. 15:1–3, RSV).

Against this attitude Paul launches phase two of his indictment of humanity. The present task is more difficult, however, for the morally upright are less obviously in need of God's righteousness than are the unrighteous. Nevertheless, the *self-righteous* are as culpable as the *unrighteous*, for the self-righteous live under an illusion, failing to see that their value judgments of others ultimately condemn themselves. Paul condemns Jews in the same language with which he condemned Gentiles: "You . . . have no excuse" (2:1; see 1:20).

The prophet Nathan condemned King David with his own value judgment, "Thou art the man" (2 Sam. 12:1–10). John the Baptist warned the Pharisees and Sadducees not to presume on their ethnic status: "Do not think you can say to yourselves, 'We have Abraham as our father.' I tell you that out of these stones God can raise up children for Abraham" (Matt. 3:7–10). Jesus too burst the balloon of moral superiority: "For in the same way you judge others, you will be judged, and with the measure you use, it will be measured to you" (Matt. 7:2). Likewise, the apostle turns from the dives of sinners in 1:18–32 to the parlors of moral respectability in 2:1ff. to evince that it is not knowledge of God's will, nor even the status of election, which exonerates Jews before God, but the *doing* of God's will. God's judgment against those who do such things is based on truth and impartiality (2:2, 11).

Paul proceeds with the present argument in three stages. In 2:1–3 he adopts a style of argumentation called diatribe. Especially common among Stoics, a diatribe was a literary technique in which an imaginary heckler or opponent was engaged in lively argumentation. Paul's opponents, of course, were not imaginary. In the synagogues and marketplaces of his missionary travels he had encountered the attitude of moral superiority and divine favoritism expressed in 2:1ff.; indeed, he had once been part of it (see Phil. 3:4–7). Paul was no friend of the illusion that the sunlight of privilege exempts one from the cloud of divine judgment.

Once the universality of God's judgment is established in 2:1–3, Paul proceeds to challenge another illusion: is not God's silence in the face of wrongdoing indicative of a lack of divine retribution (2:4–11)? Quite the contrary. God's continued goodness in the face of evil is intended to melt the icy heart of the sinner. Patience is extended in order to lead to repentance, and presumption on that patience is a fatal mistake. God is an utterly impartial judge (v. 11) who judges *deeds* (v. 6). No sporadic ethical refurbishment, no turning over of new moral leaves, lays a foundation for acquittal before God, but only practical evidence of new life (vv. 7–10). This applies to all people, to Jews as well as Gentiles (vv. 9–10). There are no incumbents, no *ex officio* members, in the kingdom of God. Knowledge of the truth, even (as in the case of Jews) inheritance of divine revelation, does not satisfy God, only a life of repentance (v. 4) and renewal (vv. 7ff.). The "obedience [which] comes from faith" (1:5), which Paul noted at the outset of Romans, controls the present thought: the evidence of faith is not good intentions or verbal confession but "persist[ence] in doing good" (v. 7).

The third stage of the argument comes in 2:12–16, in which Paul shows that God's judgment is absolutely just. If Gentiles cannot take sanctuary in the plea that they have no knowledge of divine law, neither can Jews take refuge in divine revelation. In the former case, God's judgment appeals to a rule of conscience "written on their hearts" (v. 15), a principle which the Wisdom of Solomon expressed in the words, "thy immortal spirit is in all things" (12:1). To this principle Gentiles were obliged to conform. In the latter case, God's judgment falls on Jews because they fail to keep the revelation they have received. At the end of time the secrets of all hearts will be revealed and judged according to the gospel of the Righteous One, Jesus Christ.

2:1–3 / Jesus once told a parable about a Pharisee who stood in the temple and prayed, "God, I thank you that I am not

like other men" (Luke 18:11). In 2:1–3 Paul declares that there is
a Pharisee in the heart of everyone who esteems his or her own
morality. Their error, says Paul, consists in passing judgment on
others, for in passing judgment one supposes oneself *apart from*
humanity, whereas in truth one is always and only a *part of* humanity. The accent here falls on *doing*. It is often said that it is not
what you know but who you know that counts; Paul would have
said that it is not what you know but what you do that counts.
He says bluntly, **you who pass judgment . . . do the same things**.
Such a statement rankles those who consider themselves "good
people," for they, like the Pharisee in the temple, claim *not* to do
the things they despise in others. And often they do not. Perhaps
they reason, as Paul says in 1:32, that if applauding evil is as bad
as doing evil, the opposite must also be true, that condemning
evil is as good as not doing it, and that by condemning evil one
can avoid the consequences of it. But this is treading on casuistic
thin ice, for there are more than enough pitfalls listed in 1:29–31
to catch the most scrupulous and wary moralist.

There is still more to Paul's concern over judgments. Do not
even truly moral individuals discover to their acute disappoint-
ment that the evils they detest and strive to overcome are also in
themselves? It is no coincidence that we have learned more about
the meaning of evil from the saints who have forsaken this world
than from any number of moral idealists. Little is learned about
temptation by surrendering to it; but whoever tries to resist evil
learns its force firsthand. It is senseless to judge faults by degrees
of badness. Left to themselves and given time, even seemingly
innocuous faults become loathsome evils. Franz Leenhardt says
it is futile to use "the vices of others, even their worst, as a screen
for our own faults, even the slightest" (*Romans*, p. 74). In comparison to the worst in others nearly anyone can look good, but that
is only because, in the words of Luther, "The unrighteous look for
good in themselves and evil in others; the righteous are eager to
see the good in others and overlook their own" (*Epistle to the
Romans*, p. 36). What counts is not the evil one avoids, but the evil
one does. Most honest people are not fooled, and neither is God.
"God cannot be mocked. A man reaps what he sows" (Gal. 6:7).

Who is this (self-)righteous judge who is snared by the traps
he sets for others? A literal translation of 2:1 reads, "Therefore you
are without excuse, O man, you who judge." Paul wheels around
on the morally satisfied who would have applauded his condem-

nation of Gentiles in 1:18–32 and addresses them in the second person singular, "Thou art." Direct address was not only characteristic of the Hellenistic diatribe, it is also more personal and universal. It intensifies the argument for the very persons who thought themselves exempt from it! C. K. Barrett and others suggest that the moral prosecution here takes the form of a dialogue. Thus, verse 1 is Paul's initial charge; verse 2, the opponent's defense; and verse 3, Paul's concluding charge (*Romans*, pp. 43–44).

The word **judgment** (*krinein*) appears in one form or another seven times in verses 1–3! This indicates how thoroughly the theme dominates Paul's thought. In contrast to self-serving human judgments that stack the deck in one's own favor, Paul says that **God's judgment . . . is based on truth. We know** this, says Paul. It is something we can be confident of because God's judgment is true and impartial (v. 11), an immovable rock in a sea of moral equivocation. The reappearance of **on truth** here is not without significance. Earlier Paul argued that idolatry and wickedness were a revolt against the *truth* of God (1:25). But moral casuistry and manipulation are equally odious to God, as Jewish sages agreed. First Enoch 52:7 is similar to verse 3: "In those days (the endtime) no one will be able to save himself either with gold or silver, and no one will be able to flee" (see also 1 Enoch 102:1). Nearly a century after Paul, Rabbi Akiba (d. A.D. 135) said, "The judgment is a judgment of the truth" (m.'*Abot* 3.16). But in popular Judaism of Paul's day there was widespread overconfidence that Israelites were secure with God by virtue of their heritage (John 8:33), and that their heritage would compensate for any want of conformity to the law's moral demands. In 2:1ff. Paul goes nose-to-nose with this attitude of exemption and exclusion. Although he does not specifically call it a lie, his contrasting of specious moral judgments with **God's judgment** in **truth** associates it with the lie of Gentiles in 1:25. Moral and religious humanity are also locked in battle against the truth!

The future orientation of verses 5, 6, and 16 indicates that **God's judgment** is here the final judgment at the end of time. If God judges Gentiles in the present by handing them over to the sins they desire (1:24ff.), his judgment of Jews who judge will be in the future. But, as Paul affirms in verse 4, God's delay in judging Jews cannot be mistaken as indifference to their sin. In handing over Gentiles to the consequences of their sins and in reserving judgment on Jews until the end of time, God has but one intent in mind, and that is to lead both to repentance (v. 4). God's judgment is equal and impartial. Paul will later say, "There is no one righteous, not even one" (3:10). This includes Gentiles who know their guilt and Jews who do not; both are without excuse (1:20; 2:1). Until this truth is indelibly etched in their understanding, neither Gentiles nor Jews can understand why salvation is grounded in Jesus Christ alone. It is Christ's righteousness, not human self-righteousness or supposed-righteousness, which justifies believers. Salvation rests solely on God's grace toward sinners, not on sinners' bargaining with bogus merits.

2:4–11 / **The riches of** God's **kindness, tolerance and patience** are grace. Grace is shown not only in the gift of salvation, but also in God's patience with sinners until they receive it. Paul chides his Jewish opponents for their **contempt** of God's **kindness**, for **not realizing** that God's patience has a saving intent. And well he might, for although the idea is nowhere expressed as supremely as in verse 4, its rudiments were present in Judaism. God's patience ought not be confused with weakness or indifference, however, and anyone who interprets it as leniency toward sin is simply abusing divine benevolence. The act of judging others betrays this tendency, for those who judge claim God's patience and goodness as a confirmation of their judgment, indeed as a reward for it. On the contrary, says Paul, the proper response to grace is repentance, not indulgence.

The Greek word for repentance, *metanoia*, was relatively uncommon in Greek parlance; the biblical usage reflects the Hebrew, *šûḇ*, meaning "to turn around." *Metanoia* means to recognize one's condition and do something about it, to change one's mind and make a decisive turn. It is not primarily a feeling or intention, but an attitudinal change accompanied by action. Repentance is not coerced by fear but evoked by love. People are *led* to repent by God's goodness and patience. The religious and moral person always stands in danger of separating God's gifts from the claims and responsibilities which attend them, of thinking that God's gifts bestow righteousness, whereas, in fact, God's gifts call one to it.

The greatest obstacle to God's will is the "hardened" or "uncircumcised" heart (v. 5). **Because of your stubbornness and your unrepentant heart, you are storing up wrath against yourself.** The Greek word for **stubbornness**, *sklērotēs*, means "harshness," "callousness," or "hardness." One might expect that the hardened heart would characterize the heathen and pagan world, but it is not mentioned in 1:18–32. The hardened heart is rather the problem of Jews, of *religious and moral humanity*. One would expect gratitude and joy in response to God's **kindness, tolerance and patience** in verse 4. But this is not so. God's gifts and God's goodness are met by the elect with **stubbornness and unrepentant hearts**. Those with most reason to honor God disobey him. This truth is written deep in the history of religion, from the OT to the modern church.

But if one were to accumulate capital in heaven from works of merit, then the reverse must be equally true, that resistance to God stores up judgment **for the day of God's wrath**. To describe that fact Paul chooses a rare Greek word, *dikaiokrisia*, translated **righteous judgment**, which combines the motifs of righteousness (1:17) and wrath (1:18), thus establishing that these are not contradictory attributes of God's nature, but inseparable consequences of his sovereign lordship. For those who respond in faith, God's lordship results in righteousness; for those opposed to his righteousness, that lordship results in wrath.

Paul earlier averred that God's judgment is based on doing his will, not simply knowing it (vv. 1–3). Verse 6 repeats and concludes this idea: God's righteous judgment **will give to each person according to what he has done**. God's judgment looks to deeds, not to privilege. This thought is so close to Psalm 62:12 and Proverbs 24:12 that the editors of the NIV place it in quotation marks. Evangelical Protestants may sense that this verse contradicts Paul's teaching on justification by faith. It cannot be denied, however, that both Old and New Testaments teach that God judges according to deeds. Romans begins and ends by speaking of faith as a deed, as "obedience" (1:5; 16:26). In 1 Corinthians 3:12ff. Paul speaks of "each man's work" as a "foundation" which "the Day will bring to light." Deeds are not external appendages of personhood but expressions of personal values. The Bible refers to them as "fruit," i.e., as organic growth in continuity with the stock (Amos 6:12; Matt. 7:16; John 15:5ff.; Gal. 5:22; Heb. 12:11). Far from constituting a claim on God, as the inevitable outflowing of intent, works express faith and repentance. They are not competitive with faith, but effects of it. At the last judgment no one can claim the spiritual bank account of nation or class or race or church or home or even personal achievement.

Each must present his or her own deposit book, so to speak, to receive what has been **stored up** (v. 5).

Verses 7–10 elaborate the idea of verse 6. The structure of the verses is puzzling: there are no verbs, and the argument seems circular. Verses 7 and 10 combine to explain the character of good works, whereas the intervening verses describe the character and consequences of evil works. If there is any dislocation it may be due to the problem of oral dictation (see 16:22), with Paul's mind returning in verse 10 to clarify the content of verse 7. But closer study indicates the probability of a literary pattern, a chiastic structure (A-B-B'-A'). Thus,

> A—works which lead to eternal life (v. 7)
> > B—works which lead to God's wrath (v. 8)
> > B'—God's judgment against bad works, of both Jew and Gentile (v. 9)
> A'—God's reward of good works, of both Jew and Gentile (v. 10).

The discussion of works in verses 7–10 can be summed up by "character" or "orientation." Paul is less concerned with the exceptional deeds which all people do—whether the heroic deed on the spur of the moment, or the plunge into sin. Occasional good and bad deeds are usually extremes of an individual's moral continuum which, in the overall balance of life, might be said to be "out of character." The apostle is concerned instead with root desires and fundamental orientation in life, which, in the case of good works, he identifies as **glory, honor, immortality**, and **peace**. Thus the first characteristic of good works consists in an altruism beyond self and orientation to others and God. Moral ends, of course, must be pursued by moral means. Paul expresses it thus: **Those who by persistence in doing good works seek** such things will receive **eternal life**. This constitutes the second characteristic of good works, which is contained in two key words. The first, **seek**, occurs in Greek as a present active participle and carries the idea of pursuance or *continuing* to seek. The second word, **persistence**, comes from the Greek, *hypomonē* and means "continuance" or "endurance," conveying the idea of consistency. It recalls the thought of 1:5 ("obedience that comes from faith") and implies the sum total of one's life and works. The character of good works, then, consists in both goal and means, altruism and consistency.

Verses 8–9, by contrast, speak of evil works and recall the language of 1:18ff. God's **wrath and anger** are directed against those who **reject the truth** and **follow evil**. We noted in the discussion of 1:25 how exchanging "the truth of God for a lie" leads to idolatry. The word above rendered **evil** is *adikia*, "unrighteousness" or "wickedness," the same word to which Paul contrasted God's righteousness in 1:17, and with which he began his discussion of the guilt of humanity (1:18ff.). Rejection of the truth and the resultant evil are characterized by **self-seeking** (v. 8). A very rare word in Greek, *eritheia* means "selfishness" or "selfish ambition" and forms a blatant contrast to altruism and consistency. Selfishness and egotism lie at the root of sin and are the first steps of those **who reject the truth and** do **evil**. In consequence, God's wrath brings **trouble and distress**. In Greek these two words connote "outward affliction" and "inner anguish," respectively.

In summary, works ultimately fall into two categories, those which serve and maximize self and those which serve and maximize the glory of God. The former meet with God's wrath, the latter with eternal life. One recalls the words of George MacDonald, "There are only two kinds of people in the end: those who say to God, 'Thy will be done,' and those to whom God says, in the end, '*Thy* will be done' " (C. S. Lewis, *Great Divorce*, p. 72). The seeking of self or the seeking of God can, of course, describe a religious person as well as a pagan. That is why Paul applies these verses to *both* Jew and Gentile—**First for the Jew, then for the Gentile**. He may begin with Jews in order to acknowledge their priority in the history of redemption (see Amos 3:2; Luke 12:48), but he does so with the reminder that priority in redemption entails priority in judgment!

"Paul's whole point here is that the terms of judgment are precisely the *same* for *everyone*" (Dunn, *Romans 1–8*, p. 88). This is the meaning of verse 11: **For God does not show favoritism**. The word for **favoritism**, *prosōpolēmpsia*, means "to look only on the face of things" or "to see only the masks people wear." It occurs several times in the NT (Acts 10:34; Gal. 2:6; Eph. 6:9; Col. 3:25), but always negatively, suggesting that the face or mask does not reflect the person behind it. God, says Paul, sees the person, not the mask; he sees the character of the actor, not just the role played. The character of the Gentile has been unsparingly exposed in 1:18–32, but Paul is equally severe with the Jew. It would be disastrous to mistake knowledge of the law for obedience to it, to equate the privilege of the covenant with responsibility to fulfill it, to mistake election for salvation.

2:12–16 / The discussion of Jewish and Gentile culpability is now continued from the standpoint of the law. Gentiles and Jews are not named, but the reference to those **apart from the law** and **under the law** (v. 12) clearly intends them. The **law** is the Mosaic law which included not only the Ten Commandments but the whole body of decrees and ordinances in the Pentateuch, which, according to rabbinic count, totaled 613 commandments (365 negative, 248 positive). Verses 12–16 argue that the law is an impartial standard of judgment, and they illustrate the principle of verse 11 that "God does not show favoritism."

The cutting edge of Paul's argument is verse 13: **For it is not those who hear the law who are righteous in God's sight, but it is those who obey the law who will be declared righteous.** This verse, which recalls James 1:22, 25, asserts that it is not *knowledge* of the law (for all know it, at least in part, either by revelation or by conscience), but *obedience* which matters. "Cursed is the man who does not uphold the words of this law by carrying them out" (Deut. 27:26).

Verse 14 addresses the problem of Gentiles and the law. Since Gentiles have not been given the Mosaic law, ought they not be free from its stipulations? False reasoning, says Paul. **When Gentiles, who do not have the law, do by nature things required by the law, they are a law to themselves.** Here, and in verse 15, where Paul speaks of **the law written on** Gentile **hearts,** he argues that even people without religious instruction are responsible moral agents. Cranfield understands Gentiles here to mean Christian Gentiles, but that is surely reading too much into the verse (*Epistle to the Romans*, vol. 1, pp. 155–56). Paul has not yet introduced Jesus Christ into the discussion of Jews and Gentiles (with the exception of 1:16–17). His whole argument depends on the premise that *apart from Christ* Jews and Gentiles are deserving of God's wrath. Paul is contending for an innate moral sense in humanity, to whose voice Gentiles are as bound as are Jews to the Torah. In so arguing he is in good company, not only with the Jewish tradition, but also with the pagan. There is within humanity a rudimentary but undeniable moral sense, an "oughtness," which the Hebrew tradition regarded as the "heart." Paul bears witness that it is **written on their hearts**. To **the require-ments of the law** the Gentiles are responsible, and by it they are condemned.

On the Last Day God will reveal the hidden recesses of human hearts and judge them accordingly (v. 16). Although humanity's guilt will be established by the law, judgment will be rendered **through Jesus Christ, as my gospel declares**. This verse states explicitly that there is no judgment apart from the gospel. In his inscrutable wisdom (11:33) God will **judge men's secrets** only through Christ, whose perfect love satisfied God's exact justice. Thus, in the midst of humanity's dire condition and inescapable guilt, Paul introduces a harbinger of grace. The Judge, it is true, brings lethal charges against the accused, both Jews and Gentiles, but the same Judge will be no less valiant in his defense for the accused **through Jesus Christ**.

Additional Notes §5

For a comparison and analysis of Wisd. of Sol. 11–15 and Rom. 1–2, see Nygren, *Romans*, pp. 113–16.

2:1–3 / On the problem of judgments, see Achtemeier, *Romans*, pp. 43–44. For arguments in favor of reading 2:1ff. as addressed to Jews, see Cranfield, *Romans*, vol. 1, p. 138.

It is of historical interest to note that Luther hurled Paul's condemnation in 2:1ff. not against Jews but against political rulers! "By what authority do princes and secular rulers help themselves to all game and fowl, so that no one but they can go on the hunt? If an ordinary man would do such a thing, he would rightly be called a thief . . . but when the rulers do something of this sort, they cannot be thieves because they are the rulers. . . . In the same sense, Blessed Augustine says in *The City of God*: 'What else are the great kingdoms but great robberies?' In the same place he tells this story: 'When Alexander the Great asked a pirate who had been taken prisoner how he dared to infest the safety of the sea, he got from him the very frank and insolent reply: 'And how do you venture to make the whole earth unsafe? When I do this with a small boat, they call me a robber, but when you do it with a large fleet, they call you an emperor' " (*Lectures on Romans*, p. 38).

2:4–11 / For allusions to God's patience in Jewish literature, see Wisd. of Sol. 11:23; 12:10, 19; 15:1; 2 Apoc. Bar. 59:6; 4 Ezra 7:74. In addition, see the material gathered in Str-B, vol. 3, pp. 77–78.

On presuming on God's grace, note Franz Leenhardt's words: "To know the good does not furnish us with a claim to divine indulgence. The fact that the hour of divine judgment has not yet struck does not by any means show that God judges us favourably. . . . History is the school of repentance, but we must learn the lesson and not squander our time" (*Romans*, p. 75). Of repentance Karl Barth says,

> What is pleasing to God comes into being when all human right-eousness is gone, irretrievably gone, when men are uncertain and lost, when they have abandoned all ethical and religious illusions, and when they have renounced every hope in this world and in this heaven. [Repentance] is not the last and noblest and most refined achievement of the righteousness of men in the service of God, but the first elemental act of the righteousness of God in the service of man; . . . which, because it is from God and not from men, occasions joy in heaven.

For OT references to hardness of heart, see Deut. 9:27; 10:16; Jer. 4:4; Amos 6:8; Zeph. 3:1–5. For the idea of storing up merit in Judaism, see Str-B, vol. 1, pp. 429ff. Helpful discussions of **righteous judgment** are offered by Käsemann, *Romans*, p. 56, and Schlatter, *Gottes Gerechtigkeit*, p. 78.

References to divine judgment of works occur in Ps. 62:12; Prov. 24:12; Isa. 3:10f.; Jer 17:10; Hos. 12:2; Matt. 7:21; John 5:28ff.; 2 Cor. 5:10; Gal. 6:7–9; 1 Pet. 1:17; Rev. 2:23.

2:12–16 / Not uncommonly Rom. 2:12–14 is cited as evidence that there is salvation apart from Jesus Christ. This passage does not answer the question in the affirmative. Verse 16 says explicitly that Jesus Christ will be the standard of judgment for all peoples—"on that day . . . God will judge men's secrets through Jesus Christ." The point of these verses is not that Gentiles can be saved by an inner law, but that both Jews and Gentiles have failed to live up to the laws which they have respec-tively received, and that both are justly condemned. The standards will be different for each, but the verdict will be the same for both.

On the idea of knowledge of the law versus obedience to it, the early rabbinic tradition was agreed that the practice of Torah was more important than the study of Torah, and thus in general consensus with Paul. A reversal of rabbinic opinion occurred, however, about A.D. 135 when under Hadrian the death penalty was decreed for the study as well as for the practice of Torah. At the Council of Lydda the rabbis declared that in the face of death a Jew could violate any law (with the exceptions of idolatry, unchastity, and murder), but that the study of Torah could under no circumstances be forsaken. Thus, less than a century after Paul, the rabbinate under historical compulsion rendered a legal verdict which reinforced the very point Paul argued against in Rom. 2:12–14! See Str-B, vol. 3, pp. 85–86.

On the moral accountability of humanity, see Jer. 31:30, Wisd. of Sol. 12:2, Acts 10:35. The rabbinic tradition argued that while the Mosaic law was obligatory for Jews, the more general Noahic law (Gen. 9:1–17) was obligatory for Gentiles. See Str-B, vol. 1, pp. 88–89. In the pagan tradition Aristotle states that the moral individual is "a law to himself" (*Nicomachean Ethics* 4. 8. 10). A few hours browsing through a reference work on ethics (e.g., Hasting's *Encyclopedia of Religion and Ethics*) will relieve the skeptical reader of any doubt as to the general agreement of the world's various religions and peoples on basic moral principles. So apparent was this "oughtness" that Kant formulated his moral argument for the existence of God on the basis of it. See I. Kant, *Critique of Practical Reason*, trans. L. Beck (Indianapolis: Bobbs-Merrill Company, Inc., The Liberal Arts Press, 1956), bk. 2, ch. 2. Two modern discussions of the issue are presented by C. S. Lewis in *The Case for Christianity* (New York: Macmillan, 1953) and *The Abolition of Man* (New York: Macmillan, 1962).

Psalm 51 records the confession of David when the storm of guilt from his adultery with Bathsheba and murder of Uriah broke upon him. Psalm 51 is, in fact, descriptive of the human condition, "I know my transgressions, and my sin is always before me. . . . Surely I was sinful at birth" (vv. 3, 5). It may be possible to maintain confidence in one's virtue if one limits or controls the field of comparison. It is common, for instance, in comparative studies of various kinds, to compare the strengths of one system to the weaknesses of another system in order to vindicate the superiority of the former. Jews did this in Paul's day when they compared Jewish morality with Gentile immorality, as we have seen in the Wisdom of Solomon 12–15. A modern approach would be comparing "the American way of life" to that of the Far East or Latin America, or church attendance in America to that of Europe. But what happens when the good is not contrasted to the inferior but compared with the ideal, the standard by which the judgment is itself made? A vast difference results: we find ourselves no longer in the victory circle but on the ropes.

This is the program in 2:17–29. The exacting righteousness of God's revealed will pronounces judgment on all people, and each person is forced to confess with David, "I was sinful at birth." The face of unrighteousness first becomes apparent when one "looks intently into the perfect law" (James 1:25). Thus, the reflection of Jewish righteousness and confidence is as distorted by the mirror of the law as is the obvious unrighteousness of Gentiles. Paul eliminates all possibility of a righteousness apart from the grace of God.

2:17–20 / Paul now mentions Jews for the first time in his case against humanity, although he doubtlessly had them in mind since 2:1ff. If Jews could still maintain their confidence after 2:1ff., all illusion is now dispelled as Paul calls them from their seats in the courtroom, nay, from the jury itself, and summons them to the defendant's chair. The diatribe style is again resumed (vv. 17–20), but even in verses 21ff. the style continues to be accusatory. The argument of verses 17–29 is essentially the same as that of 2:1–3, but what Paul argued on the grounds of moral logic in 2:1–3 he measures by the straightedge of the law in 2:17–29. We will understand Paul's case here only if we grant his previous conclusion that God judges according to obedience to known good. The privileges which Israel received from God do not exempt it from judgment, but increase its burden of responsibility.

Verses 17–20 form the introductory condition of a logical argument (note the repetition of **if**), known as the premise or protasis. Paul resumes the direct second person singular address with which he intensified the argument in 2:1–5. He begins the prosecution by appealing not to Jewish weaknesses but to Jewish *strengths*. One strength is the name **Jew** itself. No later than the Maccabean period (second century B.C.) "Jew" had become a name of honor (although not always in the mouths of Gentiles) for the individual who confessed the one true God in an alien, polytheistic environment. For the rabbis Mordecai became the exemplary Jew who refused to forsake the God of Israel for the idolatry of Haman (Esther 3:5). Paul's kinsfolk accepted the designation of Jew with pride as a name that fused a national faith and a strong loyalty to Torah.

A second strength is the **law**. Well might Jews **rely on the law**. "Torah" was a sacred word in Judaism, for to Israel alone the law had been given. Of all the nations Israel received Torah because it alone was *worthy* to receive it, and the possession and study of Torah were tantamount to ensuring Israel a place in the world to come. Israel might lose everything else, but the Torah remained Israel's identity and hope. The rabbis waxed prolific on Torah:

> In you we have put our trust, because, behold, your Law is with us, and we know that we do not fall as long as we keep your statutes. We shall always be blessed; at least, we did not mingle with the nations. For we are all a people of the Name; we, who received one Law from the One. And that Law which is among us will help us, and that excellent wisdom which is in us will support us (2 Apoc. Bar. 48:22–24).

The NIV says you **brag about your relationship to God** (v. 17), but **brag** slurs a reputation of which Jews were justly proud. Better to translate *kauchaomai* in verse 17 positively, "to boast," or "pride oneself in," as echoed in Jeremiah 9:23–24.

Jewish privilege and pride continue in verse 18 (note the third "if"). Torah was holy because it revealed God's **will**. This too Israel claimed to its credit, that it alone knew God's will. Knowledge of God's will gave Israel a standard by which to **approve of what is superior**. This phrase, repeated in Philippians 1:10, means the ability to differentiate essentials from incidentals, the heart of a matter from peripherals. When Jesus criticized the Pharisees for neglecting the "important matters of the law—justice, mercy, faithfulness"—and tithing "mint, dill, and cummin" instead (Matt. 23:23), he had such things in mind. The distinction between primary and secondary matters of faith would play an important role in later theology. The *diapheronta* were essentials about which Christians could not disagree without jeopardizing the faith; the *adiaphora*, however, were non-essentials about which Christians could disagree and still hold the faith. The law, says Paul, admits of judging between the content of God's will and the wrappings in which it appears. Such distinctions were important for Jews, and particularly Pharisaic Jews, who endeavored to exceed the minimal requirements of the law and fulfill it in its entirety. In these matters Jews had been **instructed by the law**. The Greek word for **instructed**, *katēcheō*, from which "catechism" is derived, means that such matters had been ingrained by formal religious instruction.

In verses 19–20 Paul lists four evidences of Jewish preeminence: Jews are **a guide for the blind, a light for those who are in the dark, an instructor of the foolish**, and **a teacher of infants**. These again are premises of the subsequent argument, introduced by **if**. It may appear from these accolades that, similar to Matthew 15:14, for example, Paul is mocking the Jews or chiding them for harboring inflated claims of their importance. But this does not seem to be the case. These and other designations appear frequently enough in the OT and rabbinic literature to assure us that Paul is not being sarcastic. Especially in the Diaspora, one frequently encountered the belief that Torah was the supreme expression of the moral law, and that the wisdom of the Greek philosophers—Pythagoras, Heraclitus, and Plato—was indebted to Jewish moral patronage. The idea is evident in the Sibylline Oracles, "[Jews] point out the way of life to all mortals" (3.195).

Such pretensions caused many Diaspora Jews to think of their Gentile neighbors as barbarians who lived in "congenital ignorance," to quote Bengel (*Gnomon*, vol. 3, p. 36). Torah was for Jews **the embodiment of knowledge and truth** (v. 20), the latter being divine truth or "orthodoxy." The Greek word rendered **embodiment** (NIV) is *morphōsis*, meaning "form" (cf. 2 Tim. 3:5). Here *morphōsis* has positive connotations. Jewish orthodoxy was not a hollow claim. Jews had been called and equipped for the special mission of being "a light for the Gentiles" (Isa. 49:6). The premise in verses 17–20 is not that Jews harbored inflated claims of themselves. They had reason to boast in God. Their problem lay not in overestimating their importance, but in failing to live up to it. God's favor entailed a responsibility, not an exemption. They understood their privileges to *excuse* them from judgment, whereas Paul argues that their privileges *accuse* them before God.

2:21–24 / Paul now proceeds from the protasis to the apodosis or main point of his argument. On the basis of their privileged status Paul delivers the sentence: the one who has taught others the truth has failed to learn it himself; the one who has moralized against theft, adultery, and idolatry has been caught in the act. This is a charge of hypocrisy, which is serious enough. But there is something worse. Failure at the behavioral level has mocked profession at the verbal level (v. 23), besmirching God's name before the Gentiles, to whom Jews were to illumine it (v. 24)!

Exactly how might these verses be understood? How many Jews, for instance, were guilty of stealing, adultery, and robbing temples? Is Paul overstating the case to make a point? Were not Jews on the whole innocent of such censorious deeds? Luther, apparently sensing hyperbole on Paul's part, says such things "refer to the attitudes of the inner man," to the *desires* of humanity to do such things, as Paul later attests in 7:16–18 (*Lectures on Romans*, pp. 57–58). Paul, in Luther's understanding, is referring not to deeds but to intentions, to the problem of the hardened heart. These are the things Jews would do "if they were permitted to," and of which they are thus guilty, since God knows the secrets of human hearts (2:16).

This interpretation disposes of Paul's crowning blow, however. His intention is to burst the balloon of Jewish pride and presumption, and he must do so by citing actual violations of the law, for it is acts—and not intentions—to which the Ten Commandments appeal. Stealing, adultery, and idolatry are thus moral offenses, not cultic offenses. Paul must have been aware that fabrication of such offenses (or even exaggeration of them) would have weakened his argument, if not destroyed it altogether.

That some Jews were innocent of such vices cannot, of course, be doubted. Paul's choice of sins is illustrative, not exhaustive. What could not be doubted, however, was that there were enough infractions of the law—even among pious Jews—to cause the most complacent Jew to shift uneasily in the chair of moral security. The rabbis themselves told stories of a man who lost his cloak and, upon going to the judge to get help in recovering it, found it spread over the bench of the judge himself; of a rabbi's wife who caught her husband in adultery by disguising herself as another woman; of a rabbi who taught against lending money at interest and against stealing . . . and who was convicted of both; of double standards such as: "Robbing a Gentile is forbidden, but if one finds a Gentile's stolen property he can keep it." That Palestinian Jews felt justified in denuding pagan temples in the name of the One God was practically axiomatic. Some four decades before Paul wrote to Rome, the Jewish community there had been scandalized by four of its members who had persuaded a wealthy Roman proselyte named Fulvia to make a generous gift to the Jerusalem temple and had then absconded with the money themselves. In retaliation Tiberius expelled the Jewish community from Rome in A.D. 19.

There is no need to dig in rabbinic archives to find such aberrations, however. Matthew 23 and Luke 11:39–52 provide a chorus of evidence against the Pharisees, as the prophets had against their people earlier (Isa. 3:14–15; Jer 7:8–11; Ezek. 22:6–12; Mal. 3:5). Paul is not accusing Jews of crimes they were either guiltless of or unaware of; he is but one voice in a jury of his own people, and also of Gentiles. The evidence is sufficient, as Dunn rightly notes, "to undermine the confidence that the Jew per se stands in a position of superiority or advantage over the non-Jew by virtue of being a member of the people of the law" (*Romans 1–8*, p. 114).

Because they have been privileged by God, Jews are like the debtor in Jesus' parable who was forgiven ten thousand talents by his master, and who then went out and grabbed a fellow debtor by the throat and threw him into jail until he paid back a hundred denarii (Matt. 18:23–30). Jews may be Exhibit A of human righteousness, yet even they cannot withstand the straightedge of the law.

2:25–29 / Paul now moderates his argument by shifting to a more reasoned and didactic approach. He resumes the general thought of 2:12–15 by taking up the trump card of Jewish confidence—circumcision. **Circumcision has value if you observe the law, but if you break the law, you have become as though you had not been circumcised** (v. 25). Paul allows no separation of sign from reality, of circumcision from observance of the law. Most of his contemporaries would not have accepted either the wording or reasoning of verse 25. Already in the first century A.D. the sign of circumcision had replaced the significance it represented and, in the words of C. K. Barrett, was regarded as a "passport to salvation" (*Romans*, p. 58). In contemporary Judaism we find such statements as, "The circumcised do not descend into Gehenna," or "at the last Abraham will sit at the entrance to Gehenna and will not let any circumcised man of Israel go down there." To the average Jew circumcision seems to have carried an unquestioned pledge of security. The same sign which differentiated Jew from Gentile assured the Jew of his inviolable status with God. Comparable to the understanding of citizenship today wherein nationality depends on birth rather than on adherence to the ideals of the nation, so salvation was assured by the ritual of circumcision.

Paul parted ways from his fellow Jews on this issue. For them circumcision *was* the covenant, for him it was the *sign* of the covenant! According to the OT, circumcision, which dated from the time of Abraham (Gen. 17:10ff.), was practiced as an act of initiation into the community of Israel as a sign of adherence to the covenant. Paul's terminology in 2:15 and 3:1 is instructive. He does not say that circumcision "justifies" (*dikaioun*), but that it "has value" (*ōphelein*). Its value depends on fulfilling the substance it signifies, i.e., the covenant of obedience, similar to wedding rings or pendant crosses today which have meaning only insofar as the vows or commitment symbolized by them are fulfilled. Failure to honor the marriage or faith commitment not only renders the symbols meaningless, it scandalizes them.

One can scarcely avoid the force of this argument with regard to the sacraments. There were theories in the later church that the effects of the sacraments were independent of the faith of those who received them, that they worked *ex opere operato*. In his battle against Donatism, Augustine, in fact, would appeal to such thinking. Verses 25ff. certainly cannot be cited as evidence for such an understanding. Paul, of course, did not despise the Lord's Supper any more than he despised circumcision. It was precisely because he valued them that he warned against their misuse (see 1 Cor. 10:20–22). When the sacraments *dispense* with obedience instead of *obligate* to obedience, they run into the same danger which Paul saw in circumcision. The apostle had an inveterate mistrust that signs and rituals could become substitutes for the will of God rather than signs of it (see 1 Cor. 13:3; 14:6; Gal. 5:2). As signs they remained expressions of the will of the believer, and hence meaningful and necessary. But as substitutes they were deceptive and dangerous.

By reverse logic, if an inner commitment is the thing of God's concern, then the doing of the law ought to compensate for the lack of the sign of circumcision. If, as Leenhardt says, "the presence of circumcision is [not] an automatic guarantee of divine favour, [neither] is its absence a sign of divine prejudice" (*Romans*, p. 88). This is the thought of verse 26, which repeats that of 2:14. The word *logizomai*, "to reckon or account" (NIV, **regarded**), conveys this idea. It means the imputing of a missing quality on the basis of an equivalent or superior quality. In the case of Abraham, God "reckoned" him righteous because of his trust in God (Gen. 15:6; Rom. 4:3). Likewise, believers are "reckoned" righteous because of the righteousness of Christ imputed to them (3:28). Uncircumcised Gentiles who do the law are reckoned as having the sign of circumcision. If the circumcised who fail to keep the law betray an "uncircumcised heart," then the uncircumcised who keep the law reveal a "circumcised heart" and are **regarded as though they were circumcised** (v. 26).

Thus, the uncircumcised Gentile who keeps the law will judge the circumcised Jew who does not (v. 27). A startling conclusion indeed! In the eyes of Jews, of course, Gentiles were transgressors or **lawbreakers** (v. 27). A non-Israelite who kept the law scrupulously was still regarded as a stranger to the covenant because of his uncircumcision. But the true economy of God is different, says Paul. The one who **obeys the law** (v. 27; the tense in Greek means continuous, ongoing obedience), even if a Gentile, will judge the one who does not, even if a Jew. "The men of Nineveh will stand up at the judgment with this generation and condemn it," said Jesus (Matt. 12:41). **The written code and circumcision** (v. 27) indeed identify Jews (v. 17), but they avail nothing apart from obedience to the law. The emphasis is shifted away from ritual and custom toward faith and ethics.

Chapter 2 concludes with reference to religion evident **inwardly** and **outwardly**. By **inwardly** Paul does not mean "private" or "closet" faith, but earnestness; and by **outwardly** he intends not to disparage ethics (which has been the thrust of his argument since 1:18ff.) but to warn against outwardness as the mask of hypocrisy. **Inwardly** and **outwardly** repeat the teaching of 2:11, 16: the true sign of the covenant is a willing (= **circumcised**) heart, which includes inner conversion and moral renewal. Apart from such commitment, circumcision of the flesh is a meaningless mark; in fact, it is a sign of condemnation because it signifies the disparity between the ideal and the failure to live it out. Circumcision thus does not *make* one a Jew, but it *reveals* the **Jew inwardly, circumcision of the heart** (v. 29).

The distinction between inward and outward was not new to Paul's readers. Through the metaphor of the circumcised heart (Lev. 26:41; Deut. 10:16; Jer. 4:4), the prophets had admonished Israel to obey the covenant and not merely to name it. There is a vast difference between the human will and the divine will. The former, according to Paul, is designated by **outwardly, physical**, and **written code**. These are human elements which, apart from the radical surrender of faith and the regeneration of the Holy Spirit, are but hollow echoes of the divine word. True religion is inward, **of the heart, by the Spirit**. It is *of God*, and what is of God receives **praise . . . from God** (v. 29). In Hebrew "praise" (*hôḏâh*) and "Judah" (*yᵉhûḏāh*; e.g., Gen. 29:35; 49:8) sound similar. Paul seems to have made a word play on this (though he cannot have expected many of his Roman readers to have understood it): not the judging Jew nor the boasting Jew, but the true Jew receives God's praise.

Additional Notes §6

2:17–20 / On the significance of the term "Jew," see Dunn, *Romans 1–8*, pp. 109–10, 116–17; and Str-B, vol. 3, pp. 96–97.

Further examples of the importance of Torah in Judaism can be found in Str-B, vol. 3, pp. 115–18; 126–33.

On the idea of minimal versus maximal performance of the law, see Schlatter, *Gottes Gerechtigkeit*, p. 102.

Further references to the characteristics of Jews in vv. 19–20 can be found in Cranfield, *Romans*, vol. 1, pp. 166–67; and Dunn, *Romans 1–8*, pp. 112–13.

On the indebtedness of Greek philosophers to the Torah, see the examples listed in Str-B, vol. 3, pp. 98–105.

Bengel's crisp formula is an example of his ability to say much in few words. He further observes that in his case against Gentiles Paul argued that their sins were first against God, then against themselves, and finally against others; but in his case against Jews the order is reversed, arguing that moral infractions against others and self ultimately dishonor God! The Jews thought of Torah as a loving father, but in reality it was an exacting schoolmaster. See Bengel, *Gnomon*, vol. 3, pp. 36–37.

2:21–24 / On the story of Fulvia, see Josephus, *Ant.* 18.81–84. For the other examples of Jewish vices, see the material gathered in Str-B, vol. 3, pp. 105–15.

Dunn's discussion of these verses is balanced and helpful (see *Romans 1–8*, pp. 108–16).

On the bankruptcy of human righteousness, see Barth, *Romans*, p. 75.

2:25–29 / For the idea that Jews were exempt from judgment because of circumcision, see Cranfield, *Romans*, vol. 1, p. 172, and Str-B, vol. 1, p. 119.

On Jewish attitudes toward uncircumcised Gentiles, see Str-B, vol. 3, p. 119–21.

Some commentators understand verse 27 to mean *Christian* Gentiles who will judge Jews, taking the "circumcision of the heart" in verses 28–29 as a reference to the new covenant foreseen by Jeremiah (31:31–34). But this blunts the edge of the verse. As we noted in 2:13–15, it is doubtful that Paul intends Christian Gentiles here. His argument hangs not on faith in Christ but on a moral righteousness grounded in the law. Moreover, righteousness by faith is not formally introduced until 3:21ff.

Dunn offers a good discussion of the distinction between "of God" and "of man" in *Romans 1–8*, pp. 123–25. Luther adds this note: "Outer righteousness is praised by men and reproved by God; inner righteousness, however, is praised by God and reproved and persecuted by men" (*Lectures on Romans*, p. 59).

§7 Israel's Faithlessness and God's Faithfulness (Rom. 3:1–8)

The logical follow-up to the preceding section is the question, "What advantage, then, is there is being a Jew?" (v. 1). Although *ultimately* Jews have no advantage, if we understand Paul rightly, they operate in the short run with a favorable handicap, for "they have been entrusted with the very words of God" (v. 2). God's revelation does not happen just anywhere. Humanity cannot conjure up God whenever and wherever it will. God must be known where he makes himself known—within Israel. "Salvation is from the Jews" (John 4:22). Paul does not say, however, that God *gave* his words to Israel, but that God *entrusted* them to Israel. This shifts the emphasis from ownership to stewardship, from possession of the law to responsibility to it. Israel's knowledge of God was, of course, for its benefit, but it was not limited to Israel. Israel was not to be a dam but a sluiceway, "a light for the Gentiles, that you may bring my salvation to the ends of the earth" (Isa. 49:6).

The diatribe style again structures these verses, in which Paul raises two objections. The first objection concerns whether the advantage of Jews in salvation history has been annulled by the argument of chapter 2. The objection is discussed by a question (v. 1) and answer (v. 2), and by a second question (v. 3) and answer (v. 4). Verses 5–8 consider the second objection, whether the doctrine of justification makes God arbitrary and unjust and spells havoc for morality in general. This objection is also discussed with questions and an answer. The questions, which quite likely repeat questions posed to the apostle in the mission field, are presented in verses 5–7, again (for the first time since 1:16) in the first person. The defense comes in the final dictum, "Their condemnation is deserved" (v. 8). The abrupt diatribe may leave the reader somewhat dissatisfied, especially in verses 5–8, where

Paul broaches questions which he cannot fully discuss until chapters 6 and 9–11.

3:1–2 / Two questions are posed in verse 1: **What advantage is there in being a Jew**, and **what value is there in circumcision?** Paul desists from further discussion of circumcision in favor of the larger issue of the advantage of being a Jew. There is a "relentless logic" to Paul's argument (so Achtemeier, *Romans*, pp. 54ff.). In light of what was said in 2:25–29 the reader might conclude that there is no advantage in being a Jew. If circumcision is of value only if practiced (2:25; 1 Cor. 7:19), and if true Jewishness is internal and not external (2:28–29), then Jews are evidently no different from other people, and their supposed advantage is but a pure illusion.

But that is a mistaken conclusion. With regard to *salvation* there is, to be sure, no advantage, for Paul will shortly conclude that on the basis of a moral righteousness "Jews and Gentiles alike are all under sin" (3:9), and that "all have sinned and fall short of the glory of God" (3:23). But there is a decided advantage with regard to *mission*, as Paul argued in 2:17–20. Along with the sign of circumcision, the law was given to Jews to equip and obligate them as "a guide for the blind, a light for those who are in the dark" etc. (2:19). Whereas earlier (ch. 2) Paul referred to the Jews' advantage as the "law," here he speaks of *logia* (v. 2; NIV, **the very words**), "oracles," the spoken utterances of God through Moses and the prophets which constitute Holy Scripture.

We have already noted the preeminent position which Torah held in Judaism. Only to Israel had Torah been given, thus setting Israel apart from the nations. Torah was Israel's source of wisdom, honor, and life, the pledge of God's love. Paul's expression for Torah here is less formal and more personal. The Jews have been entrusted with God's self-disclosure, the **very words of God** (v. 2). Torah was the chief hallmark of the Jew, as Paul seems to indicate in the words **First of all** (v. 2). The expression may suggest that Paul intended to follow it with something else, but the Greek word, *prōton*, probably means here simply the "number one," or distinguishing characteristic.

3:3–4 / If Torah was the pride of Jews, their response to it was disappointing. Torah was not a possession to be hoarded but a gift which entailed a responsibility. Calvin believed the

Jews were first to be the depositories of Torah and then the
dispensers of it (*Romans*, p. 114). But in this they failed. **What
if some did not have faith?** asks Paul (v. 3). Does Paul understand their failure to be "disbelief" in Christ as Messiah, or
"faithlessness" to the Mosaic covenant? The Greek word *apistein* can mean either. The former view is favored by the fact that
six out of seven occurrences of *apistein* in the NT mean "disbelief." Moreover, **some** (v. 3) may suggest Jews who did not
believe in Christ as opposed to the remnant which did. But
context favors the latter. The subject remains the *logia*, **the very
words** of the Mosaic law. Thus, the faithlessness of Israel is
contrasted to the **faithfulness** of God (v. 3). Since Paul is still
arguing that Jews are convicted by their failure to fulfill the old
covenant apart from their failure to believe in Christ (which he
does not formally introduce until 3:21), he probably intended
verse 3 as faithlessness to the old covenant. Nevertheless, faithlessness to the old covenant tended to lead to disbelief in
Christ; hence it may be well not to make too much of the
distinction.

**Will their lack of faith nullify God's faithfulness? Not at
all!** (vv. 3–4). God's character and behavior are not determined
by human failure. If Israel's history had taught anything it had
taught that God is faithful despite Israel's failure. To suggest that
human faithlessness could make God faithless is to make God the
object of an external and evil force. "God will not reply in kind,"
(Achtemeier, *Romans*, p. 55). "If we are faithless, he will remain
faithful, for he cannot disown himself" (2 Tim. 2:13). God is not a
contingent being whose actions depend on something outside
himself. God is an essential being whose actions are true to his
character, despite human response to it. **Let God be true, and
every man a liar**, says Paul (v. 4)! This statement, indebted to
Psalm 116:11 ("And in my dismay I said, 'All men are liars' "), was
judged by Calvin to "contain the primary axiom of all Christian
philosophy" (*Romans*, p. 116). Calvin was right, but the statement
means more than that. Verse 4 is not a philosophical abstraction
of metaphysics and anthropology; it is a truth hammered out on
the anvil of experience, a punishing truth that all are liars, and
yet a liberating hope that God is true. Whatever we must concede
about ourselves—and it will not be optimistic—we must confess
that **God is true** (v. 4). Barth affirms, "HE is the Answer, the
Helper, the Judge, and the Redeemer; not man" (*Romans*, p. 80).

God is not a speculative truth, but a living and subsistent truth who helps, aids, restores, and saves. It is precisely because God is not like us that he is able to help us.

In support of this Paul includes a quotation, **"So that you may be proved right when you speak and prevail when you judge"** (v. 4). This comes from Psalm 51:4, where David acknowledges his sin against Uriah and Bathsheba and confesses that God is true and just in his judgment of David's covetousness, adultery, and murder. David has been a **liar**, but in his lie he has known God's truth.

3:5–8 / Paul has now dealt with the first objection to his gospel, namely, that there is no value in being a Jew. He is most emphatic that there is. To the Jews God made himself known, and even their faithlessness to God has not altered God's faithfulness to them. Verses 5–8 take up a second objection related to Paul's doctrine of justification. This objection presupposes 1:16–17 and anticipates 3:21ff. It raises issues related to justification by faith which Paul has yet to discuss, and as a consequence he cannot fully develop his argument until after he has discussed justification by faith (see chs. 6, 9–11). Why Paul broaches the issue here is not altogether clear. It is not exactly demanded by what has preceded, although the result of verses 1–4 may have suggested it in his mind. Perhaps it was pressing on Paul's mind from his missionary preaching. His shift to the first person (and addition of **as some claim**, v. 8) seems to indicate its existential urgency for him.

Paul counters the objections to his doctrine of justification by four questions in verses 5–8. The critical questions are, **is God unjust in bringing his wrath on us** (v. 5), and should we **do evil that good may result** (v. 8)? If God's truth becomes fully apparent in the face of human wretchedness, then sin throws God's truth into greater relief (v. 7). And if human wickedness does not thwart God's righteousness—indeed, God uses wickedness for his righteous purposes—perhaps we should do evil so more good may come (v. 8)!

These are questions which will receive fuller treatment in 5:20–6:4, but that Paul denies them is abundantly clear. Both questions of verses 5 and 8 are prefaced by the negative particle *mē*, which in Greek demands a negative answer. Again in verse 6 Paul adds the emphatic *mē genoito*, **Certainly not!** The argumen-

tation of verses 5–8 manifestly exposes the unreasonableness of
the objection. If, as Paul maintains, God remains true in the face
of human lying (v. 4), if God remains righteous in the face of
human unrighteousness (v. 5), it does not follow that God is
unjust in his judgment of human unrighteousness (v. 5) or that
humans are somehow free to act however they please (v. 8). God
is wholly other, God is God and not human. But that does not
absolve us from being human. God's goodness is never rivaled by
human goodness; neither is God's goodness increased by human
badness (although it may be the more apparent). God is perfectly
good and just; otherwise, he could not judge the world. Human
evil is not worse because it grows, anymore than cancer is more
deadly because it infects three vital organs instead of one. Nor is
human evil less evil because God chooses to meet it with good.
That would be like saying that if a master painter could make a
bad painting into a good one, then the original painting was not
bad after all. If **our unrighteousness brings out God's righteousness** (v. 5) that does not change the fact that the unrighteousness
is *ours* and the righteousness is *God's*! "Love does not delight in
evil but rejoices with the truth" (1 Cor. 13:6).

Paul will not whitewash human achievements or compromise God's. Of humanity Paul speaks of **unrighteousness,
falsehood, sinner, evil, condemnation**. His incriminations are
relentless—and they are not limited to "bad" people. They are
true of all people—including Paul! He speaks of **our unrighteousness** (v. 5), **my falsehood** (v. 7), **I** who am **still condemned** as a
sinner (v. 7). God, however, is wholly different. God is **righteousness**, just, **judge, truthfulness, glory, good**. Only because of the
vast difference between God and humanity can God **judge the
world** (v. 6)—and judge it from a standard completely different
from human judgments (see Gen. 18:25; Deut. 32:4; Job 8:3; 34:10ff.).
That Paul says God will judge the **world** (and not only Jews as
the argument might lead us to expect), indicates that he does not
regard Jews in a fundamentally different light from that of humanity as a whole. God's judgment of the world will turn the
tables on human pride and judgments. In this age it is we who
judge God: we argue whether God exists, or whether God is
good, or why God allows this or that to happen, and sometimes
we curse and deny God. But in the age to come the One who is
so unlike humanity will judge humanity and the world from his
nature of truth and righteousness.

Additional Notes   §7

On the structure of 3:1–8 see Käsemann, *Romans*, p. 78.

3:1–2   /   For the role of Torah in Judaism, see Str-B, vol. 3, pp. 126–33.

3:3–4   /   The expression "Not at all!" *mē genoito*, is the strongest negation possible in Greek. Paul uses it frequently after rhetorical questions, but only in Romans and Galatians. It was common in rabbinic argumentation to force an absolute contrast, "Impossible!" or "God forbid!" It carries equal force in Paul's usage.

3:5–8   /   On the relationship of Jews to humanity as a whole, see Käsemann, *Romans*, pp. 84–85.

Note the dialectical thrust of Barth's discussion of this section:

> God and man are not interchangeable terms; and we are permitted neither to attribute evil to God's account nor to place to our own account the good which may come out of evil. Our action is never God's action; nor does the consequence of our action lie within our competence. Mistakenness here does but occasion a fresh obscuring of the distance between God and man as a consequence of our supposed insight into His sovereignty. But we are not God: the sovereignty is His not ours. Evil remains evil, in spite of the good which God may bring out of it; the non-sense of history remains non-sense, in spite of the sense which is in it from God; infidelity is infidelity, in spite of the faithfulness of God by which it is not permitted to wander out of the way. The world is the world, in spite of the mercy of God by which it is enveloped and established. . . . The arrogance with which we set ourselves by the side of God, with the intention of doing something for Him, deprives us of the only possible ground of salvation, which is to cast ourselves upon His favour or disfavour (*Romans*, p. 84).

§8   The Door to Moral Righteousness Is Shut! (Rom. 3:9–20)

With devastating finality Paul now concludes the long discussion of the guilt of humanity which began in 1:18. The passage falls into three parts: a summation of the argument of 3:1–8 (v. 9); a series of proof texts from the OT on the moral failure of humanity (vv. 10–18); and a conclusion that the law is powerless to save (vv. 19–20). Paul enters the final round against his fellow Jews who suppose that the advantage of the law (3:2) secures favor with God. Since 2:1 he has attacked Jewish presumption to judge Gentile sinners and Jewish pride in Torah and circumcision as their means of salvation. The result of the close and unyielding web of argumentation from 1:18 to 3:20 is that there is no possibility of a moral righteousness before God. In a concluding series of blows the apostle hammers out a chain of quotations from the Torah—the longest in Romans—to evince that "Jews and Gentiles alike are all under sin" (3:9).

3:9 / In Greek verse 9 begins with the same rhetorical question as verse 1, *ti oun?*, although the NIV translates it slightly differently. This indicates that Paul is returning to the thought of verse 1. Unfortunately the words which follow present a maze of possible interpretations. The chief problem is *proechometha* (v. 9) which is capable of several renderings. The most literal translation would be, "are we excelled?" The "we" here would mean "Jews," with the sense, "are we Jews being excelled by the Gentiles?" or, "do the Gentiles have an advantage over [Jews]?" This is the most sensible rendering grammatically, but it is virtually eliminated by the fact that Paul nowhere argues that Gentiles have an advantage over Jews. A second possibility is to understand "we" not in reference to Jews generally, but to Paul personally, thus continuing the thought and grammar of verses 5–8.

The sense would be, "are we making excuses for ourselves?" It may be attractive to read the pronoun of verse 9 as a continuation of verses 5–8, but the translation is militated against by two factors. First, the rendering "making excuses for oneself" is a bit forced, given the technical definition of *proechō*, which means "to excel," or "be first." Moreover, nowhere else do we see Paul apologizing for his doctrine of justification. A final possibility is to render the term, "do we (Jews) have an advantage?" This translation fits the context of 3:1ff., indeed it seems demanded by it. Paul has argued that Jews have an advantage in the short run (3:2), but "Not ultimately" (**Not at all!** is too strong for the Greek *ou pantōs*). The fly in the ointment of this translation, however, is that the middle, *proechometha*, must be rendered as an active, *proechō*, and this occurs seldom elsewhere, if at all. Nevertheless, of the three renderings the last seems the most preferable (or perhaps the least unsatisfactory).

Despite the textual ambiguity of *proechometha*, the meaning cannot be doubted. Jews do have an advantage in Torah, but it is not an ultimate advantage, for **Jews and Gentiles alike are all under sin**. Paul's argumentation all along has led to this conclusion, but with two modifications. First, this is a penultimate and not an ultimate conclusion, i.e., acknowledging the human condition is the prerequisite to the reception of the good news of grace. And second, there is even within his hammering condemnation of human wickedness an element of humility on Paul's part; as Calvin noted: when Paul recounts the preeminence of the Jews he speaks in the third person, but when he strips them of their advantages he includes himself among them and speaks in the first person (*Romans*, p. 124).

Paul's persistence in demonstrating the unrighteousness of Jews is not because of any malice towards them. Paul was himself a Jew who empathized deeply with his people (9:2–5). His argumentation rather has a strategic purpose to show that if the Jew, the best of the lot, cannot make the grade, then no one can. Paul's case against Jews, in other words, cinches his case against all humanity, for to exclude Jews from salvation on the basis of moral righteousness is to exclude everyone!

This universal guilt and hopelessness is called **sin**. The noun is introduced here for the first time in Romans (a verb at 2:12), although a full explanation of sin is reserved until 5:12–7:25. **Under sin** is a crucial motif in Paul. The apostle, of course, believed that persons were responsible for individual transgressions, but such transgressions were only symptoms of an inner grip of evil on the human race. Paul seldom speaks of *sins* (as individual acts), but rather of *sin* as a singular nature, which he tends to personify. Sin is an external power which enslaves humanity (6:16), and indeed all creation (8:21). Sin is more than a composite of human evil, more than a simple equation that sin equals the sum of human badness. In Paul's thinking sin carries two paradoxical and unresolved tensions: people sin willingly, but inevitably. Sin is freely chosen (otherwise it would not be sin), but there is a "gravitational pull" to sin, a tyranny or domination against which humanity is powerless to contend. Humanity, in other words, is not free not to sin. Sin is thus not an occasional slip or mistake, but a personal collaboration with a suprapersonal power (Eph. 2:2) which overshadows and tragically infects the world.

There are powers then which overshadow human life, sin being one of them, though such powers are often less than apparent. Realizing this, the Reformers interpreted **under sin** spiritually. This passage, says Luther, "does not deal with men as they appear in their own eyes and before other men but as they are before God, where they are all under sin" (*Lectures on Romans*, p. 86). That Paul regarded sin not solely as bad acts, but as brokenness, fallenness, and spiritual lostness is clear from Romans 14:23, "everything that does not come from faith is sin."

Ancient rabbis agreed in principle that all people stand under sin, since death is the result of sin. The logic was unassailable: if all die, all must have sinned. Nevertheless, they believed that many virtuous souls had not sinned, and had not died, among them Abraham, Isaac, Jacob, Elijah, Hezekiah, Benjamin, Isaiah, Moses, Aaron, and others. The rabbis understood sin to be proscribed *acts* that a virtuous person could avoid. Paul, who also was a rabbi, had once shared this opinion, boasting that he was blameless under the law (Phil. 3:6). But Paul the convert understands sin to be a power of fallenness within and over humanity from which no one, Jew or Gentile, is free.

3:10–18 / The assertion that all people (Jews included) are "under sin" is substantiated by "the very words of God" (3:2). It was a common rabbinic practice, also in evidence in the Dead Sea Scrolls, to assemble Scripture passages bearing on a common subject for catechetical purposes or as proof texts for argumentation. Paul may be utilizing a pre-formed list here, but, given the unusually appropriate fit of the list to Paul's purpose, it is not unlikely that he assembled it himself. The quotations are skillfully pieced together, five passages from Psalms, one from Ecclesiastes, and one from Isaiah. The first section of the mosaic, verses 10–12, charts offenses against God; the second, verses 13–14, sins of speech (cf. James 3:2; Ps. 34:13; Jer. 9:5), and the final section, verses 15–17, offenses and violence done to neighbors. This fearsome barrage of evidence determines that no one is exempt from God's wrath. **There is no one** (righteous, etc.) occurs six times in the quotations. The crowning blow of human unrighteousness is that **There is no fear of God** (v. 18). Failure to fear God eliminates the possibility of knowing God.

The remarkable thing about the list, as Dunn notes, is that originally the passages cited were Jewish indictments of unrighteous *Gentiles*, in the spirit of 1 Enoch 99:3–4 (Dunn, *Romans 1–8*, pp. 147–48). In Paul's hands, however, they no longer function as such. Not only are those who think themselves righteous condemned by their scriptures, they are condemned by their condemnations of others. "You are condemning yourself," said Paul at 2:1, "because you who pass judgment do the same things."

Verse 10 is quoted from Ecclesiastes 7:20; verses 11–12 from Psalm 14:2–3; verse 13a,b from Psalm 5:9; verse 13c from Psalm 140:3; verse 14 from Psalm 10:7; verses 15–17 from Isaiah 59:7–8; and verse 18 from Psalm 36:1. All quotations are from the Septuagint (the Greek translation of the Old Testament) rather than from the Hebrew. The progression of evil from **throats, tongues, lips** in verse 13 corroborates Jesus' words, "What comes out of a man is what makes him 'unclean' " (Mark 7:20). The Isaiah passage of verses 15–17, a condemnation of Israel's sins centuries earlier, is a clarion reminder that Paul's contemporaries were no less guilty than Israel of old. Thus, Jews also stand under the prophetic condemnation of Israel. Calvin notes with typical sobriety that these vices are not conspicuous in any one individual, but are characteristic of human nature. His comment on verse 18 is a fitting summary, "every wickedness flows from a disregard of God" (*Romans*, pp. 128–29).

3:19–20 / Paul follows the devastating testimony of Holy Scripture with his own conclusion: **Now we know that whatever the law says, it says to those who are under the law, so that every**

mouth may be silenced and the whole world held accountable to God (v. 19). **We know,** says Paul. There can be no doubt, no one can feign ignorance. If arguments from reason and experience fail (1:18–2:29), then Paul adds the witness of the **law**, "the very words of God" (3:2). Humanly speaking, all avenues of escape from God's wrath are sealed off. That Paul refers to the list of quotations as **law** is somewhat interesting, since none of the quotations actually comes from the Law or Pentateuch. He clearly understands **law** to mean Scripture in its entirety, law as the sum of the Old Testament (so also John 10:34). The commandments (i.e., vv. 10–18) naturally govern **those who are under the law** (i.e., Jews). As we argued earlier, if the boast of Jews is silenced, then all mouths are silenced, for no one can claim greater righteousness than they. Thus, the **whole world** (= Jew and Gentile, v. 9) **is held accountable to God** and stands under God's wrath (1:18). This is the final speech for the prosecution. Those who were initially satisfied with their moral code and behavior now find the evidence amassed conclusively and irrevocably against them. Their defense, whether glib or sincere, withers in their throats as the verdict is pronounced.

The conclusion of the discussion of the guilt of humanity in verse 20 introduces themes which will demand further development. **No one will be declared righteous in** God's **sight by observing the law.** This thought results from Psalm 143:2, "for no one living is righteous before you." The Greek of verse 20 literally reads, "no flesh will be saved." "Flesh" (Gk. *sarx*) is a crucial term in Paul. It usually means humanity in weakness and corruptibility, the mortal nature which is the willing instrument of sin, i.e., humanity apart from grace. The expression **observing the law** is unique to Paul and finds no counterpart in rabbinic literature. The rabbis normally spoke of the "study of Torah," or simply "commandment," but Paul emphasizes the doing of Torah, fulfilling its moral requirements.

Heretofore a reader might have concluded that **if** one fulfilled the law one could be saved. But, in a new slant, verse 20 excludes even this possibility, assuming one could keep the law. Total fulfillment of the law cannot produce salvation. Observing the law cannot remove a person from the cloud of condemnation which results from being "under sin" (v. 9). That is not the way to a restored relationship with the creator, because the law, even if adhered to, is not sufficient to resist the power of sin.

What then is the function of the law? One purpose of the law is to produce a **conscious**ness **of sin** (v. 20). This too is an insight unique to Paul and unknown to rabbinic Judaism. The justice demanded by the law's demands cannot be provided by the law. The law provides the knowledge of sin, but no rescue from it. It is diagnosis, not cure.

The statement that **through the law we become conscious of sin** is not a moralism, i.e., that we should learn from our mistakes. Paul means that in the law we hear our own condemnation! Only when the defendant gives up all hope of defense, all thought of parading his or her own case (= "boasting," 2:17, 23), only then can that person hear the verdict of the judge. And a surprising verdict it is! The sentence is not justice—getting what one deserves; it is grace—getting what one does *not* deserve. That is the wholly unexpected news of the gospel to which Paul will now turn.

It is important to understand Paul's perspective and purpose in Romans 1:18–3:20. It has not been the intent of this frightening diagnosis to force the patient to accept a radical cure. There is no thought in the Christian faith of coercing one into the kingdom of God out of fear of punishment. Rather, the condemnation of human unrighteousness *presupposes* grace; it is not a prelude to it. The non-believer seldom sees the hollowness of his or her righteousness apart from the light of God's love and grace. This was true in Paul's case. Far from being disappointed in himself, prior to his conversion Paul considered himself a moral and righteous individual. It was only *after* his encounter with the forgiving Lord near Damascus that he looked again into his chest of moral treasures, there to discover fakes and colored glass. "Whatever was to my profit I now consider loss for the sake of Christ" (Phil. 3:7). Thus Paul begins Romans with the word of grace (1:16–17), and only then turns to the revelation of God's wrath (1:18–3:20). One does not realize how close one came to freezing until one begins to thaw out by the fire!

Additional Notes   §8

3:9 / For discussions of the textual problem and translation of v. 1, see BAGD, pp. 705–6; and Cranfield, *Romans*, vol. 1, pp. 187–91.

Dunn's discussion (*Romans 1–8*, pp. 146–48) is also helpful, but his decision to follow N. Dahl's rendering, "What then do we plead in our defense" (variant of option 2), necessitates the omission of *ou pantōs*, words which are textually secure. Our rendering ("Do we Jews have then an advantage? Not ultimately.") still seems to do the least violence to the text. It is of historical interest to note that Paul diverged sharply from the rabbis on the question whether Jews have an advantage or not. Paul answers, "Not entirely," but his contemporaries would have answered, "Absolutely." The rabbis taught that "All Israelites have a share in the world to come" (m. *Sanh.* 10.1) and that the Goyim (non-Israelites) were en masse destined for Gehenna. Gentiles were like chaff blown by the wind, like debris underfoot, or garbage for the fire. See Str-B, vol. 3, pp. 139–55.

Adolf Schlatter describes the universality of human guilt in these words: "In everything that Paul says he describes humanity, to which the gospel of Jesus is addressed; in his language we can indeed say that he is describing the world. Those who are gathered in the synagogue are not new people, they are not different people. In the law, to be sure, they possess the teaching which those on the outside of the synagogue do not possess; but the teaching does not change them. Thus it is that just as the activity of humanity opposes divine justice and in the work of evil undercuts it, we find the proof that 'all people are under sin' " (*Gottes Gerechtigkeit*, p. 124 [my translation]).

For a clear presentation of sin in Pauline theology, see Robert Spivey and D. Moody Smith, *Anatomy of the New Testament*, 3d ed. (New York: Macmillan, 1982), pp. 366–67.

Paul's understanding of sin as a dominion of power may raise problems for moderns, not because sin and evil are foreign to us—who in the twentieth century could say that?—but because we are products of a society which believes that human reason and freedom are ultimate truths, beyond which there is no greater power. This premium on reason and freedom arose in the Enlightenment and has been responsible for much human progress, particularly in the natural sciences. But despite this progress, unsettling voices have arisen about their limits and dangers which strike a chord with Paul's conception of sin. I am referring not primarily to irrational powers, as in the teachings of Freud, or more recently to the powers of addiction or occult phenomena, but to the power of technology, for example, to create both means and ends which supersede moral values, to which Jacques Ellul and others have alluded. Ellul's ideas are presented cogently in two small books, *The Presence of the Kingdom*, trans. O. Wyon (New York: Seabury, 1967), and *The Betrayal of the West*, trans. M. O'Connell (New York: Seabury, 1978). For the rabbinic view of sin, see Str-B, vol. 3, pp. 155–57.

3:10–18 / On the universal sinfulness of humanity, hear Barth's words: "The whole course of history pronounces this indictment against itself. . . . If all the great outstanding figures in history, whose judgements are worthy of serious consideration, if all the prophets, Psalmists, philosophers, Fathers of the Church, Reformers, poets, artists, were asked their opinion, would one of them assert that men were good, or even capable of good? Is the doctrine of original sin merely one doctrine among many? Is it not rather, according to its fundamental meaning, THE Doctrine which emerges from all honest study of history?" (*Romans*, pp. 85–86).

On the mosaic of quotations, especially verses 10–12 (quoted from Psalm 14:1–3) were typically applied by the rabbis either to Esau or to Rome, two of Israel's loathsome enemies (see Str-B, vol. 3, p. 157). But Paul applies these verses not to self-righteousness but to self-incrimination (Dunn, *Romans 1–8*, p. 151). Look into the eyes of your worst enemy, says Paul, and there you will see mirrored your own reflection!

3:19–20 /   The argument of 1:18–3:20 is somewhat reminiscent of Job's argument in 9:3–10 against the caricature of God presented by his accusers. Job's friends argue that his suffering must be the result of sin, for sin causes suffering. Similarly, Paul's opponents argue that the law and circumcision secure the favor of God. Both Paul and Job argue for a bigger, less anthropomorphized God, whose purposes are less known and more sovereign, and whose mercy and justice cannot be separated or claimed for some and against others.

Bunyan offers an effective allegory on the inexorable demands of the law in the waylaying of Faithful. See John Bunyan, *Pilgrim's Progress* (New York: New American Library, Signet Classics), pp. 69–70.

Themes in v. 20 which Paul will subsequently develop are "Observing the law," 3:27, 28; 4:2, 6; 9:11; "declared righteous," 3:24, 26, 28, 30; 4:2, 5; 5:1, 9; 6:7; 8:30, 33; and "through the law we become conscious of sin," 4:15; 5:13; 7:13.

On the phrase **observing the law**, see Str-B, vol. 3, pp. 160–61.

On the distinction between the law as a moral requirement but not as a means of salvation, see Achtemeier, *Romans*, p. 60, and C. Cosgrove, "Justification in Paul: A Linguistic and Theological Reflection," *JBL* 104 (4, 1987), pp. 655–64.

§9 Jesus Christ: The Righteousness of God (Rom. 3:21–31)

We return now to the opening theme of the epistle which Paul announced in 1:16–17, righteousness by faith. There it was like a first glimpse of the Himalayas seen from the plains of Nepal, shimmering on the horizon. Then the trek began in earnest as the reader was led up the rugged terrain of argumentation and proof from 1:18–3:20, in which Gentiles and Jews were confronted with a landslide of evidence against them. The inspiring first vision was long since obscured, and more than once the trekker was brought to the brink of discouragement. "But now," says Paul (3:21). Suddenly a bend is rounded and there is a stunning massif of peaks. The original glimpse had not been a mirage after all, nor had the arduous trek miscarried. The Mount Everest of Scripture looms before us.

Like the Himalayan giants whose immensity is compromised because of their proximity to one another, Romans 3:21–31 may at first deceive the reader because of its compactness. Here is a veritable glossary of the Christian faith, and surely the most succinct and profound expression of the gospel in the Bible. The presence of so many terms otherwise unusual or foreign to Paul— and without explanation—indicates that the apostle is here resorting to familiar concepts, perhaps even to an early Christian formula.

Paul employs a wide variety of vocabulary in developing the theme of righteousness by faith. One set of terms comes from the law courts, consisting of "righteousness," "law," and "reckoning" (NIV, "maintain," 3:28). The first two terms are heavyweights; in this passage of some 150 words "righteousness" recurs nine times and "law" seven times. A second set of terms, deriving from the institution of slavery, includes "redemption" and perhaps "grace." A final set comes from the ritual of animal sacrifice and includes "expiation" (NIV, "sacrifice of atonement"), "sin," and "blood." The most common word in the entire section, "faith," recurs ten times. It is the key to the vocabulary of the whole, and the means by which these momentous truths are appropriated by the believer.

3:21 / The finale of redemption begins with a pronouncement (which is emphatic in Greek), **But now** (see also 8:1). This is not entirely surprising. Paul introduced redemption at 1:16–17, but held it in abeyance until now. Like a rail switch in a train yard, this wee phrase is a small piece of equipment with great consequences. **But now** presupposes everything Paul said in 1:18–3:20, that humanity stands justly condemned by God's wrath. This is not the final verdict, however. **But now** is an exclamation of *hope* which marks the transition from wrath (1:18) to righteousness (1:17). The transition is important both logically and temporally: logically, because it belongs to the strategy of Paul's argument; temporally, because at a given point in history God intervened to consummate the plan of redemption. The temporal sense is reinforced by **has been made known** (Gk. *pephanerōtai*). The perfect tense here specifies something which began in the past and is still valid. When someone says that he or she has been married ten years, for example, it means that ten years ago a condition was brought into existence which is still valid. When Paul says that **righteousness from God . . . has been made known** he means that the cross of Jesus Christ has inaugurated the means of salvation which is valid for all people ever after. Righteousness has now been manifested in the once-for-all redemptive act of God in Jesus Christ.

The most important issue in verse 21 is the relationship between God's righteousness and the law. Paul calls it a righteousness **apart from law**, but a righteousness **to which the Law and the Prophets testify**. There is a delicate relationship between righteousness and law, a "sweet antithesis," to quote Bengel (*Gnomon*, vol. 3, p. 47). Luther's bitter controversy over indulgences with sixteenth-century Catholicism has stamped Protestantism in general with a skepticism towards law. The result has been to overstress righteousness **apart from law** and to undervalue righteousness **to which the Law and the Prophets testify**. Verse 21 offers a more balanced understanding of the two themes. On the one hand, righteousness occurs **apart from law**, which means it is neither subordinate to law nor derivative from law; it depends wholly on God's initiative. God is not indebted to human achievement, and humanity can take no credit for the righteousness which comes to it in Christ. The thrust of 1:18–3:20 has been to prove that no one is righteous on the basis of moral achievement, and what is more, that works of law (aside from the issue of whether the law can or cannot be fulfilled) are insufficient to save one (3:20).

But having granted this, Paul does not establish an antithesis, or worse, hostility, between righteousness and law as he does, for example, between spirit and flesh. There is rather a corollary between law and righteousness. First, the law reveals sin (3:20) in that it demonstrates the need for a salvation apart from law. Moreover, the law testifies to righteousness. It bears witness to Jesus Christ and finds its proper culmination in him, as we shall argue at 10:4, "Christ is the end of the law." This does not mean that Christ is the negation of law, but he is its goal and fulfillment. This agrees with Galatians 3:24, where the law is regarded as a chaperon (*paidagōgos*) who escorts a schoolboy (Israel) to the headmaster (Christ). The law leads to Christ, but only Christ can teach salvation. Finally, as Paul will assert in verse 31, righteousness does not abolish the law, but "upholds the law." The explication of this statement must await chapters 12 and following, but Paul will argue that righteousness by faith is the necessary prerequisite to fulfill the *intent* of the law (e.g., 8:4).

The opposition of righteousness and law is largely due to a false dichotomy. Paul nowhere claims that law, rightly understood, was ever a means of salvation. It had a preparatory and subordinate function to reveal sin (3:20), and thereby to lead one to Christ (Gal. 3:24). But that salvation had always been intended by faith is evinced in the case of Abraham, who even before the law was given was promised righteousness by faith (4:1–25; Gal. 3:1–20).

3:22 / Paul repeats his leitmotif again in verse 22. **Righteousness from God** is not simply an attribute of God or an idea, a theological truth, or even a religious dogma. It is present in a person, Jesus Christ; and because Jesus is the personal manifestation of God's righteousness, righteousness must be received through a relationship of faith in God's Son.

The concept of righteousness is the seminal idea in this passage, and perhaps in all Pauline literature. The English nouns "justification" and "righteousness" (as well as their adjectival and verbal forms), all translate the same Greek word, *dikaiosynē*. Paul's use of *dikaiosynē* is guided by the same model which informs the Greek writers as well as the Hebrew OT (e.g., Ps. 98:2; Isa. 43:9), namely, a court of law and the absolute righteousness of God's judgments. The NIV correctly translates the Greek original, *dikaiosynē theou*, as **righteousness** *from* **God** (see particularly Phil. 3:9), i.e., righteousness not as God's attribute (which no one doubts), but righteousness which comes from God to guilty humanity, effecting a condition of righteousness in it. God as judge pronounces a verdict of acquittal upon a guilty party, thereby reckoning or imputing to that party a quality which it does not possess on its own, nor can it possess apart from God's pronouncement. This is primarily a forensic or covenantal understanding of righteousness rather than a moral or ethical understanding, for it begins with God's treating humanity in a way which its unfaithfulness and wickedness do not warrant. When God acquits a sinner or restores a faithless covenant partner on the basis of trust in the saving work of Jesus Christ, the forgiven party is at the time no better or worse than it was before. It is a righteousness utterly independent of merit, otherwise the reward would be a payment or obligation of God (Rom. 4:4). As it is, righteousness from God is a gift, wholly unmerited and freely given, which is motivated by grace and received by trust or faith (Rom. 4:5).

Lest the voltage of this truth dissipate into sentimentality, we must recall that a judge who hands down a lenient sentence to a guilty party (not to mention acquittal) has done a monstrous thing at law. In so doing the judge violates the *one* thing judges are obligated to do—to mete out justice by matching punishment with wrongdoing. Is then the justification of sinners an injustice on God's part? It might be regarded as such if the discussion were divorced from 1:18–3:20. Three times in 3:25–26, however, Paul declares that righteousness by faith **demonstrated God's** justice. How can this be? Moral outcries against injustice arise from parties desiring redress (i.e., from innocent parties which have been wronged), but they are never heard from guilty parties. Whether one is the wronged or the wrongdoer makes a vast difference in one's attitude towards the decision of the judge. The party in the right expects justice, a "therefore." The party in the wrong hopes for mercy, a "nevertheless." But Paul has shown in 1:18–3:20 that all people stand justly condemned by God. Neither Jew nor Gentile is innocent; both are guilty. What to the morally faultless is a travesty is to the sinner grace. There is thus no "injustice" in God's imputing righteousness to sinners—at least humanly speaking—for as sinners all humanity stands under God's wrath, and justly so. The only injustice might be to God's nature, but, as Paul will explain in verses 24–25, Jesus Christ has satisfied the requirements of justice by his "sacrifice of atonement."

God's righteousness cannot be earned (v. 28), nor is there anything one can give in return for it. It can be received only **through faith in Jesus Christ** as a gift of which one is absolutely unworthy. Faith is an attitude and action of pure receptivity. Paul does not say "*the* faith," in reference to faith as a creed or formula. Faith as an affirmation of certain truths in order to merit God's acceptance is really but a substitute for works. True faith is a response of trust in Christ and a confession that in oneself one has nothing to bring to God.

Verse 22 concludes with an emphasis on the universality of righteousness by faith, **to all who believe. There is no difference** (see also 10:12). It had been Paul's purpose in 1:18–3:20 to show that *all* stand under God's wrath; it is now his purpose to show that *all* are objects of God's grace. "For God has bound all men over to disobedience so that he may have mercy on them all" (11:32)! The gospel is the universal answer to universal need.

How might righteousness by faith have been heard in first-century Rome? In the introduction we suggested that the polarities between Jew and Gentile, which were extreme in the best of circumstances, were likely exacerbated in Rome due to the expulsion and return of Jews surrounding the edict of Claudius. This would have been due, in part, to the fact that the church, which had grown out of the Jewish synagogue, had become increasingly Gentile after Jews were expelled from Rome. Upon their return, perhaps in A.D. 54, it would be surprising indeed if friction and divisions had not developed. In light of this, Paul's protracted strategy in 1:18–3:20 must have been read as more than an abstract theological exercise. The guilt of both Gentiles and Jews is underscored, and the right of either to judge the other is undermined. Moreover, God's righteousness is offered **to all who believe. There is no difference.** We can well imagine the reconciling and healing effect which the doctrine of justification by faith must have had for Jews and Gentiles in such circumstances.

3:23 / **For all have sinned.** This is Paul's categorical summary of the human experience. In chapter 3 he repeats this judg-

ment nine times (vv. 4, 9, 10, 11, 12, 19, 20, 22, 23)! Regardless of
the distinctions humans draw among themselves, in God's sight
"there is no difference." **All have sinned** is an essential prelude
to verse 24. Only in the light of grace can humanity recognize and
lament its rebellion; only in the light of its rebellion is humanity
humbled to receive grace. If humanity is to be saved, salvation
must come from outside it, for on its own humanity stands under
wrath. The Reformers referred to this as "alien righteousness,"
salvation from outside, salvation not from humanity, but freely
and entirely from God. Karl Barth presses this idea into service
when he says, "Genuine fellowship is grounded upon a negative:
it is grounded upon what men lack" (*Romans*, p. 101). There is
no denominator common to humanity, whether social status,
nationality, race, or whatever interests, which constitutes the fellowship of righteousness. All humans share a solidarity of impov-
erishment with one another in God's sight. The one thing they
have in common is that which makes them objects of both wrath
and grace, their unworthiness before God.

Unworthiness is characterized by a **falling short of the glory
of God**. Paul said earlier of those who sought glory and did good
that "glory, honor, and peace" would await them (2:10). It might
be supposed that the human predicament is actually a failure to
"come of age" or attain its destiny. This is quite an alien thought
for Paul. **Falling short of the glory of God** is surely a reference to
Adam's sin in Genesis 3. Humanity lacks glory not because it has
failed in its potential, but because it has lost it through disobedience. The lacking of glory draws our attention not to a hopeful
evolutionary spiral, but to the state of sin ("under sin," 3:9), resultant from humanity's exchanging the glory of God for its own
will (1:21–23).

3:24 / In all Scripture there is probably no verse which
captures the essence of Christianity better than this one. Here is
the heart of the gospel, the mighty Nevertheless, the momentous
divine reversal. Everything in verse 23 was due to humanity;
everything in verse 24 depends on God. Paul slashed through the
stubborn underbrush of idolatry and pride in order to remove
any thought of a righteousness from below, for such a righteousness leads to boasting before God and distinctions among
peoples. There is another righteousness, however, founded not
on human stratagems but on the sovereign grace of God. By it

humanity is **justified freely**. **Freely** underscores that God's right-eousness is unwarranted and determined by nothing but his sovereign will; "the beneficiary has no contribution to make: he receives all and gives nothing" (Leenhardt, *Romans*, p. 100). All this is motivated **by** God's **grace**. How pleasant is the sound of this word after the incriminating argumentation which has gone before. In this word is the sum of the gospel, for in grace God acts towards sinners out of love and mercy rather than from wrath and judgment.

The heart of the matter is **the redemption that came by Christ Jesus**. Here Paul depicts the work of Christ according to a second metaphor, deliverance from slavery. The Greek word, *apolytrōsis*, translated **redemption**, was frequently used in the Hellenistic world with reference to ransom paid for prisoners of war or redemption from slavery. Not the least significant aspect of this word is its concreteness: it refers to an *event* rather than an idea, a fact which must have been of some consequence to the addressees of the epistle, many of whom (to judge from the names listed in chapter 16) were themselves slaves or freedpersons. **Re-demption** means an act on behalf of an inferior, e.g., a prisoner, slave, or sinner. In the OT it often refers to the "redeeming" or buying back of slaves, indentured servants, or land (e.g., Lev. 25). More importantly, the term is often used in the OT of God's deliverance of Israel from oppression in Egypt or exile in Babylon. But in the fulness of time, **redemption** happens *by* **Christ Jesus**. In the Christian faith redemption is defined by the person of Jesus Christ and his sacrifice on the cross. Redemption is an abstraction apart from the person of Jesus, whose name means "deliverer" in Hebrew. Redemption can never be severed from the person of Christ.

3:25 / Paul continues with Christ's agency of salvation in verse 25. In Greek the verse begins with a relative pronoun, "*whom* God put forth," which refers back to Jesus in verse 24. Everything in verses 25–26 therefore depends upon and is ful-filled in Jesus. The Greek word, *protithēmi*, here translated **pre-sented**, can mean either "to set forth publicly" or "to plan or determine beforehand." The latter meaning cannot be doubted. It is often supposed that when the human experiment went foul, God initiated a stopgap measure by sending his Son to remedy it. But Jesus Christ is far from a last minute, scissors-and-paste solution to sin (Gal. 4:4; Heb. 1:1–2). He belongs to the eternal purpose of God, and before the foundation of the world he was ordained as our saving partner (Eph. 1:3–4; Col. 1:15–20). True as this is, however, Paul likely intends the first meaning of *protithēmi*, "to set forth publicly." The following references to the **sacrifice of atonement** and **his blood** seem to indicate the crucifixion as a public demonstration of God's love. The efficacy of the various mystery cults of Jesus' day—Eleusis, Mithra, Isis, Dionysis, and Cybele, to name the most common—depended on anonymity and secrecy. But the gospel had not been "done in a corner," to quote Paul's defense before Agrippa (Acts 26:26). Jesus Christ undertook a public ministry (Luke 2:31), his crucifixion was an official and public act, and the *kerygma*, the earliest Christian preaching, was public proclamation.

The key to the verse is *hilastērion*, rendered **sacrifice of atonement**. With this term Paul changes the metaphor from deliverance to sacrifice. The rarity of the term (and cognates) in the NT (Luke 18:13; Heb. 2:17; 9:5; 1 John 2:2; 4:10) is no indication of its importance. *Hilastērion* translates the Hebrew °*apōret̲*, which designated the lid or mercy seat of the ark of the covenant (Exod. 25:17–22). The ark was *locus revelationis*, the place of revelation symbolizing the very presence of Yahweh, where Israel's sins were forgiven. Paul transfers the imagery of the ark (which had perished six centuries earlier) to the cross of Jesus Christ. What had been revealed provisionally and proleptically in the Holy of Holies has been effected consummately in the cross of Christ: God put forth Christ as the means of forgiveness of sin, finally and forever!

Exactly *how* God removes sin by Christ's sacrifice remains unresolved in theology. Various theories of the atonement attempt to present models or images of this divine mystery. That the same theories—ransom, classical, substitutionary, and moral—continue to be debated millennia after they were first proposed is evidence that each contains a germ of truth. But none exhausts the mystery. Paul's use of *hilastērion* is itself a model of a high priest throwing blood from a sacrificial victim on a holy place in order to remove the sins of those for whom it was offered. But how redemption is thereby effected is much debated. *Hilastērion* is sometimes rendered "propitiation," which means an action intended to alter God's disposition of wrath. At other times it is rendered "expiation," which means an action intended to alter

the human condition of guilt. That the wrath of God discussed in
1:18–3:20 is indeed removed by redemption in Christ Jesus argues in favor of propitiation. But other observations argue for
expiation. The emphasis in 1:18–3:20 is less on God's wrath than on
the human condition of faithlessness and unrighteousness. The
fundamental problem is not God's wrath but human wickedness
and rebellion; once the latter is resolved, the former is dissolved.
It is, after all, the human problem which redemption chiefly addresses. The thought behind expiation closely agrees with the
scriptural testimony that God initiates reconciliation (thus, **God
presented him**). The sinner has absolutely nothing to bring to
appease God's wrath. But God, out of his fathomless love and
holiness, gives what the sinner cannot give, namely, himself on
the sinner's behalf. The ultimate sacrifice of God's offering himself in the person of his Son on behalf of humanity removes the
barrier of unrighteousness and estrangement between the two.

The syntax of **through faith in his blood** should not be
construed as faith in the agency of blood. Were that Paul's meaning he would have used the preposition *eis* (into) instead of *en*
(in). Paul nowhere teaches believers to trust in Jesus' blood, but
in the blood of *Jesus* (NIV, **his blood**), whom God put forth as a
sacrifice of atonement. The OT taught that life resided in the
blood (Gen. 9:4; Lev. 17:11; Deut. 12:23), and the offering of blood
at the altar symbolized the giving of life back to God. Moreover,
the efficacy of a sacrifice consisted in the blood of an *innocent*
victim. Placing their hands upon the head of an unblemished
animal before it was slaughtered, sinners transferred their sins to
the sacrificial victim and claimed its innocence for themselves. At
the cross, however, the blood is efficacious not as blood per se, nor
as innocent blood, but as *Christ's* blood. Paul will return to this
image in chapter 12 when he speaks of Christian ethics, though
with this significant change: Christ offered of necessity a bloody
sacrifice, but the believer must offer a "living sacrifice" (12:1).

Animal sacrifice in Israelite religion served two functions.
First, it covered sin *provisionally*. This is confirmed in verse 25,
**God did this to demonstrate his justice, because in his forbear-
ance he had left the sins committed beforehand unpunished**.
This does not mean that God overlooked or disregarded sin. The
gravity of sin was equally heinous before Christ, although God
allowed a partial remedy until a complete one should come. Patience with sin should not be mistaken for toleration of it. God,

of course, would not be thoroughly good if he were content to pass over sin indefinitely. This introduces Paul's second understanding: animal sacrifice had a *proleptic* function; it was a harbinger of a final sacrifice which would remit the full consequences of sin. It is hardly surprising that early Christianity saw in such imagery the perfect prototype of "the Lamb of God, who takes away the sin of the world!" (John 1:29).

3:26 / God's righteousness is revealed in two ways in verses 25–26. In the past it was revealed in *forbearance* by "leaving sins committed beforehand unpunished" (see also 2:4). In the present it is revealed through *faith in Christ's atoning sacrifice* on the cross. In this Bengel noted a great paradox: in the law God was seen as just and condemning, but in the gospel he is seen as just and yet the justifier of sinners (*Gnomon*, vol. 3, p. 51). In both forbearance and faith God remains *just*. The cross of Christ adequately expressed both God's justice and love, and compromised neither. The cross is not a hope of the subconscious or a gestalt of the archetypical memory; it is a historical fact, a **demonstration** of God's **justice**. But in addition to its historical reality, it is an existential reality, for God **justifies** (the Greek tense indicates contemporary time) those who believe in Jesus.

The central truth in verses 24–25 is Jesus Christ who defines each of the surrounding terms and concepts. Jesus is the redemption whom God put forth as an expiation, whose blood demonstrated God's righteousness, a righteousness through faith in him who justifies the ungodly. That is, to be sure, high caliber vocabulary, but Paul is not indulging in conundrums and sophisms. He is striving to put universal and eternal verities into finite language, and his words are straining under the load. That should not surprise us. If dogs or dolphins were capable of penetrating human knowledge, we presume their language skills would be taxed in describing the Grand Canyon or a Beethoven concerto. Barth was right when he compared the desperate picture of humanity in 1:18–3:20 with the sublime restoration of grace in 3:21ff. It is indeed nothing less than *creatio ex nihilo* (*Romans*, p. 100).

3:27 / Election, circumcision, law—these were so inextricably part of Judaism, and themselves a source of pride and error, that Paul could not fail to consider them in light of the breathtaking news of righteousness in 3:21–26. He reverts here briefly to the rhetorical or diatribe style which he used in chap-

ter 2. The style of verses 27–31 is deft and decisive, likely the result
of ample experience with such issues on the mission field. **Where,
then, is boasting?** Earlier Paul spoke of boasting in Jewishness
(2:17) and the law (2:23). But God's righteousness excludes **boasting**, lest credits and privileges begin to calculate merits with God.
The NIV renders verse 27 loosely, whereas the original Greek maintains a distinct parallelism between "law of works" and "law of
faith." The exact meaning of "law of faith" is a matter of debate.
Paul may employ it as a figure of speech, conforming to "law of
works." Then again, he may mean that since the advent of Christ
the law must ever after be regarded in terms of faith, not as a
reward for virtue but as a summons to faith. What is clear is that
grace stands in conflict with boasting. Justification by works is
the presumption to calculate what God owes to one and not to
another. The arithmetic of legalism juggles the figures to show a
refund due in my column which God must pay. But the arithmetic of grace is based on a bottom-line that all have failed, but that
God has mercy on all. The arithmetic of grace shows a balance
due in my column, and yet a cancellation of debt!

3:28 / Verse 28 recapitulates the main ideas of verses
20–26 (see also Gal. 2:16; 3:12). Even more clearly than in verse
20, Paul here affirms that righteousness could not be attained by
the law. There were not a few virtuous souls in Judaism who were
believed to have fulfilled the law (Paul included, Phil. 3:6), but
not even this constituted righteousness with God. Paul introduces a word that will play a leading role in the following chapter, *logizomai*, "to reckon or impute" (NIV, **maintain**). *Logizomai* is
a strategic word logically because justification by faith is a necessary corollary of the universal condemnation of the law; it is strategic theologically because God reckons sinners righteous solely
by grace through faith, and not by works.

3:29–30 / If it is true that righteousness is received from
faith and not works, then it is universally applicable to Jews and
Gentiles. Both Jews and Gentiles are equally guilty of sin; thus,
both are equally candidates for grace. Jewish rabbis of Paul's day
would have taken strong exception to this. Writing a century after
Paul, Rabbi Simeon ben Yohai granted that God was the God of
all peoples as creator and judge, but to Israel alone God had given
his name, and to Israel alone he belonged (Str-B, vol. 3, p. 185).
Paul reminds the Romans, however, that God is not only creator

of the Gentiles but also their redeemer, because **there is only one God**. Thus, the doctrine of salvation by grace alone is rooted in monotheism, in the oneness of God. *Sola gratia* derives from *solus deus!*

3:31 / Paul concludes the discussion of righteousness with an obvious question: **Do we, then, nullify the law by this faith?** He denies this categorically, **Not at all!** The purpose of the law had never been to bring salvation, as he will argue in chapter 4 (4:13f.; see also Gal. 3:1–20). The law's function had been to reveal sin (3:20) and to demonstrate the need of a savior apart from the law. In 2 Corinthians 3:6 Paul says, "The letter (law) kills, but the Spirit gives life." In the Sermon on the Mount Jesus repeatedly reinterpreted the law in terms of its motive or intent (e.g., Matt. 5:21–22, 27–28). The purpose of the commandment, in other words, had been to engender a proper attitude and behavior toward God's will. It is this original intent or motive which faith perceives, for "the law is holy, and the commandment is holy, righteous and good" (7:12). The law drives one to Christ, and where one lives by faith in Christ, there one fulfills the intent of the law. "The righteous requirements of the law might be fully met in us, who do not live according to the sinful nature but according to the Spirit" (8:4).

Additional Notes §9

The following terms are either rare or unknown in Paul: in v. 25, "presented," "sacrifice of atonement," "demonstrate," "forbearance," "beforehand," "sins" (*hamartēmata*); and in verse 26, "forbearance" (omitted in NIV)—all of which suggest that Paul is utilizing either a confession or well-established Christian terminology.

On the variety of vocabulary in 3:21–31, see Dodd, *Romans*, pp. 51–57.

3:21 / Insightful discussions of the transition at 3:21 can be found in Leenhardt, *Romans*, pp. 98–99, and Nygren, *Romans*, pp. 144–45.

Anders Nygren's comment on 3:21 is an example of Protestant overstatement of the opposition between righteousness and law: "Wherever the righteousness of God is found, it has come apart from any co-operation of the law. It has come, and been revealed, through Christ;

and in that the law claims no share. The righteousness of God and righteousness by the law are opposite to each other and absolutely exclude
each other. Where the one is, the other cannot be. For Paul it is of utmost
importance for every one to understand that the new situation of which
he now speaks has come about 'apart from the law' " (*Commentary on
Romans*, p. 148). More recently R. David Kaylor transgresses the same
boundary in the following comment, "Freedom from the Torah is undoubtedly Paul's most radical teaching, and one that created the most
difficulty in the church of his day. Its implications have rarely been
accepted in the two thousand-year history of the church. The Torah
meant not only rules, but the whole structure of Jewish religious belief
and practice. Freedom from the Torah in its boldest, starkest terms means
freedom from all those structures, rituals, and forms by which Judaism
organized its life" (*Paul's Covenant Community. Jew and Gentile in Romans*,
p. 67).

3:22 / A thorough discussion of righteousness is offered by Quell
and Schrenk, "*dikē*, etc.," *TDNT*, vol. 2, pp. 202–10. For a less technical
discussion, see Achtemeier, *Romans*, pp. 61–66. Achtemeier favors a covenantal (as opposed to forensic) understanding of the term, but for him
also the initiative and decisive work lie with God who must restore the
unrighteous covenant partner to grace.

It is instructive to compare Paul's understanding of righteousness
with that of second temple Judaism. The "righteousness of God" was not
a common expression in the ancient synagogue. It would be an oversim-
plification, however, to say that Jews believed they earned or merited
God's righteousness. The Jew also spoke of *receiving* God's righteousness
or favor, but with this important difference: for Jews God's righteousness
acknowledges a righteousness which they possessed because of Torah,
whereas for Paul God's righteousness *establishes* a condition which sinners do not possess on their own. See Str-B, vol. 3, pp. 162–64.

Franz Leenhardt speaks of faith as the hands of a beggar which are
useful only if empty (*Romans*, p. 99).

The original Greek (*dia pisteōs iēsou christou*) could be rendered,
"through [the] faith *of* Jesus Christ," implying that righteousness comes
from Christ's faithfulness rather than the believer's faith in him. This
is possible on grammatical grounds, but it is less likely on theological
grounds. On the whole, Christ's faithfulness is not an emphasis in Romans, not because it was unimportant, but because it was self-evident.
Moreover, immediately following the phrase under discussion in v. 22
Paul stresses the role of believer, "to all who believe." *Dia pisteōs iēsou
christou* appears also in Gal. 2:16, but is immediately followed by the idea
of putting faith *in* Jesus Christ, all of which argues that Paul understands
Christ as the object of faith. See Dunn, *Romans 1–8*, pp. 166–67. For an
argument favoring the phrase as a subjective genitive (i.e., the faithfulness of Jesus Christ), see L. Keck, "Jesus in Romans," *JBL* 108 (3, 1989), pp.
452–58. For an argument favoring our understanding of Christ as the
object of faith, see D. Hay, "*Pistis* as 'Ground for Faith' in Hellenized
Judaism and Paul," *JBL* 108 (3, 1989), pp. 461–76.

3:25 / There were several traditions associated with the ark, but its general description is contained in the following. Constructed of acacia wood that was overlaid with gold, the ark's dimensions were roughly those of a footlocker. Inside were deposited the tables of stone received by Moses on Mt. Sinai. Each end of the ark was adorned by a single golden cherub with wings extended upward, and on each side were two rings through which poles could be inserted for portability. The ark was placed on a stone dais in the center of the Holy of Holies and situated on a north-south axis. The high priest entered the Holy of Holies once a year on the Day of Atonement (= Yom Kippur) and sprinkled blood on the east side of the ark as a remission for sins. The ark perished after the fall of Jerusalem under Nebuchadnezzar in the sixth century B.C. The second temple thus had no ark, although on the Day of Atonement the high priest continued to sprinkle the place where it had stood. See Str-B, vol. 3, pp. 165–85; and G. Davies, "Ark of the Covenant," *IDB*, vol. 1, pp. 222–26.

A full discussion of the theories of the atonement is presented by G. Aulen, *Christus Victor*, trans. G. Hebert (New York: Macmillan, 1969).

Dunn offers a careful and balanced discussion of the atonement (*Romans 1–8*, pp. 170–72).

3:27 / On the meaning of "law of faith," see Cranfield, *Romans*, vol. 1, pp. 219–20; and Dunn, *Romans 1–8*, p. 186.

3:28 / Note Schlatter's baroque description of righteousness in verse 28: "The meaning of 'to be justified' is the granting of total help, the offering of God's grace, the end of divine wrath and destruction that God metes out to humanity, a bonding with Christ for a life from and for God, complete salvation that is received through faith, and possession of a faith that comes not from calculation of performance" (*Gottes Gerechtigkeit*, p. 152 [my translation]).

§10 Abraham as the Model of Faith (Rom. 4:1–12)

Chapter 4 is a test case of righteousness by faith. In 3:21–31 Paul presented a position statement on salvation through faith in Christ's sacrifice of atonement. In chapter 4 he sends the class to the laboratory, as it were, to test that thesis. Here we find the compressed and nuclear thesis of 3:21–31 developed in the discursive style of Jewish midrash. Midrash was the name given to a form of rabbinic exposition in ancient Palestine which sought to penetrate the meaning of Scripture and deduce principles from it.

The thesis under consideration is that of 3:28, "For we maintain that a man is justified by faith apart from observing the law." The crucial terms are "by faith" and "apart from law." Paul invokes a daring example to verify his thesis—Abraham, the patriarch of Israel. Abraham figures more prominently in the epistles of Paul than any other figure except for Jesus. Abraham's introduction serves three purposes: first, that he was justified by faith and not by works (vv. 1–8); second, that his justification took place before he was circumcised (thus proving that righteousness is for Gentiles as well as Jews, vv. 9–12); and finally, that the promise of God to Abraham was fulfilled not through law but through faith (vv. 13–25). Abraham was thus not only the father of Israel, he is the prototype of Christian faith. Because Abraham trusted in God, God counted him righteous even before he was circumcised and before the law was given. Once the primacy of faith is established, the position of the law is clarified. The law is subsequent to faith and is rightly understood only in light of faith, as Paul stated in 3:31.

4:1 / Resuming the rhetorical style now familiar to readers of Romans, Paul adduces Abraham as conclusive evidence that righteousness comes by faith and not by works. Verse 1 is awkward in Greek and has been altered somewhat in the NIV. A literal translation might read, "What therefore shall we say that Abraham our forefather according to the flesh has found?" The word translated **discovered** (Gk. *heurēkenai*, "has found") seems oddly suited to the verse and may derive from 1 Maccabees 2:52 and Sirach 44:19–20, which utilize the same word. The language suggests that Paul is appealing to a Promethean figure in Israelite tradition whose name has long been encoded in formulaic phraseology. Abraham was a brave choice on Paul's part because Paul hoped to prove by his example a point quite at variance from the established rabbinic understanding of him. The rabbis believed that Abraham was counted righteous because of his works; Paul endeavors to show that he was justified solely by his faith, *apart from* works.

It would be difficult to overestimate Abraham's importance in Judaism. A hero who worshipped the one true God in the midst of idolatrous peoples, Abraham's legacy had been polished with a rich patina of miracle and legend. Indeed, in the nearly two millennia since his death he had been elevated to a quasi-divine status. His grave (actually a cenotaph) in Hebron was honored as a holy place. He was believed to have obeyed perfectly God's commandments before they were given, and he was extolled as the embodiment of Psalm 1. Rabbis spoke of God's having ordained the Torah before the foundation of the world "for Abraham's sake," and, along with Isaac and Jacob, he was regarded as "one who has not sinned against Thee." A familiar passage in the Greek OT eulogized his life in these words,

> Abraham, the father of a multitude of nations, suffered no blemish to his honor and had no equal in glory, observed the commandments of the Most High and entered into a covenant with Him. God was near to him in his flesh and faithful to him in his temptations. Therefore God swore a firm oath with him, that in his offspring he would bless nations, and that their possession would stretch from sea to sea, from the river Euphrates to the ends of the earth (Sir. 44:19–21, Charlesworth, *OTP*).

As a reward for his meritorious life Abraham was called the friend of God (Isa. 41:8) and a helper for salvation to later generations of Israel.

4:2 / In light of such credentials, both real and imagined, it was no wonder that Jews were proud to be known as "children of Abraham" (see Matt. 3:9). When they appealed to "Abraham our forefather" (v. 1) they identified, to be sure, with his righteousness, but also with the fame and honor which attended it. People are flattered to think that the achievements and renown of their ancestors convey like qualities to themselves—and deny them to others. There is a point, however, at which self-esteem overripens into pride, desiring to prove itself better than others. It is this pride which Paul addresses in verse 2. He does not say that Abraham had nothing to boast of. If Abraham chose to present his credentials as a pretext for God's favor, then he was, as we say, a "self-made man," and he need not give credit to God, for his justification was his desert, not God's gift. This was how first-century Judaism regarded Abraham. The rabbis taught that God's favor had been a *reward* to Abraham for his observance of Torah, even before it had been given. A common proof-text was Genesis 26:4–5, which said that God would give the patriarch the blessings of numerous descendants and lands *"because* Abraham obeyed me and kept my requirements, my commands, my decrees and my laws."

4:3 / Paul confronts this preening attitude with a proof-text which he used more than once in his battle over faith and works, **"Abraham believed God, and it was credited to him as righteousness"** (Gen. 15:6; see also 4:9, 22; Gal. 3:6). Ironically, this verse played a prominent role in Jewish discussions of Abraham, being used to show the *merit of faith*, i.e., that Abraham's faith was itself a work of obedience and thus a ground for justification. It was a bold venture for Paul to cite a verse which his opponents assumed supported their position, and by it to demonstrate a diametrically opposite view.

In mounting his counterattack Paul emphasizes two words: **believed** and **credited**. Abraham was justified because he *believed*, not because he did something (v. 2). Paul's Jewish contemporaries understood the word **believed** as *an act of faithfulness*, which was itself a meritorious work. Paul, conversely, understood **believed** as *radical trust* in God. It was common in Jewish midrash to take a verse (sometimes out of context) to try to prove one point or another. On the basis of Genesis 15:6 alone it would be quite impossible to say whether Paul or his opponents were right. But in considering the life of Abraham as a whole (Gen. 12–25) one is struck by the fact that Abraham repeatedly stood before the dilemma of believing in God's promise of a son *in spite of* circumstances to the contrary: Abraham's old age, Sarah's barrenness, Eliezer's ineligibility, Ishmael's rejection, and always, the interminable waiting. And yet, despite the obstacles and setbacks, Abraham is nonetheless called by God to believe. There is nothing that Abraham can *do*—although he tries in vain to assist the fulfillment of the promise in the Eliezer (Gen. 15) and Hagar (Gen. 16) episodes. The only avenue open to him was faith. How telling that Paul says simply that **Abraham believed.** Paul does not say that he believed this or that as a quantum of faith, but that **Abraham believed God,** personally and completely. Considering that Abraham was the first person summoned into the drama of salvation history, his achievements—forsaking the civilized world of Ur for the nomadic stretches of Canaan; his long and perilous journeys; his great herds, many servants, and victorious battles; his intercession for Sodom; his willingness to sacrifice a beloved son to a largely unknown God—were utterly remarkable. But worthy and noble as these things were, they were of no consequence in realizing God's promise. Abraham stood before the awful choice of trusting in the credibility of God, despite howling evidence to the contrary. His faith was not a work, not a virtue, not an expression of the heroic will, but a resignation in weakness, a powerlessness in the face of overwhelming opposition to the sovereign word of God. God's promises to Abraham were not a reward for his obedience, for God called Abraham and promised him land, progeny, and blessing *before* he had obeyed (Gen. 12:1–3). It was God's word alone which created and determined Abraham's existence, and to which he relinquished himself by a commitment of trust.

Faith is a form of poverty, says Ernst Käsemann, in which the believer must wait for blessing. "It is the place where the Creator alone can and will act as such" (*Romans*, p. 111). Calvin adds that faith is "deriving from another what is wanting in oneself" (*Romans*, p. 155). Faith is born only where personal hopes are exhausted and God's word is expected, where personal claims and doubts give way in humble submission, "May it be to me as you have said" (Luke 1:38). It is an attitude of resigning and receiving, and consequently Paul cannot speak of Abraham's having earned or deserved God's righteousness. He says rather that **Abraham believed God, and it was** *credited* **to him as righteousness.** The word *logizomai*, here rendered **credited,** can also mean "to reckon" or "impute." It occurs 11 times in this chapter and is the second key word in verse 3. The passive voice **it was credited** is a divine passive, meaning actually "God credited it." This is an essential nuance in Paul's argument. Righteousness was not Abraham's due but God's determination, "the act of a gracious will," in the words of Bengel (*Gnomon*, p. 55). Righteousness is God's attribute, not Abraham's, and if Abraham is to participate in it he must receive it solely as a gift from the kindness of God. But faith is not a substitute for works, for if it were, then it would be a condition or work itself. There is indeed a work of righteousness—the death of Jesus Christ as a "sacrifice of atonement" (3:25). The ground of righteousness is the work of Christ alone, and this righteousness can only be appropriated by faith.

> The question is not, what men are in themselves, but how God regards them? not that purity of conscience and integrity of life are to be separated from the gratuitous favour of God; but that when the reason is asked, why God loves us and owns us as just, it is necessary that Christ should come forth as the one who clothes us with his own righteousness (Calvin, *Romans*, p. 157).

4:4–8 / It remains for Paul to demonstrate that his understanding of faith is the proper one. He does this in verses 4–5 by a lesson in logic: When one works, argues Paul, compensation is calculated in terms of wages or earnings; but if one is justified without working, then compensation as such is excluded, and justification is a free gift. Paul reduces the difference to the following formulas: traditional Judaism accepted the continuum **works – credited – obligation** (v. 4); but Paul argues otherwise for **trust – credited – righteousness** (v. 5). For Paul the difference is between grace and rewards, and there exists an unbridgeable chasm between the two. The mentality of rewards denies that it is "under sin" (3:9), it affirms that God's values are more or less the same as human values, indeed, that God is essentially a personification of the moral law. Paul finds this stereotypical picture of God rancorous because it denies God's sovereignty, and with it his grace, making of God a cosmic automaton whose reactions are determined by human causes and moral systems. Paul faulted the accepted Jewish interpretation of Genesis 15:6 as identifying God too closely with human judgments, and thus being in danger of making God in humanity's image.

Only the latter way of thinking, the mentality of faith, opens up the possibility of grace. But grace is offensive, as we noted in the discussion of 3:22. The problem is repeated and intensified when Paul says that **God . . . justifies the wicked** (v. 5). That phrase posed an utter contradiction for Paul's Jewish contemporaries. In Judaism **God justifies** only those within the covenant, whereas **the wicked** stand outside the covenant and thus outside the possibility of salvation. To acquit, much less justify, the ungodly was abhorrent to the morally conscientious (Exod. 23:7; Prov. 17:15; Isa. 5:23). Paul, however, understood **wickedness** or "ungodliness," as the Greek *asebēs* could also be rendered, far more radically than did normative Judaism, for, as he argued in 3:9–20, not just the morally reprobate, not just Gentiles, but all humanity stood "under sin." Ungodliness was a description of the human condition—a condition, indeed, which included Abraham! This was assuredly an incendiary statement in a milieu in which, at least in some circles, Abraham was accepted as sinless.

Paul did not regard Abraham as sinless any more than he regarded Israel as sinless. In its reflective moments Israel realized that God had chosen it not because it was more numerous or powerful or important than other peoples, but from a deeper, more mysterious inclination called **grace**. "The Lord did not set his affection on you and choose you because you were more numerous . . . but because the Lord *loved* you" (Deut. 7:7–8). Neither Abraham nor Israel had meritorious checks written against their accounts. Luther rightly recognized that "God does not accept a person on account of his works, but the works on account of the person, and the person before the works" (*Lectures on Romans*, p. 123).

In verses 6–8 Paul continues with the thought of justification. This is shown by the repetition of verse 3 in verse 6, **God credits righteousness apart from works**. This truth is illustrated by King David as well as by Abraham. If there were any doubt about Abraham's sin, there could be none about David's (cf. 2 Sam. 11). The quotation in verses 7–8 comes from the opening lines of Psalm 32, which was believed to have been written by David. The purpose of the quotation is to contrast **blessedness** (mentioned three times) with **sins** (also mentioned three times). Paul, of course, does not say that David did no good works. Like Abraham, any number of laudable things could be said of him. But his works were insufficient to cover his sins. That he could speak from a condition of **blessedness** was due to the forgiveness of his sins which were remitted solely by grace. Here particularly

Paul interprets **righteousness apart from works** by the forgiveness of sins (vv. 7–8), thereby implying that reckoning righteousness and not imputing sin are essentially the same thing.

4:9–10 / Thus, (1) Abraham was justified by faith, and (2) his faith was itself not a work. There remains yet one objection which could be raised against the thesis that Abraham—and with him the whole OT—advocates justification by faith. The objection is found in verses 9–10. Paul's kinsfolk would naturally have understood Psalm 32 and the forgiveness of sins therein to apply exclusively to Israel. The text itself almost shouts out a rejoinder, "Of course Abraham was accounted righteous, as was David forgiven, *because they were Jews!*" A midrash on Psalm 32, in fact, reads, "On the day of atonement God cleanses Israel and atones for her guilt, as it says, 'For on this day atonement will be made for you. . . .' And if you would ask, 'Does [God] cleanse any other nation?' Know this, 'No, only Israel. . . . Only Israel does he forgive.' "

In light of this Paul returns to Genesis 15:6 in verse 9 and raises the question of circumcision. If it can be shown that God's promise came to one who was circumcised (i.e., a Jew), then his argument is scuttled, for Paul would only have demonstrated righteousness by Judaism, not righteousness by faith.

But Paul denies that forgiveness of sins in Psalm 32—and God's grace in general—are limited to Israel. The opposite is the case. Returning to a rhetorical style, Paul asks, **Is this blessedness only for the circumcised, or also for the uncircumcised?** (v. 9). That is to say, under what circumstances was righteousness credited to Abraham? Was Abraham declared righteous after he was circumcised or before? The answer, of course, is that "God credited to him righteousness" *before* he was circumcised. Abraham's justification is recorded in Genesis 15:6; his circumcision not until Genesis 17:10ff. According to rabbinic calculations, Abraham received the promise of Genesis 15:6 at age 70, but he was not circumcised until age 99. Thus, circumcision cannot be a prerequisite for righteousness. Otto Michel correctly notes that Paul's strategy here is exactly the opposite of that at 3:10–18: there he faced the danger that the Jews would shift the sentence of judgment exclusively onto the Gentiles; here he faces the danger that Israel will reserve God's blessings solely for itself (*Der Brief an die Römer*, p. 119).

The conclusion that Abraham was blessed before he was circumcised was like a sonic boom in a china cupboard. If God had called and justified Abraham before he had a son, then he was not at the time a patriarch; and if God had justified him before he was circumcised, then he was not at the time a Jew! In other words, Abraham was an uncircumcised (and therefore, unrighteous) Gentile when he was reckoned righteous by God! The logic of grace may be offensive but it is irrefutable; the same logic will prompt Paul to exclaim, "While we were still sinners, Christ died for us" (5:8).

4:11–12 / Since Abraham was justified *before* he was circumcised, his circumcision was a **sign** of righteousness, not a cause of it. Whereas Judaism came to regard circumcision as a good work, as something *achieved*, Paul refers to it as something *received* (v. 11). Judaism emphasized the doer of the act; Paul emphasizes the Giver of the sign. Circumcision is **a seal of the righteousness that** Abraham **had by faith**, i.e., a visible corroboration of righteousness already granted to Abraham through his trust in God. Circumcision was not an acknowledgment of Abraham's observance of Torah, as the rabbis taught, but a guarantee of his righteous standing with God. If circumcision was an acknowledgment of Abraham's moral rectitude, then it was in fact a reward, a payment, an "obligation" of God (v. 4). But circumcision was not God's duty to Abraham, it was a sign of his grace to him.

One way of grasping Paul's distinction between faith and works is to compare the use of **father** in verses 1 and 12. When Paul speaks of "Abraham our forefather" (v. 1) he speaks as a Jew. Only Jews (or proselytes who had undergone circumcision) spoke of Abraham as "*our* forefather," and in Abraham's circumcision Jews saw the inauguration of the covenant of salvation which included themselves. Paul argues, however, that circumcision is not merely a "sign of the covenant" (Gen. 17:11), but a **seal of righteousness**, which is something more primary and fundamental. Abraham was reckoned righteous not by circumcision, but by faith, which preceded his being circumcised. The consequence of this is portentous, even if not at first apparent: Abraham was the father of Gentile believers before he was the father of Jewish believers, for he was **the father of all who believe but have not been circumcised** *before* he was the father of the cove-

nant. His becoming forefather of the Jews was a subsequent spec-
ification of an original fatherhood of all who believe, namely, of
Gentiles. Thus, both Gentile Christians and Jewish Christians
(and in that order!) may appeal to Abraham as father.

Six times in this section Paul affirms that "righteousness is
credited to them" by faith (vv. 3, 5, 6, 9, 10, 11). Its repetition
assures its veracity, that by faith believers receive from God what
is lacking in themselves. Because Abraham was counted righteous by faith he is the father of uncircumcised (Gentiles) *and*
circumcised (Jews) believers. Both groups are included in Abraham's fatherhood of faith, and neither is pitted against the other.
There is not one way for Jews to be saved and another for Gentiles, but all have Abraham as their father, who is the prototype
of saving faith. God did not institute salvation by law in the first
covenant and salvation through Christ in the second covenant,
but salvation through faith in both covenants. Justification by
faith is not a late idea, not an emergency measure instituted when
a crisis developed in the original plan, but the oldest and truest
idea of redemption, conceived by God in love before the foundation of the world, exemplified by Abraham of old, and consummated by Jesus in the fulness of time. " 'I tell you the truth,' Jesus
answered, 'before Abraham was born, I am!' " (John 8:58).

Additional Notes §10

4:1 / On the use of "has found," 1 Macc. 2:52 reads, "Was not
Abraham found faithful in temptation, and it was accounted to him as
righteousness?"; similarly, some 13 times in Gen. (e.g., 18:3; 19:19, etc.)
Abraham is spoken of as having "found favor" (= grace) in God's eyes.

On the hagiographic standing of Abraham in late Judaism, see
Str-B, vol. 3, pp. 186–201; and J. Jeremias, "*Abraam*," *TDNT*, vol. 1, pp. 8–9.

4:3 / See the discussion of Gen. 15:6 and the role it played in
Judaism in Cranfield, *Romans*, vol. 1, pp. 228–30.

Of faith, Hans Urs von Balthasar says, "Faith is a surrender by man
to the fidelity of God in which he agrees with God from the very beginning (it is faith *in* God's word) and adapts himself to that agreement"
(*Convergences* [Ignatius Press, 1983], p. 69).

4:9–10 / The midrash on Ps. 32 is Pesiq. Rab. 45 (185b); quoted
in Str-B, vol. 3, pp. 202–3 (my translation).

Paul hacked his way through a thicket of works, circumcision, and pride in 4:1–12 in order to create a clearing where faith might grow. The second half of the chapter continues with the example of Abraham but furthers the discussion by showing how faith is anchored to the promise of God. One scholar puts it this way, "In the preceding verses we learned *that* Abraham is our father in the faith. In these verses we learn *how* he is our father" (Achtemeier, *Romans*, p. 81). Paul develops his argument in three stages. He first argues that God's promise to Abraham was independent of the law (vv. 13–16). He then argues that Abraham's faith was analogous to believing in the resurrection from the dead (vv. 17–22). Finally, he concludes that Abraham's faith anticipated the resurrection of Jesus from the dead and was fulfilled by it (vv. 23–25).

4:13 / This verse restates the conclusion of 4:1–12. Paul has argued that God's call and promise to Abraham were independent of the latter's works or achievement; **it was not through law that Abraham and his offspring received the promise**. The same point was demonstrated more factually in Galatians 3:17, "The law, introduced 430 years later, does not set aside the covenant previously established by God and thus do away with the promise." Had the law been the doorway to the promise, then Abraham first would have had to receive the law in order to inherit the promise. But this he had not done. God had declared him righteous before the giving of the law, thus demonstrating that righteousness was prior to and independent of the law. Abraham was an **heir** not by virtue of family lineage or works, but **through the righteousness that comes by faith**, that is, by grace.

Paul could have alluded to the same motif in the life of Jesus. The call of Levi the tax collector manifestly illustrates the offense of grace (Mark 2:13–17). Had Levi been a *former* tax collector who had washed his hands of a dirty profession, his call might have been understandable. True, Jesus called him *from* tax collecting, but the call came while he was *at* his tax table, during business hours. The outcry was immediate: "Why does [Jesus] eat with tax collectors and 'sinners'?" Romans 4 is a similar probe of the impulse of grace, an impulse which Paul sees already at work in Abraham. Abraham's justification lies in the justification of Gentile sinners "apart from the law." Abraham is therefore a theological prototype for Paul and the father of faith for both Jews and Gentiles. It is also possible that Paul may have intended Abraham to be an ethical prototype for Jews and Gentiles following the edict of Claudius, as a point of convergence where their differences could be overcome and their unity in faith recovered.

The promise to Abraham (repeated frequently in Genesis) includes possessing the land and having offspring more numerous than stars in the sky or sand on the seashore. Since the promise came to Abraham before the law was given and even before he was circumcised, it could be received only as a gift in faith, for Abraham had done nothing to merit it. This was an about-face from the conventional view of the synagogue. The rabbis taught that the promise came to Abraham because of his observance of Torah, and the faith with which he received it was itself a meritorious achievement. For Paul, however, grace depended not on a *because of* but on an *in spite of*. He orients the discussion around two contrasting sets of terms. Verse 15 speaks negatively of law, transgression, and wrath, whereas verse 16 speaks positively of faith, grace, and promise. Abraham had to elect one option or the other. Where one endeavors to make oneself worthy of a gift, there one tries, however subtly, to take credit for something intended freely. Where there is no faith as the humble and grateful response to God's promise, there can be no righteousness. When God makes a promise, one either receives the promise by faith or forfeits the promise. "For if the inheritance depends on the law, then it no longer depends on a promise; but God in his grace gave it to Abraham through a promise" (Gal. 3:18).

That the promise could be received only by faith and not by works was for Paul *status confessionis*, which could not be conceded without destroying the faith. He devotes a protracted discussion to this issue in Romans 4 and Galatians 3. Although the promise is not a prominent motif in the OT, it was for Paul a sublime expression of grace, for the promise was rooted in and guaranteed by the character of God. The God who issues the promise is fully able to fulfill it (4:21) because he brings the dead to life, and he creates from nothing (4:17). Since the law cannot impart life (Gal. 3:21), it is therefore subordinate to faith. The promise presupposes God's gracious will and favor (4:16) and can be received only through faith, not by calculations of merit. A faith which doubts God's ability to honor his promise constitutes a theft against God's glory (4:20) and a challenge to his truthfulness (15:8).

The promise is more than a favorable disposition of God towards humanity, such as the "benevolence" of Buddhism or "bounty" of the older hymns. The promise comes as a concrete word of hope to individuals and peoples, to **Abraham and his offspring** (v. 13). Paul speaks of the promise variously as inheritance (v. 13; Gal. 3:18); life (v. 17; Gal. 3:21); righteousness (Gal. 3:21); a gift of the Spirit (Gal. 3:14; Eph. 1:13); or adoption as children of God (Gal. 4:5). These are not abstract qualities but characteristics of Jesus Christ in whom the promises of God take on human form (15:8). "All the promises of God find their Yes in him" (2 Cor. 1:20, RSV). God is not a divine killjoy, a cosmic sadist bent on "getting even" with the world. God says *Yes* to the world in the promise to Abraham, even before Abraham knows God's name, his person, or his will. To say that the world is fallen and sinful is to say that it is the object not of God's damnation but of his love. " 'For I know the plans I have for you,' declares the Lord, 'plans to prosper you and not to harm you, plans to give you hope and a future' " (Jer. 29:11). The promise of God is an expression of his faithfulness (3:4), his "for us-ness" (cf. 8:31).

Abraham is the **heir of the world**. Genesis records extraordinary promises to Abraham—that he would become a great and powerful nation, that his descendants would be countless in number, and that future nations would be blessed through him (Gen. 12:1–3; 18:18; 22:17–18). In later tradition Abraham's reputation evolved even further to the cosmic proportions that we saw in 4:1–12. A midrash on Numbers reads, "You [Abraham] have made my name known in the world; by your life I will enable you to inherit princes and paupers, as it says: blessed be Abram, the heir of heaven and earth from God on high." That Paul also calls Abraham **heir of the world** reveals the influence of such thinking on him. He presses the tradition, however, into the service of his argument that Abraham's offspring (Gk. "seed") would surpass the bounds of Israel and include the Gentiles; that is, the object of God's promise to Abraham was the *world* (vv. 17–18; also Acts 2:5f.). The promise, first spoken to a solitary pilgrim nearly 2,000 years before Paul, did not perish in the sands of time; neither was it to remain the possession of one branch of humanity. Rather like yeast permeating the whole, it lays hold of the world! "All things are yours," wrote Paul to the Corinthians, "whether . . . the world or life or death or the present or the future—all are yours, and you are of Christ, and Christ is of God" (1 Cor. 3:21–23).

4:14 / The concept of inheritance played an important role in the OT and subsequent Jewish thought. When Paul speaks to **those who live by law** he refers to the attitude he attacked in chapter 2, namely, that circumcision and observance of Torah qualified one to inherit righteousness. But in Paul's mind this led to "boasting" (3:27), to the calculating of merits, and to the laying of charges to God's account. Claiming inheritance on the basis of law empties faith and annuls the promise (5:12–20; Gal. 3:18–19). When one attempts to secure by one's own efforts what is intended as a gift, the attention is shifted from the giver to the gift. The thing promised takes precedence over the one who promises, and a consideration of dues replaces a relationship of trust. The argument is not unrelated to what Martin Buber terms "I–Thou" versus "I–It" relationships. There is an implicit admonition in verse 14 against any form of religious belief that values the things God does more than the God who does them. This is tantamount to loving God not for *who* he is, but for *what* he does, which is idolatry (1:25).

4:15 / The progression of thought leads Paul to a startling conclusion, **law brings wrath**. If by **law** Paul means Torah (the definite article in Greek implies this), he could hardly have penned a more offensive statement. Pharisaic Judaism taught that the law brought grace, not wrath. If the law was given by God, how could Paul assert that it provokes his wrath? In the present context the statement is somewhat problematic. The progression of Paul's thought does in fact introduce the statement, but the constraints of the argument prohibit him from developing it until 7:7ff.

In order to unpack verse 15 we must recall 3:20, "through the law we become conscious of sin." This complements the latter half of verse 15, **where there is no law there is no transgression**.

A society which does not regard stealing as a crime, of course, has no thieves. The offensive word is **wrath**, the same word used of God's wrath against "all godlessness and wickedness" in 1:18. The word *katergazomai* (**brings**) clearly implies that the law not merely reveals sin, but that it *produces* sin. There is a cause-and-effect relationship between law and sin. Calvin's interpretation that the law shows the right way to live but supplies no power to live it falls short of explaining the verse (*Romans*, p. 171). A proper understanding depends on two observations. First, there is a missing link in the logic of the statement (**law brings wrath**) which the remainder of the verse attempts to clarify. As a whole the verse implies that the law makes humanity deserving of wrath because it reveals **transgression**; thus, transgression, and not the law, produces wrath. Nevertheless, the law is more than an impartial standard of justice, for it *incites* sin, as Paul will argue in chapter 7. **Transgression**, *parabasis*, hints at this, for a transgression is a willful overstepping or violation of a commandment. Paul suggests that the prohibition of something actually produces a desire for it. In prohibiting theft, adultery, covetousness and so forth, the law subtly creates a desire for the things it condemns. For this reason the **law brings wrath**. This idea, of course, is not nearly so foreign as it may seem. "Reverse psychology" and the "created desire" syndrome of Madison Avenue are two modern illustrations of it.

4:16 / To law, wrath, and transgression Paul contrasts **faith, grace**, and **promise**. **Faith** and **grace** are inseparable for Paul. Grace is God's sovereign and gratuitous decision to redeem rebellious and estranged creation. Grace is "God's very presence and action within us. . . . the sanctifying energy of God acting dynamically in our life" (Thomas Merton, *Life and Holiness*, p. 30). "Man shall not quite be lost," said Milton, "but sav'd who will, Yet not of will in him, but grace in me Freely voutsaft" (*PL*, 3.173–75). The decision to act salvifically on behalf of the world derived solely from God. Faith in God's saving action is not the will to achieve it, but the will to receive it. Salvation must depend on grace and not on works, for if salvation comes by grace then it depends on God and is therefore certain; but if it depends on works or law, then it is as unreliable as the human heart and will. "God is for us" (8:31). God's grace assures us of that which we cannot assure ourselves.

The latter half of verse 16 may be misleading. The juxtaposition of **those who are of the law** with **those who are of the faith** might suggest that some (Jews) are saved by law and others (Gentiles) by faith. That, of course, would contradict Paul's entire argument. The phrase deserves comment in two respects. First, like verse 12 above, it is a technical reference to Jews and Gentiles. **Those who are of the law** refers to Jews, who, like Gentiles, must receive the promise through faith. The latter half of the verse is contingent on the first half. The **promise . . . to all Abraham's offspring** includes Jews and Gentiles. Second, and equally important, the phrasing does not pit Jews and Gentiles against each other or require that one adapt to the other to receive salvation. They have different stations, but they have a common faith (cf. 1:16–17). Paul again emphasizes the universality of the promise and of the faith symbolized by Abraham, who **is the father of us all**.

4:17 / In Genesis 17:5 God reaffirmed the promise that Abraham would be the "father of many nations." God declares to him, **"I have made you a father"** (Gk. *tetheika se*, literally, "I have set you or established you"). Abraham's fatherhood, in other words, depended not on him but on God. The plural, **nations**, is equally instructive. Abraham's heirs were to be all peoples who walk by faith, "the world," according to verse 13, which includes—but is not limited to—the Jewish people.

The remainder of the verse describes the kind of God in whom Abraham believed, **the God who gives life to the dead and calls things that are not as though they were**. **In the sight of God** is a bit cumbersome in Greek due to the expression *katenanti hou*, which probably derives from the Hebrew, *lip̄e nê*, meaning "in front of, before." Paul pictures Abraham not as assenting to a theological truth, but as standing or perhaps bowing before the Almighty. There was a latent danger in God's awesome works. Like Simon the Magician (Acts 8:9–25), Abraham may have been tempted to worship the power rather than the person behind it, the thing made alive rather than the life giver. Abraham's trust, however, was in God rather than in the works which God did for him.

When Paul speaks of God as the one **who gives life to the dead and calls things that are not as though they were**, he appeals to the highest characteristics of God in the Hebrew tradition. Both manifestations—giving life to the dead and creating out of nothing—were also experiences of Abraham. His body and

Sarah's, long beyond childbearing age, were dead to the possibility of producing an heir. Yet God made a promise to that heir as though he existed, and the son born to Abraham and Sarah inherited that promise. Later, on Mount Moriah Abraham was called to sacrifice his son, and at the moment when Isaac was doomed, God restored him to life. For Abraham—and for Paul—there was no separation between the God of creation and the God of redemption. Both creation and redemption were for Abraham results of the one promise of God. Abraham did not have a vague notion of a "divine presence," he did not recite platitudes about an "ultimate power." Abraham's God gave life—to himself, to his wife, to his son. He brought into being a posterity which, from a human perspective, was an impossibility. Abraham's God was a God of the impossible. And so was Paul's God, as he testifies in 2 Corinthians 1:8–9. The numbing darkness of the impossible was a terrible but necessary prelude to receiving the promise of the God who spoke and it was, of the God who breathed into clay and flushed it with life.

The God who raises the dead cannot be tamed or controlled. He can be received only by faith, and by faith God transforms frozen impossibilities into springs of hope and resurrection. "Faith beholds life and existence where the man of the world sees nothing but death and non-existence," says Barth, "and contrariwise, it sees death and non-existence where he beholds full-blooded life" (*Romans*, p. 141).

4:18–19 / Faith in the God of the impossible gives birth to hope, and hope, in the words of Hebrews (6:19), is "an anchor for the soul." **Against all hope**, or as the Greek might be rendered, "hope upon hope," is how Paul describes Abraham's situation in verse 18. When Abraham surveyed his circumstances **he faced the fact that his body was as good as dead—since he was about a hundred years old—and that Sarah's womb was also dead** (v. 19; cf. Gen. 17:17). There was no hope for Abraham in circumstances. But Paul says Abraham saw his circumstances **in faith**, i.e., not from the perspective of mechanistic determinism, but from the viewpoint of God, who makes all things new. God's promise transformed Abraham's weakness and despair into hope. This did not mean that Abraham closed his eyes to the bleakness of his circumstances. A textual variant on verse 19 reads that Abraham did *not* observe the deadness of his body, which implies that he avoided sizing up his circumstances. This is surely a corruption of Paul's meaning. It was precisely because Abraham had faith that he could see his terrible prospects for what they were. But that was not all he saw. Menacing and prohibitive though his circumstances were, because Abraham's faith was in a God of mercy, he did not see the obstacles as insurmountable. God's promise made them potential for something beyond his dreams. Abraham's faith was not a safe faith: "If the Bible says it, I believe it, and that settles it!" Rather, his faith was beset with opposition. The passage of time sucked the winds of hope from his sails, and more than once he was driven to the brink of despair.

Despite all this, Paul makes a preposterous claim: Abraham's faith *grew*. There was a disproportionate relationship between his obstacles and his faith. There was more involved in Abraham's faith than Abraham himself, more than self-reliance or the tapping of inner reserves in times of crises. The older and more impotent he became, the stronger he grew in the conviction that God was faithful to fulfill his promise. His faith, in other words, was not bound by his sight. Calvin aptly observed that "there is nothing more injurious to faith than to fasten our minds to our eyes" (*Romans*, p. 176). It was not from his senses that Abraham found hope, but from his faith. What he saw filled him with despair, but the word of promise inspired him with hope "in him who raised Jesus our Lord from the dead" (v. 24).

4:20–22 / Faith is not an inoculation against the germs of life. Faith is a fierce struggle. The hardest thing in life is to believe God above circumstances. Abraham questioned God, "O Lord, what can you give me?" (Gen. 15:2). He pleaded with God (Gen. 18:16ff.). His wife laughed at God (Gen. 18:11ff.). One command—to sacrifice young Isaac—struck so hard that he was left reeling in confusion. But he obeyed the command, repeating to himself "God will provide" as he trudged up the mountain (Gen. 22). His obedience, however, was not the obedience of despondency. How could he be passive before the God of the impossible? Abraham questioned God and struggled with God. The decision of faith was not then and is not now an easy one. Calvin was right when he said,

> All things around us are in opposition to the promises of God: He promises immortality; we are surrounded with mortality and corruption; He declares that he counts us just; we are covered with sins:

He testifies that he is propitious and kind to us; outward judgments threaten his wrath. What then is to be done? (*Romans*, p. 180).

Yes, what is to be done? In the tempest of struggle Abraham
did not allow himself to be swept into the vortex of disbelief. His
questions did not cancel his belief; he did not become a nihilist.
Things, facts, statistics, the hard evidence of life—these were
inescapable for him, but they did not rule him. His faith neither
minimized nor finalized his outward circumstances, but the final
word for him was **the promise of God**. Abraham chose to believe
the promise rather than become immobilized by the arguments
against it—and his choice **strengthened . . . his faith**.

True faith is strengthening faith, which exists in tension
with doubt and disbelief. The ideal, of course, is that the human
will might become one with the divine—and someday it will be.
But the initial lessons in the classroom of life are not so easily
learned. " '*Abba*, Father. . . . Take this cup from me. Yet not what I
will, but what you will' " (Mark 14:36). Jesus too knew the struggle of faith. Faith does not exist in a vacuum. We may worship
God in a sanctuary, but we do not normally find our faith in one.
Faith is more often born in a boxing ring of choices—of doubt,
disbelief, impossibility, and meaninglessness. To adhere to the
promise of God in spite of everything to the contrary is to give
glory to God. If Abraham can do nothing to receive God's promise except to believe, neither can he honor and glorify God except
by believing (1:21). "No greater honor can be given to God," says
Calvin, "than by faith to seal his truth, and no greater dishonor
can be done to him than to refuse his offered favor, or to discredit
his word" (*Romans*, p. 180). God is honored by the believing will.
Leenhardt concludes,

> [Abraham] believed what God had said because God said it, and
> not because he might have found in what had been said good
> reasons for adherence. His faith neither made a calculation of the
> probabilities of accomplishment nor a quick estimate of the advan-
> tages to be gained. Abraham thought only of that Being who had
> spoken (*Romans*, p. 126).

Abraham was **fully persuaded** of the promise because of the
character of God who stood behind it, and **This is why "it was
credited to him as righteousness."**

4:23–25 / What Paul says in verses 23–24 will come as no
surprise to the reader. The righteousness accorded to Abraham

was **not for him alone, but also for us**. Paul had no intention of
treating Abraham as a museum piece; neither is his review of
righteousness in this chapter undertaken from purely historical
interests. Paul saw in Abraham's experience a model for the Gentiles, whose hope for salvation was as dead as Abraham's body.
Abraham was for Paul the first fruits of a process of salvation
which extended from the patriarch to Jesus Christ. Abraham's
faith in God's promise is expressive of the faith of believers in the
God **who raised Jesus our Lord from the dead**. Everything Paul
has said finds its culmination in Jesus, who is here mentioned for
the first time in chapter 4. Whoever believes that God raised
Jesus from the dead testifies to the God of the promise "who
gives life to the dead" (v. 17). As Abraham and Sarah believed
despite the deadness in themselves (vv. 19–20), so believers are
justified through faith in the God who raised Jesus from the
dead. It is the same faith in the same God who brings the dead
to life.

A refined couplet concludes the chapter: **He was delivered
over to death for our sins and was raised to life for our justification**. The parallelism—death for sin, raised for righteousness—
points doubtlessly to an early Christian formula or confession.
Christ's achievement on both accounts was *for us*. The passive
voice, **He was delivered over**, a divine passive, is a reverential
reference to God without using his name (lest it be profaned),
meaning "God handed him over." The couplet is apparently a
christological reflection on the final verse of Isaiah's hymn to the
suffering servant, where (in the LXX) the servant "was handed
over on account of our sins" (53:12). The verb behind **delivered**
(Gk. *paradidōmi*) is doubly suited to the context, for it embraces
the idea that Jesus was *betrayed* by Judas (and others) as well as
handed over by the providence of God. The themes of dying and
raising which appear throughout the section are here completed.
As the deadness of Abraham and Sarah typifies the death of the
sinner and ultimately the death of Christ for sins, so God's promise to quicken them typifies the forgiveness of sins and the resurrection of Christ from the dead.

God called forth Isaac from the "dead" body of Abraham,
he called forth Jesus from a sealed tomb, and he calls forth believers from the death of sin and endows them with new life (6:13).
Wherever God's sovereign purpose prevails over mortal circumstances, there "is a new creation" (2 Cor. 5:17).

Additional Notes   §11

4:13 / Str-B cites a large number of rabbinic sources arguing that Abraham had knowledge of Torah through personal intuition, scriptural tradition, and divine revelation before its revelation at Sinai (vol. 3, pp. 204–6). The artificiality of such argumentation is for the historical critic evidence of the need of the ancient synagogue to ground Abrahamic righteousness in Torah obedience.

The promise to Abraham is repeated in Gen. 12, 13, 15, 17, 18, 22. The Zionist movement of the last hundred years and the formation of the state of Israel in the aftermath of the Holocaust have focused intense interest (not least among Christians) on the promise of land (e.g., Gen. 17:8). Nowhere in Paul, however, or in the NT as a whole, is the theme of the land again taken up. In Romans 4 Paul understands the promise to Abraham to be fulfilled in Jesus Christ (v. 24; see also 2 Cor. 1:20). It would be instructive for the church to consider the implications of the promise of land in Genesis 17 *in the light of Christ*, as does the NT.

The midrash quotation is from Num. Rab. 14 (173ᵃ). Quoted from Str-B, vol. 3, p. 209 (my translation). For further extrabiblical references to the same effect, see Dunn, *Romans 1–8*, p. 213.

4:14 / For Buber's thesis, see *I and Thou*, trans. W. Kaufmann (New York: Scribners, 1970). Similarly, writes Barth, "When the law claims to possess in itself ultimate reality and to be like God, it becomes *ungodliness* and *unrighteousness* (i.18), and attracts to itself the wrath of God" (*Romans*, p. 135–36). Hence, when the gift of God takes precedence over God it becomes the enemy of God. When humanity looks to the law to bring life (which it cannot) instead of to God (who can), idolatry lurks at the door. This results in an object-centered relationship (i.e., I-It) instead of a person-centered relationship (I-Thou).

4:15 / For helpful discussions of the phrase **law brings wrath**, see Schlatter, *Gottes Gerechtigkeit*, pp. 167–68; and Michel, *Der Brief an die Römer*, pp. 122–23.

For a poetic development of Paul's understanding of the law, see Milton's *Paradise Lost*, 12.282–302.

4:17 / On raising the dead and creation from nothing in the Hebrew tradition, see the following: giving life, Deut. 32:39; Ps. 71:20; Tob. 13:2; Wisd. of Sol. 16:13; Jos. As. 20:7; T. Gad 4:6; creation from nothing, 2 Macc. 7:28; Wisd. of Sol. 11:25; 2 Enoch 24:2; Jos. As. 12:2.

Note Käsemann's comment on justification by faith as a creative-redemptive act:

> As hardly anywhere else the full-radicalness of Paul's doctrine of justification is brought out here. When the message of this justification is accepted, there is unavoidably linked with it a reduction to nothing which deeply shakes the righteous by associating them

with the ungodly. No one has anything of his own to offer so that a new creature is both necessary and possible" (*Romans*, p. 123).

4:18–19 / On the textual variant in v. 19, see Metzger, *TCGNT*, p. 510.

4:20–22 / The phrase, "for us, to whom God will credit righteousness" (v. 24), need not be restricted to a future sense. Paul has a dynamic understanding of righteousness, beginning in the response of faith and being consummated in the world to come.

§12 The Transforming Love of God
(Rom. 5:1–11)

Romans 5:1–11 is a victorious passage. "In the whole Bible there is hardly another chapter which can equal this triumphant text," said Luther (*Epistle to the Romans*, p. 72). It is like a mountain pass from which one revels in scenery after having labored through the inclines and switchbacks of argumentation in the earlier chapters. The view cannot be fully appreciated without the effort it took to get there.

Commentators are divided whether the passage is the conclusion of Paul's argument so far or the beginning of a new section. On the one hand, the passage concludes much of what has been said before. Previous themes, in particular those of righteousness, boasting, wrath, grace, hope, glory, and blood, culminate here. But, on the other hand, new terms are introduced, most notably that of reconciliation. Moreover, various themes of chapter 5 will be developed in succeeding chapters; in particular, 5:1–11 is elaborated in chapters 6–8, and (to a lesser extent) 5:12–21 in chapters 9–11. Evidently, therefore, 5:1–11 is not exactly an end or a beginning, but a *bridge* between two distinct phases of Paul's argument. It is like the overlapping ends of a carpenter's folding rule: the justifying act of Christ is recapitulated and the justified life is introduced; the work of reconciliation is reviewed and the life of righteousness is anticipated.

The structure of 5:1–11 falls into three units. First, Christ's work of reconciliation ushers the believer into a condition of righteousness, characterized by peace and hope (vv. 1–5). The condition of righteousness is then shown in verses 6–8 to rest on the death of Christ, the supreme expression of God's reconciling love. Finally, in addition to effecting reconciliation, the death of Christ guarantees future salvation and eschatological hope (vv. 9–11). Paul begins (v. 1) and ends (v. 11) with the idea that the believer's hope and life are rooted in "God through our Lord Jesus Christ." Thus, the *magnalia Dei*, the mighty acts of God, are encompassed within the work of Jesus Christ.

No less remarkable than the triumphant content of this section is its tone. In order to establish the truth of righteousness by faith Paul had to build his case on logical argumentation demonstrated by proofs and examples from Scripture. But guarded reasoning from both Scripture and history now yields to inner confidence and the certainty of salvation in the present and future. Shifting to the first person, Paul raises the voice of the justified sinner to hymnic heights. A greater contrast between 1:18f. and 5:1f. could not be imagined. The desperate straits of the sinner have been transformed to peace and reconciliation with God. "The night is far gone, the day is at hand" (13:12, RSV).

5:1 / Therefore, since we have been justified through faith. Everything Paul has said in the last four chapters has paved the way for this exclamation. The aorist passive tense of "justified" (Gk. *dikaiōthentes*) means an accomplished condition, something which is finished as opposed to something pending or in progress. Verse 1 resounds with this decisive note and new train of thought: the problem of sin has been resolved by the death of Christ, and sinners, like Abraham, stand in a new relationship with God. They **have been justified through faith,** and, as Paul says in verse 2, they "have gained access by faith into this grace in which we now stand." Justification is access to grace, as a consequence of which the believer is no longer under wrath but has **peace with God.** A variant tradition in verse 1 (noted in the NIV) reads, "let us have peace with God," thus exhorting the reader to fulfill or enter into the condition established by Christ. Although this reading claims the stronger support among the ancient manuscripts, it remains the weaker reading. Internal evidence suggests that Paul's original wording was not an exhortation but an indicative, **we have peace with God.** In general when Paul speaks of peace between humanity and God it is God who effects it. This is exactly his point in verse 10 where "God's enemies . . . were reconciled to him through the death of his Son." Peace, like justification, comes exclusively from God. Both conditions depend on God's action; neither is something humanity can bring on itself.

There are important practical implications of this truth. Nearly all Christians confess that Christ's death effects salvation, but not infrequently they try (perhaps unconsciously) to live the Christian life on their own. Both righteousness as the act of saving and peace as the condition of being saved, however, come **through our Lord Jesus Christ**. The Christian life is from Alpha to Omega a life of faith, and the progress of the new life is as much a part of God's grace as was Christ's death for the sinner in the first place.

When Paul speaks of **peace with God** he means virtually the same thing as being a "new creation" (cf. 2 Cor. 5:17). The English word "peace" has a variety of meanings, not all of which are compatible with Paul's understanding of the term. The expressions "peaceful coexistence," or "peace and quiet," for instance, connote absence of conflict, whereas "peace of mind" implies contentment. In the Bible, however, peace is neither the absence of adversity nor a sensation of euphoria. The Hebrew *šālôm*, normally rendered in the Greek OT by *eirēnē*, means a condition in which life can best be lived. A review of this common OT word reveals that it seldom refers to a purely inner peace, whether psychological or emotional. Especially in the prophetic literature peace is a condition established by God which characterizes the age to come. The triumphant assertion in 5:1 claims that the long-awaited peace of the future has dawned in Jesus Christ. There is a certainty in Paul's expression uncharacteristic of rabbinic authors. As the sinner in 1:18ff. stood in a condition of hostility to God, and thereby under wrath, so now, having been justified by faith, the believer stands in a condition free from obstacles in his or her relationship with God. In neither case does Paul say how the individual may have *felt* in those conditions, which means that wrath and salvation are not subjective human experiences but decrees of God. Verses 9–10 describe the condition as one of reconciliation instead of hostility. When one is at peace with God, for the first time one fulfills one's purpose with God, others, and the world.

Peace with God, therefore, is neither anesthetic bliss nor the repose of a graveyard. The removal of sin, like the removal of an obstruction from one's windpipe, restores one's vital signs. The life of peace is not a life free from adversity; neither do adverse circumstances necessarily threaten the believer's peace with God. In verses 3–5 and 10 Paul speaks of struggle and suffering in the

Christian life. The life of faith may indeed create adversity, but adversity is not necessarily a sign of divine judgment or abandonment. In faith, adversity may be a sign of life, just as exercise brings sore muscles in a person who has been bedridden. In chapter 3 we spoke of the forensic or legal connotations of righteousness, whereby a judge, who may not know a defendant or ever see that person again, declares the sinner righteous. Paul now moves beyond that official metaphor. If justification produces release for the prisoner, peace is the life of freedom. If justification results from the crack of a gavel, peace results from the outstretched hand of a Father, drawing the estranged child into a new experience of freedom and hope.

5:2 / The prepositional phrase **through whom** reinforces the pivotal importance of Jesus Christ. Through Jesus Christ **we have gained access by faith into this grace in which we now stand.** The Greek word for **access,** *prosagōgē,* carries the solemn sense of being granted an audience with a monarch or afforded unhindered access into God's presence (cf. Eph. 2:18; 3:12). The verbal form of the word *prosagō,* for example, occurs numerous times in the LXX with reference to bearing sacrifices to the altar or entering the Holy of Holies. The verbs **gained** and **stand** are also instructive. Both are in the perfect tense in the Greek, meaning that their effect began in the past at the point of faith and continues into the present. Moreover, **stand** carries the sense of something firm and lasting, the opposite of a short-term, fair-weather relationship with God. To stand in grace is to possess a footing and anchor from God which is able to withstand all opposition to the life of faith.

Here, and again in verses 3 and 11, we encounter that vintage Pauline word, "to boast" (**rejoice**), occurring in various forms 55 times in Paul, but only four times elsewhere in the NT. Normally, Paul regards boasting as an expression of pride, the flaunting of the sinner's independence of God. On rare occasions, however (and this is one of them), Paul employs the term positively of boasting not in self but in God (Jer. 9:24; 1 Cor. 1:31; 2 Cor. 10:17). To fail to rejoice in God is to rob him of glory (1:21), whereas turning to God in faith renders him rightful glory (4:20) and promises **the hope of the glory of God.** Christians are able to take courage in present afflictions because they know that the present reality is not the final reality. This passage sets the believer's sights confidently on the future where God's glory will overcome sin and pain, where "what is mortal may be swallowed up by life" (2 Cor. 5:4). The Christian's hope is that of being a participant in God's very nature (2 Pet. 1:4), for "when he appears, we shall be like him" (1 John 3:2).

5:3–5 / It is one thing to be a Christian with the wind at one's back. How frequently the Christian life is depicted as a state of insulation and ease, where believers are supposedly endowed with some sort of "executive clemency" from the knocks of life. Increasingly in our day the Christian life is depicted in terms of triumphalism and success.

Paul, however, says that the believer must learn to rejoice not only in the future hope of glory, but also **in our sufferings**. This is a paradox, because sufferings and afflictions appear to deliver us up to death, not to glory. But for Paul *faith* enables sufferings and afflictions to aid God's grace, not oppose it. Throughout salvation history human suffering plays an unavoidable and necessary role of identification with God's way in the world. David confesses that God does not lead him around the valley of the shadow of death, but through it (Ps. 23:4). Suffering is the necessary prelude to the exaltation of the Servant of Yahweh (Isa. 52:13–53:12). The Lord of Glory himself suffered a violent and ignominious death on the cross. The apostle Paul's witness to his faith led to such persecution that he could have written a guide to the jails of the Roman world. Suffering is an essential part of the Christian's identification with the fate and work of Christ. Paul was not an exponent of a health and wealth gospel. He knew firsthand that the Christian life is one of "conflicts on the outside, fears within" (2 Cor. 7:5; see his list of hardships in 2 Cor. 11:32ff.). He knew that suffering, loathsome as it is, strips away false securities and drives believers to God, the source of all hope and compassion. He knew, bewildering as it may seem, that hardships and sufferings were necessary to prepare believers for the weight of glory prepared for them (2 Cor. 4:16–18).

In verses 3–4 he presents the consequences of suffering as a chain reaction: **we also rejoice in our sufferings, because we know that suffering produces perseverance; perseverance, character; and character, hope**. The Greek word for **perseverance** is a compound of "under" and "remain," meaning the ability to endure, or staying power. The word for **character** is found nowhere in Greek literature prior to Paul, and appears to be unique to him.

It means the quality of being approved after testing, or character, and hence the distinguishing attribute of the mature individual. The Greek word is a contrastive word play with the "depraved mind" (Gk. *adokimon*) of 1:28 which leads to wrath and the mature **character** here (Gk. *dokimē*) which leads to salvation. **Hope**, which both begins (v. 2) and ends (vv. 4–5) the sequence, means to live by the promises of God. The stimulus to this chain reaction is *faith*. That is to say, Paul does not here provide us with a fail-safe formula for virtue. By itself tribulation does not necessarily produce perseverance; it often produces bitterness and resignation, and hardship may simply produce hardness instead of character. **Perseverance, character,** and **hope** are marks of grace, and they develop only where the believer stands justified before God and responds to them in faith.

Especially important is Paul's statement that **hope does not disappoint us** (v. 5). The Greek word for **disappoint**, *kataischynein*, is a cognate of the same word in 1:16, "I am not ashamed (*epaischynein*) of the gospel." It recalls, despite everything to the contrary, that the believer's trust in the gospel is no empty fantasy. The Jewish Christian concept of hope dwarfs the ancient Greek idea of hope. For the Greek hope was little more than an eventuality, a possible outcome of current circumstances. But for Jews and Christians hope is anchored to the person and promises of God. Käsemann captures the distinction well, "[Hope] is no longer in Greek fashion the prospect of what might happen but the prospect of what is already guaranteed" (*Romans*, p. 134).

Hope is also tempered by the fires of adversity, but again only through faith. Apart from faith, hope is the opiate of a false and bitter illusion. But apart from love, hope has no basis. **God has poured out his love into our hearts**, says Paul (v. 5). The original Greek reads "in our hearts" (not **into our hearts**), implying that the Holy Spirit is already active in the hearts of believers. God is not a big brother dispensing miserly increments of goodwill to his minions. God is a compassionate Father who literally **pours out** his love within us. The Greek word for **poured out**, *ekchein*, suggests a lavishness on God's part, reminiscent, perhaps, of the occasional torrential rains in arid eastern regions. The verb is in the perfect tense, indicating that the gushing forth began at a specific point in the past and continues into the present. The same verb recurs several times in the Acts 2 narrative (vv. 2:17, 18, 33), which may indicate that Paul locates its inception at

Pentecost. At any rate, in prophetic literature the outpouring of
God's Spirit was anticipated as the inauguration of the new age,
and Paul saw in Christ's death and resurrection and in the subsequent bestowal of the Holy Spirit the dawning of the eschatological order.

For the first time in Romans Paul mentions the love of God
(v. 5). In Christian usage the Greek word for love, *agapē*, means
unconditional love originating solely from the giver and independent of any merit in the recipient. It is not conditional love,
love "if"; not earned love, love "because of"; but unwarranted
love, love "in spite of." Verse 10 attests that God expressed his love
in Christ "when we were God's enemies." Ordinarily, to bestow
love on a worthless or treacherous person is madness. But God's
love does not justify itself, as Franz Leenhardt notes, by pointing
to the value of the beloved object (*Romans*, pp. 136–37). Neither
does it justify itself by reciprocity from the beloved. Rather, God's
love gives that which its object does not possess in itself; its
transforming power is its own reason for existence. Jesus commanded his followers to love not because of expected returns, but
"in spite of" the apparent worthlessness of the other (Luke 6:32–
36). Love is the blueprint for the plan of salvation and the Christian life. "We love because he first loved us" (1 John 4:19).

God's love is no abstraction. The supreme expression of
God's love is the death of Christ "on our behalf" (vv. 6–8). The love
of God, therefore, must be understood objectively rather than
subjectively, i.e., as God's love for us rather than our love for God.
Interestingly, Paul does not say "the love of Christ," as verses 6–8
would suggest. This implies that the crucifixion promotes not the
heroism of Jesus, but rather the saving purpose of God to redeem
hostile humanity. God's love is expressly mediated **through the
Holy Spirit, whom** God **has given us** (v. 5). Paul is not yet prepared to introduce a discussion of the Holy Spirit, which must
await chapter 8. He continues rather with the love of God as it
was expressed in Christ's atoning death. Mention of God's pour-
ing out **his love into our hearts by the Holy Spirit** does, however,
establish the significant points that God's love is personal love
communicated through the Spirit and that the Spirit is the companion of believers. The verb **given**, an aorist (past) participle in
Greek, indicates that the Holy Spirit has entered the lives of
believers at a point in the past (at their justification by faith, v. 1;
Gal. 3:2) and continues to abide with them.

5:6–8 / Verses 6–8 present one of the most profound descriptions of divine love found in Scripture. *Poor Richard's Almanack* said that "God helps them that help themselves." That is vintage deism, but it is not biblical Christianity. Romans 5 teaches that God helps them that *cannot* help themselves. Note Paul's descriptions of the human condition: **when we were still powerless** (v. 6), **ungodly** (v. 6), **sinners** (v. 8), "God's enemies" (v. 10). A miserable list of credits if ever there was one! God's love is not a matching fund bestowed on the worthy. God's love is love for the undeserving. Christ died for humanity not when it made amends or turned over a new leaf, but for humanity as rebellious **sinners** (v. 8) and "God's enemies" (v. 10). This is a shocking thing to realize, indeed quite an offense to moral people who nurse the idea that their goodness is somehow responsible for God's love. The radical news of the gospel is that Christ died for the godless, which means that God loves the godless. And to say that God loves the godless is to say that God justifies the godless. The offense remains: to say that a person is a sinner is to say that that person is the object of God's love!

God demonstrated his love **at just the right time**. Paul was of the conviction (Gal. 4:4; Eph. 1:10; Phil. 2:6f.), as were other NT writers (Mark 1:15; John 1:14; Heb. 9:26), that the Christ-event was no arbitrary happening, but an integral part of the divine economy, the constituent element in the plan of salvation which happened "in the fulness of time," according to Galatians (4:4), "once for all at the end of the ages," according to Hebrews (9:26). God did not send his regards to the human race, he did not merely possess noble intentions for the human race, but he did something absolutely without precedent or analogy—God became a human being. The word "incarnation" in Latin literally means "in human flesh," and the enfleshment of God in Jesus Christ is the supreme manifestation of God's love (v. 8).

In verse 7 Paul considers the limitlessness of God's love, a love which, in comparison with human guardedness, must appear utterly profligate. Verses 6–7 are not a little awkward, however. Verse 6 is complicated by a textual variant in Greek. This is followed by a redundancy in verse 7, the first half of which says that death on behalf of a righteous person hardly ever occurs, with the implication that death on behalf of an unrighteous person *never* occurs. But the second half of the verse continues that death on behalf of a good person is still thinkable. Exactly how

we should understand the difference between a **righteous** and
good individual is debatable. Attempts to argue an interpretation
of the passage from these two words alone ring a sour note. More
plausible is Barrett's suggestion that Paul, realizing that he overstated the case at the beginning of the verse, attempted to rectify
it in the latter half, but that Tertius, his amanuensis (16:22), failed
to omit the first statement, thus accounting for the repetitiveness
of the verse (*Romans*, p. 105).

There can be no doubt about Paul's meaning, however, for
verse 8 avers that God's love is humanly inconceivable. God's
love for the ungodly is greater than human love for the godly. Three
times in as many verses Paul includes the little Greek particle *eti*,
"yet" or "still," driving home that God's love and Christ's sacrifice
were offered contrary to all expectation, while we were *still* sinners and enemies. Here is no bloodless essay on "the idea of the
good." Paul speaks of an enactment, a manifestation, a **demonstration** of divine love in the death of Christ for sinners that has
transformed history itself. The German artist Matthias Grüne-
wald (1460[?]–1528) captured something of Paul's sense in his
"Crucifixion." Dwarfing the mortals who surround him, including
John the Baptist who points to him with outstretched finger, Jesus
hangs heavy in human agony on the cross as an awesome demonstration of the weight of sin and the magnitude of divine love.

The climax of the passage comes in the final pronouncement, **Christ died for us** (v. 8). Here is the gospel in four words,
a combination of history and theology, event and interpretation.
Christ died is a historical statement; **for us** is a theological interpretation. Both are essential to the gospel. Without theological
interpretation Christ's death becomes a meaningless datum of
history; but without history theology evaporates into speculation
and idealism. Each word in this confession is a vital tenet of
salvation. Not just anyone, not even a very good person, but
Christ, who appeared at the **right time, died** for our salvation.

The Greek text of verses 6–8 contains four sentences, each
of which ends with reference to Christ's death. Thus, when Paul
speaks of God's love, or of righteousness, or of eschatology, he
must speak of the cross, for the cross is the constitutive criterion
of salvation. Whoever thinks God begrudges the world a pittance
of goodwill finds that notion dispelled forever by verse 8. Christ
did not die of natural causes. In the face of animosity and rejection he *offered* his life as a supreme sacrifice **for us**. The Greek

preposition translated **for** means "on behalf of." Unlike most prepositions, this one is concrete: Jesus took *our* place. It is one thing to say Christ died; quite another to say Christ died for me! Thus, **Christ died for us** is not only the gospel distilled to four words, it is by necessity the personal confession of every Christian.

5:9–11 / Paul's magisterial exposition of the transforming love of God reaches its apogee in verses 9–11. Paul utilizes a rabbinic comparison from lesser to greater, or from light to heavy, known in Hebrew as *qal wāḥômer*, the object of which is to inspire confidence that God is utterly trustworthy to complete the work of salvation, for if God's love delivered Christ to death for sinners, how much more will it save them from his wrath! God has already done the really difficult thing in justifying rebellious sinners; how much more may those who are justified take confidence that God will preserve them in the state of reconciliation. If God delivered Jesus from death, the same God will also deliver believers from sin and death to life, a point Paul reemphasizes in 8:11. Chapter 5 began with the present state of righteousness, but it now shifts boldly to the future: the cross not only forgives past sins, it assures the justified of their future hope and glory.

Paul continues his decisive contrast between God's will and human resistance, describing unjustified sinners as **God's enemies** (v. 10). The story is told that as Henry David Thoreau lay dying he was asked by his sister if he had made peace with God. Thoreau reportedly answered, "I did not know we had argued." It was a witty reply, but wide of the gospel. Thoreau evidently believed that human nature is basically good, and that apart from a fault here and there God finds little objectionable in the human race. Paul disagrees. Humanity cannot reconcile itself to God. If there is to be reconciliation it must be effected from God's side, not ours. On our own and apart from grace we are entrenched in rebellion. We are not distant relatives of God; we are insurrectionists against a worthy king (Mark 12:1–12). It took nothing short of **the death of** God's **Son** to persuade humanity to lay down its arms and accept the gift of reconciliation.

The verb tenses in verses 9–11 encompass the entire life of the believer in God's love: **we were God's enemies, we have been justified, we shall be saved**. God's redeeming love is past, present, and future. In theological terminology Paul is speaking of justification, the *act* whereby we were made right with God; sanctification, the *process* by which God renews us according to his purpose; and eschatology, the *completion of salvation* in the future and the fulfillment of hope. For the present, the believer lives between two worlds, a theme which Paul will develop in chapter 6. Paul refers to the renewed life variously as a race (Phil. 3:12; 1 Cor. 9:24), dying and rising (2 Cor. 4:16), a fight (1 Tim. 1:18; 6:12), a struggle (Rom. 5:3–5), and a battle (Eph. 6:10–20). But in one thing the believer takes confidence: the cross stands as an irrevocable demonstration of God's faithfulness in the past, and hence believers can trust God for all things in the future. His love is our hope. St. Chrysostom put it thus, "If God gave a great gift to enemies, will he give anything less to his friends?"

The passage concludes with a new term in verses 10–11, **reconciliation**. **Reconciliation** is the act whereby God makes the sinner right with himself, thus ushering the justified sinner into real participation in the life of the risen Christ, which is characterized by peace (v. 1) and hope (v. 2). The concept of reconciliation builds a bridge into chapters 6 and 7. *Katalassein*, "to reconcile," was rare, if not unknown, in Hellenistic usage, and consequently no more familiar to Paul's first readers than it may be to us. In writing to the Corinthians Paul used the term with reference to being a "new creation," meaning first to be reconciled to God, and second, the surrendering of self as an "ambassador of reconciliation" (2 Cor. 5:16–21). **Reconciliation** thus carries the double significance of God's doing something *for* us and *with* us.

The parable of the prodigal son in Luke 15:11–32 wonderfully illustrates reconciling love. Willful and defiant, the younger son demanded his share of the father's blessing, later to be rudely awakened in the outside world. Returning to his father and expecting what he deserved—censure, humiliation, and (if lucky) probation—the boy received what he did not deserve—shoes, ring, robe, banquet, and most of all, his father's delight in the infinite worth of one who was lost and now found. Reconciliation is being found by—and surrendering to—the love of God.

Additional Notes   §12

Arguments favoring 5:1–11 as a conclusion of the foregoing chapters can be found in Leenhardt, *Romans*, pp. 131–32; those favoring it as a beginning of upcoming argumentation in Michel, *Der Brief an die Römer*, p. 129. Dunn (*Romans 1–8*, p. 243) also regards the unit as a bridge.

5:1 / For discussions of the textual variant as an indicative or hortatory subjunctive, see Metzger, *TCGNT*, p. 511; and O. Kaiser and W. G. Kümmel, trans. E. Goetchius, *Exegetical Method. A Student's Handbook* (New York: Seabury Press, 1963), pp. 51–52.

Regarding uncertainty of salvation in rabbinic authors, see Str-B, vol. 3, pp. 218–20.

5:2 / Calvin's comment on standing in faith is insightful: "And by the word *stand*, [Paul] means, that faith is not a changeable persuasion, only for one day; but that it is immutable, and that it sinks deep into the heart, so that it endures through life. It is then not he, who by a sudden impulse is led to believe, that has faith, and is to be reckoned among the faithful; but he who constantly, and, so to speak, with a firm and fixed foot, abides in that station appointed to him by God, as to cleave always to Christ" (*Romans*, p. 189).

5:3–5 / For lists of virtues similar to the sequence of vv. 3–4, see Hos. 2:19–20; Amos 5:14–15; 2 Pet. 1:5–7; Wisd. of Sol. 6:18–21.

Gaugler offers a trenchant description of hope: "In the testimony of the apostle hope is, according to the original Hebrew sense, a connection stretching from God to us, in which the human creature, even in the midst of the pressure of opposition, possesses an eternal standpoint. Hope is like a rope stretching between the Now and Then, so that the Then in Christ is already realized. Hope is thus essentially another word for faith, which again does not look to itself but solely to the way in which God goes with us. Hope has nothing to do with conjecture, nor with our 'fate,' nor with possibilities, nor even with the 'hidden God.' Hope rather is concerned with what has been revealed in Christ, and with the promise which has been given in him" (*Der Römerbrief*, vol. 1, pp. 114–15 [my translation]).

5:6–8 / Attempting to follow the logic of vv. 6–7 literally, Bengel argues that it is more thinkable to die for a good person than for a righteous person because "Every good man is righteous; but every righteous man is not good" (*Gnomon*, vol. 3, p. 65). Somewhat better is Cranfield's interpretation: "We understand Paul's meaning then to be that, whereas it is a rare thing for a man deliberately and in cold blood to lay down his life for the sake of an individual just man, and not very much less rare for a man to do so for the sake of an individual who is actually his benefactor, Christ died for the sake of the ungodly" (*Romans*, vol. 1, p. 265).

5:9–11 / The Chrysostom quotation is cited from Cranfield, *Romans*, vol. 1, p. 268. Similarly, Pelagius commented, "If God loved sinners in such a manner, how much more will he preserve them now that they are justified!" (ibid., p. 266 [both translations are mine]).

§13 Paradise Lost, Paradise Regained (Rom. 5:12–21)

Paul now embarks on a bold typological contrast between Adam and Christ. He continues the train of thought already begun in chapter 5, however, for verse 12 begins, "on account of this," or **therefore**, which links 5:12–21 to 5:1–11. Paul's purpose is to illustrate that the work of redemption has universal significance. The focus shifts from *our redemption* in the first person plural in 5:1–11 to the two seminal figures of humanity, Adam and Christ, in the third person singular. Heretofore the gospel has been discussed primarily in relation to Israel (e.g., the law, chs. 2–3; and Abraham, ch. 4), but Paul now extends his purview to show that Jesus not only fulfills the promise given to Abraham, but also mends a deeper, fundamental rift stemming from Adam himself. In so doing he elevates Christ from a figure of parochial importance to universal significance. The vast sweep of history is embraced in two prototypes, Adam and Christ.

The two epochs signified by Adam and Christ stand in stark antithesis and are underscored by contrasting language: "just as" in Adam, "so also" (or "how much more") in Christ. Paul introduces the typology by saying that "[Adam] was a pattern (Gk. *typos*) of the one to come" (v. 14). A "type" is a particular person or thing that foreshadows or prefigures something true of a larger group to follow. Sparta was a type of the military state, Machiavelli of the despotic ruler, Jefferson of the liberal democratic mind. Adam and Christ are types too. Like the "lesser light" of Genesis 1:14ff., Adam represents humanity apart from salvation. There are many satellites in his orbit: "trespass" (v. 15), "sin" (v. 20), "disobedience" (v. 19), "judgment" (v. 16), "condemnation" (v. 16), "law" (v. 20), and "death" (v. 12). But Christ is the "greater light" whose starry host is far brighter. He governs "obedience" (v. 19), "justification" (v. 16), "grace" (vv. 15, 17, 20, 21), and "life" (v. 17). Paul, however, does not resign the world to a cosmic tug-of-war between two equal but opposite forces—God and the devil, light and darkness, good and evil—each vying for humanity. On the contrary, Christ is vastly superior to Adam, for the last Adam's power to save is far greater than was the first Adam's power to destroy.

Arguments from typology intend to present global or universal truths, not unlike Paul's use of allegory elsewhere (Gal. 4:21–31). The general nature of typology, however, limits its effectiveness in dealing with details and exceptions. Types are yardsticks, not calipers. Their effectiveness consists in the essential truths they convey, not in every logical possibility they imply, and to push them beyond such limits runs the danger of logical casuistry. In verse 19, for example, Paul says that one man's obedience overcame another man's disobedience. This clearly implies that Jesus' obedience in the wilderness won what Adam's disobedience in the garden lost; but it is not at all clear, despite what some commentators say, that this verse teaches universal salvation.

What effect might the Adam-Christ typology have had on Jewish–Gentile rivalry in Roman Christianity (see Introduction)? In progressing from Abraham and Christ in chapter 4 to Adam and Christ here, Paul signifies that Jewish-Gentile differences are secondary to the more fundamental categories of condemnation and grace, and of sin and salvation. At the bedrock of existence all humanity holds a common hope in life and faces a common enemy in death. "There is no difference" (3:22). The ultimacy of human destiny relegates ethnic and even religious disputes to penultimate categories.

5:12 / Verse 12 recapitulates the story of the fall in Genesis 3. The accent falls not on the particulars of the temptation but on the all-encompassing consequence, namely, that disobedience brought death into the world. **Sin entered the world through one man, and death through sin, and in this way death came to all men**. Milton captured the thought of this verse in the title of his epic poem, *Paradise Lost*. Paul omits the name Adam, stressing instead the universal correspondence between the **one** and **all**. Although he does not explain exactly how Adam's sin affected humanity, he understands Adam's sin to have infected the race so that it is not free not to sin. Sin is not a coincidence, it is a contagion. Sin is a compelling power at work both within and without. Jesus said, "The Son of Man will go just as it is written about him. But woe to that man who betrays the Son of Man!" (Mark 14:21). This verse probes the ineffable tension between the inevitability of sin, on the one hand, and human responsibility for sin, on the other. Humanity is not free to choose not to sin, and yet each sin is freely chosen. Sin is derivative from **one man**, and, like a despot, sin controls its subjects. Three times Paul emphasizes that **sin** (or **death**) reigns (vv. 14, 17, 21). And yet **all sin** willingly, thus deserving condemnation (v. 18). Adam's sin was the root, ours are its offshoots, says Bengel (*Gnomon*, vol. 3, p. 76).

In Genesis 3 the serpent tempts Eve to "be like God" (v. 5). There are two ways of being "like God." One is positive, in which we honor and emulate God, whereby to "be like God" is admirable. But the temptation story carries a negative sense of rivaling God and willing to displace God. It begins with a desire to discredit God (" 'Did God really say?' "), and ends with a willful disobedience of God's concrete command. In a mysterious and terrible way Adam's sin becomes our sin. Genesis 3 is the story of every sinful act. All humanity disputes God's word and usurps God's authority.

In the history of theology verse 12 (also 1 Cor. 15:22) has been the breeding ground of the doctrine of original sin. The OT links sin with death ("when you eat of [the tree of the knowledge of good and evil] you shall die," Gen. 2:17), but it is silent concerning *how* sin and death were transmitted to the race. By the first century A.D., however, a theory had developed in Jewish thinking linking Adam's sin and human corruption and death. Fourth Ezra says, "You laid upon [Adam] one commandment of yours; but he transgressed it, and immediately you appointed death for him and for his descendants" (3:7). From Second Baruch, "O Adam, what did you do to all who were born after you? And what will be said of the first Eve who obeyed the serpent, so that this whole multitude is going to corruption?" (48:42). Again from Second Baruch, "For, although Adam sinned first and has brought death upon all who were not in his own time, yet each of them who has been born from him has prepared for himself the coming torment. Adam is, therefore, not the cause, except only for himself, but each of us has become our own Adam" (54:15, 19). The last passage in particular speaks of sin's origin in Adam, but its responsibility in individual transgressions. More than three centuries after Paul, Augustine (354–430) stamped West-

ern thinking indelibly with the theory that sin and guilt are transmitted sexually. This theory, which is indebted more to neo-
Platonism than to the Bible, is one reason why the church has
tended to regard sex as sinful. During the Reformation Luther
and Calvin differentiated between human nature and personal
guilt. Adam, they maintained, corrupted human nature so that it
is not free from sin, which they referred to as "total depravity."
This oft-misunderstood term does not mean that humanity is
incapable of good; it simply means that humanity is incapable of
saving itself. But Adam has not, continued the Reformers, con-
ferred his guilt on the race. Human nature is hereditary, but guilt
is a matter of personal responsibility.

From a human perspective the problem of original sin is an
unsolvable mystery. The boat will capsize whether one jumps to
the one side or the other. On the one hand, there are those who,
with Augustine, overemphasize Adam's progenitive role in sin
and the damning consequence of death. Relying on the Latin text
of verse 12 (*in quo omnes peccaverunt*), Augustine derived the interpretation "in whom (i.e., Adam) all sinned." But this jeopar-
dizes human potential and responsibility, as well as the divine
mandate for genuine moral change. At the same time, the modern tendency is to relegate sin to the level of moral lapses, slips,
flaws, mistakes, and so forth. Not only does this fail to deal with
the crucial question of the origin of sin (i.e., *why* all people sin), it
underestimates the power and gravity of sin. God would not
have sent his Son to Calvary for moral peccadillos.

Verse 12, in fact, does not actually discuss the problem of
sin from a theoretical perspective. The premise of the argument
is not sin but death: if all die, all must deserve to die because of
sin. Thus, a more plausible antecedent for the much-debated
Greek phrase, *eph' hō*, would be *death*, and not Adam as Augustine
supposed. At any rate, nearly all Greek authorities agree that
eph' hō pantes hēmarton should be rendered **because** (of death) **all
sinned**, rather than "in whom (i.e., Adam) all sinned." Paul's starting
point is thus the empirical reality of death. The grim stalker of life
is, to be sure, the result of an equally horrid disobedience to God
by the rebellious human will, but Paul does not explore this connection or the way in which human sin and death result from
Adam's disobedience. His purpose here is not the development
of a doctrine of original sin but the establishment of a typological
contrast between Adam and Christ. He is content to say typologi-

cally what he said in 3:23, "All have sinned and fall short of the glory of God." The curse of Adam's sin is death, and death, as Paul taught elsewhere, is "the last enemy to be destroyed" (1 Cor. 15:26).

5:13–14 / The protasis "just as" (v. 12) leads the reader to expect a completion of the Adam-analogy in Christ. But in order to discuss the effects of **the law** and **Moses** on sin, Paul refrains from introducing Christ until verse 15. Verses 13–14 are therefore something of a footnote to verse 12, clarifying what Paul said before, that "through the law we become conscious of sin" (3:20), and that "where there is no law there is no transgression" (4:15). Verse 13 repeats that sin was in the world before Moses gave the law, whether or not sin was recognized as such. The reign of death from Adam onward proves as much. Sin thus precedes death, but the universality of death became apparent before the universality of sin which caused it. This is the sense of the statement, **sin is not taken into account. Taken into account** (Gk. *ellogeitai*) was a commercial term meaning "to charge to someone's account." Since sin existed before the law, it was independent of the law. Sin was hence as offensive and punishable before the law as it was afterward when it became fully recognizable, and consequently, **death reigned** even before people knew why.

The wording is somewhat misleading, but the latter half of verse 14 attempts to elucidate this point. A literal translation is, "death reigned from Adam to Moses and upon those who had not sinned in the likeness of Adam's transgression." This might suggest that there were persons before Moses who did not sin, which, of course, would contradict Paul's trump argument that *all* humanity stands under sin (3:9, 23; 5:12). Despite what some commentators suppose, it is unlikely that this verse refers to infants who died before the (illusive) age of accountability. The key to its meaning rather seems to be the phrase, "those who had not sinned in the likeness of Adam's transgression," i.e., those who had not consciously disobeyed a divine commandment as Adam did. The NIV renders the passage, **those who did not sin by breaking a command, as did Adam**. This is an interpretative translation, but the sense seems to be justified. Even where a deliberate rebellion against God was lacking, there was still the presence of sin and its terrible consequences.

As disastrous as sin's effects were, they were in one respect a harbinger of hope: as Adam initiated an epoch which determined the beginning of time, so Christ initiates an epoch which determines the end of time. Both Adam and Christ have universal significance, Adam for death and Christ for life. In the one respect that his sin has universal consequences Adam becomes a type for Christ. Thus, Paul calls Adam **a pattern of the one to come.** The Greek word for **pattern,** *typos,* means "the impression made by a blow," hence a "stamp," "model," or "pattern." In all other respects, however, Adam and Christ are antitypes, for the wrong which Adam did in his disobedience, Christ in his obedience did not do; and the good which Adam could not do because of his sin, Christ did in his righteousness. In 1 Corinthians 15:45 Paul calls Christ "the last Adam." He is not called the "second Adam," i.e., a repetition or even improvement of the first Adam. Christ is not Adam's successor, but his redeemer, the final word of God who, though not part of the old, redeems the old in the new.

5:15–17 / Now for the first time in verse 15 Paul completes the analogy between Adam and Christ. **If the many died by the trespass of one man . . . the gift that came by the grace of the one man, Jesus Christ,** will **overflow to the many!** Adam and Christ may be antitypes, but they are not equally balanced, as Paul's opening line indicates (**the gift is** *not like* **the trespass**). It took less effort for Adam's disobedience to release sin and death than for Christ's obedience to overcome sin and death. It was easier for Adam to lead to ruin than it was for Christ to lead to life. The effects of each are conveyed by the **one** and **many,** a familiar distinction in the ancient world. As one led to condemnation, so will a greater one lead to righteousness. The term **many,** which reappears in verse 19, is an inclusive term, roughly equivalent to "all" in verses 12 and 18. It does not mean that some do not share in Adam's transgression, or that there are some for whom Christ's death is not efficacious. Again Paul employs the rabbinic argument from the lesser to the greater that we saw in 5:9–10. Its logic contains the key to the Adam-Christ typology, the **how much more** of grace! Calvin said it well, "Christ is much more powerful to save, than Adam was to destroy" (*Romans,* p. 206).

Verse 16 repeats that the propositions about Adam and Christ are not equal: **The gift of God is not like . . . one man's sin.** Adam's **sin** resulted in **condemnation,** but Christ's **gift** prevailed over it and brought **justification.** There is a word play in Greek between **judgment** (*krima*) and **condemnation** (*katakrima*). **Con-**

demnation means both the pronouncement of a sentence and its execution—death. Sin, condemnation, and death may be self-evident, needing no proof, but Paul's vocabulary regarding Christ's work is no less conclusive. The Greek word rendered **gift**, *charisma*, does not mean, as it does in 1 Corinthians 12, the various manifestations of grace; rather, it concerns the work of grace already accomplished on the cross. Likewise, the word for **justification**, *dikaiōma*, is a cognate of Paul's preferred term and means the *result* of being justified, namely, being reconciled with God.

Paul extends the contrast between Adam and Christ to its zenith in verse 17. Again he employs the *qal wāḥômer* analogy from lesser to greater: **how much more** efficacious is Christ's gift of life than Adam's road to ruin. Paul speaks of **God's abundant provision** to denote the excess of grace over sin. The word for **abundant**, *perisseia*, recurs five times in this section (vv. 15, 17, 20 [3x, in various forms]). Moreover, Paul says that believers **reign in life . . . through Jesus Christ**. The Greek word for **reign** is the verbal form of "king," meaning to rule with final authority. **Grace** and **righteousness** are sovereign gifts of God which break the hegemony of Adam's fall.

From a human perspective one or the other will rule: disobedience or obedience, sin or righteousness, death or life. It is not a question *of whether* we will submit to such masters, only to *which* ones we will submit. Either death reigns or life reigns, but not both. To be human is to stand at a crossroads of choice: there is the way of the past, the way of death, or the way of the future, the way of life in Christ. There is the first Adam, and there is the last Adam. But that is only the human perspective. Paul writes from the divine perspective, assuring us that the influence and effect of Christ's work defeat the tragic effects of Adam's **trespass**. The sin of one is cancelled by the righteousness of the other; the curse of one is overcome by the grace of the other. The one causes death, the other swallows up death in life. In every way Christ surpasses Adam.

5:18–21 / The Adam-Christ typology is repeated in verse 18, and for the first time in perfect parallelism. The Greek construction behind **Consequently** at the beginning of verse 18, *ara oun*, indicates a conclusive, summary statement. Milton fashioned a key passage in *Paradise Lost* after the Adam-Christ typology, concluding that "Heav'nly love shal outdo Hellish hate" (3.287–

301). Especially noteworthy is Paul's emphasis on **all men**. St. Chrysostom said that Adam and Christ are types in this way: as Adam became a source of death to those who followed him, although they had not eaten of the fruit of the tree, so Christ has become the provider of righteousness to those belonging to him, although they have not performed what is righteous (see Bengel, *Gnomon*, vol. 3, p. 71). There are for Paul no exceptions to Adam and Christ. Adam's sin corrupts all, and Christ's righteousness justifies all. Paul's language should be taken quite seriously. It is an undeniable fact of experience that all persons are sinners. It is an undeniable fact of logic that if Christ died for sinners, indeed for the *ungodly* (5:6), his righteousness clothes all. Both are biblical truths. This is not necessarily to assert universal salvation, however. In verse 17 Paul spoke of "those who *receive* God's grace and righteousness." Salvation by grace is not salvation by fiat, much less coercion. Grace is only grace where it grants the other freedom to receive—or reject—Christ's self-sacrifice for forgiveness at the cross.

The typological balance continues in verse 19 where Paul introduces a new set of contrasts, Adam's **disobedience** and Christ's **obedience**. Adam's fall was not due to an oversight, lapse, or mistake. Adam was not a tragic hero, but a treacherous rebel. His act was one of **disobedience**, a willful choice to break God's commandment, and his **disobedience** could be overcome only by Christ's **obedience**. Christ's **obedience** need not be understood as his substitutionary death on the cross alone; the word directs attention to the whole course of his life, from his obedience in the wilderness (Matt. 4:1–11; Luke 4:1–13) to his obedience in Gethsemane (Mark 14:32ff.), wherein he reversed the **disobedience** of Adam.

It is often assumed that since Jesus shared a greater likeness to God than we do—indeed *is* God, according to the implication of Scripture and explication of the creeds—that it was easier for him to be obedient than it is for us. Both Scripture and logic would rigorously contest that assumption. According to Hebrews, "[Jesus] learned obedience from what he suffered" (5:8), and Philippians says that "he humbled himself and became obedient to death—even death on a cross!" (2:8). Who can read the intensity of Jesus' temptation and suffering in Gethsemane as a mere sham (Mark 14:32–36)? C. S. Lewis reminds us that the *higher* one is in the order of being, the *greater* are one's temptations. A dog cannot be either as good or as bad as a child, nor a child as good or as bad as a genius. Christ's temptations exceeded ours to the degree that his divine nature exceeds ours. Hence, his obedience effects a righteousness that we cannot achieve for ourselves.

The verb in verse 19 is also instructive. Paul says that **the many** were made to share the condition of their prototype: in Adam they **were made sinners**, in Christ they **will be made righteous**. The future tense here (and in v. 21) indicates that the completion of salvation must await the future eschaton. Equally significant is the verb itself, *kathistēmi*, meaning "to appoint, **make**, cause," or "to constitute according to (an image)." It is clearly implied that the effects of the prototype are applied to the lot: **the many** are *acted upon* by a force outside themselves. People do not fashion their fate as much as they like to think. It is rather they who are fashioned by the masters they serve, a point Paul will elaborate in 6:15ff. Ultimately, both sin and salvation are *extra nos*, as the Reformers taught. They originate not within us but *outside us* in Adam and Christ, and they manifest themselves as persons adapt to their pattern.

Paul now returns to the **law** (v. 20), although both stylistically and theologically its interjection disrupts the antithetical parallelism between Adam and Christ. The law does not play a determinative role in the contest between Adam and Christ because the law did not bring sin and death into the world, nor can the law remove sin and death from the world. The law thus promises no ultimate solution to the meaning of existence. This was assuredly no small offense to Paul's Jewish readers, as it is to the moralistic of every age, for it excludes "living a good life"— the way of legal piety—from the whole question of salvation. Beyond Adam and Christ there is no third alternative of moralism, legalism, or good works.

The law, in fact, belongs to the way of sin and death in Adam. Earlier Paul said that the law makes us "conscious of sin" (3:20) and "brings wrath" (4:15). Here he heightens the offense to include those who take refuge in moral scrupulosity. **The law was added so that the trespass might increase**. As Paul will argue in chapter 7, the law not only reveals sin, it actually *incites* it! The prohibition, "Do not," creates an appetite in the sinful will for the thing it forbids, thus exposing the depth of human complicity in sin. That was its intent from the beginning. Its purpose was not to convince Israel of its goodness and separate it from the Gentiles, but to expose Israel's solidarity *with* the Gentiles in sin. Here again, Paul undercuts Jewish legal pride and narrows the gap between Jews and Gentiles—a shot we trust was not wasted on the two quarrelsome factions in early Roman Christianity. Until we stand in grace we cannot see how we are mired in sin; and yet, until we learn what we lost in Adam we cannot appreciate what we have gained in Christ.

But where sin increased, grace increased all the more. This verse provided John Bunyan with the title of his autobiography, *Grace Abounding.* However prevalent, nay rampant, sin may be, grace is more rampant yet, says Paul. Grace outweighs sin, indeed overwhelms it. After Bethlehem, evil can never again tip the scales in its favor! In his meditation, *On the Incarnation*, Athanasius celebrates the power of redemption in Christ that outstrips the power of destruction in sin—no small hope in a world such as ours where the specter of nuclear holocaust can reduce the earth to vapor and ash, or where injustice and social decay threaten the world with a dark age of moral and political anarchy. God, however, has not consigned the world to its madness. Barth speaks of *"total help* over against *total guilt"* (*Dogmatics in Outline*, p. 107). Milton's poetic pen again bespeaks an infinite wonder, that grace turns even wickedness to good.

> While [Satan] sought
> Evil to others, and enraged might see
> How all his malice served but to bring forth
> Infinite goodness, grace and mercy shown
> On Man by him seduced (*PL*, 1.215–20).

Adam, evil, and sin will be engulfed in an avalanche of love. "Death has been swallowed up in victory" (1 Cor. 15:54).

Joshua challenged the Israelites to choose between the Lord and alien gods (Josh. 24:15). Elijah forced a decision between Yahweh and Baal (1 Kings 18:24). The Psalmist taught of the way of the blessed or the way of the wicked (Ps. 1). A Christian homily in Paul's day began in the words, "There are two Ways, one of Life and one of Death, and there is a great difference between the two Ways" (Didache 1:1). Paul speaks of Adam and Christ. Ultimately, life is an *either–or*. Either submission to death and the negation of all longing and hope, or submission to **the reign of righteousness and eternal life**. Life, however, is greater, for death is not eternal. It is life which is eternal, **through Jesus Christ our Lord**.

Additional Notes   §13

5:12 / Fourth Ezra and 2 Apoc. Bar. originate from the late first and early second centuries A.D., respectively, making them only slightly later than Romans. The passages are quoted from James Charlesworth, ed., *The Old Testament Pseudepigrapha*, vol. 1 (Garden City: Doubleday, 1983).

The infectious nature of sin and its tenacity are powerfully illustrated in Augustine's *Confessions*, bk. 8.

Among the many discussions of Adam and Christ and the problem of sin, two may be mentioned for their helpful summaries. A spirited and readable presentation for the general reader is offered by Achtemeier, *Romans*, pp. 95–100. A scholarly and technical discussion is presented by Swee-Hwa Quek, "Adam and Christ According to Paul," in *Pauline Studies. Essays Presented to Professor F. F. Bruce on his 70th Birthday*, ed. D. Hagner and M. Harris (Grand Rapids: Eerdmans, 1980), pp. 67–79.

5:13–14 / On the idea that sin precedes death, but that only death reveals sin, see Bengel, *Gnomon*, vol. 3, p. 68.

Faithful's meeting with Adam the First in *The Pilgrim's Progress* remains a classic of Adam–typology. The aged Adam promises Faithful "the lust of the flesh, the lust of the eyes, and the pride of life" (1 John 2:16) in an attempt to lure him from the pathway. But the truth finally breaks upon Faithful, "Then it came burning hot into my mind, whatever he said and however he flattered, when he got me home to his house, he would sell me for a slave" (John Bunyan, *The Pilgrim's Progress* [New York: New American Library, 1964], pp. 68–69).

5:18–21 / On the issue of universalism Käsemann declares that "all-powerful grace is unthinkable without eschatological universalism" (*Romans*, p. 157). Cranfield offers a more balanced judgment, "[righteousness] is truly offered to all, and all are to be summoned urgently to accept the proffered gift, but at the same time [we ought] to allow that this clause does not foreclose the question whether in the end all will actually come to share it" (*Romans*, vol. 1, p. 290).

That law and morality cannot be a third alternative in addition to Adam and Christ, see Schlatter, *Gottes Gerechtigkeit*, p. 193, and Käsemann, *Romans*, p. 158.

§14   The Death That Brings Life (Rom. 6:1–14)

In Romans 6 we note a shift in the argument. The quotation from Habakkuk 2:4 in Romans 1:17, literally translated, "The one who is righteous by faith will live," provided Paul with a general outline for the epistle. Until now his primary concern has been with the first part of the quotation, "The one who is righteous by faith." But being right with God is not the end of the matter. Chapter 6 evinces that righteousness is a commencement, not a commemoration; reveille, not taps. In chapters 6–7 Paul takes up the relationship of faith to the new life which it inaugurates, and thus broaches the final topic of the Habakkuk quotation (which he will further explore in chs. 12–15), "will live." He shifts, theologically speaking, to "sanctification" (NIV holiness), a word appearing in 6:19 that denotes the new life that follows in the wake of justification by faith.

Sanctification, of course, is not a separate phase of Christian development. We consider childhood and adulthood as distinct stages of life, but we may not conceive of justification and sanctification in this manner. Sanctification is justification in action; indeed, it is "realized righteousness." Sanctification is righteousness before the throne of God *and* in evidence in the world. Israel was commanded to "be holy because I, the Lord your God, am holy" (Lev. 19:2). Christians are privileged to be the vessels of grace in and for the world, and their call and ordination to be such indicates their inestimable worth in God's eyes. Justification is the impetus of sanctification, and sanctification is the unfolding of justification. Without justification sanctification is cut off from its source of renewal and becomes moralistic; without sanctification justification is incomplete and remains speculative. "A [person] is saved by faith alone, but the faith that saves is not alone—it is followed by good works which prove the vitality of that faith" (B. Metzger, *The New Testament: Its Background, Growth, and Content*, p. 254).

The introduction of sanctification is signalled by a strategic use of the theme of *death*. In the fifth chapter Paul spoke five times of *Christ's* death; in chapter 6 he speaks thirteen times of the *believer's* death in Christ, again in the first person plural. Christ's death is not only the means of our salvation, it is the pattern of our sanctification. In chapter 5 Christ dies for sinners; in chapter 6 believers themselves must die to sin. The ongoing importance of dying to sin is emphasized by sixteen references to sin in this chapter of twenty-three verses! Colossians speaks of "Christ who is your life" (Col. 3:4). In a most dramatic way Paul's use of death—almost always, in fact, as "the act of dying"—weaves the new life in Christ to the death of Christ. The woof of the Christian life crisscrosses the warp of Christ's death.

The discussion of sanctification, however, is not relegated to a theoretical plane. The apostle stands before the task of making intelligible and practical the theological megaliths of chapter 5. Chapters 6–7 are clearly a response to certain objections to Paul's gospel, namely, that justification by faith encourages sin and denigrates the law. Paul shores up his gospel by answering three false conclusions, each delineated at 6:1, 6:15, and 7:7. First, he challenges the perverse notion that if grace increases with sin, why not sin all the more (6:1–14). He then confronts the objection that freedom from the law leads to moral anarchy (6:15–7:6). Finally, in a very existential argument, he dismisses the objection that if the law reveals sin—indeed incites it—the law itself must be evil (7:7–25).

6:1 / In 5:20 the apostle made a daring pronouncement: "where sin increased, grace increased all the more." Without clarification this statement could lead (and often has) to antinomianism. Paul broached this problem back in 3:8, "Why not say—as we are being slanderously reported as saying and as some claim that we say—'Let us do evil that good may result'?" He could not afford to discuss the problem then, but he cannot afford to dismiss it now.

What shall we say, then? Shall we go on sinning so that grace may increase? Heretofore the discussion of sin and redemption has been largely relegated to the past, but with this question Paul now focuses on the future. One wonders how many times the apostle had met this objection on the mission field. Barth's calling the question a "pseudo-dialectical game" makes light of a genuine difficulty which repeatedly emerges in church history (*Romans*, p. 190). There is an undeniable (though perverse) logic to verse 1, especially to someone who does not appreciate the wonder of grace: if grace is given in proportion to sin, why not sin extravagantly? The greater the sin, the greater the grace! Put more respectably: if God has done everything for us, and if our efforts achieve nothing for salvation, why make the effort to live a good life? The issue at stake here lies at the root of Jesus' breach with a common Pharisaic attitude which he exposed in the parable of the Pharisee and the tax collector (Luke 18:9–14). If a bad person receives justification before a good person, what is the value of the moral life?

The point of 5:20, however, as Luther rightly noted, was not "to excuse sin, but to glorify divine grace" (*Epistle to the Romans*, p. 83). The question of 6:1 reveals perhaps the greatest temptation the Christian faces, namely, to take advantage of grace. The rank sinner is not nearly so vulnerable to this temptation as is the Christian who is the beneficiary of grace. Who has not presumed on God's grace? Paul understood the temptation, but he could not tolerate its motive. Whoever would remain in sin has forgotten that sin was the cause not only of Christ's death, but of his own death (5:21). But Christ through his righteousness has bestowed life and hence overpowered sin. God's grace is indeed freedom, but freedom *from* sin, not freedom *for* it. "You . . . were called to be free. But do not use your freedom to indulge the sinful nature" (Gal. 5:13; see also 1 Cor. 6:12; 10:23). Whoever sees in grace a pretext to get away with as much as possible is simply showing contempt for Christ who died for sin. The freedom created by grace leads not to license but to obedience. Obedience honors God's boundless love and responds to that love in the freedom which love creates.

6:2 / Paul counters the rhetorical question of verse 1 with a categorical rejection, **By no means!** Christ came to free us from our vices, not to feed them. Another rhetorical question sums up the contrast between Adam and Christ in a principle which deflates the swollen error of verse 1. **We died to sin; how can we live in it any longer?** The death-to-sin theme will guide Paul's discussion through verse 11. Adam (= humanity apart from grace) led humanity like a prisoner to the gallows. If in Adam life leads to death, in Christ the sequence is reversed: death leads to life (**we**

died . . . we shall live). By faith Christians share Christ's death and resurrection. Whoever dies is free from sin (v. 7). Conversely, whoever remains in sin remains in death. Thus, the question of verse 2 arrests the folly of verse 1. Justification (death) leads to sanctification (life); we must first be made right before we can be made good. In Galatians Paul expressed this truth thus:

> I have been crucified with Christ and I no longer live, but Christ lives in me. The life I live in the body, I live by faith in the Son of God, who loved me and gave himself for me (2:20).

Paul's language of death, burial, and resurrection (vv. 2, 4), here applied to believers, is reminiscent of an older confession in 1 Corinthians 15:3–4, "that Christ died for our sins, . . . that he was buried, that he was raised on the third day." Paul thus welds the experience of believers to that of their Lord. But what is the meaning of, **we died to sin**? Rather than releasing its grip at conversion, sin usually tightens it, as Paul well knew. He admonishes his readers in verses 12–14 not to succumb to sin, and in chapter 7 he will confess his own struggle with sin. Had Paul said, "Let us die to sin," we might take it as an appeal to the believer's will and a call to ethical arms. But there is no hint here of imitating the example of Jesus or of a moral crusade for the virtuous life. Paul says categorically, **we died**. This is neither empty creedalism, nor implicit asceticism. It is an objective reference to Christ's death and to the reality that in Christ's death something decisive has happened *to* believers. When Christ died for sinners, sinners died in God's sight. "One died for all," said Paul, "and therefore all died" (2 Cor. 5:14). Christ's death *for* us has broken the power of sin *over* us, as verse 11 attests, "count yourselves dead to sin but alive to God in Christ Jesus." The strong Son of God has wasted the strong man's house, to allude to Mark 3:27. Since Christ has broken the claim of sin over our existence, sin no longer determines our existence. Christians are like citizens who have been liberated from a long and oppressive dictatorship. Something has been done to them: the liberator has broken the power of tyranny.

6:3–4 / The believer as the recipient of the benefits of Christ's death is reinforced by the reference to baptism in verse 3: we **were baptized into** Christ's **death**. Mention of baptism, of course, is an explicit reference to the sacraments and presupposes the reality of the church. Paul knows of no faith that is not attested to publicly via the sacraments and corporately in the church. And neither did the early church, for in prefacing verse 3 with, **Or don't you know**, Paul obviously appeals to accepted tradition before him. The phrase, **into Christ Jesus**, is an abbreviation of the traditional baptismal formula, "into the name of Christ Jesus" (e.g., Matt. 28:19). Like the phrase, "taken into account" (5:13 above), this phrase derives from the language of accounting, wherein believers are "entered upon Christ's account," so to speak. Elsewhere Paul says believers were baptized into Christ's body, thus stressing the corporate nature of faith (1 Cor. 12:13), but here the idea is one of personal union with Christ.

In speaking of union with Christ it is improbable that Paul borrows either thought or language from the various mystery religions of his day. Whereas the mysteries stressed the initiates' experience, Paul stresses God's decisive act on behalf of believers that is both signified and assured by baptism. The word "forensic," which we used earlier of Paul's understanding of righteousness, also applies here, for Christ's death and resurrection usher believers into a new condition. With God they stand on the ground of faith instead of wrath, and they are freed from the pull of sin and death. What happened to Jesus on the cross happens to believers in baptism. Baptism is a sign of participating in Christ's death and resurrection, of "charging our lives to his account." Neither mechanical (i.e., something which occurs apart from human involvement), nor magical (i.e., the manipulation of supernatural power), baptism is an act of faith wherein God communicates the effects of Christ's death and resurrection to the receptive heart.

The train of thought continues in verse 4: **we were buried with him**. The metaphor proceeds from the act of dying to the fact of death. Baptism denotes the state of death in which the power and effects of sin are annulled. In addressing converts baptized as adults, Paul correlates the immersion of baptism to the burial of the dead, in which the old life has ceased and has been committed to a foreign element. This is not the death of Nothingness, however, which awaits the old Adam, but a necessary prelude to resurrection and life. "Unless a kernel of wheat falls to the ground and dies, it remains only a seed. But if it dies, it produces many seeds" (John 12:24; see 1 Cor. 15:36). When Paul speaks of the death of believers in relation to the death of Christ he is not suggesting some kind of cultic identification, but rather the fellowship of Christ with his own, in which Christ's death and resurrection are made fruitful for the church.

Union with Christ recurs throughout 6:1–8 in waves of repetition. "[We] were baptized into Christ Jesus," "[we] were baptized into his death" (v. 3), "we were . . . buried with him" (v. 4), "we have been united with him" (v. 5), "our old self was crucified with him" (v. 6), "we died with Christ," "we will also live with him" (v. 8). Paul's cup overflows with syn-compounds (meaning "with" or "together" in Greek). The new existence is never spoken of apart from Christ because the new existence is Christ. He is our life (Col. 3:4). In the Gospel of John Jesus says, "apart from me you can do nothing" (15:5). So too with Paul, the Christian life is not an isolated effort but a corporate existence linked inextricably with Christ.

Believers share Christ's fate, including his tomb! Only thus can they share his resurrection. Christ's resurrection is a precursor to our own, so that **we too may live a new life**. The Greek preserves a more concrete summons to the moral life, "so also let us *walk* in newness of life." Christ's resurrection is thus presented not to indulge the readers in dreams of future glory, but to exhort them to moral resolution here and now. To be sure, Christ's resurrection is a prelude to believers' resurrection at the endtime, but it bears fruit *today* by calling believers to moral regeneration and responsibility. The Christian life is not a new attitude or better philosophy, but the release of righteousness into everyday life in an inexorable movement, step-by-step, toward Christ-likeness.

6:5–7 / Continuing with the theme of death and resurrection, Paul changes the metaphor from baptism to horticulture. The word **united** comes from the Greek, *symphytos*, meaning "to grow together," or perhaps "to graft onto." The perfect tense, **we have been united**, encompasses everything from the point of conversion to the present hour. The image of growth implies that believers' lives merge with Christ's and take on his characteristics. If the word means, "to graft," then the bond is closer yet: the ingrafted shoot, severed from its native stock, derives life from the new stock. The NIV renders verse 5 in balanced parallelism, omitting, however, a characteristic Pauline word. The Greek reads, "For if we have been united to the *likeness* of his death." Dunn identifies "likeness" as "the form of transcendent reality perceptible to man" (*Romans 1–8*, pp. 316–17). This means that Christ's death is not a vague and general reference for believers, but an exact pattern. The resurrection is, of course, an equal pattern, but the future tense of the verb, **we will be united in his resurrection**, means that its full realization awaits the future.

The same idea reemerges in verse 6 under the image of slavery. **For we know** suggests that the gospel provides an intellectually meaningful explanation of life. **Our old self** and **the body of sin** recall human nature apart from grace (5:12ff.). Noteworthy is the phrase, **so that the body of sin might be done away with**. In calling sin a **body** Paul implies that sin is not isolated offenses or aberrations, but a totality capable of sustaining its own existence. This phrase sheds an additional light on sin. In verse 2 the believer "died" to sin, and its power was cancelled and finished. Here, however, the **old self** must be **crucified**, which is a slow and agonizing form of death. The **body of sin** is not instantly wiped out but gradually **done away with**. Paul envisions a struggle, indeed a *battle* that confronts the believer throughout life. His metaphors of changing clothes in Colossians 3:9, or of the contest between flesh and spirit in Galatians 5:17ff., imply similar processes in overcoming sin.

Authentic Christian existence always stands with one foot in the old life and one in the new. The Christian life is one of tension between Adam and Christ, sin and grace, flesh and spirit, death and life. Fallen human nature, which is with us from birth to death, pulls in one direction, and the regenerated life in Christ, which extends from conversion to eternity, pulls even more powerfully in the other. Christian life is hence life between the times and between two worlds: it is not yet free from the old nature, and not fully at home in the new. The following diagram may help to illustrate the dilemma:

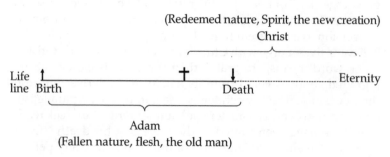

The life of faith exists between conversion (†) and physical death (↓). If it is subjected to the fierce jealousy of the old life, it is worked upon even more by the upward pull of the new. In earthly existence the believer cannot escape fully the old Adam or inherit completely the new life in Christ. Paul himself knew this tension. Though the outer person is failing, the inner person is being renewed within us (2 Cor. 4:16). We are handed over to doubts, troubles, and death, but we are not annihilated. In the midst of "birth pangs" (Mark 13:8; 2 Cor. 4:7ff.; Gal. 4:19) we are born to faith, hope, and life eternal in God.

6:8–11 / The focus now shifts to Christ as the pioneer of the Christian experience. Paul endeavors to show that what is true of Christ is equally true for believers. Thus, **if we died with Christ, we believe that we will also live with him** (v. 8). Christian existence is not mechanical or automatic, like the law of gravity or the germination of a seed in springtime. In otherwise balanced statements Paul inserts, **we believe,** which means that believers live by the claim of faith, by the conviction of and commitment to God's redemption of the world in Jesus Christ. For the present, faith believes more than it experiences, and thus it lives in hope, looking inevitably toward the future (**we will also live with him**) when Christ will be fully revealed. The wonder and reality of Christ's death and resurrection can be realized only by a faith relationship with him who died and lives, Christ the Lord, the pioneer of salvation.

Faith is neither grounded in an illusion nor hitched to the cart of wishful thinking. **We know that since Christ was raised from the dead, he cannot die again.** Faith is grounded in the risen Christ who is witnessed to through the apostolic proclamation and who is present in the lives of believers through the indwelling of the Holy Spirit. The resurrection of Jesus Christ is the anchor of faith and the assurance of our future resurrection (1 Cor. 15:12ff.). Many religions believe in nature gods who, in accordance with the rhythm of nature, reappear in the cycles of death and renewal. This, however, is not the meaning of Christ's resurrection, for his resurrection is unique, for **death no longer has mastery over him** (v. 9). The death and resurrection of Christ resound like a trumpet blast through the corridors of time—*once for all.* Not even the raising of Lazarus (John 11) is a prototype of Christ's resurrection, for Lazarus died again. Jesus lived in per-

fect obedience to the eternal God. Because he lived for God he
did not live for self; because he did not live for self he knew no
sin; because he knew no sin death held no mastery over him. The
cross swallows up the grave. Death can claim neither Christ again
nor those who through faith "charge their lives to his account"
and grow into his likeness.

Faith in the resurrected Christ is thus no pipe dream, but
the fulcrum of history, the hope of the ages, the clarion truth that
in Jesus eternity beams brightly into the dark shed of human
history. Such a truth admits of no languid and nominal acceptance; a strain so rich pulls us from our seats to join the dance of
life. The gospel is like the last train to freedom: it must be seized
at all costs. "So also you," says the original, "must count yourselves dead to sin but alive for ever more to God in Christ Jesus."

6:12–14 / We now encounter the first moral exhortation
in Romans! The cross and resurrection of Jesus have broken the
power of sin, and believers at last stand before a real choice. They
now have a fighting chance, for they can choose not to sin. Verses
12–14 hum with energy and urgency as Paul drafts believers into
action. He shifts from the indicative to the imperative mood, and
also from first person plural to second person plural. What God
has done for believers at baptism is the indicative of grace; what
God wills from believers as a consequence of grace is the imperative of ethics. The two are inseparable and witness to the unity
of justification and sanctification. When a minister unites a couple
in Christian marriage he or she enjoins them to make their vows
actual, to become what they are. This is Paul's appeal to the Romans.
Christians are dead to sin, so let them henceforth live to God!

Sin is viewed as an armed tyrant who exacts obedience. But
Christ has stopped sin's despotic drive in its tracks. Because of
Christ's resurrection and assurance that God is for them, believers are now free. They are not to return abjectly to their gangster
lord. Paul calls them to arms! Christians must not allow sin to
reign unopposed in their lives, but, in the words of Cranfield,
"revolt in the name of their rightful ruler, God" (*Romans*, vol. 1,
pp. 316–17). These are the marching orders of a militant faith as
Paul summons believers not to offer their bodies as "weapons"
(**instruments**) **of wickedness**, but rather—as inmates on death
row whose sentences have been pardoned—"to **offer** their parts
. . . to God as **instruments** of righteousness" (v. 13). The Greek

tenses of the verb **offer** are themselves instructive and might be paraphrased, "Do not continue offering yourselves to sin, but offer yourselves up once and for all to God." The reference to **parts** (of your body) in verse 13 need not be limited to the physical body, for it surely includes in a figurative sense all human talents and abilities. The Christian life pictured in verse 13 is not an idealized watercolor but a bold (albeit simple) sketch of the rigors facing the faithful. The essence of the new life is not a concept or feeling detached from reality, but a trumpet call to active combat in the cause of righteousness against evil (Gal. 5:16ff.).

For sin shall not be your master, because you are not under law, but under grace, concludes Paul (v. 14). Since believers stand in grace, sin has neither the right nor the power to enslave them. Sin can rule only when it is obeyed, and Christ has broken its power. Sin need no longer be obeyed. Jesus said that no one can serve two masters (Matt. 6:24). Believers are like soldiers who have deserted the ranks of a rebel unit to rejoin their rightful leader: the orders of the rebel captain have no further authority over them. Death can no longer be Christ's lord, and sin will no longer be the lord of the believer. The Lord of the believer is Christ. This, as we noted earlier, does not mean that sin has no power over believers, but that believers are not helpless in the face of sin's assaults. They are free to rebel against it. Indeed, they are commanded to do so, empowered by grace, and guaranteed the ultimate triumph (8:37).

To be under grace instead of law is to be led by the Spirit (Gal. 5:18). The law makes sin known (3:20), whets one's appetite for the forbidden (5:20), and hence leads to condemnation. The law is not thereby the opponent of grace, but its prelude (Gal. 3:24). The law demands righteousness, but cannot produce it, and those who try to fulfill it on their own become oppressed by its demands. To be **under grace** is to be free from the guilt of knowing the right but falling short of doing it. Grace means "that there is now no condemnation for those who are in Christ Jesus" (8:1). It means that despite ourselves God is for us (8:31), God is faithful (2 Cor. 1:18), and God frees us for himself (Gal. 5:1).

Additional Notes   §14

A word count of "righteous" in Romans is illuminating: the verb "to make righteous" occurs eleven times before chapter 6, and only three times afterwards; the adjective "righteous" (or "just") occurs six times before chapter 6, and once afterwards; the noun "righteousness" (or "justification") occurs seventeen times before chapter 6, and (outside chapters 9–11 where the problem of the righteousness of Jews is again considered) only seven times afterwards.

One of Dietrich Bonhoeffer's most valuable contributions to theology was his conviction that one cannot separate justification and sanctification, faith and obedience, and still be faithful to the gospel. "The following two propositions hold good and are equally true: *only he who believes is obedient, and only he who is obedient believes.* It is quite unbiblical to hold the first proposition without the second" (Bonhoeffer's emphasis; *The Cost of Discipleship*, trans. R. H. Fuller [New York: Macmillan, 1966], p. 69).

6:3–4 /   On the idea of Christian faith as public faith, Augustine tells a story which played an important role in his own conversion. Victorinus, a renowned philosopher, became a believer late in life, but because of his prominence in Roman society, declined public profession of faith and baptism. Confiding privately to Simplicianus, the bishop, Victorinus said, "I want you to know that I am now a Christian." "I shall not believe it or count you as a Christian until I see you in the Church of Christ," replied the bishop. Victorinus laughed and said, "Is it then the walls of the church that make a Christian?" The bishop remained undaunted, for he knew that there is no such thing as a private believer, that Christian faith is always public faith. Later, Victorinus approached the bishop and said, "Let us go to the church, I want to be made a Christian." This, in the words of Augustine, resulted "in the wonder of Rome and the joy of the church." See Augustine's *Confessions*, bk. 8, ch. 2. In a similar vein, until the "Wende" in East Germany in 1989 the Communist government denied membership in the Party not to persons of religious conviction but specifically to church members!

On comparisons of initiation into the mysteries and baptism, see Gaugler, *Der Römerbrief*, Part 1, pp. 156–61, and Dunn, *Romans 1–8*, pp. 308–11, both of whom dismiss any direct influence of the mystery cults on Paul's understanding of baptism. The attempt to adduce a parallel between Apuleius (*The Golden Ass*, ch. 11) and Christian baptism is far-fetched. Lady Charites' immolation over the grave of her lover Lepolemus is scarcely an initiation into the mysteries by death, but quite obviously a story of unrequited love, by no means an unfamiliar theme in romantic literature (cf. *Romeo and Juliet*).

James S. Stewart offers a dynamic discussion of the believer's union with Christ in *A Man in Christ* (New York: Harper & Row, n.d.), pp. 186–94.

6:8–11 / Several important Greek manuscripts append "our Lord" to Christ Jesus at the end of verse 11, but this is probably a "liturgical expansion" (cf. v. 23). See Metzger, *TCGNT*, p. 513.

6:12–14 / The ancient manuscripts are divided whether **its evil desires** (v. 12) refers back to **mortal body** or to **sin**. The manuscript weight would appear to tip the balance in favor of **mortal body** (hence, *autou* rather than *autē*). This is reinforced by the sense of v. 13. Bengel comments that "the bodily appetites are the fuel; sin is the fire" (*Gnomon*, vol. 3, p. 80).

§15 The Slavery That Liberates
(Rom. 6:15–23)

In chapters 6–7 Paul discusses the Christian life using four metaphors: baptism (6:1–14), slavery (6:15–23), marriage (7:1–6), and psychology (7:7–25). The present section on slavery continues the interplay between indicative and imperative: what God has done leads to what we *ought* to do. Paul presents his ideas in a series of antithetical statements: "under law / under grace" (v. 15), "sin which leads to death / obedience which leads to righteousness" (v. 16), "free from sin / slaves to righteousness" (v. 18), "slavery to impurity / slavery to righteousness" (v. 19), "slaves to sin / free of righteousness" (v. 20), "free from sin / slaves to God" (v. 22), "result in death / the result is eternal life" (vv. 21–22), and "the wages of sin is death / the gift of God is eternal life" (v. 23).

The antitheses are built throughout on the foundation of slavery. The institution of slavery in the ancient world is without parallel in the contemporary West. A modern employee, or even a servant, is indebted to an employer for a certain number of hours each week. Any time outside the employment contract is, of course, at the employee's disposal. The employee can, in other words, serve a number of masters.

Ancient slavery was something entirely different. A modern employee owes an employer a certain amount of productivity; an ancient slave owed a master time, labor, and life. That slaves were held under moral obligation to obey their masters indicates they were considered human beings (and not simply chattel), albeit inferior human beings. Unlike American slavery in the antebellum South, race or ethnic origin played little if any role in ancient slavery. Ancient slaves came from every background imaginable and performed the most varied roles in society; most slaves, of course, performed labors of drudgery, but some were bureaucrats, artisans, teachers, and even physicians. But like their American counterparts, ancient slaves were considered the property of their masters, literally *bonds*persons. They were acquired through a variety of means, including birth, war, and auctions. Some slave traders acquired babies exposed in temples or at public dumps, and in times of famine adults not uncommonly sold themselves into slavery to avoid starving. The exact percentage of slaves in Greece and Rome varied, but roughly a quarter of the work force belonged to slave classes. Regardless of their functions, slaves possessed few civil rights and virtually no legal rights. If a master freed a slave it was considered a merit, not a duty. Slaves could be sold at the master's whim, and punishment of slaves, including torture or capital punishment, was permissible as long as social formalities were observed. Lack of rights was due to the most odious, if essential, aspect of slavery, that slaves were considered by nature inferior—children or morons—and named accordingly, "little one," or "boy." Always and everywhere the slave psyche was shackled by two thoughts: a slave was an unfit human being who owed absolute loyalty to his or her master. The cardinal virtue of slavery was *obedience*!

To illustrate the Christian life by such an institution was in many respects an inappropriate comparison, and the apology in verse 19 indicates that Paul was not unaware of a possible offense. But despite its negative connotations, the master-slave relation provided the apostle with a supreme illustration of his core argument at this stage of the epistle, namely, the total indebtedness and absolute accountability of the forgiven sinner to the grace of God.

6:15 / Somewhat surprisingly, 6:1 is repeated in verse 15: **Shall we sin because we are not under law but under grace?** Why does the apostle plow the same field twice? It has been said that where the gospel is most faithfully proclaimed it is most vulnerable to misunderstanding and misuse. In no article of faith is this truer than of grace. This doctrine is susceptible to the slightest imbalances, resulting in absurd distortions. In verse 1 Paul defended grace against wanton abuse. Here, with a slightly different spin on the ball, he must defend it against antinomianism. Someone might conclude from verse 14 ("you are not under law, but under grace") that when the restraint of law is removed there remains no distinction between good and evil. At least one purpose of the law had been to check sin, but once the check is removed and the floodgate opened, what is there to prevent the waters of chaos from erupting?

Whenever the gospel fell victim to such a patent misinterpretation Paul often reacted sharply, as he does here, *mē genoito*, **By no means!** Freedom from law does not mean license to do whatever one pleases. That is wide of the mark, and "missing the mark" is exactly what **sin** meant in classical Greek. Sin, of course, is often a willful offense against the moral law of God, but it is also a falling short of God's glory (3:23), a failure to inherit the high calling of God in Christ Jesus (Phil. 3:14). There are sins of commission or trespasses (i.e., bad things done) and sins of omission or debts (i.e., good things left undone). The danger inherent in verse 15 is the latter, the failure to "live up" to grace. Both the costliness and free bestowal of grace obligate believers to special accountability. Grace is a form of indebtedness, a happy indebtedness, to be sure, that permits its servants no neutral ground. To live **under grace** means freedom to do not what we want but what we ought! It means, as Paul will continue in the following verse, freedom *for* obedience, not an excuse for disobedience.

6:16 / Paul hopes to make his reasoning apparent by a rhetorical question: **Don't you know that . . . you are slaves to the one whom you obey?** This resumes the thought of verses 12ff., and, as there, the present tense of his verbs implies continuous or habitual action. He is not thinking of occasional sins, but of an ongoing alliance with sin, an obedience to sin that leads to enslavement. " 'I tell you the truth, everyone who sins is a slave to sin' " (John 8:34; see also 2 Pet. 2:19).

Paul's blunt alternatives—obedience to sin or obedience to righteousness—may strike our sophisticated age as overly simplistic. Are not "either–or" answers, especially in matters of ultimate reality, the mark of ignorant or narrow minds? In Pauline anthropology the essential truth is that a human being is a creature. To be free in the sense that any human being could be lord of his or her own life, or of the world around, is a total illusion. Was not the fall of Adam and Eve due precisely to their attempt to reach beyond their creatureliness, to put themselves above obedience, or to find some neutral ground where they would be exempt from the divine commandment? Is that not the quest to be God?

Freedom from choices and obligations, or freedom from the constraints of being a creature, was out of the question for Paul.

The question was not *if* one would bow before a master, but before *which* master one would bow! One may stand on this plot of ground or that, but not in mid-air. One may obey this master or that, but the choice to obey no master is granted to no one. To be free from one power is simply to be drafted into the service of another; and to serve the one excludes service of the other. The issue of obedience was not, like other problems that Paul discusses in Romans, a problem of sin or the law. The command to obey was given along with the breath of life. It is inherent in being human, for it sets freedom itself in motion and is thus the primal condition of knowing and loving God. In *Paradise Lost* the angel Raphael admonishes Adam and Eve in pristine Eden, " 'That thou art happie, owe to God; That thou continu'st such, owe to thy self, That is, to thy obedience; therein stand.' "

Freedom, then, obligates one to obey grace, and only in obedience to grace is one free. The auto racer who drafts or slipstreams a car in front of him experiences this freedom in a rough sort of way, for by pulling into the wind pocket of the car ahead and "obeying" it, the second car achieves a speed and economy of fuel impossible on its own. It is neither the dispassionate ascetic nor the supposedly unbiased critic who exemplifies grace, but the individual indebted and bound to righteousness. Had not the Incarnate One taken the form of a slave (Phil. 2:7)? The second word of Romans is *doulos*: "Paul, [a] *slave* of Jesus Christ" (1:1). The uncommitted life has yet to be lived. Jesus told a story about a householder who rid his house of an evil spirit, swept it clean, put it in order, . . . and left it empty. The expelled demon searched for seven demons more wretched than itself, and they all returned to seize the house in fury (Matt. 12:43–45). The owner's mistake was not in ridding the premises of the demon, but in leaving it unoccupied. Unless the vacuum left by sin is filled with righteousness, the heart is vulnerable for a more violent takeover. The point is obvious. The human experience does not offer us a state of limbo. Deliverance from evil does not leave one in a neutral zone. There is no no-man's-land in moral and spiritual matters; indeed, that is the most dangerous ground to stand because it is raked with fire from all sides. Rather, to be delivered from the power of evil is to be delivered over to the power of God. It is an exchange of lords, a good one for a bad one, to be sure, but an exchange nevertheless. A Christian is still a slave—but the Christian has changed masters! One is either under grace or under sin;

these are the two primal authorities, and both obligate their servants to obedience, the one to life, the other to death.

In his *Nicomachean Ethics* Aristotle offers the following insight on slavery in moral and spiritual matters. Each action which we do in life is voluntary, he says, but with each voluntary action our *disposition* becomes increasingly involuntary. We continue, of course, to make choices, but over a period of time the choices are influenced by a disposition which is increasingly determined, either for better or worse. In Paul's words, **you are slaves to the one whom you obey**!

6:17–18 / We have then two masters, grace and sin, vying for control of both individuals and the world. A scene of two slave buyers, each bidding against the other at a slave auction, is not inappropriate to Paul's thought. **Thanks be to God**, the benevolent master has won, for the service of sin would be *actual bondage*, whereas the service of grace is *actual freedom*. Paul does not praise believers for having made a better choice of grace over sin. Salvation is not a game show where the panelist who knows the right answers wins the prize. An overweening confidence in human freedom leads us to think we have done God a favor by believing in him. Paul, however, demonstrates that the sovereign human will is a chimera. Our miserly faith scarcely does God any favors. Salvation is far more a matter of desperation and *need*, a rescue operation from the grim and hopeless servitude of sin to the freedom of sons and daughters. Grace is not honored by mere lipservice, by admitting the existence of God, or even by assenting to Christian morality. Grace is not something we grant; it is the ineffable love of God which lays claim to us as the one treasure which is worthy of our heart and will—or worthy of nothing. Paul speaks of obeying this grace **wholeheartedly** (Gk. *ek kardias*, "from the heart," which means from the center and source of the inner life). Obedience cannot be one with faith unless it comes from the heart. Bengel was surely right when he said that Christians gain a oneness of heart and will in the act of goodness which is denied to persons in their badness (*Gnomon*, vol. 3, p. 82). A wicked person is plagued by at least some stirrings of conscience and hence cannot be wicked with the same freedom that good persons can be good from the heart.

The wording of the statement, **the form of teaching to which you were entrusted** (v. 17), appears rather backward.

Would it not be more correct to speak of handing over doctrines to hearers than hearers to doctrines? In defense of the
wording Barrett notes that "Christians are not (like the rabbis) masters of a tradition; but are themselves created by the
word of God, and remain in subjection to it" (*Romans*, p. 132;
see also 2 Cor. 2:9; Gal. 1:6). Käsemann is more specific, seeing
the form of teaching not as the gospel in general, but as an
early baptismal creed to which believers were entrusted at
their baptism (*Romans*, p. 181). Precedent for the latter can be
found in the early church's course of instruction for believers
at their baptism; the Didache (ca. A.D. 75), which means "Teaching" or "Instruction," indeed may have been an early baptismal
manual. In response to Barrett and Käsemann, however, it
should be noted that **form**, *typos*, is almost always in Paul used
of persons, not things. Moreover, **the form of teaching** is nowhere else used of a baptismal creed. It seems more likely,
therefore, that Paul intends the phrase with reference to Jesus
Christ, which is entirely possible in Greek, i.e., "but you
obeyed from your heart the model (*typos*) of teaching to whom
(= Jesus Christ) you were entrusted." At any rate, whether the
phrase refers to Christ or the gospel, the main point is that **the
form of teaching** does not belong to us, but we belong to it. We
do not change Christ (or the gospel) to fit our culture and
mores, but we must be changed and converted by it. Only thus
are we **set free from sin**. This freedom, which Paul introduces
for the first time in Romans (and again in vv. 20, 22), originates
from the cross of Christ and from the believer's engrafting into
Christ at baptism.

6:19 / Paul was not unaware that comparing Christianity to the brute conditions of slavery risked offense to the
gospel. He defends the analogy, however, **because you are
weak in your natural selves**. Paul had meditated deeply on
the incarnation (e.g., Phil. 2:5–11), and if Christ did not think
it undignified to walk the streets of Palestine, then his apostle did not think it undignified to speak of him in street
language. Paul would risk offense to the sacred in order to
communicate the sacred to the secular. There are religions
which consider their saving stories too sacred to be couched
in the vernacular; Paul considered the saving story of the
gospel too important not to be!

The remainder of verse 19 is structured according to contrasting parallelism: **just as you used to . . . so now. . . .** The same **parts of your body** once used for **impurity** are now to be used for **holiness**. How brilliant the mind and indefatigable the will in the pursuit of evil. But now that they have been baptized into Christ, they are to become equally resourceful and tireless in the cause of righteousness and holiness. The injunction to **offer** your parts **in slavery to righteousness** is not a return to the burden of the law, but the way the justified individual expresses grace in daily life. Because we are freed from sin we are to be as creative and energetic for God as we once were for sin and self. The release from slavery to sin does not relieve us of responsibility, but shifts our responsibility to God.

The word Paul uses of the new responsibility is **holiness**, which, along with **impurity** and **wickedness**, was a prominent Jewish word. The Greek original, *hagiasmos*, means "holiness," "consecration," or "sanctification." It was a moral term, in which, according to several OT passages (Lev. 11:44–45; Deut. 7:6; 26:19), God laid claim to the believer as his "treasured possession" and transformed the character of the believer so as to share in God's likeness. Here Paul expressly links justification and sanctification as **righteousness leading to holiness**. The debate whether Paul intends a process of sanctification or an end result is ultimately an artificial distinction and foreign to Paul's thought. The point is that justification by faith leads to concrete moral change. What the law demanded but could not fulfill is now possible through Jesus Christ. Both the process of moral renewal and the result of moral perfection are present in perhaps Paul's most explicit statement on the subject: "Since we have these promises, dear friends, let us purify (*hagiazein*) ourselves from everything that contaminates body and spirit, perfecting holiness (*hagiasmos*) out of reverence for God" (2 Cor. 7:1; see also Heb. 12:14). The first reference to sanctification, the verb "purify," is an *act*, whereas the second reference, the noun "holiness," is a *condition*.

6:20–22 / Verses 20–22 summarize the transition from sin to salvation. Verse 20 is not entirely clear in Greek, of which the NIV offers an interpretive rendering, **When you were slaves to sin, you were free from the control of righteousness**. The sinner imagines that sin is true freedom. It is an illusory freedom, however, for it is preoccupied with self, resulting inevitably in license, lawlessness, and chaos. Only righteousness truly frees because it leads away from self and *to* "holiness" (v. 19). Under the dominion of sin one has no responsibility for righteousness and is consequently ordained for death (v. 21). **What benefit** (Gk. "fruit") **did you reap at that time from the things you are now ashamed of?** The answer is "nothing," for death is scarcely a benefit. But because God is sovereign love, the present is never irrevocable, and repentance and change are possible. Here Paul speaks of *shame* as the condition of repentance (see Ezek. 16:61–63; Ezra 9:7–15). As long as one takes delight in sin (no matter how subtly) and inwardly desires its furtherance, one secretly hopes for some gain from sin, forbidden though it may be. There one is still under sin's opiate. But where one sees the final consequence of sin as death, there sin's guise of delight is defrocked and exposed as utter shamefulness. Sin's deceitfulness is then shattered and one is freed for slavery to God, which is eternal sonship.

Inward obedience comes to outward expression in **holiness** (v. 22). Sanctification is not something we achieve, it is something we inherit and participate in by active obedience. **You have been set free from sin and have become slaves to God.** Paul is not applauding human achievement; he is rather testifying to God's liberating intervention in the cross on our behalf, the result of which **is eternal life**. Literally translated the verse reads, "you *have* the fruit of sanctification, the end of which is eternal life" (v. 22b).

6:23 / The contrast between sin and grace is now sharpened to a razor's edge. **For the wages of sin is death, but the gift of God is eternal life in Christ Jesus our Lord.** The imagery of fruit (NIV, "benefits") is here abandoned for the military imagery of verse 13. Sin and God are depicted as warlords, the one paying the wages of death, the other offering release and freedom for life. There is a telling contrast between **the wages of sin** and **the gift of God**. Hans Heidland notes that *opsōnia*, "wages," were subsistence payments to soldiers. Thus, in the present context, sin promises to pay subsistence wages, to provide for our needs, but that is an illusion, for in reality it pays death. Again, *opsōnia* were not a flat sum but installments paid over the duration of a soldier's service. If Paul is true to the metaphor, the **death** he refers to would not be death as a "lump sum," i.e., physical death, but the shadow and consequences of death already in life. Most importantly, **wages** and **gift** are two entirely different things. In Heidland's words, "Man has rights only in relation to sin, and these rights become his judgment" (*TDNT*, vol. 5, p. 592). Because of sin humanity gets what it has coming to it; death is our due or "right." But God does not pay the wages of "rights" nor compensate according to deserts. He freely forgives those who renounce the "rights" of sin. God, who is rich in mercy, remits our debts and freely grants what we do *not* deserve—eternal life in Christ Jesus. That is the meaning of grace.

Additional Notes   §15

An informative discussion of ancient slavery is presented in *A History of Private Life from Pagan Rome to Byzantium*, ed. Paul Veyne, trans. A. Goldhammer (Cambridge, Mass. and London: Belknap Press of Harvard University Press, 1987), pp. 51–94.

6:16 / The Milton quotation is from *Paradise Lost*, bk. 5, lines 519ff. Elsewhere, Adam admonishes Eve to everyday obedience rather than extraordinary virtue: "Seek not temptation then, which to avoide Were better. Trial will come unsought. Wouldst thou approve thy constancie, approve First thy obedience" (bk. 9, lines 364ff.).

Paul Achtemeier likens the thought of v. 16 to a liberated prisoner who sheds one authority (prison) for another (society). Failure to obey the new authority (society) will of course return one to the old (prison) (*Romans*, pp. 109–10).

A Jewish rabbi some fifty years after Paul echoed Aristotle. "Hasten to fulfill an easy commandment and flee a transgression; for one commandment obeyed leads to another, just as one transgression brings another after it" (*'Abot* 4.2 [my translation]; see Str-B, vol. 3, p. 233).

6:17–18 / For a vigorous exposition of the idea of two masters, see Nygren, *Romans*, pp. 255–57.

6:20–22 / The Greek of v. 20 reads literally, "you were free to righteousness," whereas we would expect, "you were free *from* righteousness." The idea seems to be that you were free *with respect to* righteousness.

One of the oldest commentators is also one of the most modern. More than two centuries ago J. A. Bengel said of the idea of shame in v. 22 that Paul commended the Romans for being ashamed of sin, but "the multitude of Christians are now ashamed of sanctification." How little things change! See Bengel, *Gnomon*, vol. 3, p. 85.

§16 Widowed from the Law and Married to Christ (Rom. 7:1–6)

Paul at last turns to the problem of the place of the law in salvation, a problem he has mentioned in passing but has not discussed in depth. Like all Jews, Paul made certain affirmations of the law. The law was given by God and was thus "holy, righteous, and good" (7:12). It was the definitive expression of God's will for the ordering of human life (2:1ff.), and as such it was worthy of endorsement (3:31). But in the wake of his conversion, and unlike most of his Jewish contemporaries and even many of his Christian contemporaries, Paul saw also a negative side of the law. The law makes us aware of sin (3:20), it reveals transgressions and thus brings God's wrath (4:15), and, most disturbingly, the law has a dangerous liaison with sin. Apart from the law, sin was not even reckoned as sin (5:13), but now the law actually incites and triggers it (7:5). This crescendo of indictments severely qualified the role of the Jewish law in the Christian scheme of things. Although it is not clear exactly how Paul viewed the law prior to his conversion, it is certainly true that even though he may not have attributed his salvation to Torah observance, the latter was at the very least a "matching contribution," so to speak, on his part to God's prior inclusion of him in the covenant. But after his conversion he realized that God accepts sinners by grace alone, apart from legal observance, and henceforth he understood his relationship with God in a totally new light, "not under law, but under grace" (6:14). Justification by faith restored law to its rightful place in the drama of redemption. It retains its function naturally as a straight-edge of sin, thus revealing our need of a savior, and after salvation it remains a norm for righteous behavior. But it is no longer—indeed never was—a means of salvation. Its function, in other words, is diagnostic, not therapeutic.

We might distill Paul's thoughts concerning the law in the present chapter to three conclusions: the law is *holy*, but it is *provisional* and *limited*. The law is holy because it was given by inspiration and reveals the will of God. But it is provisional because, like an escort or chaperon which leads believers to Christ, it has largely fulfilled its function (see Gal. 3:24–25). Finally, it is limited because it provides knowledge of sin but is powerless to produce the holiness and obedience it demands. "What a wretched man I am! Who will rescue me from this body of death?" (7:24).

Since the law was so closely allied in Paul's mind with the problem of sin, the present section shares several parallels with the previous chapter. In chapter 6 Paul argued that Christians are free from sin; in chapter 7 he argues that they are free from the law. Chapter 6 began with sin (v. 1); chapter 7 begins with law (v. 1). There "we died to sin" (6:2), here "you died to the law" (7:4). There Paul admonished Christians to "live a new life" (6:4), here to "serve in the new way of the Spirit" (7:6). There he spoke of release from sin (6:7, 18), here of release from the law (7:3, 6).

7:1 / **Do you not know, brothers**, begins Paul. This is only the second time Paul has addressed the Romans as **brothers**, and he uses the term advisedly both here and in verse 4 below as an appeal to their mutual trust on the sensitive issue of the law. **For I am speaking to men who know the law** indicates that even among his Gentile readers Paul could assume a familiarity with the law, which indicates that in Rome, as elsewhere, many of the Gentile converts had previously been adherents to the Jewish synagogue or were "God fearers." The **law** under discussion is scarcely Roman law, despite the fact that the Romans, as Paul well knew, were eminent jurists. The marriage illustration that follows clearly refers to Jewish and not to Roman practice.

The law, says Paul, **has authority over a man only as long as he lives**. The word for **has authority**, *kyrieuein*, was applied to the **authority** of death and sin in 6:9 and 14, and here it casts a cloud of suspicion over the law. Moreover, because the law holds sway only during one's life, its authority is temporary. It is not eternal, nor is its authority ultimate. It had once been regarded as such, but with the advent of Jesus Christ the law was assigned its proper place, that of a penultimate guide to an ultimate savior.

7:2–4 / The provisional claim of the law is illustrated by the analogy of marriage. A wife is bound in fidelity to her husband as long he lives, but if he dies she is absolved from his authority. What formerly would have been adultery is now a legal right: she may marry another man. The analogy was drawn from Jewish marriage customs rather than Roman. Jewish thinking on marriage began with the prescriptions in Deuteronomy 24:1–5, and subsequent rabbinic tradition was unanimous that the death of the husband annulled the marriage contract, freeing the woman to marry again, all of which is consonant with Paul's analogy.

The analogy is not exactly appropriate to illustrate the point of verse 1, however, because it fails the test of logic at the end. In verses 2–3 the husband (= law) dies, whereas in verse 4 it is the believer (= wife) who dies to the law. Obviously, it is not the law which dies but the believer who dies in Christ, as Paul says in verse 4. Because the analogy does not correspond in every respect to the point it illustrates, it is unwise to press it too far, and it is not necessary to do so, for it is simply an analogy, not an allegory. It is, however, eminently clear in the one respect in which Paul intended it—that death ends obligations. Christians are like the wife in the story: the law has lost its claim over them, and they are free to transfer their allegiance to **another**. Believers are widowed from the law and free to marry Christ.

The marriage analogy must be understood in light of what Paul said in chapter 6. Freedom from the law does not leave one in a neutral, noncommitted state. One cannot remain "unmarried." Either one transfers allegiance to Christ or one falls back under the authority of the old Adam. "Anyone who has died has been freed from sin" (6:7). The law maintains its hold on humanity through sin. When sin is abolished (6:6; 7:6), so too are the penalties and condemnations of the law (8:1). This is summarized in verse 4, **So, my brothers, you also died to the law through the body of Christ**. The NIV rendering, **you also died**, is a passive in Greek, meaning "you were put to death." It connotes that something *was done* to believers in Christ's death. This is probably a "divine passive," by which reverent Jews avoided using the name of God lest they profane it. It means, "God put you to death," and it testifies to God's initiative in the work of salvation. It was God who "killed" the effects of law, sin, and death in us, and raised us in Christ to live in freedom and fruitfulness for himself.

This becomes a reality **through the body of Christ**. Several commentators take this as a reference to the familiar Pauline metaphor of the church as **the body of Christ** (e.g., 1 Cor. 12:27), or perhaps to the sacraments (e.g., 1 Cor. 10:16). But one wonders if the doctrine of the church is not premature at this juncture of the argument. It is more natural, and probably more correct, to understand **the body of Christ** as Christ's redeeming work on the cross and our identification with it; in the sense of 6:2, "We died to sin" (cf. Col. 1:22; 2:14). **The body of Christ** is vividly and rightly anti-docetic. It reminds us that Christianity is not a noble ideal wherein Jesus simply appeared in the guise of a human being, although in reality he was spared both temptation and suffering. **The body of Christ** recalls a historical fact upon which redemption hangs, that through his body and the wounds inflicted on it by his enemies, Jesus "abolish[ed] in his flesh the law with its commandments and regulations" (Eph. 2:15).

Death is brutal. In the world as we know it no creature experiences death without pain and suffering. Death is the robbery of life, the curse of existence. And yet, in the mystery of faith, death is a necessity. It may seem in our daily dyings and in our final physical passing that death is the final trick of a universe as meaningless as it is vast, but this is not so. God's mercy is active in death, freeing us from whatever would enslave us so that we may be joined **to him who was raised from the dead**, for only in him can we **bear fruit to God** (see John 15:1ff.).

7:5–6 / Verse 5 reverses the image of fruitfulness. The old marriage to **the sinful nature . . . bore fruit for death**. The rendering, **the sinful nature**, is too restricted and pejorative in light of the Greek, "in the flesh." "Flesh" (Gk. *sarx*), of course, is a key Pauline concept. **Sinful nature** suggests something evil, whereas "flesh" in Paul's understanding (when it does not simply mean "physical") pertains to all aspects of life—including individual aspirations, culture, politics, economics, and even religion (2:28)—that resist or stand apart from God's redemption.

Although "flesh" suggests the material side of human nature in contrast to the spiritual, reminiscent of the body/soul dichotomy, this is not Paul's understanding. He does not have in mind two parts of a person, but rather two possibilities of existence. Flesh and spirit are two realms, two authorities under which we may live. Flesh is the fallen nature, humanity apart from grace, which is descriptive of the condition of Adam in 5:12ff. It is a gravitational force-field determined by the pull of sin and death. The law, it might be hoped, would have arrested our fall into this perilous vortex, but it was of no help. Indeed, it made matters worse, for **the sinful passions** were **aroused by the law**. True, the law judges and condemns sin, but it also exacerbates sin, for it provides the specific handles by which sin seizes us.

But this is not the last word, for the Christian belongs to a different realm. Paul begins verse 6 with an emphatic contrast, **But now**. The power of the "flesh," which is condemned though uncured by the law, is finished. The Greek verb for **we have been released**, another "divine passive," means "to abolish or wipe out" and testifies that something decisive has been done for us by God. **Dying to what once bound us** repeats the theme of verse 4: we "died to the law." Paul again contrasts the exclusive alternatives of sin and law to Christ and the Spirit. To drive the nail home he leaves the analogy of marriage and returns to that of slavery, **so that we serve in the new way of the Spirit, and not in the old way of the written code**. Slavery to Christ leads to freedom in Christ, "whose service," as the Book of Common Prayer says, "is perfect freedom."

The new way of the Spirit and **the old way of the written code** present a double contrast between newness and oldness, or the Spirit and the letter. It is tempting to see here a contrast between the old and new covenants, or law and grace, but that would overlook an important nuance of the argument. Paul does not contrast the law with the Spirit exactly, but the **written code** with the Spirit. In the next verse he emphatically rejects the idea that the law is sin (7:7), and later adds that the law is holy (7:12) and spiritual (7:14). By the **written code** he evidently understands the scrupulous interpretation of the Torah characteristic of the rabbinic tradition, the "tradition of the elders" according to Mark 7:3, which later developed into the elaborate legal systems of Mishnah, Gemara, and Talmud. The **written code** is what religion becomes when the word of God is separated from the Spirit of God. It belongs to the "old self" (6:6), to Adam, and to the "flesh." It puts legal proscriptions in place of persons, and substitutes legal technicalities for the original and driving intent of the law. The Spirit alone can breathe life into the word of God, making it "God-breathed" (2 Tim. 3:16), regenerative rather than moribund. The **new way of the Spirit** is what Ezekiel foresaw when he spoke of need for a heart transplant in humanity, for the

removal of the heart of stone and its replacement with a new
heart and Spirit which would "move you to follow my decrees"
(Ezek. 36:26–27). The **written code** is an external taskmaster, but
the Spirit dwells within believers and *moves* (though not coerces!)
their hearts, making obedience both possible and pleasing to God.

Additional Notes   §16

There are verbal as well as thematic parallels between chapters 6
and 7, e.g., *katargeisthai* ("be done away with," 6:6; "released," 7:6), *kyrieuein* ("master[y]," 6:9, 14; "authority," 7:1), *karpos* ("benefit," 6:21, 22; "bear
fruit," 7:4, 5), *doulos–douleuein* ("slaves," 6:20, 22; "serve," 7:6), *thanatos*
("death," frequently in both chapters).

7:1 / Eliminating the idea that Paul has Roman law in mind in
v. 1, Dunn notes that it would have been presumptuous for Paul, who
had never visited the capital, to lecture its residents on Roman law (*Romans 1–8*, p. 359).

7:2–4 / Roman marriage customs were palpably different from
those assumed by Paul in vv. 2–4. As far as we know, marriage in Rome
was normally a private matter with scant means of verification, not unlike
engagements today. It did not require the sanction of a public authority,
and there was no official ceremony or written documentation. The sole
legal transaction concerned the wife's dowry. The role and rights of
women in Roman marriages were, in certain respects, more egalitarian
than in Judaism. Divorce could be initiated as easily from the wife's side
as from the husband's. Roman men did not hesitate to marry divorced
women, and many men could and did carry on affairs with mistresses or
slave women outside their marriages with impunity. Adultery on the
woman's part was regarded in a similar vein, not specifically condemned
by Roman law as it was in Judaism, but regarded as something of a
misfortune which might be tolerated with stoical reserve on the husband's part. See *A History of Private Life from Pagan Rome to Byzantium*, ed.
Paul Veyne, trans. A. Goldhammer (Cambridge, Mass. and London: Belknap Press of Harvard University Press, 1987), pp. 33–49.

On Jewish marriage prescriptions, see Jacob Neusner, *Judaism. The
Evidence of the Mishnah* (Chicago and London: University of Chicago Press,
1981), pp. 59–60.

7:4 / Regarding Paul's emphasis on **the body of Christ**, Bengel
says that Paul stresses the death of Christ's body rather than his soul
because the flesh is "the theatre and workshop of [our] sin," and hence
Christ's flesh must be the site of its redemption! *Gnomon*, vol. 3, p. 87.

7:5–6 / The distinction between "law" and "written code" might be illustrated by the distinction between "biblical" and "biblicist." The former hears the commandment to forgive seventy times seven (Matt. 18:22), for instance, to mean unlimited and unconditional forgiveness; the latter counts up to 490!

Note Ernst Käsemann's pronouncement on the **Spirit** versus **the written code**: "Christianity is not just a Jewish sect which believes in Jesus as the Messiah. It is the breaking in of the new world of God characterized by the lordship of the Spirit. The intensification of the Torah which shaped Judaism in the days of the apostle is impossible for Paul even in the form of an internalizing of the law. . . . The presence of the risen Lord in the power of the Spirit takes the place of the Torah of Moses and makes holy the world which otherwise, even in its piety and ethics, is unholy" (*Romans*, p. 191). Käsemann is right that Christianity is something new and transforming and not simply an addendum to Judaism, but he runs the risk, in contrast to Paul, of denying the validity of the law as a moral guide for believers.

§17 The Power of Sin Within (Rom. 7:7–25)

We noted in section 14 that chapters 6–7 are something of a theological entrenchment on Paul's part designed to defend his gospel against three objections. In 6:1–14 he contended against a misunderstanding of 5:20 ("where sin increased, grace increased all the more"), which would argue that if grace increases with sin, why not sin all the more? In 6:15–7:6 he answered a second objection that freedom from the law leads to moral anarchy. Now in the present section (7:7–25) we hear his final defense, in which he endeavors to clarify the exact relation between the law and sin, and, in particular, to dispel the idea that if the law reveals and increases sin then law itself must be evil.

With the choice of the first person singular in verse 7 and the present tense after verse 13, Paul establishes a more personal and immediate bond with his readers than anywhere else in this or in his other epistles. Why does Paul interject himself so dramatically here? And from what perspective is he writing? Is chapter 7 a flashback to Paul's pre-conversion experience, or is it a present portrayal of the Christian's ongoing struggle against sin? At no point in Romans do the fevers of interpreters reach a higher pitch. Solid arguments have been advanced in monographs or lengthy excurses for each view, and it is quite impossible to cinch the argument either way. We can do no more than present the general arguments for each position and choose the most reasonable path—which in this instance is the least *un*satisfactory path—over the terrain.

Twentieth-century scholarship has tended toward the view that verses 7–25 describe Paul's pre-Christian experience. The chief supporting argument contends that if the Christian—including Paul—has died to sin and now lives a new life in Christ (6:22; 7:4; 2 Cor. 5:17), then how can Paul consider himself "sold as a slave to sin" (v. 14), or "a prisoner of the law" (v. 23) and exclaim, "What a wretched man I am!" (v. 24)? Nowhere else do we hear an outcry of such frustration from the Christian. Verses

7–25 must therefore be a lament, it is asserted, of Paul's condition before his conversion on the road to Damascus.

Against this view there is a long tradition of interpretation, beginning with the church fathers (in particular Augustine), and continuing to the Reformers and a number of modern scholars, which sees Romans 7 not as a pre-Christian elegy but as a description of the *believer's* experience. This view, I believe, in the end provides the more plausible understanding of chapter 7 and of its place in the epistle.

We begin our defense of this judgment with the place of Romans 7 in the structure of the epistle as a whole. In 1:16–17 Paul proclaims the gospel of salvation through faith. He then introduces the guilt of humanity in 1:18–3:20, but only *after* he has announced the good news of God's love and forgiveness in the cross. Thereupon he expounds the gospel (3:21–31), defines the meaning of faith (ch. 4), and moves to the life of faith (chs. 5–8). If chapter 7 is a pre-conversion reflection, then it is a digression from an otherwise consistent and purposeful development of the epistle thus far, the whole of which is patterned after Habakkuk 2:4: "The one who is righteous [chs. 1–3] by faith [chs. 4–11] will live [chs. 12–15]." On the other hand, if chapter 7 is descriptive of the believer's experience it is entirely consonant with the development of the epistle.

Internal arguments in chapter 7 argue in a similar vein. The unusual present tense in verses 14ff. certainly appears to represent Paul's mind at the time of writing Romans, rather than prior to his conversion. Moreover, nowhere in Paul's pre-conversion experience do we find, as we do here, a dirge of such desperation. A review of his pre-conversion life, in fact, reveals not frustration and struggle, but confidence ("as for legalistic righteousness, faultless," Phil. 3:4–6). Paul had boasted of fulfilling the law as a Pharisaic Jew (Gal. 1:14). Any number of pious Jews could (and did) make such claims, which we might expect from those who had measured their lives according to a law of *deeds* as opposed to a law of love that examined *intentions*. The real battle with sin, of course, begins when an individual is transferred by faith from the authority of Adam to Christ. "Therefore do not let sin reign in your mortal body," said Paul in this context (6:12). It is true, as those who argue for a pre-Christian context of Romans 7 maintain, that 7:14 ("sold as a slave to sin") is a mystifying utterance from the mouth of a Christian. But there is no need to get cramps over it, as do a number of commentators. It is a metaphor, dramatic to be sure, but still a metaphor of the ongoing battle with sin in the process of sanctification. The darkness and desperation of chapter 7 may strike us as untypical of the Christian Paul, but his words are echoed, to some extent at least, elsewhere in Romans and Galatians. The struggle between the first Adam and the last Adam as diagrammed earlier (see p. 162) and the tug-of-war between flesh and Spirit in Galatians 5:16–18 are not dissimilar. "For the sinful nature desires what is contrary to the Spirit, and the Spirit what is contrary to the sinful nature. They are in conflict with each other, so that you do not do what you want" (Gal. 5:17). The final confession of chapter 7, "In my mind [I] am a slave to God's law, but in the sinful nature a slave to the law of sin" (7:25) is reminiscent of 6:17–20. And last but not least is the evidence of Romans 8:18–20. There Paul projects the "*present* sufferings" of his own experience onto a cosmic canvas of the "creation [which] was subjected to frustration," and "bondage to decay," only after which will dawn the final liberation of "the glorious freedom of the children of God" (8:21).

It is not without reason, therefore, that we argue for a post-conversion understanding of chapter 7. Paul's use of the first person singular flows from his own struggle of *becoming righteous after having been made righteous*. It is his own experience, but it is not only his experience. Chapter 7 is an apt illustration of the adage that what is truly individual is truly universal. Who can deny that the voice of the apostle echoes in the experience of all Christians and in their frustration at the persistence of sin? "The world is too much with us," said Wordsworth, and this is no less true for Christians. Indeed, at times it seems to be more so. If believers appear as raw recruits, offering but miserable resistance to the veteran forces within them and against them, then they must seize the manifest grace of God as the only antidote to their own wretchedness.

7:7 / For Judaism, Torah was the supreme gift of God. But Paul's critique of Torah brought him perilously close, at least in the minds of his Jewish hearers, to blaspheming that gift. Statements like "law brings wrath" (4:15), "sin is not taken into account when there is no law" (5:13), and especially 7:5, "the sinful passions aroused by the law were at work in our bodies" (see also 5:20), must have suggested to Paul's Jewish contemporaries that he was equating Torah with sin. He now gives voice to this suspicion, **Is the law sin?**, and he retorts, **Certainly not!** A century after Paul, Marcion (ca. A.D. 140) would drive an iron wedge between law and gospel by his heretical teaching that the God of the OT, the so-called Demiurge, was an inferior and evil God in contrast to the God and Father of Jesus Christ. To this day anti-Semitism more often than not reasserts this claim. Paul naturally recoils from this terrible idea. The law, to be sure, is of divine origin and is holy and good (vv. 12, 14), but it cannot rescue humanity from its bondage to sin.

Paul then repeats a position he has stated before: **I would not have known what sin was except through the law** (v. 7; also 3:20). It is true that in the absence of law people still sinned, but they did not fully recognize their sin. The law stands in a similar relationship to sin as a physician does to illness. The patient may sense a loss of vitality, but not until the disease is diagnosed does the patient know the full extent of the problem. The diagnosis, of course, is not the illness, nor did it cause the illness–but neither can it cure it.

Paul illustrates this by citing the tenth commandment, "**Do not covet**" (Exod. 20:17; Deut. 5:21). Although this commandment did not play nearly so prominent a role in Jewish theology as did the commandments about idolatry or the sabbath, for example, Paul alights on it because, of all the commandments in the Decalogue, this one penetrates to the inner life of the believer. The first nine commandments forbid *actions*, but the tenth forbids *desires*. Not all desires are forbidden, of course, for the Bible knows many good desires. The desire prohibited by the tenth commandment is that of the "flesh," the *yēṣer hārā'*, or "evil impulse," as the rabbis called it. It is possible, of course, for a person to refrain from doing any number of forbidden actions. But this is not to say that one did not *desire* to do them. The tenth commandment penetrates behind evil deeds to the evil *intentions* which motivate them as the wellsprings of behavior and the command center of living.

7:8 / Until now the law has been depicted rather like a watchdog which keeps trespassers out of private property. But that is only the half of it. The same law can become a hound dog nipping at the heels of a trespasser and chasing him further *into* forbidden territory. **Sin, seizing the opportunity afforded by the commandment, produced in me every kind of covetous desire,**

says Paul. Rabbinic Judaism saw two drives in humanity, one bad
and one good. Torah was believed to be the God-given means of
quelling the bad one. Paul's assessment of Torah, however, was
not so optimistic. The quelling of evil desires belonged to the
province of the Spirit of God, not to Torah. At one level the law
may have been like the safety lock on a gun, but on another level
it was the trigger! Sin **seized the opportunity**, says Paul. **Opportunity** (Gk. *aphormē*, vv. 8, 11) means "point of departure," "origin
of a war," or "the base camp of an expedition." Thus, far from
checking sin, the law actually triggers it.

It might appear that Paul anticipates the findings of modern psychology here. It is well known that the prohibition of a
course of action is normally an invitation to pursue it. When a
mother orders her son *not* to wash his face—only to watch him
run to the bathroom and do the opposite—she is using this phe-
nomenon to her own advantage. "Reverse psychology" may approximate Paul's thought, but it does not explain it, for Paul is not
speaking psychologically but theologically. His concern is not
with human personality but with *sin* as a latent power which is
awakened and activated by the law, *in spite of* the faith and will
of the believer.

St. Augustine gave a graphic testimony to this in his own life:

> There was a pear-tree near our vineyard, loaded with fruit that was
> attractive neither to look at nor to taste. Late one night a band of
> ruffians, myself included, went off to shake down the fruit and
> carry it away. We took away an enormous quantity of pears, not
> to eat them ourselves, but simply to throw them to the pigs. For of
> what I stole I already had plenty, and much better at that, and I
> had no wish to enjoy the things I coveted by stealing, but only to
> enjoy the theft itself and the sin (*Confessions* 2.4).

7:9–12 / These provocative verses allude to the Edenic
beginnings of the race. The dramatic use of **I**—for the first time
in Romans—identifies Paul (and all humanity) with Adam, the
archetypal father of the race. Adam's fate anticipates the human
race to follow (except for Christ), and the entire race (except for
Christ) is implicated in Adam's fall. **Once I was alive apart from
the law** refers to the epoch of innocence reflected in Genesis
1:26–2:16, before there was either sin or commandment. But the
prohibition against eating from the tree of the knowledge of good
and evil (Gen. 2:17) disturbed humanity's primal bliss. Paul seems
to imply that sin existed before the actual choice of Eve and Adam

to eat the forbidden fruit (Gen. 3:1–6), although as a latent condition rather than as an actuality. But once the commandment was issued—the commandment which was necessary to create the condition of freedom—**sin sprang to life and I died**. Like gasoline, sin is something of a theoretical hazard until a match is struck, and the match which ignited sin was the law. The serpent (neither Genesis nor Paul calls it Satan) had no means by which to attack Eve until the prohibition of Genesis 2:17 had been given. The purpose of the commandment, of course, had not been nefarious. Its purpose was positive, **to bring life** and create the condition of freedom which in turn created the possibility of free and joyful obedience to the Creator. But with its violation, **the very commandment that was intended to bring life actually brought death**. This thought echoes an idea Paul had written earlier to the Corinthians, that the law is a "ministry that brought death" (2 Cor. 3:7). This does not mean the law *is* sin and death. Its nature is **holy, righteous, and good**, and were it not for sin it would, as the rabbis taught, have promoted life. But sin spoils fundamentally and forever the law's purpose. The law, of course, condemns sin, but it also incites it. The commandment not to eat the forbidden fruit had been given for the purpose of life, but the commandment contained within itself the possibility of death—a death which resulted when it was transgressed.

The thought reaches its climax in verse 11, Sin **deceived me, and through the commandment put me to death**. Literally, it tricked me and killed me! A critical distinction must be made between the *occasion* for sin and the sin itself. The occasion for sin, according to Paul's line of reasoning, is the commandment which the power of sin seized and turned against me, but the actual sin was the desire *to usurp God's authority*. Thus, **sin, seizing the opportunity afforded by the commandment , . . . put me to death**. So then, the law is holy, and the commandment is holy, righteous and good. Here is the answer to verse 7, "Is the law sin?" The law results in death, but death is not due to the law. It is due to sin which the law both illumines and inflames. Because the law is of God it is not abrogated (3:31), for it reveals the moral will of God and humanity's obligation to it.

7:13 / Verse 13 compresses the train of thought in verses 7–12 into a single verse. Is the law which is "holy, righteous and good" in reality a curse? Paul again thunders a denial, **By no**

means! (see 3:6; 6:2, 15; 7:7). The culprit is sin, not law. The law plays a divine role in relation to sin for it reveals sin (3:20), and by arousing the slumbering demon to life makes sin's true character the more apparent. But sin abuses the law, producing the opposite of what the law intended. The law, however, cannot be blamed for death any more than a detective who discovers a corpse can be said to be the killer.

7:14 / From verse 14 onward the first person singular pronoun and the present tense command center stage. Although some commentators doubt that Paul is speaking here personally, he gives every impression of shifting from a historical identification with Adam in verses 7–13 to a personal and existential lament in verses 14ff. The contrast between the spirituality of the law and the unspirituality of humanity dominates the thought until the end of the chapter. The style and mood evoke startling pathos. **We know**, confesses Paul, **that the law is spiritual**. That is not an isolated opinion, but the summary judgment of Judaism: "And these are they that have no share in the world to come: . . . he that says that the law is not from heaven," declares the Mishnah (*Sanh.* 10.1). The law is spiritual because it is given by inspiration and reflects God's righteous will.

What Paul says of the law, however, he cannot say of himself. Surely the emphatic "I" is Paul's personal testimony, but it also carries universal significance. Paul's experience is no more isolated from our common humanity than is Job's struggle with suffering. In his heart Paul confesses that he is **unspiritual, sold as a slave to sin. Unspiritual**, *sarkinos*, means "carnal" and "fleshly," i.e., subject to the gravitational pull of Adam. This is not simply an admission that Paul, like everyone else, is a mortal of flesh and blood. Any moralist can point out failures in human "oughtness," but the apostle is thinking of the higher summit of divine righteousness. It means that the law is God's ideal, an ideal which people acknowledge and affirm, but which no one can attain. At the very point where the divine aura of the law becomes apparent, human fallenness (which Paul describes in 8:18ff. as part of the tragic pain of creation itself) wells up and frustrates all obedience to it. It is not a matter of trying harder. Indeed, the harder people try the more deeply they become mired in the quicksand of failure. The lament of verse 14 is nothing less than the horrid recognition that in *oneself* there is to be found the cosmic corruption and fallenness which we condemn in the world around us.

The Greek word for **sold** reinforces this thought. *Pipraskein* often refers to the export and sale of slaves. In the present context it describes someone possessed by the supernatural slave owner of sin. If our tack on Romans 7 is correct, **sold as a slave to sin** refers not to the non-Christian life but to the Christian life. People who cave in to sin know very little about it; they normally think themselves as good or better than other people. One discovers the force of the current not by floating with it but by rowing against it. So it is with sin. It is saints, after all, not gangsters, who teach us the meaning of sin. The "flesh" does not roll over dead at conversion; neither does it die easily thereafter. When threatened it fights for its life.

7:15 / The crux of the problem of being "sold as a slave to sin" (v. 14) is explored in verses 15ff. There is within the Christian a division caused by knowing the good but not doing it. **I do not understand what I do**, sighs Paul. **I do not understand** (*ou ginōskō*) apparently means, "I cannot figure myself out," or "I am a mystery to myself." With one foot in the kingdom of God and the other in the world, the believer is a bewilderment to self. At the cognitive level there is a discernible good which one ought to do. This extends also to the volitional level, for Paul exclaims, **what I want to do I do not do, but what I hate I do**. Paul is not depicting a split personality or a battle between Spirit and flesh; the devil is not to blame here for Paul's problems. There are not two command centers of personality, not two "I's," but only one, the same "I" which *wills* the good yet *does* the bad. Above all, Paul is not thinking of base and wicked people who neither know nor value good. The individual under discussion is the moral person, indeed the godly person, who knows and wills the good but is frustrated by an unwillingness and inability to do it.

7:16–20 / The litany of lamentation in verses 16–20 repeats the foregoing thought—often in the same words—in ever deepening anguish. The thesis remains constant, **I have the desire to do what is good, but I cannot carry it out** (v. 18). But the thesis is augmented and clarified by two additional ideas. The first is, **If I do what I do not want to do, I agree that the law is good** (v. 16). The tragic irony of our contrary behavior does not negate the law, but actually confirms it. If the good remains good despite our doing the opposite, then it is all the truer. When a nihilist, for example, decries that the world is meaningless, this betrays that the nihilist has at least some concept of what a meaningful world would be like. Likewise, when I do what I do not will to do, my will at least testifies to the good as revealed in the law.

Second, verses 17 and 20 disclose the final consequence of what it means to be "sold as a slave to sin" (v. 14). Paul's inability to do the good he wills to do is ultimately the result of **sin living in me**. The Greek says sin "residing" or "setting up house" in me. A rabbinic saying centuries later repeats the imagery, "Sin begins as a guest and ends up as master of the house" (Str-B, vol. 3, p. 239 [my translation]). The implications of this are more radical than they first appear. We normally think that as subjects of their actions individuals choose whether or not to sin. Paul, however, does not say the individual does sin but that sin is a power dwelling within an individual which causes a person to do what he or she does not will to do! The individual is not the captain of the ship, but a prisoner of it. Freud might have echoed the imagery, claiming that the ship is not steered from the observation deck of the conscious but from the cargo bay of the subconscious. Paul's picture is similar but more forbidding: it is not even the subconscious which pilots the vessel, but *sin*.

We must hasten to add that Paul does *not* say that humanity is all bad and can do no good. All people are capable of some good, and many are capable of great good. What Paul does say is that no one does the good that he or she *wills* to do. Whatever good one does, it is less than one ought to (and could) have done. Notice that Paul says nothing of character or convictions. Strong convictions and noble character are not enough. Sin is active disobedience, the failure to do the will of God as it is revealed in the law. This is not in the least diminished for Christians, but actually compounded, for Christians know better than others what is expected of them, and hence they are made increasingly aware of their shortcomings in doing it.

Sin living in me testifies that the source of evil is not somewhere "out there," not even in the great social evils of Paul's day or ours. Paul would have agreed with James (4:1ff.) that oppression, war, poverty, materialism, militarism, etc. were but magnifications on a national or international scale of a nucleus called sin within each person. This is not to say that Paul discounted sin in its social ramifications. He would not have seen the inside of jails from Jerusalem to Rome had not his preaching challenged economic values (Acts 19:21ff.), exploitation and oppression (Acts 16:16ff.), slavery (Philem.), and religious intolerance (Acts 22:22), to name but a few. Spiritual recluses are not accused of "caus[ing] trouble all over the world" (Acts 17:6). But these things did not blind Paul to the fact that the problems of the world, whatever they were, were inherent in *himself*. The essential problem of sin is its **living in me**, and hence its solution is the transformation of the human heart.

7:21–23 / The argument now takes a complicated turn, for Paul begins speaking of two laws, the **law of my mind** and the **law waging war against** it **in the members of my body** (v. 23). Some argue that this is only a manner of speaking, that Paul has one and the same law in mind, in the first instance seen from the perspective of faith, in the second from the perspective of sin. The plain sense of the text argues against this, however. In verse 23 the apostle contrasts **another law at work in the members of my body** from **God's law** (which must be the Torah) in verse 22. A review of Paul's argument implies that **my inner being** (v. 22), **the law of my mind** (v. 23), and the "I" that wills the good (v. 19) and that **delights in God's law** (v. 22) are only different idioms for "the law [that is] holy, righteous and good" (v. 12). Ranged against this law is **another law at work in the members of my body** that makes **me a prisoner** (v. 23). If we ask what this other and nefarious law might be, the context of 7:7ff. demands that it is *sin*. Paul concedes this at the end of verse 23: **the law of sin at work within my members** (see also v. 25b). There is thus an inescapable tension, a **war**, between the law and sin in every person. Paul again resorts to military imagery as he has throughout the discussion: "instruments" (6:13), "wages" (6:23), "opportunity" (7:8,11), "hostile" (8:7). Although not all these words carry military connotations in English, their Greek originals do. Even in the best person there is an ugly residue of sin, and even in the worst person the ineffaceable image of God. Thus, not even the best person can achieve justification by works, and not even the worst person is beyond the reach of redemption and justification by faith.

7:24–25 / In this emotionally laden panegyric Paul gives utterance to the agony and ecstasy of the Christian life. **What a wretched man I am! Who will rescue me from this body of**

death? Thanks be to God—through Jesus Christ our Lord! He does not say, Praise God, even though I often fail, at least I have my ideals, my good intentions, my dignity, my character, and convictions! He concludes rather in crashing finality: What good are these things if I still do evil? When one discovers not only a power at work within oneself against one's best desires, but also a powerlessness to combat it, then one must look for help beyond oneself. Paul is not in the market for a self-help program. He is not hoping for a lucky break or turning over a new leaf. He is a drowning man crying out for **rescue!** The word for **wretched,** *talaipōros,* means that the situation is critical and beyond his power to change it. If salvation is to come it must come from a *who,* not a *what.* It must come from the *outside,* and apart from his own resources . . . or it will not come.

This cry of dereliction is not the last sound in an empty universe. It is a prelude to grace. **Thanks be to God—through Jesus Christ our Lord!** The Greek word for **thanks** is the word "grace." This encomium exposes the nerve of Paul's gospel that reverberates in triumphant refrain throughout chapter 8. While we were in the pit of despair, God demonstrated his grace in Jesus Christ. When human hope is exhausted, salvation is at hand. Where nothing can be expected from humanity, everything may be hoped for from God. Creation out of nothing will happen again. "I have seen . . . the misery of my people . . . I have heard them crying out, . . . and I am concerned about their suffering. So I have come down to rescue them" (Exod. 3:7–8).

The end of verse 25 poses a problem for commentators who suppose Paul is speaking of his pre-Christian experience. How can the recipient of grace and salvation end on a note of slavery to sin? Many commentators and translators, in fact, either omit 25b or place it after verse 23. There is not a shred of evidence in the textual tradition for such a transposition, however, and a transposition is unnecessary if our thesis is correct. The chapter closes with a reminder that the Christian life is one of tension and struggle (so v. 23). The Christian, as Luther said, *simul justus est et peccat*—is both justified and yet a sinner (*Epistle to the Romans,* pp. 98–99). To be righteous with God is not to be fully free from the effects of sin. Believers must run the race with perseverance, and though there is progress, sin and sorrow and death do not in this life fade away. These remain enemies, death the greatest of them. Through all this the Christian learns to walk "by faith, and not by

sight" (2 Cor. 5:7). Our one anchor is the promise and presence
of the resurrected Lord who gives grace for the present struggle
and eternal life in the world to come.

Additional Notes   §17

For a survey of Rom. 7 in the history of theology, see Michel, *Der
Brief an die Römer*, pp. 175, 181–83. For a pre-Christian understanding, see
W. G. Kümmel, *Römer 7 und die Bekehrung des Paulus* (Munich: Chr. Kaiser,
1974), and Gaugler, *Der Römerbrief*, vol. 1, pp. 233–46. For a variant view
that Rom. 7 is a Christian reflection on the pre-Christian life as it was lived
under the law, see Achtemeier, *Romans*, pp. 119–24. For thorough discussions of the post-conversion view presented here, see Nygren, *Romans*,
pp. 284–303, and Cranfield, *Romans*, vol. 1, pp. 340–47.

7:8 / **Produced** (*katergazomai*) is a thematic key in ch. 7. Paul
used the word earlier of the shame *resulting* from homosexuality (1:27) or
of "the law *bring[ing]* wrath" (4:15), but in this chapter it appears in a
six-round volley (vv. 8, 13, 15, 17, 18, 20) denoting the tragic and inevitable
outworking of sin to death.
For Torah as the antidote to evil desires in rabbinic thought, see
Str-B, vol. 3, p. 237.
For a further literary allusion beyond Augustine to the idea that
law incites sin, see Milton, *Paradise Lost*, 12.287ff.

7:9–12 / The same distinction between the occasion for sin and
the sin itself is apparent in Genesis 3:1–6. The occasion for sin is in v. 6:
"When the woman saw that the fruit of the tree was good for food and
pleasing to the eye, and also desirable for gaining wisdom, she took some
and ate it." Pleasure, beauty, and wisdom were, of course, God's gifts.
Neither then nor now is there anything sinful about them. They became
an occasion for sin only in light of the evil motive of v. 5: "For God knows
that when you eat of it your eyes will be opened, and you will be like God,
knowing good and evil." There is nothing wrong with wanting to be like
God; indeed, believers are commanded to be such (Lev. 19:2). The sin was
in choosing to receive God's gifts from the tempter's hand rather than
from God's, and thus usurping God's authority. The desire to *play God* is
the motive of sin—a desire which may be stronger in a good person than
in a bad person, which was Paul's thesis in ch. 2. Sin is thus a parasite or
perversion of good. Without good there could be no sin.

7:15 / There are many echoes of 7:15 in history. Immediately
before his conversion Augustine fell into desperate straits, "torn between
conflicting wills," "a house divided against itself," "trembling at the bar-

rier," "hanging in suspense," "utterly bewildered," "saying, 'Let it be now, let it be now,' but being held back" (*Confessions*, bk. 8, chs. 7–12). Likewise, while serving as a missionary in Georgia, John Wesley found himself "beating the air," repeating Romans 7:15ff. to himself, and saying, "Before, I had willingly served sin: but now it was unwillingly; but still I served it" (H. Kerr and J. Mulder, *Conversions*, Grand Rapids: Eerdmans, 1983, pp. 57–58).

7:16–20 / On sin as active disobedience, see Gaugler, *Der Römerbrief*, vol. 1, p. 219.

7:21–23 / On the possibility of one and the same law under consideration in vv. 21–23, see Dunn, *Romans 1–8*, pp. 377, 392–95. It is more likely, however, that Paul has two different laws in mind; so Cranfield, *Romans*, vol. 1, pp. 361–62, and Gaugler, *Der Römerbrief*, vol. 1, pp. 221–27.

7:24–25 / Compare vv. 23–25 with 1 Cor. 15:56–57, "The sting of death is sin, and the power of sin is the law. But thanks be to God! He gives us the victory through our Lord Jesus Christ."

§18 The Advocacy of the Spirit (Rom. 8:1–17)

In sublime contrast to the questions which have beset the argument since chapter 6 (6:1, 15; 7:1, 7, 13ff.), chapter 8 begins with a thunderous proclamation, "Therefore, there is now no condemnation for those who are in Christ Jesus." Especially in 7:7–25, Paul's blow-by-blow account of indwelling sin reminded one of a ringside announcer reporting a losing struggle. But the long and doleful report is now interrupted with ecstatic news. The contest has been decisively reversed. Sin and law may have been the overwhelming favorites, but victory belongs to "those who are in Christ Jesus." The fires of hope had dwindled to a cold flame when reinforcements finally arrived.

Credit for the victory, as irrevocable as it was unexpected, belongs to the Spirit. Unforeseen and from the outside, like a ray of hope extending backward from the future to the present, the Holy Spirit has broken into the dreary domain of sin, law, and death with freedom from oppression, strength for the struggle, and hope for the future. Paul had alluded to the Spirit briefly in 7:6 when he mentioned "the new way of the Spirit." But because of the need to clarify the problem of indwelling sin (7:7–25) he had to hold the subject in abeyance until now. But in chapter 8 the Spirit commands center stage. Before this chapter the Spirit is mentioned only five times, and afterwards only nine times. But in chapter 8 the Spirit occurs twenty-one times—a record for any chapter in the NT.

The Spirit's activity can be roughly divided into two foci. The first half of the chapter (vv. 1–17) describes the advocacy of the Spirit in the lives of believers even now dogged by the "flesh." The chapter concludes (vv. 18–39) with the completion of salvation and the transformation of believers into the image of God's Son. The Spirit thus resolves the two major problems between humanity and God, the problems of condemnation and alienation.

The Hebrew and Greek words for spirit, *rûaḥ* and *pneuma* respectively, mean "breath" or "wind," thus air in motion. God's

Spirit was the animating breath of life at creation (Gen. 2:7), the inspiration of prophecy (Ezek. 2:2), and the divine force that swept over the church at Pentecost (Acts 2:4). For Paul, Spirit "give[s] life to your mortal bodies" (v. 11) by breaking the reign of sin and flesh. The Spirit is not to be confused with an enlightened though inherent component of human personality (e.g., body, mind, and *spirit*). The Spirit is God's creative presence, both in believers and in the church, which bears witness to Christ, provides liberation from sin and death (v. 2), and guarantees the completion of salvation in the world to come (2 Cor. 1:22; 5:5).

The Spirit belongs indissolubly to the person and work of Jesus Christ. It is not an impersonal force or energy field or an intensified "noosphere," as certain evolutionary thinkers claim. The Spirit is God's will and capacity to act as manifested in Jesus Christ. Paul can speak interchangeably of "the Spirit of God" and "the Spirit of Christ" (8:9), or he can say, "the Lord *is* the Spirit" (2 Cor. 3:17). Through the Spirit the resurrected Lord carries forth his redemption and lordship of the world. Any spirit not bearing witness to Jesus Christ and not drawing believers into obedient discipleship to him and fellowship with one another is not God's Spirit. The Spirit empowers believers (v. 9; Gal. 3:3) and is their ethical guide (v. 14; Gal. 5:22–25). The Spirit not only unites believers to Christ and his body, the church (Eph. 4:4), but also through that body the Spirit shapes believers into the very image of Christ (Eph. 4:13).

8:1 / Chapter 8 begins with the triumphant crash of Beethoven's "Emperor Concerto"—**Therefore, there is now no condemnation for those who are in Christ Jesus**. The Greek behind **Therefore** (*ara nyn*) signals an emphatic break from the preceding train of thought. To be **in Christ Jesus** is to experience something not offered by the law of Moses. Paul's tireless labors have shown that the law reveals sin (3:20), aggravates sin (7:8–9), and condemns both sin and sinner (7:11); and the burden of this awareness causes him to cry out, "What a wretched man I am!" (7:24). His only recourse is to cry for help outside himself, and help he finds in Jesus Christ.

Without diminishing the force of verse 1, we must not mistake its message. Paul does not say that those in Christ Jesus no longer sin or that they are exempt from the struggle against sin so dramatically portrayed in 7:7–25. Romans 8 is not an apology for Christian perfectionism. What he does say is that there is no *condemnation* for those who are in Christ. The antecedent idea is found in 5:16 where, in speaking of Adam's sin, Paul said, "The judgment followed one sin and brought condemnation" (also 5:18). It is that condemnation which is revoked in Jesus Christ. Verse 1 is therefore a victorious summary of 5:12–6:11. The ongoing skirmishes with sin do not defeat believers, but the thought of being cursed or abandoned by God does. Believers need to know that they do not stand condemned by God. Christ has cancelled the bond of indebtedness against humanity (Col. 2:14). The accent throughout falls on Christ's victory, not on human merits.

When Paul says, **there is now no condemnation**, he means that the sentence of death and judgment on the Last Day has been commuted. Verse 11 will repeat the idea of 7:24: believers remain in "mortal bodies" (see also 2 Cor. 4:7–11). But the consequences of sin are annulled through Christ's death, and even now the Spirit begins in believers a work of regeneration that will be completed in the world to come. Grace is knowing that God is for us and with us even in our "body of death" (7:24).

8:2 / Paul now resumes the thought of 7:6 concerning the "new way of the Spirit." Paul's Jewish contemporaries were familiar with the belief that the day of the Messiah would be accompanied by an outpouring of the Spirit. Keying off the theme of **law**, Paul says, in effect, that a higher **law of the Spirit** supersedes **the law of sin and death**. We know of instances in nature where the effects of one law are cancelled by another. When an airplane wing provides the necessary "lift" to raise a plane upwards, one law (that nature abhors a vacuum) prevails over another (the law of gravity). In like manner, **the law of the Spirit of life set me free from the law of sin and death**. This is a development of 5:20–21, "Where sin increased, grace increased all the more." The Spirit now stands where the law formerly stood. It is the **Spirit of life through Jesus Christ** which **set me free**. The past tense, **set me free**, refers to a decisive point, most probably Christ's crucifixion, but possibly the believer's conversion. At any rate, it is no vague, undefined spirit which stands there for **me**. Paul expressly links the Spirit with the redemptive and liberating work of Jesus Christ. What God did through the historical Jesus on Golgotha, he now applies and extends to believers through the Spirit in the community of faith. The emphasis again falls on God's initiative. Christ's work, and its ongoing effect as applied by the Spirit, brings peace and freedom. "Grace renders that most easy, which seems difficult to man under the law, or rather does it itself," said Bengel (*Gnomon*, vol. 3, p. 98).

There is, to be sure, a bristling tension between being a "prisoner of the law of sin" (7:23) and being **free from the law of sin**. But the inherent intellectual contradiction does not cancel the fact that both represent the experience of believers (see also 2 Cor. 4:7–12). In their earthly frames Christians are never free from the hold of sin, yet there is a marked difference between their response to that grip and that of non-Christians. Augustine said prior to conversion, "My sin was all the more incurable because I did not think myself a sinner" (*Confessions* 5.10). Christians are alerted to the ways of sin and are no longer ignorant and unresisting accomplices to its work. They recognize the power and deception of its tyranny and fight against it in the name of Christ and in the power of the Spirit.

Christians may still live with the effects of sin, but they do not live under its *authority*. When Paris was liberated in 1944 the Allies declared France free, even though a large portion of the country still lay under Nazi control. With the loss of the capital, however, the Nazi power base was broken, and it was only a matter of time until the remaining forces were driven from the land. The Christian experience is similar. The cross of Christ has once and for all broken the claim and power of evil over the lives of believers. The capital belongs to Christ, so to speak, even if mopping-up operations are still in effect. The liberating edict of the Spirit is now effecting Christ's victory throughout creation. The future is assured even if the present is still uncertain. "He must win the battle" proclaimed Luther in the hymn, "A Mighty Fortress is Our God."

8:3–4 / Verse 3 is a classic formulation of redemption. The beginning of the verse lacks a verb in Greek and is somewhat defective, reading literally, "For the inability of the law because of the weakness of the flesh." But there is no doubt of its meaning: the law was rendered ineffective because of the "flesh." Paul does not say the law was unable to condemn sin; that it *could* do because it was "holy, righteous, and good" (7:12). The law is not bad, but its good counsels are undermined by a bentness and gravitational pull in human nature toward evil. The law offers a proper diagnosis of the disease, but no cure.

To accomplish what neither the law nor human will could carry out, God entered decisively and historically **by sending his own Son**. God had, of course, dispatched messengers and prophets to Israel in the past. "From the time your forefathers left Egypt until now, day after day, again and again I sent you my servants the prophets" (Jer. 7:25). More than forty times in the OT God sends something or someone to lead Israel back to God. But the sending of the Son is something entirely different. God no longer represents himself through a surrogate, like the law of Moses, nor does he send someone in his behalf. In the Son, God comes in person. **His own Son** emphasizes the filial intimacy between Jesus and the Father. In Jesus, God takes the problem of sin into his own hands. In Jesus, God takes personal responsibility for humanity's salvation.

"God sent his Son" was a heavily freighted expression in the early church (John 3:16; Gal. 4:4; Phil. 2:6f.; 1 John 4:9). It was both a theological and liturgical capsule of the mystery of the incarnation: the preexistent Son of God had been sent for the salvation of the world. The yeast of this truth continues its redemptive fermentation in the world. Pop religion tells us we can do something for God; sociology, that we can do something for others; and psychology, that we can do something for ourselves. But the gospel says that God has done something for *us*, apart from which we are caught in a tailspin of futility (vv. 18ff.). This brief phrase rearranges the axis of the world. "God sent his Son" means that God—not humanity or the world—is the source and center of reality; it means that where there was no help within creation, God intervened from outside it; and it means that God's help is not a pious intuition, but a historical manifestation in first-century Palestine. "God sent his Son" is salvation in four words: enacted from the fullness of divine love, evoked by the fallenness of the world, and effected by the incarnation of Jesus Christ.

Of special importance is the meaning of **the likeness of sinful man**. On the one hand, Paul doubtlessly wants to avoid saying that Christ became as "sinful man," for in the first eleven verses he employs that term, or "flesh [of sin]" as the Greek reads, eleven times with reference to sin and death. Moreover, in 2 Corinthians 5:21 Paul states that Christ "had no sin." On the other hand, Paul does not use **likeness** abstractly, as did the Docetists when they taught that Christ only *appeared* human (from Gk. *dokein*, "to seem or appear"). Docetism characteristically taught that Jesus could not have been tempted, nor could he have sinned, nor did he really suffer. It was, however, fallen humanity which needed redeeming, not an ideal or apparent humanity, and Christ had to become fully human if he were to **condemn sin in sinful man** (v. 3). If human flesh is the stage of sin, that same flesh must become the stage of redemption. **Likeness**, therefore, means that Christ did not take on any nature other than *our* nature, though apart from sin. **In the likeness of sinful man** agrees with Philippians 2:7–8, "being made in human likeness, and being found in appearance as a man, he [Jesus] humbled himself." "God achieved his purpose for man," says Dunn, "not by scrapping the first effort and starting again, but by working through man in his fallenness . . . and remaking him beyond death as a progenitor and enabler of life *according to the Spirit*" (*Romans 1–8*, p. 421). The critical difference between Christ's humanity and ours is that whereas we yielded to sin's dominion, he rendered perfect obedience (Phil. 2:8; Heb. 5:8). **In the likeness of sinful man** almost certainly recalls the Adam typology of chapter 5. This offers an explanation why Christ obeyed, whereas all other humanity disobeyed. The answer is that the Son entered humanity with a nature like Adam's before the Fall. It was possible for him not to sin, though for all others it was not possible not to sin. As a human being he was tempted by sin, and he could have sinned, but he was not *subject* to sin as was humanity after Adam. Where the first Adam disobeyed, the last Adam obeyed. And whereas our yielding to sin brought our condemnation, Christ's obedience to God brings sin's condemnation!

The mission and goal of the incarnation were **to be a sin offering**. God did not send the Son primarily as a moral reformer. The essential aspect of the incarnation is not ethical but sacerdotal: **He condemned sin in sinful man** (v. 3). Before humanity can live it must be freed from death. It is a delusion to think that humanity needs only a better model for life. Its plight is more desperate. It needs a savior from bondage to sin, and the price of deliverance was the suffering and death of a sacrificial victim. In the old covenant God had established the practice of animal sacrifice in anticipation of the future and ultimate sin offering of the new covenant, the "Lamb of God, who takes away the sin of the world" (John 1:29). And thus the death which had until Christ's advent been sin's ally became in Christ's death sin's defeat.

Understanding the progression of thought in verses 2–4 is essential. Paul begins with the Spirit who brings liberation from "the law of sin and death." The Spirit, however, is not a free agent. The Spirit attends to Jesus Christ and is the divine auxiliary who makes Christ's redemption efficacious. Moreover, the Spirit salvages the law as a moral standard, **in order that the righteous requirements of the law might be fully met in us, who do not live according to the sinful nature but according to the Spirit** (v. 4). Paul does not say *"righteousness* of the law," for he has argued that righteousness comes by faith. Rather he speaks of the **righteous requirements of the law** (see 2:26), meaning that which the law demands, even if the law cannot provide it. Those who live in the Spirit are for the first time enabled to acknowledge the true intent of the law, and they are empowered to begin fulfilling it. This is the first positive role of the law in Romans so far. The Spirit is the supernatural reinforcement of God's grace who empowers Christians to fulfill the intent and requirements of the law. Paul does not say that one must keep the law in order to be saved but that one must be saved in order to keep the law! Augustine understood Paul correctly, "The law is given that grace might be sought; grace is given that the law might be fulfilled" (quoted by J. Stewart, *A Man in Christ*, p. 109). The reader familiar with the OT cannot resist the allusion here to Jeremiah 31:31ff. and Ezekiel 36:26ff. Both prophets agonized over the fatal flaw in Israel which thwarted Israel from fulfilling the law and pleasing God. Both foresaw the need for a new covenant and new spirit, not coercing Israel by external dictates but *moving Israel from within* to fulfill God's righteous will. And the longing and anticipation of both are fulfilled in Christ.

Does not Paul's confidence in fulfilling the law in verse 4 **(that the righteous requirements of the law might be fully met in us)** contradict his frustration in *not* fulfilling it in chapter 7? According to verse 4, the Spirit reveals the essence of the law and enables Christians to conform to its fundamental intent, even if not to its every detail. The Christian is like a man who has the right tune in his head but cannot remember all the words. Accordingly, when Paul says that love fulfills the law (13:8; also Gal. 5:14), that is not to assert that Christians are perfect, but that they **live . . . according to the Spirit**. The present tense of the Greek *peripatein,* "to walk" or **live,** connotes continued action, forward progress, a pattern of behavior under the Spirit's leading. The idea is one of direction, not perfection; orientation toward a goal, if not yet attainment of it. Otto Michel correctly notes that the willingness and strength to resist sin is the unmistakable sign of the Spirit. "The claim to possess the Spirit of God is justified only where it is accompanied by the battle against the flesh" (*Der Brief an die Römer,* p. 180 [my translation]).

8:5–8 / It is usually possible to gain an idea of something unknown by describing what it is *not.* This is Paul's tack in verses 5–8, where, in a Jekyll-and-Hyde contrast, he sets the Spirit in antithesis to the flesh (NIV, **the sinful nature**). Paul has employed global contrasts before with Adam and Christ, slavery and freedom, death and life. In these verses he begins with the negative consequences of the flesh, and later in verses 12ff. he highlights the positive consequences of the Spirit.

The antithesis of Spirit and flesh is to this day often mistaken as a dichotomy in morals (good and bad), or in religion (dos and don'ts), or in personality (mind and body, spirit and matter, etc.). But Spirit and flesh are not descriptive of a theological or ethical schizophrenia, or of higher and lower principles in the same person, one Christian, the other unchristian, or one saved, the other unsaved. Spirit and flesh are rather two exclusive realms, two authorities or governing powers. One is *either* in the Spirit *or* in the flesh, but not in both at the same time. The language indicates a sense of sovereignty and totality of the one or the other: to **live according to the sinful nature / Spirit** (v. 5), "controlled by the sinful nature / Spirit" (v. 9), "belonging to Christ" (v. 9), "if the Spirit . . . is living in you" (v. 11), in "obligation . . . not to the sinful nature / Spirit" (v. 12–13).

In verses 5–8 Paul speaks of **the mind** of the Spirit or flesh. *Phronēma* means "thought," conveying the idea of the sum total of inner dispositions, literally a "mindset" that leads to a goal. "Flesh" then connotes not base instincts or the material side of life, but that which human nature in its rebellion against God has made of itself. Spirit, likewise, is not a noble or ideal self, but God's transmitting of the effects of Christ's salvation to believers and God's infusing himself into them.

We noted that there are twenty-one references to the Spirit in chapter 8. Only slightly less important is *sarx,* "flesh," which occurs thirteen times in the first thirteen verses of the chapter. Paul sets the two in opposition, like flint sharpened by flint, in verse 6: **The mind of sinful man is death, but the mind controlled by the Spirit is life**. Flesh and Spirit, and death and life are polar opposites. The disposition controlled by sin leads to death, and *is* death even in life. The disposition controlled by the Spirit participates even now in the life and peace that will be fully realized in the world to come.

In 5:10 Paul contended that unreconciled humanity is "God's enemy." It is not unusual to find people who do not believe in God, but it is unusual to find people who claim to hate God. Paul resumes this offensive idea in verse 7 by saying that **the sinful mind is hostile to God**. It is a commonplace in the modern West to regard human nature as basically good, or at least as neutral. Blatantly wicked persons or events are regarded as aberrations of an innate moral norm and are thus the less explainable because of it. One could more easily make alligators into house pets than convince Paul of this. He has argued that humanity honors the made above the Maker, condemns others and exonerates self, serves self and denies others, and loves self in place of God. Left to itself human nature is red in tooth and claw, locked in combat against God. Whether or not the expressions of human egotism are socially acceptable does not change their fundamental enmity from God and others. **Those controlled by the sinful nature cannot please God** (see Heb. 11:6).

8:9–11 / Paul now departs from the fulminations of the flesh and turns to the hopeful certainty of the Spirit. The mood shift, accompanied by a shift in person from the third to second person, thus reassures Paul's readers of the Spirit's personal advocacy in their lives. The chief idea is that the Spirit unites the objective achievement of Christ's sacrifice of atonement to the lives of believers. The Spirit integrates and internalizes the work of Christ with the response of faith. Hence, the Scriptures speak of Christ dying *for* us, and of the Spirit dwelling *in* us. It is thus the Spirit who actualizes the doctrine of justification by faith in believers' lives and guards it from becoming a sterile intellectual dogma. Paul highlights this with the ambiguous wording of verse 9, **You, however, are controlled . . . by the Spirit,** *if* **the Spirit of God lives within you**. The Greek word *eiper* can mean either "since" or "if." If it means the latter (so NIV) it may function as a gentle prod to Paul's readers to encourage them to consider whether or not they belong to the Spirit. For the solid church members in Rome it would have been an inducement to humble self-examination, and for inquirers about the faith, an invitation to its grateful acceptance.

Above all, the Spirit accentuates the experiential nature of faith. Paul says expressly that possession of the Spirit is the criterion for belonging to Christ: **If anyone does not have the Spirit of Christ, he does not belong to Christ** (v. 9). God does not hold his children over the fires of anxiety regarding their salvation; neither is it his pleasure to keep them guessing whether or not they belong to him. God has sent his Spirit into the heart of each believer and each community of faith to produce an inner conviction based upon demonstrable change in character and conduct, reassuring Christians of God's sovereign and irrevocable love for them, thus freeing them for praise, witness, and service.

Verses 9, 10, and 11 all contain a condition prefaced by **if** (protasis), followed by "then" (apodosis). The purpose of these statements is hortatory, and their effect resembles an orchestra's crescendo, or climactic finale. Paul does not deny the lingering effects of the fallen nature on believers. Believers are still *human* believers in the present age. God has not yet transposed believers into a heavenly state, but he has transformed their earthly state, and this means the battle with sin and death continues, though the victory is won. Paul testified to that struggle when he complained of "sin living in me" (7:17, 20). But he recognizes another and more compelling agent in believers, God's **Spirit, who lives in you** (v. 11). In both passages Paul uses the Greek word, *oikein*, meaning "to dwell or inhabit." The old regime is no longer the only regime, for the power of life, the Spirit who raised Jesus from the dead, even now resides within believers. The Spirit's present succor in their lives is the prolepsis that his vivifying power will quicken them fully in the final resurrection. "Though outwardly we are wasting away, yet inwardly we are being renewed day by day" (2 Cor. 4:16).

The Spirit is therefore the decisive answer to the agonizing struggle of 7:7–25, help from deep heaven for the world's deepest need. Through the Spirit the saving work of Jesus is present for us and at work in us. The Spirit is the divine answer to the human question, "Who will rescue me from this body of death?" (7:24). Justification by faith is the means by which believers appropriate

Jesus' death for salvation, and through the Spirit they receive Jesus' life for sanctification. The Spirit is the divine guarantee that "God is for us" (8:31), both in present struggles and for future glory.

8:12–13 / The transition in verse 12 is more emphatic in Greek than the NIV (**Therefore**) indicates. Again in verse 13 Paul includes two conditional statements beginning with **if**, which are followed by apodoses. This, combined with a switch again to the second person, intensifies the note of admonition to the readers. Believers may be in the flesh, but they are not obligated to it. It would be an error to consider sin like a mugging from which Christians could get up, brush themselves off, and continue on their way, the wiser for it. A Christian is a "debtor," as Paul says literally (NIV, **obligation**, v. 12). The Adam-Christ typology taught that all humanity stands under the rule of either Adam or Christ (5:12–21). This domination extends also to moral commitments (6:12–23, 8:2–4). Both the rule of Christ and its moral obligations are actualized as believers forsake their selfishness and sinful nature and relinquish themselves to the Spirit.

Freedom is not simply doing what we want; that is a capitulation to the flesh, sin, slavery, and death. Freedom is the decision to act according to God's Spirit, for **if by the Spirit you put to death the misdeeds of the body, you will live** (v. 13). The Greek of the verb **put to death** is in the present tense, which indicates continuous action. The battle with sin is not a momentary event, no matter how sincere, but a lifetime commitment. The Spirit is not a promise to those who succeed in overcoming sin, but God's abiding presence in the midst of the flesh or sinful nature. The ability to sustain warfare against sin signals the Spirit's presence. The Spirit emancipates believers from slavery to sin and joins them in sonship with Christ (vv. 15, 29).

8:14–17 / **Those who are led by the Spirit of God are sons of God** (v. 14). With this subtle transition Paul ushers believers into abiding fellowship with God and their spiritual inheritance in Christ. The imagery is that of a family. Sin abducts, God adopts. Sin makes slaves, God makes children. Sin provokes fear, the Spirit evokes trust. Sin foments rebellion and hostility, the Spirit leads believers to appeal to God in the most intimate and urgent cry, "*Abba*, Father." The paradox of grace is that those who deserve death are granted life.

The relationship of a slave to its master is ultimately one of fear. The law itself contributed to the status of servitude by making its promises on the basis of conditions, for conditions create anxiety and fear. When humans fail to meet conditions, as they inevitably do, they find themselves condemned. But grace cancels condemnation, as Paul heralded in verse 1; indeed grace short-circuits the whole downward spiral of law, sin, and death because grace is *unconditional*, that is, it is bestowed not on the basis of human merit, but on the basis of *God's* love.

The alternative of grace is expressed in *pneuma hyiothesia*, rendered **Spirit of sonship** (NIV, v. 15). *Hyiothesia* literally means "adoption," which clearly implies that believers are not naturally begotten children of God, but constituted children. Since adoption, as far as we know, was not practiced in Jewish society, Paul must have taken over the metaphor from Hellenism where it was practiced. The point, however, is not where the metaphor came from, but what it means. That answer is found only in the life and teaching of Jesus. In its conception of God as Father, and in its intimate address, **Abba**, meaning "Daddy," or "Papa," the early church bore witness to the central element in Jesus' relationship with God (see v. 23, 9:4; Eph. 1:5, and esp. Gal. 4:4–6). In all rabbinic literature there is no passage where the Spirit of God aids believers in prayer. Neither is there any clear evidence in that same immense corpus that Jews customarily addressed God as "my Father," much less with the intimacy of *Abba*. Jews, to be sure, knew how to pray, and they prayed fervently, but they avoided pronouncing God's name when possible; and when not, they accompanied his name with a blessing, for fear of profaning it. But in a remarkable break with tradition, Jesus dared to address God simply and intimately as "Father" in all his prayers—indeed probably addressing God as *Abba*, since the Aramaic *Abba* appears to lie beneath the Greek *patēr*, "Father"—and he invited his followers to do the same!

According to verse 15 God is by nature Father, not distant and forbidding, but near and intimate. The Spirit witnesses to believers that they too share Christ's *Abba*-relationship with the Father. **The Spirit himself testifies with our spirit that we are God's children** (v. 16). And if believers are on a "first name" basis with God, if they participate in the trust and confidence which Christ shared with the Father, they also receive the same benefits as **heirs of God and co-heirs with Christ** (v. 17). Heirs of what?

Of glory! Sin deprived humanity of God's glory (1:23). Once glory was marred in humanity, it was marred in the whole creation (1:23). But God restored his glory by the cross of Christ to fallen creation (5:2; 8:30).

If in the mystery of God the suffering of his Son became the gateway to glory, then believers and the church must also participate in Christ's suffering if they are to share in that glory. In the history of theodicy the problem of suffering has normally been posed as an obstacle to belief. But in verse 17 this problem is wholly absent. Suffering and glory are not presented as a theological dilemma, or in diametrical opposition, but in identification with Christ: they are **his sufferings** and **his glory**. Suffering is not a glitch in the divine purpose or a lapse on the part of believers. Suffering is an unavoidable and necessary part of God's purpose for Christ and his church. The power of resurrection is known only through suffering (Phil. 3:10). "No cross, no crown" is not a trite cliché; it expresses God's saving purpose, for both suffering and glory are the believer's inheritance with Christ.

Additional Notes §18

8:1 / The clause appended to v. 1 in several late manuscripts ("who do not live according to the sinful nature but according to the Spirit") is almost certainly an interpolation from v. 4. See Metzger, *TCGNT*, p. 515.

8:2 / For references to the outpouring of the Spirit in Jewish literature, see T. Jud. 24; T. Levi 18; Jub. 1:23; and the material gathered in Str-B, vol. 3, p. 240.

The Greek text presents a difficult choice at 8:2. The NIV reads, "through Jesus Christ the law of the Spirit of life set me free from the law of sin and death." The pronoun "me" is supported by many and varied ancient manuscripts, plus it agrees with the eight occurrences of the first person singular pronoun in chapter 7, all of which argue in its favor. But an alternative reading of "you" (singular), although it claims fewer manuscripts in its favor, nevertheless claims the most important ones, in addition to being the less obvious reading, which would argue in its favor since copyists may have changed "you" to "me" in order to harmonize it with chapter 7. Against "you," however, is the fact that in Greek the second person singular pronoun consists of the same letters as the last syllable of the preceding word and may have arisen from accidental repetition by a copyist. Nevertheless, "you" appears to be the stronger reading, and Cranfield is correct in noting that "Paul, being aware of the momentousness and amazingness of the truth he was stating ... wanted to make sure that each individual in the church in Rome realized that what was being said in this sentence was something which really applied to him personally and particularly" (*Romans*, vol. 1, p. 377).

8:3–4 / Note Calvin's explication of the atonement: "And thus what was ours Christ took as his own, that he might transfer his own to us; for he took our curse, and he freely granted us his blessing" (*Romans*, p. 282).

OT references to sin offerings can be found in Lev. 5:6–11; 16:3–9; Num. 6:16; 7:16; 2 Chron. 29:23–24; Neh. 10:33; Ezek. 42:13; 43:19.

8:5–8 / R. David Kaylor offers a helpful discussion of the often misunderstood terms of Spirit and flesh in *Paul's Covenant Community, Jew and Gentile in Romans*, pp. 143–48.

8:9–11 / References to "the Spirit," "the Spirit of God," and "the Spirit of Christ" suggested to J. A. Bengel an incipient testimony to the Trinity in verse 9. See *Gnomon*, vol. 3, pp. 100–101.

The outpouring of the Spirit was a common expectation in first-century Judaism. *Exodus Rabbah* (48, 102d) reads, "God spoke to Israel, 'In this world my Spirit has given you wisdom, but in the future my Spirit will make you alive (or resurrect you), as it is written, I will put my Spirit within you, that you may live' (Ezek. 37:14)" (quoted from Str-B, vol. 3, p. 241 [my translation]). Paul, of course, identifies the outpouring of the Spirit with the advent of Jesus!

8:12–13 / Luther said of v. 13: "Therefore, we cannot overcome death and its evils by power and strength and we cannot escape them by running away from them in fear but only by bearing them patiently and willingly in weakness, i.e., without lifting a finger against them. This is the lesson Christ teaches us by his example: he went confidently to meet his Passion and his death" (*Lectures on Romans*, p. 230).

8:14–17 / The name associated with *Abba*-research is Joachim Jeremias. A full discussion of Jesus' unique relationship with the Father is presented in his *Prayers of Jesus*, trans. J. Bowden (Philadelphia: Fortress, 1978), pp. 11–65. Str-B, vol. 3, p. 243, presents additional and corroborative material. Jeremias asserts that "in the literature of early Palestinian Judaism there is no evidence of 'my Father' being used as a personal address to God" (p. 57), whereas in the gospels Father appears on the lips of Jesus no less than 170 times. A growing number of scholars would argue that Jeremias overstated the case somewhat, as is evidenced by the use of "Father" in personal address to God in Sir. 23:1; 3 Macc. 6:3–11; 1QH 9.2–10.12 in the Dead Sea Scrolls; and in the Apocryphon of Ezekiel, Frag. 2 (Charlesworth, *OTP*, vol. 1, p. 494 [although the last passage may reflect 1 Clem. 8:3]). Although we are too ill-informed about Jewish prayer life prior to A.D. 70 to speak as categorically as did Jeremias, the latter is correct that Jesus' numerous and exclusive appeals to God as *Abba* underscored his unique filial intimacy and authority with God, in which (as Rom. 8:15 evinces) he was followed by the early church.

§19 The Hope of Glory (Rom. 8:18–30)

As we near the conclusion of the first half of the epistle Paul summarizes a number of vintage ideas. From the immediate context he continues the themes of liberation from slavery (vv. 2, 21), resurrection (vv. 11, 23), sonship and adoption (vv. 14–17, 19, 21, 23), and the role of the Spirit. From earlier portions of Romans he reintroduces the themes of creation (1:20, 25; 8:19, 21), futility (1:21; 8:20), and likeness (1:23; 8:29). The two dominant themes, however, are suffering and glory (see v. 17). That which humanity lost through Adam's bid to usurp God's authority (1:22–23), and which resulted in a "depraved mind" (1:28), has been restored in Christ. The firstfruits of this restoration are already in evidence among believers, and they guarantee salvation's glorious culmination.

It is, however, with heavy feet that Christians run the race set before them. Amid this effete and transitory age they await future glory with sighs and groans. Frustration at the incompleteness and purposeless of the present order forms the backbone of this section. In verses 19–22 Paul speaks of the whole creation groaning, in verses 23–25 of Christians groaning, and in verses 26–27 of the Spirit groaning for them. Such sighs have meaning only when seen in light of God's eternal purpose in verses 28–30.

If in chapter 7 Paul looked inward and found a tragic conflict between his will and God's law, here he looks outward and, with poetic sensitivity, sees the same conflict in the travail of creation. His inner wretchedness (7:24) is part of the outer world (8:20). In heartfelt empathy he speaks of creation "subjected to futility" (v. 20, RSV), in "bondage to decay" (v. 21), and "groaning as in the pains of childbirth" (v. 22). But with equal conviction he speaks of God. The Spirit is God's "fifth column" who infiltrates this unhappy plot, creating *hope* between suffering and glory (vv. 20, 24, 25). Like Abraham, believers have been allotted the ground of hope as the only ground between the promise of God and the contradictory circumstances of the world. Human hopes derive from earthly resources and circumstances; the hope of the Spirit by contrast is a gift of God. Hope does not deny "our present sufferings" (v. 18), but it engenders confidence that God's purpose is at work in *all things* to make believers fit partners for glory (2 Cor. 4:16–17).

8:18 / The section begins with a pronouncement: **I consider that our present sufferings are not worth comparing with the glory that will be revealed in us. Consider** (*logizesthai*) implies not a mere opinion but a statement of gravity, an authoritative judgment. The sufferings of the present seem slight when compared to the glory that will be revealed. Sufferings are not illusory or mere surface scratches, however. Some religions, like Hinduism, maintain that matter, including evil and suffering, is only an illusion, and that relief from the illusion can be achieved by proper mental control. The Bible's testimony is vastly different. No one reading the story of Gethsemane (Mark 14:32ff.) or Golgotha (Mark 15) can doubt the reality of suffering. We may wish **our present sufferings** were bad dreams, but that is only a bad wish. Not answering the telephone does not make the call from the emergency room go away. Paul concedes that suffering is numbingly, painfully real, but *in comparison with glory* it looks different than when viewed alone, for it is dwarfed by the grandeur of glory awaiting believers. Moreover, it is only "for a season." The Greek word for **present**, *kairos*, means a momentary, limited duration of time. Suffering is limited to this life and pales in comparison to God's coming glory. The apostle is not minimizing suffering but maximizing glory.

8:19 / Verse 19 is charged with all the expectation of children on Christmas eve, and in Greek it nearly collapses under the weight of anticipation. The noun translated **eager expectation,** *apokaradokia*, appears only in the vocabulary of Christian writers and carries the sense of "craning one's neck" or "straining for a glimpse." Not only believers await the final revelation, but all **creation**—sub-human and supra-human—longs for **the sons of God to be revealed,** i.e., for Christians to inherit glory. According to Genesis 3:17 the ground itself was cursed because of Adam's disobedience; and if creation suffered Adam's defeat, the same creation must be renewed by Christ's victory (see also Isa. 11:6ff.; 65:25). Paul's scope of salvation far exceeds the saving of human souls, important as that is. Salvation is not like a space launch in which the booster rockets and fuel tanks are expended and then jettisoned after hurling a tiny manned capsule into orbit. Such a concept may have appealed to Gnostics who awaited the solitary heavenward flight of the soul as the evil material world around it perished, but it did not appeal to Paul. All creation longs for wholeness and freedom from pain, and all creation will also be the arena of salvation. In Gnosticism less of the world is redeemed than was created, like a germ of wheat in comparison with the full head, but for Paul the created world is the world God intends to redeem.

The focus of verse 19 concerns not the world as it *is*, but the world as it *will be*. The world may be a sorry place, and Paul would not deny it; but rather than lamenting that it is so he directs his gaze *in hope* toward the future. Believers groan in their creatureliness, but they also know they will not forever remain as they are. Creation is not God's final work. They learn to take God more seriously than their sufferings. Redemption is God's final work, when believers will no longer be simply creatures, but sons and daughters in glory with Christ.

8:20–22 / The present condition of creation is one of futility, for **creation was subjected to frustration** (v. 20). The word translated **frustration**, *mataiotēs*, means the inability of something to fulfill its intended purpose, and hence it suggests "emptiness," "futility," or "absurdity." How remarkably verse 20 echoes the message of Ecclesiastes, " 'Meaningless! Meaningless!' says the Teacher. 'Utterly meaningless! Everything is meaningless' " (Eccles. 1:2). The past tense of the verb, **was subjected**, probably refers to the curse of creation in Genesis 3:17–18. The voice of the same verb is again probably a divine passive, i.e., a deferential reference to God without using his name for fear of profaning it. It is sometimes thought that the creation was subjected by either Satan or Adam, but if that were so the result would hardly be **hope** (v. 20). God must be **the one who subjected** creation, though a bewildering condition results, for **The creation was subjected to frustration, not by its own choice** (v. 20). The curse of God which fell on guilty humanity extended also to guiltless creation, thus implicating creation in humanity's fate, though without its guilt. Consequently, if creation's curse is due to the external agency of Adam, its redemption will have to depend on the external agency of Christ.

Is not the past century a standing commentary on this verse? Our knowledge leaps exponentially and our problems no less so. Books proliferate and ignorance abounds, harvests increase and hunger spreads, production grows and poverty deepens. Mechanization makes our lives easier but threatens our worth as persons, and the time it saves us reveals only the meaninglessness of life around us. People live longer but fear growing old, they worship sex but fear getting pregnant. Counselors, clinics, and agencies abound, but the divorce rate soars and youth lose their way. Symbolic of it all is nuclear weaponry which, with each advance in technology, makes the world less secure. Human solutions, which once rose like a Phoenix from the ashes of the past, return like Harpies to prey upon us!

The truly remarkable feature in this is that the travail of creation leads not to despair but to **hope**! Were **bondage to decay** (v. 21) the only thing the world knew, or its final state, then despair would be the only possible result. But creation has been given the promise that it **will be liberated from its bondage to decay and brought into the glorious freedom of the children of God** (v. 21). The subjected world must give way to the liberated world, creaturely existence must yield to existence as heirs and children of God. The "when" of hope is not yet known because liberation from bondage lies in the future; but the "what" of hope is already known, for God wills to restore humanity to "the likeness of his Son, that he might be the firstborn among many brothers" (v. 29).

At present, **the whole creation has been groaning as in the pains of childbirth** (v. 22). Both **groaning** and **pains of childbirth** are Greek *syn*-compounds, i.e., they bespeak the experience of suffering common to all creation. There is no thought of a dualistic escape from creation, but rather of suffering with it! Hardship is not an anomaly; it is endemic to life. The metaphor **pains of childbirth** pictures hope in two respects. On the one hand, pain of childbirth is a NT expression for the coming of the messianic kingdom (Matt. 24:8; Mark 13:8; Rev. 12:2). But birth pains are pains of hope; they are not death pains, but life pains that promise a new existence. Whatever the pains of the present may be, they are not in vain. Paul confirms this with a judgment similar to verse 18, **We know**. That the groanings of creation will one day open up to the glory of sonship is a certainty based not on rational observation but on claiming the promise of God in faith. Apart from faith, suffering and evil are infernal and meaningless. But through faith in Christ's resurrection, "whom God raised after wiping out the birth pains of death" (Acts 2:24), our present sufferings are not the final cries in an empty universe, but the prelude of joy at the final liberation. If at the resurrection God will give believers spiritual bodies to inherit glory (1 Cor. 15:42ff.), so too will he renew the "body" of creation. "Then I saw a new heaven and a new earth" (Rev. 21:1).

8:23–25 / Paul now applies what he said of creation (vv. 19–22) to believers. Verse 23 contains two emphatic first person plural pronouns in Greek, stressing that *we ourselves* . . . **groan inwardly as *we* wait eagerly for our adoption as sons.**

Paul is found to be fighting on two fronts in verses 18–30. On the one hand, he stresses human solidarity with fallen creation, which is in "bondage to decay" (v. 21). Christians too are part of this bondage. Their bodies are susceptible to cancer, their businesses to failure, their families to brokenness. But this is not the sum of the matter (**Not only so**, v. 23), for the **firstfruits of the Spirit** guarantee their future **adoption as sons** and daughters and **the redemption of our bodies** (v. 23). This is Paul's second front. Believers are determined not by **groanings**, but by the Spirit; not by the way things are, but by the way they will be. The word for **firstfruits**, *aparchē*, which originally derived from the practice of OT sacrifice, carries here a metaphoric sense of something given by God in pledge of a full gift to come, similar to the guarantee of the Spirit in 2 Corinthians 1:22 and 5:5. The Spirit is God's **firstfruits** or pledge, the ground of hope for living in the tension between suffering and glory.

The theme of hope continues in the memorable phraseology of verses 24–25. The opening phrase, **For in this hope we were saved**, is vexingly ambiguous. In Greek, **hope** is thrust to the beginning of the sentence and is therefore emphatic. It is unlikely that Paul means we were saved *by* hope, for salvation normally comes by faith or grace, not by hope. It seems more probable, as the Greek duly allows, that we were saved to live in the condition of hope, or saved *for* hope. The aorist passive indicative, **we were saved**, would make salvation the premise upon which hope rests. As in verse 20, then, hope is the condition in which those who are saved live.

What has been done *for us* on the cross permits us to say, **we were saved**, but what remains to be done *in us* requires that

we wait for it patiently. Hope does not belong to the empirical world. It is unseen and its goal is as yet unpossessed, and hence hope is inseparable from patience (v. 25; Heb. 6:15). The Greek word for **patience**, *hypomonē*, suggests perseverance and endurance, especially in the face of toil and suffering (cf. 5:3–5). Patience renounces the ego and its claims and submits to God's will, way, and timing. Like patience, hope is purified through submission. Only where one has forsaken personal aspirations and agendas can one stake one's hopes on the promises of God. Hope belongs to the One who holds the future, not in the things which occupy the present.

8:26–27 / Paul now returns to the advocacy of the Spirit, a subject broached in verses 16 and 23. The Spirit, he says, **intercedes for us with groans that words cannot express**. There is again no hint of dualism between the sacred and profane, for the profane, the very **weakness** or insufficiency that divides us from God, becomes the stage for the Spirit's intimate and effective work. The present tense of the Greek verb translated **helps** (itself a *syn*-compound that denotes the Spirit's identification and solidarity with weak humanity) conveys an abiding, ongoing succor **in our weakness**. God is not an absentee slumlord, but our active advocate through the Spirit; and nowhere is God more present than in human weakness.

The reference to prayer in the Greek of verse 26 is more pronounced than in the NIV. It might be translated, "For we do not know how we ought to pray." God wills that believers adapt their prayers to his saving purpose in history. But in this we fail. In the parable of the Pharisee and tax collector, Jesus taught that effective prayer is based not on virtuosity and profuseness, but on sincerity (Luke 18:9–14). Paul knew firsthand that sincerity sometimes issues in weakness and speechlessness (2 Cor. 12:6–10). In prayer, as in every facet of faith, God does not command what he does not give. We noted at 8:16 that there is no precedent in Judaism for the Spirit's intercession in prayer, and this risked limiting prayer to a human work. But the early church called on the Spirit to "translate" its feeble stammerings, appealing to the God within to intercede with the God above. In verse 27 Paul hints at this divine interplay between him **who searches our hearts** (= God) and **the mind of the Spirit** (= God's Spirit). Even in human weakness prayer is participation in a divine conversation. Prayer is not a human work, but, like all of God's gifts and commands, it is evidence of God's work in believers.

In a probing and daring exposition of Paul, Luther pondered why Christians often experience the *opposite* of what they pray for.

> [God] contravenes all our conceptions . . . because it is his nature first to destroy and to bring to nothing whatever is in us before he gives us of his own. . . . When, therefore, everything about us seems to be hopeless and all that happens goes against our prayers and wishes, then those "groanings" commence "that cannot be uttered." And then "the Spirit helps our infirmities," for without the help of the Spirit we could not possibly bear up under God when he acts in this way to hear and fulfill our prayers (*Lectures on Romans*, pp. 240–41).

Luther is not accusing God of sadism. Rather, God uses human need to create receptivity, and receptivity is the prerequisite to acknowledging God's lordship, which is active *in our behalf*, although not always in accordance with our expectations.

8:28 / Verse 28 is a widely quoted and often misunderstood passage. It is sometimes interpreted to mean that good fortune favors nice people, or that things are not as bad as they seem and that everything "will work out in the end." But this is to confuse wishful thinking with Christian faith.

The first part of verse 28 was in fact an axiom in both Hellenism and Judaism. Plato says in the *Republic*:

> This must be our notion of the just man, that even when he is in poverty or sickness, or any other seeming misfortune, all things will in the end work together for good to him in life and death: for the gods have a care for any whose desire is to become just and to be like God (*Republic*, 10.613).

Judaism likewise abounded with stories (e.g., Ruth, Esther, Judith) in which adverse circumstances came to a good end. A saying attributed to Rabbi Akiba (ca. A.D. 130) stressed God's providence over all things, "Everything which the All Merciful does is done for the good of his servants" (for this and further quotations, see Str-B, vol. 3, pp. 255–56). Paul also repeats this precept, which he prefaces with a solemn affirmation, **We know that in all things God works for the good of those who love him**. Interestingly, Paul seldom speaks of human love for God as he does here. This is probably accounted for by the fact that he was reluctant to attribute to humans the quality of *agapē* which was so characteristic of God (e.g., 5:5–8). At any rate, the statement is not a general law of life. It is a theological statement valid for **those who have been called according to his purpose**, which is embodied in Jesus Christ. It does not mean that all things are good. They are not, and to call evil good is a grievous error under any circumstances. It means that for those who love God no evil may befall them which God cannot use for their growth and his glory. Paul includes yet another *syn*-compound, meaning "working together with." God works in all things—even horrible things—to accomplish his eternal will. This verse testifies to God's sovereignty, not to the beneficent outworking of circumstances. God does not will all things, but he is at work in all things. Similarly, Paul enjoins believers to give thanks "*in* all circumstances," not *for* them (1 Thess. 5:18).

8:29–30 / These verses, reminiscent of 5:3–4, rise in a crescendo of inspiration, filling readers with confidence in the promise of hope. Each statement forms a link in a chain—**foreknew, predestined, called, justified, glorified**—which secures believers to their future glory in Christ. Salvation does not just "happen." It is the result of God's eternal will! God's will is not a groping of divine benevolence. Salvation is not a matter of harps and golden streets, or the amorphous release of Nirvana. If believers want to know what God is like, and what they by his grace will become, they must look to Jesus Christ (Eph. 4:13; Phil. 3:21; Col. 1:15). Salvation is God's personal, eternal plan to make believers **conformed to the likeness of his Son, that he might be the firstborn among many brothers** (v. 29). The NT normally refers to Christians as believers, disciples, slaves, apostles, sheep, etc., but in this rare passage they are called **brothers** and peers of Christ! As **the firstborn among many brothers** Christ desires to share his glory with believers in a sibling relationship. What is more, believers will actually be peers of God, for, as Christ is the image of God, and believers are the image of Christ, believers will one day inherit their original image restored by Christ (Gen. 1:26; also Heb. 2:6–10). Conformity to Christ will reach its final and glorious completion at the Second Coming, but even now it is taking shape in believers' lives through faith and obedience (12:2; Col. 3:9–10). To be **conformed to the likeness of** God's **Son**—what a breathtaking hope in a world in which the image of humanity is presently so disfigured!

The Greek vocabulary of verses 29–30 is directed emphatically and proleptically toward the future. Three words in verse

29 (**foreknew, predestined, firstborn**) carry the Greek prefix *pro*, underscoring God's prevenience and control of the process of redemption. **Foreknew** refers to God's eternal purpose, and **predestined**, which follows it, refers to God's eternal power to effect that purpose. God's purpose and power come to fruition in Jesus Christ. The NT does not dwell heavily on predestination, but whenever the idea occurs it is anchored to the person of Christ. The sacrifice of Jesus on behalf of the world is the culmination of God's eternal will for the world, a will which is past (**foreknew**), present (**called**), and future (**glorified**). Predestination is a doctrine not of tyranny or terror, but of assurance that God is *for us* (8:31), that he ordains to bring believers to the glory of his Son.

Verses 29–30 are cast in the past tense, as though Paul were looking back on God's will, though some of it still remains to be realized. The affirmations of these verses are therefore grounded more in experience than in reason and logic. They are a revelation from God's perspective which sees the embroidery of human life not as we see it, from the backside of knots and tattered ends, but from the finished side of the pattern. The challenge of the present is to believe that by God's grace the knots and rough ends are actually weaving a pattern which is already known to God, even if unclear to us. The glory of the future will be to see the completed pattern, but even now something of it is visible in hindsight. C. H. Dodd comments,

> A man who is the object of grace, when he looks back upon himself, feels more and more that he has become what he is by no act or activity of his own, that grace came to him without his own will or power, that it took hold of him, drove him, led him on. Even his most intimate, his freest, acts of decision and assent become to him, without losing their quality of freedom, something that he *experienced* rather than *did* (*Romans*, p. 141).

On the threshold of such ineffable mysteries, however, it is the hymn writers, not theologians, who are the best commentators.

Additional Notes   §19

8:20 / According to Genesis 3:14ff. certain aspects of creation were cursed because of human disobedience. Subsequent rabbinic tradition universalized the idea, teaching that all things, though initially good, were corrupted by Adam's sin. Humanity, in particular, bore the brunt of the curse by a diminishing of its radiance, life span, and stature, but the fruitfulness of the earth and trees was also diminished, as was the brilliance of the stars. All these would be restored by the advent of the Messiah. See Str-B, vol. 3, pp. 247–55.

Paul's statements on the matter are more measured. He says only that the present languishing of creation is **by the will of the one who subjected it**, namely, God. Without lessening the consequences of Adam's sin (5:12), Paul seems to allow that the mystery of suffering is greater than a simple causal relationship between human sin and the futility in creation.

8:23 / Dante picks up the theme of suffering and glory in a conversation between himself and Virgil in *The Inferno*,

So we picked our way among the shades
of filthy rain speaking of life to come . . . .
speaking of pain and joy (Canto 6, lines 97ff.).

For a discussion of redemptive suffering in Paul, see J. Beker, *Suffering and Hope. The Biblical Vision and the Human Predicament* (Philadelphia: Fortress Press, 1987), pp. 57–79.

On a textual note, there is some doubt whether "adoption as sons" stood in the original text. See Metzger, *TCGNT*, p. 517.

8:24 / Two helpful discussions of the meaning of **For in this hope we were saved** can be found in Michel, *Der Brief an die Römer*, p. 206, and Käsemann, *Romans*, p. 238.

8:26–27 / Human weakness plays a key role in Romans. At 5:6 Paul says, "when we were still powerless, Christ died for the ungodly," and in 8:26, **the Spirit helps us in our weakness**. Both "powerless" and "weakness" come from the same Greek root. Thus, both the Son's work of redemption and the Spirit's work of sanctification are directed to human weakness!

Bunyan illustrates God's help in affliction by the story of the fire beside the wall. The devil casts water on the fire, but the fire (which represents the work of God in the believer's life) continues to burn. Interpreter then takes Christian to the other side of the wall where he is shown Christ sustaining the fire by oil. "Christ continually with the oil of his grace maintains the work already begun in the heart, . . . but it is hard for the tempted to see how this work of grace is maintained in the soul" (*Pilgrim's Progress* [New American Library, 1964], p. 37).

8:28 / The textual tradition of verse 28 is uncertain. One tradition reads, "all things work together for good," whereas a second specifies, "*God* works all things for good" (followed by the NIV). Evidence for both readings is roughly divided. Either way, however, the verse testifies to the sovereignty of God over circumstances.

§20 The Invincible Love of God
(Rom. 8:31–39)

In a rhapsody of grace Paul brings the first half of Romans to a climactic conclusion. In an unrestrained volley of rhetorical questions, dramatic repetitions, and contrasting universals, Paul is borne by a thermal current of assurance that "God is for us." At least six of his eleven sentences are rhetorical questions (the exact number is debatable since ancient manuscripts normally contained no punctuation). We can imagine the effect such rhythmic questions must have had as they were first read aloud in Rome, moving Christians joyously to praise God for his faithfulness. The certainty of that faithfulness is celebrated in brisk repetition, like a sixteen-gun salute, with sixteen references to God or Christ in only nine verses. The scope of God's faithfulness is heralded in seraphic universals: there is *no* condemnation for Christians, *no* power against them, *no one* to bring charges against them, *nothing* that can separate them from the love of Christ; for *all* is given to them, *all* things work for them, and in *all* things they are more than conquerors in Christ. "The gate of heaven is thrown open," in this triumphant conclusion, says Bengel (*Gnomon*, vol. 3, p. 111).

There is, to be sure, deliberate crafting here, as there has been throughout Romans. The first strophe (vv. 31–32) celebrates omnipotent grace; the second (vv. 33–34), vindicating grace; the third (vv. 35–37), overcoming grace in the face of physical dangers; and the final strophe (vv. 38–39) heralds victorious grace in the face of cosmic dangers. In tone and theme the section is strongly reminiscent of 5:1–11, though its hymnic language exceeds the former in grandeur. Grace is not an escape from this world and its dangers. Rather, grace stands before the yawning abyss and stark terror and confesses that they are no match for the invincible love of God. God's love cannot be defeated, nor will it let us go.

8:31–32 / At decisive stages in the epistle Paul sums up
the argument with a rhetorical question, **What, then, shall we say
in response to this** (v. 31; also 3:5; 4:1; 6:1; 7:7; 9:14, 30). This is
the most summary transition so far, concluding the argument at
least back to chapter 5, and perhaps back to the foundational 1:17,
"He who through faith is righteous shall live" (RSV). Paul hastens
now to conclude. No further diatribes, digressions, qualifica-
tions, typologies, or exacting expositions. The homestretch is before him, the tape is in sight, every effort and exertion must
purchase the only thing that matters—the essence of the gospel.
Its final articulation, like all great truths (though this is the truth
by which *all* truths will be measured), is disarmingly simple—
God is for us.

In many religions God is unknowable, indifferent to human need, and sometimes beyond good and evil. In others God
is largely a personified moral order. In still others God is a distant
and often impersonal first cause, a remote high god of endless
and lesser manifestations. In such religions "god" is largely an
abstraction capable of description only in varying degrees. But
Paul's God, the God revealed to Abraham and by Jesus, is qualitatively different. This God is both higher ("nor anything else in
all creation," v. 39), and nearer ("we cry, '*Abba*, Father,' " v. 15).
God is for us reverberates throughout the finale of Romans 8 (vv.
31, 32, 34). Here is another summary of the gospel in four words
(cf. 5:8), the most concise definition of grace in the Bible. **God is
for us** is not a conceptual statement of God's gracious disposition;
it is a historical statement testifying to God's *action* on our behalf.
The preposition, **for**, *hyper* in Greek, means "on behalf of," and
here expresses God's love in the vicarious sacrifice of his Son
Jesus. God **did not spare his own Son, but gave him up for us all**.
God is for us is a reality which is verified in the person of Jesus
Christ who died, was raised to life, and is now at the right hand
of God, and is interceding for us (v. 34).

It is easy to miss the significance of **God is for us**, seeing in
it some sort of vague benevolence, analogous perhaps to a con-
gressperson who is "for" his or her constituents, though none of
them may be known personally. Its meaning is appreciated only
when one realizes the extent to which God went to demonstrate
its truth. Recounting the stubbornness of humanity in chapter 1,
Paul three times said that "God gave them over" (Gk. *paradidōmi*)
to their "sinful desires" (1:24), "shameful lusts" (1:26), and "de-

praved mind" (1:28). Here in verse 32 he uses the same word for the sacrifice of Jesus: **He who did not spare his own Son but** *gave him up* (Gk. *paradidōmi*) **for us all**. God delivered his Son to the same depravity to which he consigned defiant humanity, *in order to redeem humanity.* "He was delivered over (Gk. *paradidōmi!*) to death for our sins" (4:25). "Christ died for the ungodly" (5:6). "God demonstrates his own love for us in this: While we were still sinners, Christ died for us" (5:8). God manifests his love not in a Japanese tea garden, but in the hammer blows of Skull Hill. The love of God *is* the cross of Jesus, a verdict on human sin and a vindication of God's righteousness. **God is for us** means "Christ died for us" (5:8).

To illustrate God's love Paul alludes to two OT images in verse 32. **He who did not spare his own Son** echoes Abraham's sacrifice of Isaac ("you . . . have not withheld your son, your only son," Gen. 22:16). The linguistic similarities between these two passages, particularly in the original languages, are unmistakable. Abraham's love for and sacrifice of his only son became a foreshadowing of God's sacrifice of his only Son—but with the significant difference that whereas Isaac was spared, Jesus was not!

The following phrase, God **gave him up for us all**, recalls the suffering servant of Isaiah 53 ("the Lord has laid on him the iniquity of us all," vv. 6, 11, 12). Isaiah 53 is the only passage in all the OT that speaks of vicarious human suffering. The scapegoat (Lev. 16:21–22), to be sure, relates vicarious suffering to animal sacrifice, and the lament psalms are replete with references to unjust human suffering. But nowhere except in Isaiah 53 are sins acquitted by the suffering of an innocent human ("by *his* wounds *we* are healed," Isa. 53:5). This is why Isaiah 53 plays such a significant role in the accounts of Jesus' passion, for only vicarious suffering discloses the meaning of the cross. The first part of verse 32 (**He who did not spare his own Son**) thus testifies to God's love. But that alone is not an adequate testimony to the cross, for the crucifixion is more than an expression of *agapē*. The full effect of the cross becomes clear only in the following statement, God **gave him up for us all**. The cross was the means by which Christ became a sin offering, "bore the sin of many" (Isa. 53:12), and reconciled sinners to God.

If the cross represents both God's love and Christ's atoning sacrifice, can God's favor be doubted? **How will he not also,**

along with him, graciously give us all things? (v. 32). The logic (as was also true of 5:9–10) is irrefutable: if God paid the highest price, why would he quibble about anything less? The cross is the assurance that God is for us in **all things** necessary for salvation both now and in the world to come.

8:33–34 / Grace is also the vindication of God's chosen. Verses 33–34 begin by asking, **Who** will bring a charge against believers? If the Almighty has declared them righteous, who can reopen the case against them? This thought echoes Isaiah 50:8–9, where God is proclaimed the vindicator of his servants. Perhaps Paul is thinking of Satan's accusing of God's elect (Job 1–2; Zech. 3:1ff.), but Satan is no match for Christ. True, believers are sinners, but Christ died for sinners; who then will be found to condemn them? Only God or Christ is left to condemn them, but God has pledged at the cost of the Son's life to preserve believers, not destroy them.

The nucleus of 8:31–39 is verse 34: **Christ Jesus . . . died . . . —was raised to life—is at the right hand of God and is also interceding for us**. This chain of statements was hammered out on the anvil of eternal providence. The one who **died** redeemed humankind from sin and judgment. The one who was **raised** guarantees victory over death and assurance of eternal life. The one who **is at the right hand of God** (a quotation from Psalm 110:1—a passage more frequently applied to Christ than any other OT passage!) attests that Jesus is the enthroned *Lord*, reigning in power and honor. And the one who **is interceding for us** repeats what was said of the Spirit (v. 27), that the enthroned Lord employs his might **on behalf of us**. "He always lives to intercede for [believers]" (Heb. 7:25; also 1 John 2:1). Every statement in the chain is spoken of Jesus Christ. Jesus assures us that God is for us, not only in his sacrificial love on the cross, but even now in his sustaining love as resurrected Lord.

In referring to believers as **those whom God has chosen**, Paul transfers the name and honor of Israel to the church (1 Chron. 16:13; Ps. 105:6, 43). This is highly significant, for in speaking of the church as the **chosen** or "elect" (16:13; Col. 3:12) NT writers were testifying that the church of Jesus Christ, like Israel, was "called according to [God's] purpose" (v. 28). The church is not a stop gap remedy when God's earlier plan with Israel went awry, but the culmination of salvation history.

8:35–37 / Now to the third part of this concluding doxology. **Who shall separate us from the love of Christ? Shall trouble or hardship or persecution or famine or nakedness or danger or sword?** Each noun refers to dangers to faith from physical adversities. The list shares much in common with Job's adversities in the OT, but still more in common with Paul's hardships as recorded in 2 Corinthians 11:23–29. These terms likely stem from Paul's recent and painful memory. Apart from two notes they need no explanation. The word for **persecution**, *diōgmos*, refers primarily to *religious* persecution in early Christian literature. And **sword**, which more likely refers to execution than to war, is a fitting final term, for the sword is the one peril that no one can survive. In Paul's case it takes on added significance if, as tradition records, he perished by the sword in the city to which this epistle was addressed.

Paul's concern in verses 35–37 is not to argue theodicy, i.e., why suffering exists in a world made by a good and omnipotent creator. His concern is less theoretical and more practical, for within a decade of Paul's writing to Rome believers would have to undergo Nero's horrors. How can Christians consider themselves saved and yet continue to suffer misfortune? Does that not deny their salvation, or God's existence, or both? It is an ancient problem. Jewish rabbis agreed that adversity has always been the lot of those who dedicate themselves to God. This is the point of quoting Psalm 44:22 in verse 36. The psalm does not refer to misfortune, but to persecution which arises *because of* faith: **"For your** (God's) **sake we face death all day long."** This psalm was applied to martyrs in Israel during the Maccabean persecutions (2nd cent. B.C., 2 Macc. 7; 4 Macc. 13) and under Hadrian's persecutions (early second century A.D.). Violent death has always been the lot of the faithful. More mystifying yet, the Psalm testifies that our daily dying is *for God's sake*, which means that such suffering is a sign not of failure but of God's will.

Come what may, answers Paul, no adversity **shall separate us from the love of Christ**. Victory takes place through suffering, not apart from it. Our tribulations and sufferings serve God's purpose when they are surrendered to him (**For your sake**). **We are more than conquerors through him who loved us** (v. 37). **More than conquerors**, itself a militant expression, means that God works through harsh realities (v. 28), and the present tense in Greek means that he does not do so once (in a while) but always. The victory comes not by escaping suffering, nor even in courage in the face of suffering, but in God's love in the midst of suffering. If human works cannot earn salvation, then neither can the human will sustain faith during persecution. It is not our hold on Christ which sees us through, but his hold on us. The victory is God's love "that will not let me go"—in life or death.

8:38–39 / The physical threats to faith in verse 35 are now heightened to cosmic and supernatural powers which are paired in global antitheses: **death / life, angels / demons, present / future, height / depth**; only **powers** and **creation** disrupt the contrasting parallelism (see 1 Cor. 3:22). It may be possible, as Bengel thought, to relate the list to verse 34:

Neither **death** shall hurt us,	for Christ died;
nor **life**,	Christ was raised to life;
nor **angels, nor demons,**	Christ is at the right
nor the present nor future	hand of God;
nor **powers, nor height**	Christ is interceding
nor depth, nor anything else	for us.
in all creation (*Gnomon*, vol. 3, p. 114).	

Paul believed that there were both malevolent and benevolent powers at work in the universe. He begins with **death** perhaps because he ended with the "sword" in verse 35. Nor can the seductive impulses of **life** inhibit God's love. **Angels, demons,** and **powers** refer to orders of superhuman beings. **Height** and **depth** are astrological terms denoting a star's closest or farthest point from its zenith, and hence personified sidereal powers.

But as the dangers heighten, so does the apostle's confidence in God's love, transporting him to an ecstatic doxology. **I am convinced** (a perfect passive indicative in Greek) means an utterly unshakable conviction based on past experience. The source of confidence is the career of Christ summarized in verse 34: our hope began at Christ's victory at Calvary and is as invincible as Christ's reign in heaven.

These powers, however mysterious and menacing, cannot overwhelm God's love. The cross of Christ was the decisive defeat of all mutinous authorities (Col. 2:15; Eph. 1:21; 1 Pet. 3:22). Though the universe is bent in hostile and savage rebellion, Paul asseverates that nothing **in all creation will be able to separate us from the love of God that is in Christ Jesus our Lord**. In this chapter, as we have seen from chapter 5 onward, the lordship of Jesus Christ is the final word (5:21; 6:23; 7:25; 8:39)! "I have told you these things, so that in me you may have peace. In the world you will have trouble. But take heart! I have overcome the world" (John 16:33).

Additional Notes   §20

8:35–37 /   The role which Psalm 44:22 played in Jewish martyrology can be seen in Str-B, vol. 3, pp. 258–60.

Gaugler is correct in observing that Paul is not attempting to justify God's love in the face of evil, but that he celebrates the triumph of God's love over evil (*Der Römerbrief*, vol. 1, pp. 351ff.).

§21   The Election of Israel (Rom. 9:1–13)

What remains of God's promises to the Jews now that the Messiah has come and the Jews from whom and for whom he came have, for the most part, failed to recognize him? That is the theme of Romans 9–11. Finding the exact term to describe Paul's discussion of the theme is somewhat difficult. On the one hand, Romans 9–11 is more or less an excursus complete in itself. The beginning declaration (9:1) and the concluding doxology (11:33–36) delimit it clearly from the remainder of the epistle. The chapters are thematically coherent, with an uncharacteristic reliance on quotation (thirty percent of 9–11 is quoted from the OT, of which forty percent comes from Isaiah). The numerous studies and monographs devoted to Romans 9–11 further evince a history of interpretation unique to itself.

On the other hand, the question of Israel's salvation flows out of the argumentation of Romans 1–8 and is demanded by it. Earlier themes are reemployed and applied to the question: e.g., Jews and Gentiles (1:16–17 / 11:1–32), ethnic versus spiritual Israel (2:28–29 / 9:6), the advantage of Israel (3:1ff. / 9:4–5), salvation for all (3:21–26 / 10:5–13), God's faithfulness (8:31–39 / 11:25–32), and doxologies (8:38–39 / 11:33–36). These chapters are therefore an excursus not in the sense of a digression from the theme of the epistle, but as a development of it. Romans 9–11 is therefore *a thematic focus of the righteousness of God applied specifically to Israel's enduring place in salvation history.*

With typical Johannine simplicity the Fourth Gospel notes the same problem addressed in these chapters: "He came to that which was his own, but his own did not receive him" (1:11). The problem, as Paul develops it, can be elaborated in a series of questions: Why did God's chosen people reject the Messiah, and, having done so, what further role do they play in God's plan? What is the relationship between the old and new covenants, and between Israel and the church? If Israel has rejected its calling, has God rejected Israel? Does Israel's rejection of God's Messiah thwart God's providence and Israel's election? These questions determine Romans 9–11.

With "great sorrow and unceasing anguish" (9:2) Paul enters the fray. Will the God who proved faithful to errant sinners be found equally faithful to an errant *nation*? Does the grace involved in justification by faith apply also to salvation *history* and Israel's place in it? To this end Paul develops the argument in three stages. Chapter 9 vindicates God's freedom and mercy in the face of Israel's stubbornness. Chapter 10 demonstrates that even though Israel is chosen by God, Israel is free to reject God's overtures—and is responsible for its exclusion from salvation when it does. In chapter 11 Paul argues that Israel's rejection does not frustrate God's sovereign purpose, but that God uses it for the inclusion of the Gentiles—and ultimately of Israel itself!—in salvation.

Paul was a Jew, and he remained one all his life. He was deeply distressed by the fact that those who had been the recipients of God's promises had failed to inherit them. Important as this was, however, the "Jewish question" was for Paul but a test case of a larger problem. In the face of human rejection, does God renege on his promises? Does the rejection of the Messiah relieve God of fulfilling his promises to the Jews? This theological problem was not merely of historical interest to Paul the Jew, but of existential interest to Paul the Christian. For, if God cancels his promises to Jews because of their hardness, under similar circumstances might God cancel his promises to Christians in the gospel? Paul does not fully resolve the problem, but he concludes that God's choices are not provisional, but sovereign and eternal, sealed by his invincible faithfulness and guided by his mercy.

9:1–5 / The chapter opens with the seriousness of a court proceeding. The gravity of the matter and Paul's authority are underscored by a chain of assertions: **I speak the truth in Christ—I am not lying, my conscience confirms it in the Holy Spirit** (v. 1). This is not simply an introductory formality. It is a declaration which involves Paul deeply in its outcome, in **great sorrow and unceasing anguish of heart**. He does not formally define the cause of his distress, but verse 3 reveals his torment over the failure of his people to receive Christ. One might expect the Apostle to the Gentiles to distance himself from his unbelieving Jewish kinsfolk, but he does nothing of the sort, referring to them

rather as **my brothers** and **my own race**. So inseverable is Paul
from his fellow Israelites that he would be willing to forfeit his
own salvation if it would gain theirs: **I could wish that I myself
were cursed and cut off from Christ for the sake of** Israel.

To anyone familiar with the Pauline formula "in Christ"
(some 70 instances in his epistles, including the Pastorals), it is
startling to hear the apostle speak of wishing to be **cut off** *from*
Christ! The ultimate price anyone can pay is life itself, a price
which Paul prominently volunteers: **I could wish that** *I myself*
were cursed. Following Israel's debacle with the golden calf, Moses
prayed that God would "forgive their sin—but if not, then blot
me out of the book you have written" (Exod. 32:32). The Greek
word for **cursed**, *anathema*, derives from the Hebrew *ḥērem*, which
means a sacrifice (whether of an animal or heathen people) devoted to the Lord for total destruction (Lev. 27:28ff.; Deut 7:26;
Josh 6:17). Nothing was more dreaded for a Jew than banishment
from the elect community of Israel. For Paul separation from
Christ was worse than banishment because it meant separation
from eternal salvation. The idea reveals the extent to which Paul
thought "messianically." Had not Jesus himself become accursed
for the sake of Israel's salvation (Gal. 3:13; 2 Cor. 5:21)? The Greek
preposition *hyper*, translated **for the sake of** in verse 3, is the same
word Paul used throughout 8:31–39 for God's sacrificial love *on
behalf of* believers. Paul's sorrow over Israel's rejection of the
Messiah, combined with his willingness to take Israel's curse upon
himself if it would gain Israel's salvation, could hardly bespeak a
more earnest sacrifice (cf. 2 Cor. 12:15)—especially since he has
just asserted that nothing "in all creation will be able to separate
us from the love of God that is in Christ Jesus our Lord" (8:39).

From a Jewish perspective, Israel was preeminent among
the nations. The name "Israelites" (NIV, **the people of Israel**, v. 4)
derives from Jacob, the patriarch who wrestled with God and
prevailed (Gen. 32:28). It means the elect, covenant people of
God (Isa. 43:1). Who else could claim **adoption as sons** (Exod.
4:22; Jer. 31:9; Hos. 11:1)? What other people had beheld **the
divine glory**, the very presence of God in theophanies (Exod.
3:2ff.; 24:10), in the desert (Exod. 13:21–22), in the temple (1 Kings
8:29; Ps. 11:4), and in the ark of the covenant (1 Sam. 4:4; 2 Sam.
6:2)? With what other nation had God entered into **covenants**,
first with Abraham (Gen. 15:17f.), later with Israel at Mount Sinai
(Exod. 19:5) and on the plains of Moab (Deut. 29:1) and in the

promised land (Josh. 8:30f.), and finally with David (2 Sam. 7:21ff.)? What people could boast of **receiving . . . the law**, the Torah, Israel's crown and eternal instruction? Was not **temple worship** ordained and pleasing to God (2 Chron. 7:11ff.; Ps. 11:1)? Did not God make **promises** to the **patriarchs**, to Abraham (Gen. 12:7), Isaac (Gen. 26:3ff.), Jacob (Gen. 28:13ff.), and David (2 Sam. 7:12)? Not surprisingly, Israel's crowning hope was the advent of the **Christ**, the final deliverer of the ages. Truly, "salvation is from the Jews" (John 4:22). And why does Paul rehearse this glorious heritage? To magnify the mystery that Israel, who had been arrayed so divinely, had in the end rejected its crown!

9:6–9 / Verse 6 is the crux of Paul's argument. Israel (for the most part) has failed to receive the Messiah, but **it is not as though God's word had failed**. Significantly, the phrasing primarily emphasizes God's purposes, not Israel's failure. Moreover, Israel's failure to fulfill its calling does not annul God's word and sovereignty (3:3–4). God's sovereignty remains operative through a principle of two Israels: **For not all who are descended from Israel are Israel**. The first Israel (**all who are descended from Israel**) refers to ethnic Israel, whereas the second refers to Israel that received the gospel, the "Israel of God," according to Galatians 6:16. Herein lie the seeds of the idea of the remnant, a true Israel within nominal Israel, which will be developed in chapter 11.

Paul defends the principle of an Israel within Israel by arguing that God made limiting choices among Abraham's various descendants. Thus, as every Jew knew, Abraham was the father of many descendants, including Ishmael (Gen. 16:15) and the sons of Keturah (Gen. 25:1ff.), but God chose to fulfill his plan of salvation only through Isaac (Gen. 17:20–21). In the language of verses 7–8, the former were **descendants** of Abraham, or **natural children**, but only Isaac and his line were **God's children**, or **children of the promise**. Obviously, what constitutes Israel is not biological generation, but the supernatural endowment of God's promise. This is the point of verse 9, where Isaac's conception and birth are foretold again during a visit from three divine messengers (Gen. 18:10–14). All of this is the result of divine decree. Abraham's wider descendants were not rejected for any failure, nor was Isaac chosen for any virtue; both choices and their consequences lay in the sovereign will of God. What role, if any, Ishmael, for example, played in God's broader economy we do not know, although we are told that God blessed and cared for him (Gen. 16:10–14; 17:20; 21:13–21). The salvific line as the line of promise, however, remained with Isaac.

9:10–13 / It might be asserted that God chose Isaac because he was the first (and only) legitimate son of Abraham and Sarah, Abraham's other children being born of mistresses or second wives. This argument was in fact advanced by those Jews who believed they were heirs of the promise because of physical descent. But God's way was less calculable, as the case of Esau and Jacob proved. Both were twins of Rebekah, yet while they were still in the womb and before they **had done anything good or bad**, God rejected the **older** Esau (the obvious choice) and chose the **younger** Jacob. If God chose Jacob before he demonstrated any worthiness, then certainly God's election was **not by works but by him who calls**. Israel's election is the result, therefore, of the eternal decree of God, not of its merit. Jacob became Israel, the people of God, not because of deserving works but because of a divine resolution as merciful as it was unsearchable; and Esau became Edom, a people of the earth like any other, not because of failure but because of the same inscrutable will of God. Luther correctly saw here the same gracious will operative in justification by faith: "Hence, it follows irrefutably: one does not become a son of God and an heir of the promise by descent but by the gracious election of God" (*Lectures on Romans*, p. 266).

The heart of the matter is **that God's purpose in election might stand**. The crucial word, **purpose**, *prothesis*, appeared in 8:28 concerning those "who have been called according to his purpose." There, as here, it is shrouded in ineffability. But what God had ordained before creation he executed in history. The reason God chooses Jacob and rejects Esau is not because God is arbitrary or unjust, but because God wills for his eternal purpose to **stand**. The Greek word for **stand**, *menē*, means "to remain or endure," thus relieving any anxiety from verse 6 that God's word might have failed. If God's purpose is not ours, neither are his ways and reasons ours. " 'For my thoughts are not your thoughts, neither are your ways my ways,' declares the Lord" (Isa. 55:8). The mystery of God's purpose is not cause for anxiety or terror, however, but for confidence, because "God is for us" (8:31ff.). Following the exodus, Israel concluded that God had elected it for a purpose (Deut. 7:6; Ps. 135:4; Isa. 41:8–9), but the only reason Israel could discover for that purpose was God's unmerited love (Deut. 7:8; 10:15; Isa. 44:21–22). Not because Israel was more numerous or powerful did God choose it, but simply because he loved Israel, although it was the *least* of the nations.

At this point we find ourselves in a maelstrom of theories "Of Providence, Foreknowledge, Will, and Fate, Fixt Fate, free will, foreknowledge absolute," as Milton put it (*PL*, 2.559–60). The idea of predestination has always had an unfair ring to it, and particularly the idea of double predestination, which teaches that before the foundation of the world God determined who would be saved and who would be damned. With regard to the latter doctrine it must be said, at least from a NT perspective, that double predestination is not as compelling *theologically* as it may appear *logically*. At root, predestination is simply God's way of assuring that his gracious will in restoring creation to glory does not fail, i.e., **that God's purpose in election might stand**. In the present context Paul is not discussing the eternal salvation of individuals, but God's purposeful choices in history from Abraham to Christ. The question is how God separated the thread of Israel, through which he would fulfill his promises, from the fabric of all the nations. It was to that end that God chose Jacob and rejected Esau. The intent is functional rather than eschatological. The question is *how* God operates in history rather than *what* is the final fate of individuals or nations.

Predestination as it is here understood is a doctrine presupposed throughout Scripture, although (apart from Rom. 9 and Eph. 1) seldom discussed. When Deuteronomy speaks of the choosing of Israel, or when John's Gospel tells of the sending of the Son, or when Paul relates the plan of redemption, the fundamental issue is God's free and sovereign engagement for saving his people, which is predestination. The idea is presented from a positive perspective (and only from this perspective), that in Jesus Christ God is for the world, electing believers in grace and equipping them by the Spirit for his saving purposes in the world. God's choices within history—of Jacob over Esau, or Moses over Pharaoh, or Gentiles over Jews (ch. 11)—are interim choices to serve his salvific ends. They are not presented as final choices. The eternal destiny of all things lies solely with God, who is perfect love and perfect justice. As a means of salvation, predestination has an inclusive "ripple-effect": like a stone thrown into a pool, God intervenes at a point in history (e.g., the call of Abraham) and extends the effects of his intervention outward in ever-widening circles. "God our savior . . . wants all men to be saved and to come to a knowledge of the truth" (1 Tim. 2:3–4). "For God so loved the world that he gave his one and only Son, that whoever believes in him shall not perish but have eternal life" (John 3:16).

If verse 13 has an antagonistic ring (**"Jacob I loved, but Esau I hated"**), it must be understood that the statement arose from centuries of antipathy between Israel (Jacob) and Edom (Esau). The source from which it is quoted makes this clear (Mal. 1:2–5; also Gen. 36:1). In the present context it simply attests to God's unfettered, unconditional election of Israel and rejection of Edom in history. It says nothing about the salvation or damnation of individuals in the respective groups. Although Edom as a *nation* was rejected, *Edomites* were beyond neither Israel's compassion nor God's (e.g., "Do not abhor an Edomite, for he is your brother," Deut. 23:7). If at one point in history God rejects Edom and chooses Israel, and at another point rejects Israel and chooses the Gentiles, then both choices originate in his inscrutable wisdom and promote his salvific will. Moreover, if God wills to regraft the severed branch of Israel back onto the stock of his saving purpose (11:17–27), then we ought not dismiss the possibility that God has cards in his hand with regard to the Edoms of the world which he has not yet played.

Additional Notes §21

9:1–5 / Paul's **wish that I myself were cursed and cut off from Christ for the sake of my brothers** reflects the idea of vicarious suffering, which was discussed at 8:31–32. The thought that the voluntary innocent suffering of one person could expiate the sins of others had gained currency in synagogue thinking by Paul's day. See Str-B, vol. 2, pp. 275–79; and vol. 3, p. 261.

The punctuation of verse 5 is a minefield in NT scholarship. Early Greek manuscripts were without systematic punctuation, which necessitated the supplying of punctuation appropriate to the meaning by later editors and translators. If a comma is placed after Christ, then the following doxology (**God over all, forever praised!**) refers to Christ and ascribes deity to him. This is the way the NIV punctuates the text. If, on the other hand, one places a full stop (period or semicolon) after Christ, the ensuing doxology refers to God (a reading presented in a footnote in the NIV). The chief argument against the first reading (i.e., that the doxology refers to Christ) is that nowhere in his undisputed epistles does Paul explicitly call Christ God, and that doing so would have been nearly unthinkable in Jewish monotheism. Nevertheless, Paul comes close to calling Christ God elsewhere (2 Cor. 4:4; Col. 1:15; 2 Thess. 1:12; Phil 2:6 "equality with God"). The syntax of the sentence also favors the first reading, whereas ascribing the doxology to God abruptly introduces a new subject. Moreover, had Paul desired to ascribe blessing to God and not to Christ, he should have placed **praised** *before* God rather than after it, as was always customary in Jewish doxologies. However compelling one regards the argument that Paul nowhere explicitly calls Christ God, grammatical, syntactical, and thematic reasons seem to argue that he did so here; and if so, Romans 9:5 is one of the clearest references to the deity of Jesus Christ in the NT (see Titus 2:13). Complete discussions of the problem are presented by Metzger, *TCGNT*, pp. 520–23; Michel, *Der Brief an die Römer*, pp. 228–29; Cranfield, *Romans*, vol. 2, pp. 464–70; Dunn, *Romans 9–16*, pp. 528–29.

9:6–9 / For many Jews physical descent from Abraham and circumcision were sufficient to assure salvation, to which Paul countered in 2:28–29 that "outward" Jewishness must be confirmed by "inward" Jewishness or "circumcision of the heart." He maintains a similar distinction in 4:14–16 in speaking of Abraham's offspring "of the law" versus offspring "of faith." For Paul, redeemed Israel could never be a matter of race or biology, for then it would be other than God's doing; true Israel is the result of receiving the divine promise and election by grace. This distinction was not entirely foreign to Israel. The difference between nominal Jews and true Jews was a matter of occasional debate in Judaism, true Jews being those who were faithful and obedient to God's will. This answer, however, was untenable for Paul, because "those who were faithful and obedient to God" lays the responsibility of salvation on the shoulders of human merit, thus denying grace. *Grace* as received by faith is the sole condition of individual justification *and* of God's sovereign will in history.

This section continues the theme begun in 9:6, in which Paul defends God's historical choices leading from Abraham to the establishment of a church consisting of Jews and Gentiles. On the one hand, God blessed Israel immeasurably as the chosen people (9:4–5), but Israel resisted or became hardened to God's final overture in Jesus the Messiah (9:32; 11:7), thus placing itself under wrath and outside salvation. The problem is summarized in 11:28: "As far as the gospel is concerned, they are enemies on your account; but as far as election is concerned, they are loved on account of the patriarchs." The logical mind asks, Is Israel's hardening the *cause* of God's rejection, or the *result* of it? That is, has God rejected Israel because of its unbelief, or has Israel been unable to believe because God rejected it? Many theologians have put the question this way, and as tempting as it may be to do so, it runs the risk of channeling the river of providence into a straight and shallow sluiceway of theory. What is logical is not always theological.

The error of the first option is apparent from verse 6: "It is not as though God's word had failed." The creator is not determined by the creation any more than a potter is determined by a pot (9:20–21). God's will achieves its purpose despite sin, adversity, and rebelliousness, even from elect Israel. The second position is equally erroneous. If it were true that Israel *could not* believe because God blinded it, why would Paul struggle so vehemently with Israel's unbelief (9:1–5; 10:1–3), thereby calling into question the eternal decree of God and violating the principle of 9:20, "Who are you, O man, to talk back to God?" In reality the discussion of Romans 9–11 is more nuanced and subtle, however. Sometimes Paul implies that God predestined Israel to unbelief (11:7–10) and other times that Israel is responsible for its unbelief (9:32). In contrast to many interpreters who regard the dilemma of Romans 9–11 from the side *either* of predeterminism *or* of Israel's failure, Paul preserves a *tension* between the two, similar to the tension which Exodus preserves regarding Pharaoh's hardness of heart. The tension, in fact, is the very tension of faith, which is both a divine gift and a human response. At present divine providence and human free will look like two rails of a train track which will never meet. There is, however, a point in the distance beyond human knowing where they converge, in God's "unsearchable judgments" and "inscrutable ways" (11:33, RSV). To speak otherwise on such matters is to confess with Job, "Surely I spoke of things I did not understand, things too wonderful for me to know" (Job 42:3).

9:14–18 / The rhetorical defense in verses 14ff. is not of God's nature or attributes, but of his sovereign acts, and the diatribe style again is employed to that end. Does not Scripture suggest an arbitrary and capricious God when it says " 'Jacob I loved but Esau I hated' " (v. 13)? Anticipating the challenge to God's righteousness, Paul asks rhetorically, **Is God unjust?** (v. 14). He vigorously denies the charge (Gk. *mē genoito*) and counters with a quotation from Exodus 33:19, "I will have mercy on whom I have mercy, and I will have compassion on whom I have compassion." A Targum to this verse reads, "I will spare whomever is worthy of being spared, and I will have mercy on whomever is worthy of being pitied." The idea of worthiness is exactly what Paul does *not* want to suggest. God chose Abraham before the Torah had been revealed; God chose Jacob over Esau before either had merited or forfeited the blessing; God revealed his Son to Paul while he was still a persecutor of the church; God justifies persons by grace through faith while they are still sinners (5:8) and apart from works of the law. In saying that he will have mercy on whom he will have mercy, God is not, like a mad dictator, saying he can do whatever he pleases. It is rather a promise that in his behavior towards humanity God will be true to his character of love and justice. God's character guarantees his actions. **I will have mercy on whom I have mercy** is simply the experiential form of "I am who I am" (Exod. 3:14).

We can hear the pious rejoinder of Jews—and of all morally upright peoples—in verse 16. Does **man's desire and effort** then count for nothing? The term, **effort**, is literally "running" (Gk. *trechein*), suggesting the devotion of an athlete in training and competition. **Desire** and **effort** were in fact very much part of

Paul's commitment to Christ (Phil. 3:12–16), but they had nothing to do with his (or Israel's) choosing by God. Human effort is a necessary response of gratitude and commitment to God for his grace in Jesus Christ, but it neither merits nor maintains grace. With regard to election God remains totally free, not to employ arbitrary (or worse, malevolent) designs, but to express **mercy**.

It is, then, God's freedom and mercy which Paul advocates in these verses. God's superior power, his ability to execute what he desires, is, of course, everywhere acknowledged. Our fear, however, is that God will use his power arbitrarily and without regard to his subjects, or even against them. Everyone agrees that God is free; but is he just? Here, as elsewhere in Romans 9–11, Paul takes a surprising tack, for he does not defend God's justice but champions his mercy. A God determined by justice would have to deliver the world to wrath and punishment because of its greed and lust and war. But a God whose nature is love is free to make the dictates of justice penultimate to those of compassion.

But what is the relation between God's mercy and his judgments? That is the issue of verses 17–18. That Paul connects a verse on judgment (v. 17) to a verse on mercy (v. 16) with **for** (which normally defines a causal relationship) reveals how closely judgment and mercy (which ordinarily are deemed contradictory) are in his mind. The quotation of verse 17 comes from Exodus 9:16. The case of Pharaoh poses a knotty problem because the hardening of his heart is sometimes attributed to God (Exod. 4:21; 7:3; 9:12; 10:1, 20; 11:10) and sometimes to Pharaoh himself (Exod. 7:14, 22; 8:15, 19, 32; 9:7, 35; 13:15). Thus, the same tension is maintained in Pharaoh's case which Paul maintains with regard to the Jews. Pharaoh freely chooses what God ordains. The Book of Exodus is clear that in his hardening Pharaoh pits himself not against Moses but against God, and that God uses Pharaoh's hardness in order to demonstrate his glory! The effect of Pharaoh's hostility, in other words, accomplishes the *opposite* of its intent, for it results in the liberation of the Israelites. Pharaoh's hardening thus not only benefits those whom it was intended to harm (the Jews), but it ultimately works to the advantage of his own descendants, for it initiates a process of redemption which will include Gentiles. Thus, through Pharaoh's resistance God's **power** and **name** are **proclaimed in all the earth**.

Verse 18 repeats and intensifies the idea of verse 13, **God has mercy on whom he wants to have mercy, and he hardens**

whom he wants to harden. The terminology obviously derives from the hardening of Pharaoh's heart. Like verse 13, this verse has an unfair ring to it, but also like verse 13, it conveys a functional rather than eschatological sense, i.e., it is an interim, penultimate, causal judgment, not necessarily an ultimate judgment. Not that we have any interest in defending Pharaoh; he was a cruel and oppressive ruler. Nevertheless, the subject remains one of redemption and not damnation. If God used Pharaoh's obdurateness to save the Jews, God now uses the obdurateness of the Jews to save the Gentiles. God imprisons sinners within their own refusal in order to provoke them to repentance (1:24, 26, 28; 2:4). Throughout salvation history, God has often employed severe immediate measures in order to serve gracious ends: "God has bound all men over to disobedience so that he may have mercy on them all" (11:32).

9:19–21 / The diatribe style continues in verse 19 with Paul countering in the words of an imaginary objector: If God pities some and hardens others, who can be blamed? In resisting **his will** is not one only acting out a role predetermined by God? And if this be the case, how can one be held morally accountable? This echoes the refrain of 3:7, "Someone might argue, 'If my falsehood enhances God's truthfulness and so increases his glory, why am I still condemned as a sinner?' " A careful reading of verses 19ff. erects a roadblock, or perhaps a detour, to an understanding of the prevailing thought here as a reference to the final salvation or damnation of individuals, for these verses steer away from that issue. Rather, the apostle already has his eye set on verse 24, that God has **called** (also v. 12) a new society **not only from the Jews but also from the Gentiles**. The subject continues to be the purposes of God from the call of Abraham to the establishment of the church, thus conveying a functional understanding of predestination.

Neither in Paul's day nor since, of course, has eschatological determinism lacked proponents. A Targum on Daniel 4:32 reads, "All the inhabitants of earth are regarded as nothing; God deals with the host of heaven and the inhabitants of earth alike according to his will, and there is no one who can resist his hand by saying, 'What are you doing?' " (Str-B, vol. 3, pp. 269–70; see also Wisd. of Sol. 11:21; 12:12). In a similar vein the Dead Sea Scrolls record, "Before things came into existence [God] determined the plan of them; and when they fill their appointed roles, it is in accordance with His glorious design that they discharge their functions. Nothing can be changed. In His hand lies the government of all things" (1QS 3.15–16; see also 1QH 15.14–20).

Paul asks similarly, **who resists God's will?** and follows with an illustration of a potter throwing a pot (vv. 20–21). Dodd finds it "the weakest point in the whole epistle," maintaining that a person is not a pot but a responsible moral agent (*Romans*, pp. 158–59). But this is to press the illustration too far. Calvin is right that the limitedness of human understanding cannot fathom the divine purpose, and errs when it tries to do so. There is a "madness in the human mind," says the Reformer, which is more ready "to charge God with unrighteousness than to blame itself for blindness" (*Romans*, p. 354). Paul is not here constructing a theodicy in an attempt to justify the ways of God. A theodicy puts humanity and its questions at the center, whereas Paul maintains the focus on God's sovereign purposes.

Who are you, O man, to talk back to God? The address, **O man**, is more than dramatic flair; it is surely a reminder of the wide chasm which separates humanity from God. There is indeed a "madness in the human mind" which presumes to fathom God's every purpose and which calls him to account when it cannot. That is the point of the potter illustration, which was well-known in Judaism (Isa. 29:16; 45:9; Wisd. of Sol. 12:12). A potter makes vessels for various purposes. God likewise ordains times and events and peoples for purposes of his choosing, some **for noble purposes and some for common use.** Even if those purposes are not apparent, that is no reason to doubt that God's righteousness and holy love are also operative in them. It would be an odd potter who made vessels simply to destroy them.

We ought to be clearer on one point than are many of the commentators. This passage might be interpreted to mean that if God is almighty, no finite creature dare question his judgments. But that is to transpose an ethics of "might makes right" onto God. Egoistic ethics are involved in either case, resulting in tyranny on earth and fate in heaven. Right is not right because God does it; rather, God does it *because* it is right. God's righteous will, as revealed in the Ten Commandments and in the rules of fairness and justice associated with them, is ultimate, and not even God can transcend it. The devil can lie; God cannot (and still be God). There is a moral order in creation only because there is a corresponding moral order in the Creator. This passage does not depict or defend a cosmic bully. God is perfect love and perfect justice, at the same time and forever, with which his creative freedom coincides perfectly.

9:22–24 / Verses 22–23 are difficult and ambiguous in Greek, leaving Paul's thought uncompleted. One interpretation is that God demonstrated his wrath by bringing vessels of wrath to destruction, and that he demonstrated his glory by showing mercy to those vessels ordained for glory. This is a justifiable rendering, which, if adopted, conceivably argues for double predestination. It would be, as Käsemann says, "an eschatological equivalent of verse 17" (*Romans*, p. 270).

Despite the fact that some of Paul's contemporaries from the rabbis and Qumran can be found in support of such thinking, it is not clear that this is Paul's meaning. Verses 22–23 are obviously predestinarian, but, as in verse 17 which they repeat, the accent falls on God's power and glory, and especially on his compassion ([bearing] **with great patience the objects of his wrath**). The NIV (which itself is not altogether clear) tries to bring this out in the form of a question. The gist is that although God desired to demonstrate his wrath against objects prepared for destruction (the Greek is unclear whether God prepared them or they prepared themselves), he restrained himself with patience in order to show mercy to the objects of his mercy. The ambiguity and incompleteness inherent in verses 22–23 are further complicated by a difficult textual variant (see Additional Notes). Both verses at any rate funnel into verse 24, which clearly celebrates God's calling of Jews and Gentiles in the gospel. Since verse 24 stresses the realization of God's will in history rather than at the end of time, it is again reasonable to conclude that the intent of verses 22–23 is functional as opposed to eschatological. It is predestination directed to soteriology; i.e., eternal election effected in historical calling. **Objects of wrath** and **objects of mercy** are alike instruments of God's saving work in history.

It would be incorrect to conclude that **objects of wrath** and **objects of mercy** (vv. 22–23) refer to Jews and Gentiles respectively, for in verse 24 the church is comprised of both (cf. 1:16–17). Like a shaft of light, the call of grace pierces the remotest corners of society. The first person plural pronoun is thrust prominently to the beginning of verse 24 in both Greek and the NIV, emphasizing that the new community consists of *us*, both Jews and Gentiles. The church is not a Jewish society or a Gentile society, but Christ's society. It is not an accident of history or a result of social evolution. The church exists because God **called** it, and it bears witness always and everywhere to his prevenient grace (8:28–30).

Despite the antithesis between **destruction** and **glory** (vv. 22–23), there is a distinct bias toward God's grace and mercy in verses 22–29. Even vessels of wrath prepared for destruction are borne with much patience (v. 22)! Wrath is subservient to mercy throughout Romans 9–11. Again, "God has bound all men over to disobedience so that he may have mercy on them all" (11:32). Although Israel deserves destruction, it will not be destroyed. At present unbelieving Israel is "hardened," as was Pharaoh, but the hardening is temporary in order to permit Gentiles access to the gospel. That Israel was chosen in the first place was a matter of sheer mercy; it should come as no surprise, least of all to Israel, that through its hardening God again extends his call to the nations. Ultimately, hopes Paul, Israel's hardening will lead to repentance (2:4) and salvation (11:26). The final result will be to the benefit of Jews and Gentiles.

9:25–29 / Verses 25–29 adduce three passages from the OT as proof texts that the church, by God's plan, consists of Jews and Gentiles. The quotation in verses 25–26 comes from Hosea 2:23 and 1:10. A Targum on this text reads, "I (God) will love the unloved because of their works" (Str-B, vol. 3, p. 273). Paul, by contrast, says that the Gentiles, like the Jews, belong to the covenant not by works but by grace. In its original context Hosea applied the saying to the Israelites who had forsaken the kingdom of God for the affluent and indulgent northern kingdom of Jeroboam II. But, with no little audacity, Paul applies it here to the Gentiles! A Jewish apocalypse a generation later would scorn the Gentiles: "O Lord, you have said it was for us (Jews) that you created the world. As for the other nations (Gentiles) which have descended from Adam, you have said that they are nothing, and that they are like spittle, and you have compared their abundance to a drop from a bucket" (4 Ezra 6:55; Charlesworth, *OTP*, vol. 1, p. 536). In applying the Hosea prophecy to the Gentiles, however, Paul affirms that they too are heirs of the promises to Israel.

The two quotations in verses 27–29 come from Isaiah 10:22–23 (and Hos. 1:10) and 1:9. The themes of *calling* and *people* predominate, bearing witness that Israel's existence depends not on itself but on God. It is God's call which constitutes Israel as God's people (9:8). The effect of both quotations is that a remnant, and not all Israel, will be saved. The quotation in verse 28 is somewhat problematic. The original Greek (lit., "The Lord completes and cuts short his word on earth") is rendered ambiguously by the NIV, **the Lord will carry out his sentence on earth with speed and finality.** Paul evidently means that God currently accomplishes his purpose through a diminished Israel. But even a remnant in Israel is a testimony to God's grace. Had God not had mercy on a remnant, Israel **"would have become like Sodom . . . and Gomorrah."** The plight of most damnable societies in the OT, in other words, would be the fate of Israel were it not for God's grace. Thus, both the inclusion of Gentiles in salvation and the preservation of a Jewish remnant testify to the grace of God.

The OT prophets developed the idea of a saved portion of Israel within the larger nation (Isa. 4:3; 10:22–23; 46:3; 65:8; Amos 3:12; Mic. 2:12; 5:7). Thus began the doctrine of the *remnant*. Paul appeals to the same idea with regard to the Jewish response to the gospel: only a few would respond, as was foretold in Scripture (so 9:6). The present believing remnant, however, is not the last chapter. Paul's continuing burden for the Jews (9:1–5; 10:1–3; 11:25–29) develops into the hope that the remnant is but an interlude in the divine drama, after which greater Israel will embrace the gospel of Jesus Christ and be joined to the church (ch. 11).

Additional Notes   §22

9:14–18 / The Targum on Exodus 33:19 is quoted from Str-B, vol. 3, p. 268 (my translation). A Targum was a paraphrase or explanatory note in Aramaic of an OT text in Hebrew.

Paul Achtemeier appropriately sums up the emphasis on mercy in the process of election: "[Paul] is not writing about the fate of each individual. He is making a statement about how God dealt with Israel, and continues to deal with it, even when it rejects his Son; namely, he deals with it in mercy, even when it deserves wrath. . . . These verses tell me

244 Additional Notes: Romans 9:14–29

that the same gracious purpose at work in the election of Israel is now at work in a new chosen people to whom I can now also belong, by that same gracious purpose of God. The passage is therefore about the enlargement of God's mercy to include gentiles, not about the narrow and predetermined fate of each individual" (*Romans*, p. 165).

On the issue of eschatological determinism Calvin interpreted 9:18 with reference to the elect and reprobate: "it seems good to God to illuminate some that they may be saved, and to blind others that they may perish" (*Romans*, p. 361). The Westminster Confession (1646) echoes Calvin: "Some men and angels are predestined to everlasting life, and others foreordained to everlasting death" (3.3). This position has recently been argued by John Piper, *The Justification of God: An Exegetical and Theological Study of Romans 9:1–23* (Grand Rapids: Baker, 1983).

9:19–21 / Anders Nygren makes a perceptive comment on v. 19: "But when everything is thus placed in God's hands, human reason rises up to say that that is not just" (*Romans*, pp. 364–65). There is no small irony in the fact that humanity, condemned by its own impure motives and destructive ends, would itself raise a claim against God's character of holy love!

9:22–24 / The textual variant in verse 23, *kai hina* ("*and* in order that"), establishes a parallelism between God's power revealed through objects of wrath and God's glory revealed through objects of mercy; whereas *hina* alone ("in order that") establishes a causal relationship: God bore objects of wrath patiently *in order that* his mercy might be revealed (which is the point of the NIV). The first reading, however, claims better manuscript support and is to be preferred.

9:25–29 / Dunn provides a helpful discussion of the OT quotations. See *Romans 9–16*, pp. 569–74.

§23 Righteousness: Gift or Reward?
(Rom. 9:30—10:4)

So far Paul has considered the case of Israel from God's side. God made choices from among Abraham's descendants to create a peculiar people for himself. The election of Jacob over Esau was independent of human merit or responsibility, since the choice was made when both were still in Rebekah's womb. If in subsequent generations God hardened Pharaoh and blessed Israel, it was "in order that [his] purpose in election might stand" (9:11), a purpose rooted in mercy and directed toward salvation (9:16–17). And if in Paul's generation the divine will which once hardened an Esau or Pharaoh for Israel's benefit now hardened Israel for the benefit of the Gentiles, that was but further evidence of God's righteous purpose.

In 9:30–10:21 Paul considers the case of Israel from the human side. Israel bears responsibility for its rejection because it trusted in righteousness by law instead of righteousness by faith. The Jews "sought to establish their own [righteousness, and] did not submit to God's righteousness" (10:3). Thus, Israel's demise is not the result of an arbitrary decree of God, but of its own willful resistance to the righteousness of God by faith.

9:30–33 / In 9:30–10:4 Paul relies less on OT proof texts and more on summarizing the argument, as indicated by the rhetorical question, **What then shall we say? Righteousness** (Gk. *dikaiosynē*), occurring three times in the Greek text of verse 30 and another five times through 10:4, is the theme of the section. The pursuit of righteousness, to be sure, was normally thought to be a Jewish rather than Gentile ideal, but in verses 30–31 Jews and Gentiles are set in competition over this ideal, and the outcome is dumbfounding. The Jews who pursued righteousness so intently found that it eluded them, whereas the Gentiles **who did not pursue righteousness, have obtained it**. This last phrase is

more startling in Greek: "Gentiles who *do* not pursue righteousness have obtained it," stressing that they received the gift of
righteousness not after repenting but in the midst of their unrighteousness (cf. 5:8). It was certainly a case of "salvation by
surprise," in the words of Earl Palmer. The NIV is somewhat misleading when it says *the* Gentiles obtained a righteousness by
faith, as if all Gentiles were saved. The Greek omits the definite
article, meaning simply *some* (i.e., believing) Gentiles (9:24). The
righteousness under consideration is not moral righteousness,
for Gentiles were, by their own admission, less circumspect in
matters of morality than were Jews. Rather, it summarizes the
argument of chapters 3–4 and means the righteousness imputed
to sinners through faith in Jesus Christ. **Righteousness** is a gift—
that is the surprising thing about it. As God surprised Isaac by
passing over Esau to bless Jacob (9:10–13), God now surprises the
Jews by passing over them in order to save Gentiles by free,
unmerited grace. Both Gentiles and Jews, in other words, were
taken by surprise, for what was unexpected by Gentiles was misunderstood by Jews.

   **Israel, who pursued a law of righteousness, has not at-
tained it** (v. 31). The reference to **Israel** probably indicates that
Paul is thinking of the people's self-understanding and not of
individual Jews. He does not say "righteousness by law," as we
would expect, but **law of righteousness**. The implication is that
Israel pursued the law rather than righteousness. Works create a
barrier and distance between humanity and God, whereas faith,
which casts one solely on God's mercy, draws God near and cries,
" '*Abba*, Father' " (8:15). Works of law were not worthless (7:12),
nor was Israel wrong to pursue them (both Jews and Christians
should, 3:31), but the pursuit of morality and the gift of righteousness are two separate matters, and this Israel confused. The law
is righteous (7:12), but it cannot give life (Gal. 3:21).

   Israel **pursued** righteousness **not by faith, but as if it were
by works**. Israel's problem was not that it was irreligious, but if
anything, that it was too religious. Confident that by works of
righteousness it could establish and justify its existence before
God, Israel was no longer open to what God alone could give.
This resulted in pride, or as Paul would say, "boasting." Faith, on
the other hand, means coming before God with empty hands and
admitting that our works, however good they are, are not good
enough. Faith looks only to God's mercy and forgiveness for

having "left undone those things which we ought to have done; [and having] done those things which we ought not have done" (*Book of Common Prayer*). That the Gentiles could do, and their faith became their righteousness. Faith directs one's attention to God and others and frees one from preoccupation with self and the merit of works.

But Israel's guilt was more than misdirected zealousness, as though Israel were a schoolchild so engrossed in its work that it missed the recess bell. Above all, Israel failed in righteousness because it refused to recognize the meaning and goal of the law, which is Jesus Christ. To make this point Paul cites an OT passage about **a stone that causes men to stumble** (v. 33). The quotation is either a loose paraphrase of Isaiah 28:16 or a combination of that passage and Isaiah 8:14. Neither passage is quoted often in rabbinic literature, although there is evidence from the Talmud (b. *Sanh.* 38a) and the Targum to Isaiah 28:16 that even within Judaism the passages were believed to refer to the messianic king.

It was the early church, however, which cemented this stone into the edifice of Christology, thereby demonstrating that Jesus Christ is either a stumbling block or a cornerstone. The image of the stumbling block was often used as a proof text to explain the Jewish rejection of Jesus (11:11; 1 Cor. 3:11; Eph. 2:20; 1 Pet. 2:4–6). At no point was Christ more of a stumbling block than at the cross. The idea of a crucified Messiah was an offense to the Jewish ideal of a messianic king, as Paul himself admitted: "the message of the cross is foolishness to those who are perishing. . . . but we preach Christ crucified: a stumbling block to Jews and foolishness to Gentiles" (1 Cor. 1:18–25). To Jews who **pursued a law of righteousness . . . by works** Christ was an offense, a "**stumbling stone.**" But for Gentiles Christ was a cornerstone of faith, "**and the one who trusts in him will never be put to shame.**"

10:1–4 / Paul begins chapter 10 as he began chapter 9, lamenting the disbelief of Jews. The opening address, **Brothers**, is spoken not to his Jewish kinsfolk, but to his fellow Christians in Rome who understood the problem of Israel's unbelief. The first three verses are solemnly confessional. On the one hand, Paul betrays an emotional bond with his fellow Jews, attesting to **my heart's desire** for their salvation. That phrase is emphatically reinforced in Greek: **my** is emphatic, the reference to **heart** denotes Paul's innermost sincerity, and the word for **desire**, which is practically unknown outside the Bible, means in this instance God's will or good pleasure. The solemn tone continues in verse 2 with **I can testify** (Gk. *martyrein*), which bonds Paul to his Jewish kinsfolk.

But there is also a measured distance between Paul and his fellow Jews. He is no longer testifying *to* "my brothers" and "my own race" (9:3), but **testify**ing *about* **them** in the third person. This is more evident in Greek than in the NIV. Nevertheless, through **prayer** Paul takes the place of an advocate, and not a prosecutor, of Israel. His prayer and advocacy are sure evidence that he did not consider the Jews foreordained to damnation or beyond being reconciled to Christ.

Israel's rejection of the gospel was more than a puzzling quirk of history; it was for Paul a cause of remorse and affliction. **They are zealous for God, but their zeal is not based on knowledge** (v. 2). "Zeal," said Paul Billerbeck, the great rabbinic scholar, "characterizes every page of rabbinic literature" (Str-B, vol. 3, pp. 276–77). Had not Paul once described himself as "extremely zealous for the traditions of my fathers" (Gal. 1:14)? But such zeal also masked a pride and subtle rebellion (Phil. 3:4–9), leading Paul to the persecution not only of Christians (Acts 7:58; 8:3), but also of Christ (Acts 9:4). It also led his fellow Jews to reject the Messiah. Religious zeal is not necessarily a sign of trust and commitment; it may betray a doubt and insecurity that faith depends on believers rather than on God, and that whatever is lacking in God's grace must be compensated for by their virtue. How desperately humans want to be something, to prove their worth to God, to take (and deserve) at least some credit for their salvation. How humbling and offensive to confess that grace must do it all!

That Israel's **zeal is not based on knowledge** (v. 2) is, on the face of it, a preposterous assertion. The literature of Judaism is immense. The OT is a big book which in turn is followed by the larger Mishnah, and the Mishnah by the larger Talmud, which, in its Babylonian version, rivals the *Encyclopedia Britannica* in length. It was not uncommon for rabbis to know the better part of the Torah by heart, as well as significant portions of the oral tradition upon which it evolved. In religious *knowledge* Jews dwarfed their contemporaries, including many Christians. Their rigorous observance of the law, down to minute details in many cases, exposed the superficiality of the other religions of the day. Only one who himself had been a Pharisee and knew firsthand the achievement of Judaism (Gal. 1:14; Phil. 3:4–9) could accuse the Jews of ignorance.

Of what then was Israel ignorant? **They did not know the righteousness that comes from God and sought to establish their own**, says Paul (v. 3). This recalls 9:31–32 above. There was a rivalry between **the righteousness that comes from God** and **their own** righteousness, something Paul had known in his own experience (Phil. 3:9). The critical words are, **sought to establish their own** righteousness. That is a revealing phrase, for it signifies an attempt to establish their status before God and their zeal *for God*. But that is the righteousness of works. The righteousness of faith knows only one thing, that *God is for us*. Human goodness is often rooted in a stubborn determination to excel even in humility and self-sacrifice. It can be a refusal to allow oneself—and others—to be human and to be saved by God. True righteousness is not a possession or *our* righteousness; it is only God's righteousness, alien righteousness. Righteousness comes as a gift of grace and is received by faith in the One who b(r)ought it. Righteousness by works, no matter how zealous, competes with grace; righteousness by faith **submit**s to grace.

God's righteousness is a gift in Christ, not a reward for works. Therefore, **Christ is the end of the law** (v. 4). This statement is deceptively simple, for the word **end** can mean either the completion or culmination of a process (e.g., the end of the birth process), or the termination or annulment of something. The first idea means that Jesus Christ is the goal or completion of the law (so Matt. 5:17); the second that he dispenses with the law (so 2 Cor. 3:13–14; Heb. 8:13). Reference to the Greek only complicates the matter, for *telos* (NIV, **end**) carries at least four different meanings in the NT. The meaning of the phrase in 10:4 has been the subject of long debates and monographs (Gaugler, for example, devotes twenty-four pages to these seven words).

The dogmatic distinction in theology between law (OT) and grace (NT), which is particularly common to Protestantism and Orthodoxy, normally interprets verse 4 in the second sense, i.e., that Christ annuls the law. "When God revealed His righteousness in Christ, He put a definite end to the law as a way of salvation," said Bishop Nygren (*Romans*, p. 379). But if our understanding of chapter 4 was correct, Paul argued that from Abraham onward righteousness had always been by faith, even if Judaism mistakenly thought otherwise (e.g., 10:5–6). In reaction to this position, and in a desire to avoid anti-Semitic overtones, recent scholarship usually favors the first view that Christ is the goal and fulfillment of the law, i.e., the law still stands, but "apart from [Christ] it cannot be properly understood at all" (Cranfield, *Romans*, vol. 2, pp. 516–20). This interpretation is supported by the fact that in Romans **end** (Gk. *telos*) normally signifies the completion of a process rather than its termination (e.g., 2:27; 6:21–22). Nevertheless, the latter interpretation is vulnerable to passages like 6:14 and 7:6, which imply a supersession of law by grace.

Neither side can claim high ground in the debate because Paul's understanding appears to combine both ideas, although favoring the latter. Two passages, above all, reveal his understanding. "So the law was put in charge to lead us to Christ that we might be justified by faith. Now that faith has come, we are no longer under the supervision of law" (Gal. 3:24–25). Both ideas of completion and termination are present in this passage: the law "leads us to Christ" (= completion), but is superseded by Christ (= termination). And in perhaps the closest parallel to 10:4, Paul says in 3:21 that the righteousness of God is "apart from the law," and yet "testified to by the Law and Prophets." By exposing sin the law leads us, indeed drives us, to seek salvation in a savior who has been foretold by the prophets; but the law is not the savior. Jesus Christ is the savior, and Jesus fulfills his ministry of reconciliation apart from the law. The law, as we noted earlier, is the diagnosis of sin, but only Christ is its cure. Christ is both completion and termination of the law: he confirms the law as the just expression of God's moral purpose for humanity, and he supersedes the law by offering forgiveness and salvation when that moral purpose is transgressed. The law is like a father who escorts his daughter down the aisle on her wedding day. At the altar the father must give the bride over to her husband, who is Christ.

Additional Notes   §23

9:30–33 / The full title of Earl Palmer's book is *Salvation by Surprise: Studies in the Book of Romans* (Waco: Word, 1975).

Paul Achtemeier says this of Israel's zeal for righteousness: "They were so religious that they did not want to settle for something God could give them. They wanted to be religious enough so that they could become partners with God in the matter of their salvation" (*Romans*, p. 167). The idea that Israel is a partner with God in salvation is still today a part of Jewish theology. See E. Frerichs, "The Torah Canon of Judaism and the Interpretation of Hebrew Scripture," *HBT* 9 (1, 1987), pp. 13–25; and J. Neusner, "Parallel Histories of Early Christianity and Judaism," *BibRev* 3 (1, 1987), pp. 42–55.

For the use of Isaiah 8:14 and 28:16 in rabbinic literature, see Str-B, vol. 2, pp. 139–40, and vol. 3, p. 276; also, Gaugler, *Der Römerbrief*, vol. 2, pp. 86–88.

10:1–4 / The NIV surprisingly (and mistakenly) substitutes the poorly attested **for the Israelites** (v. 1) in place of "in behalf of them," which "is decisively supported by early and representative witnesses" (Metzger, *TCGNT*, p. 524).

On the meaning of **Christ is the end of the law**, Gerhard Delling lists four possible meanings of the Greek *telos*: goal, exit, end, and cessation ("*telos*," *TDNT*, vol. 8, pp. 54–56). For Gaugler's treatment of v. 4, see *Der Römerbrief*, vol. 2, pp. 94–118.

For treatments approximating the view of 10:4 presented herein, see Dunn, *Romans 9–16*, pp. 589–91; Achtemeier, *Romans*, p. 168; Barrett, *Romans*, pp. 197–98; and Leenhardt, *Romans*, p. 266.

The present section continues the theme of human responsibility begun in 9:30. Israel's predicament is not the result
of ignorance or of divine arbitrariness, but of willful disobedience. Support for the argument is again drawn heavily from the
OT, particularly from Deuteronomy and Isaiah. God's word was
not distant but near (v. 8), a word which Israel both heard (v. 18)
and understood (v. 19). The gospel had been clearly presented
to Israel, and this made Israel's rejection of it the more blame-
worthy. Like the message of Hosea (ch. 11) centuries before,
Paul depicts God as a spurned lover: "'All day long I have held
out my hands to a disobedient and obstinate people'" (10:21).
But Israel's rejection of Christ was neither unforeseen nor un-
provided for. As chapter 11 will reveal, the void Israel left was
filled by the Gentiles, a circumstance that will prompt Israel to
return to the covenant. "In all things God works for the good of
those who love him, who have been called according to his
purpose" (8:28).

10:5–8 / These verses elaborate the theme of 10:4 by contrasting two kinds of righteousness: **the righteousness that is by
the law** (v. 5), and **the righteousness that is by faith** (v. 6). The
irony of righteousness by law, noted Bengel, is that one "does not
find in the law what he seeks; and he does not seek, what he
might find in the Gospel" (*Gnomon*, vol. 3, p. 140). Concerning
righteousness by law (see 2 Apoc. Bar. 67:6) Paul says, **"The man
who does these things will live by them"** (v. 5; quoted from Lev.
18:5). In Leviticus the injunction meant that once the Israelites
entered the Promised Land they were to live by God's commandments, not by Canaanite customs. But Paul lays the accent on
works (**live by them**), thus casting one back on his own power
rather than on God's. He quotes the verse to the same effect in
Galatians 3:12. As a means of righteousness the law pits one
against God. It demands that believers are ultimately responsible

for their relationship with God, and this results in an impossible dilemma: if they *could* fulfill the law's requirements they would swell with pride and make God their debtor; but, in fact, they inevitably fail the test of the law, and judgment results.

The solution, of course, is that "Christ is the end of the law so that there may be righteousness for everyone who believes" (10:4). Faith short-circuits the rationalizations and casuistries of righteousness by law by casting the believer solely on God's power and promises. This is the point of verse 6, which may reflect the thought of Deuteronomy 9:4: "After the Lord your God has driven [the nations] out before you, do not say to yourself, 'The Lord has brought me here to take possession of this land because of my righteousness.' " God did not owe Israel anything; his benevolence was not a reward for human righteousness, but an expression of his grace.

To further this idea Paul quotes loosely from Deuteronomy 30:11–14: **"Do not say in your heart, 'Who will ascend into heaven?' " (that is, to bring Christ down) "or 'Who will descend into the deep?' " (that is, to bring Christ up from the dead)**. Deuteronomy 30:11–14 originally referred to the law, but Paul freely applies it to Jesus Christ! Calvin was rocked on his heels by Paul's cavalier use of Scripture here. Comparative studies, however, reveal that Deuteronomy 30:11–14 was freely handled in Jewish tradition, Paul's interpretation being but one example. For Paul the meaning of the OT and of salvation history is fully comprehensible only in Jesus Christ (2 Cor. 3:12–16). He implies the same in verse 17 when he says that "the message (of the OT) is heard through the word of Christ." Paul's radical substitution of Christ for the law can only mean that he sees in Jesus Christ not a new revelation, but a completed revelation which supersedes everything before it. The OT is thus truly a Christian book. Had Israel perceived the essence of the law it would have acknowledged its fulfillment in Jesus Christ.

What is humanly impossible—to scale the heights or descend the depths—has been revealed by God in the law, but ultimately in Christ. All noble, pious, and heroic attempts to demonstrate human righteousness are only active unbelief. It is not we who bring Christ to people, but Christ who sends us to them with his saving word. We do not raise Christ from the dead; our proofs for the existence of God or the historicity of the resurrection, for example, do not secure their reality. We do not establish

God and his work, but God establishes us. Our task, in other words, is not to be responsible for salvation, but to be *respond*able to it.

It is not we who seek God, but God who has sought us. **"The word is near you; it is in your mouth and in your heart"** (v. 8; quoted from Deut. 30:14; cf. Eph. 2:13, 17–19). God is not a principle, distant and undefinable, but a person, near and intimate, present in the *word* of the gospel. He is known not through sentiments and feelings, or by proofs and deductions, or through mystical and ineffable experiences. God imposes upon himself the limits of knowability; he is known only as he makes himself known through the Word incarnate and through the witness to the Word in preaching and proclamation. That is **the word of faith we are proclaiming** (see Eph. 6:17; Heb. 4:12; 6:5).

10:9–10 / The **word** which is near is Jesus Christ who fulfills the law (10:4). Verses 9–10 are a chiastic (A-B-B'-A') construction:

A **if you** *confess* **with your mouth**
B **and** *believe* **in your heart**
B' **for it is with your heart that you** *believe*
A' **and it is with your mouth that you** *confess.*

The whole has the ring of a confession used in worship, perhaps at baptism. Paul is likely taking up an ancient creed as he did at 1:3–4, here perhaps the earliest Christian confession that "Jesus is Lord." Early Aramaic-speaking believers already recited at the Lord's Supper, *Marana tha*, "our Lord [Jesus] has come" (1 Cor. 16:22; Did. 10:6). Especially as the gospel made its way into pagan regions, the accent on Jesus' lordship over all other lords and powers increased (1 Cor. 8:5; Phil. 2:9–11). We saw at 9:5 that Paul very likely called Christ "God." The formula *kyrios Iēsous* here would have been equally provocative for his Jewish readers, for the title "Lord" (Gk. *kyrios*; Heb. *Yahweh*) occurs as a proper name for God some 5000 times in the OT. Paul could not yet define the nature of Jesus (in the later words of the Nicene Creed) as "being of one substance with the Father," but the fact that he freely applies the personal name of God in the OT to Jesus implies that Jesus shares the dominion of Israel's God. What is true of God's lordship is also true of Jesus' lordship. To speak of Jesus is therefore to speak of God, and speech about God must begin and end with Jesus, for Jesus is "the word of faith" (v. 8).

A Christian is one who confesses that **Jesus is Lord** over all (Col. 2:15) and who believes that **God raised him from the dead.**

The lordship and resurrection of Jesus are the essence of salvation, and they achieve their full purpose only through confession and belief: **if you confess . . . if you believe**. The variable (the subjunctive) is with humanity, **if**; the certainty (the indicative) is with God, "you will be saved." One might expect belief to precede confession, but the reversed order doubtlessly reflects the order in the preceding quotation (i.e., "mouth . . . heart," v. 8). Their order, however, is less important than their inseparability. Belief without confession is betrayal; confession without belief is hypocrisy. The righteousness of faith consists of belief *and* confession. Belief means active trust in God's goodness to us in Jesus Christ, as opposed to mere intellectual assent to a propositional truth. And confession means a deliberate and public witness to that belief. Belief and confession forsake all hopes of establishing their own righteousness (10:3). They direct hope outward, *extra nos*, to the righteousness of *God*.

10:11–13 / In support of verses 9–10 Paul again (see 9:33) quotes Isaiah 28:16, **"Everyone who trusts in him will never be put to shame."** In Isaiah the passage meant that whoever believes in the cornerstone of Zion would not be ashamed. Paul understood the cornerstone to refer to Christ and thus applies the whole reference to Jesus. By prefacing the quotation with **Everyone** he emphasizes that salvation is available to Jews and Gentiles without distinction. He continues in verse 12, **For there is no difference between Jew and Gentile**. Paul made this same assertion in 3:23 with reference to sins: "There is no difference, for all have sinned." But neither is there any difference with reference to grace (cf. 11:32)! Jesus is **the same Lord** of both Jews and Gentiles. **"Everyone who calls on the name of the Lord will be saved"** (v. 13; see Joel 2:32). The gospel is not the possession of a privileged few—not even of the chosen people. The gospel is salvation without limits, a universal promise for everyone who believes.

Grace comes solely from God, who **richly blesses all who call on him** (v. 12). There is no partiality with God, nor is grace a miserly concession on his part (2:11; Eph. 6:9; Col. 3:25). Gentiles are not the objects of God's reluctant benevolence. On the contrary, God **richly blesses all who call on him**, even Gentiles "who did not pursue righteousness" (9:30). Herein lies the offense of grace, as Jesus illustrated in the parable of the workers in the vineyard (Matt. 20:1–16). It is indeed bad business to pay laborers

who have worked one hour the same wage as those who have
worked twelve. Jesus' parable, however, is not about economics,
but about grace. There was a Roman coin (an assarion) worth
one-twelfth of a denarius, a day's wage; but there is no twelfth
part of the grace of God!

10:14–21 / But have Jews had a fair opportunity to "call
on the name of the Lord"? To answer that question Paul keys off
the quotation from Joel 2:32 in verse 13 and presents us with
another sorites (see 5:3–5 and 8:29–30), a series of propositions in
which the predicate of the preceding becomes the subject of the
following (thus, **call . . . believed / believe . . . heard / hear . . .
preaching / preach . . . sent**). Here Paul works backward, so to
speak. We would expect the sorites to progress from beginning
(sending) to end (believing), but Paul reverses the order, beginning with the Jews' guilt because of their failure to believe. Each
link in the chain of assertions holds fast except the final one, and
that was Israel's refusal to believe.

The quotation in verse 15 ("**How beautiful are the feet of
those who bring good news!**" Isa. 52:7) originally referred to the
messengers who reported the Jewish release from Babylonian
captivity in the sixth century B.C. In later Judaism, however, it was
almost universally applied to the coming of the Messiah. Paul
has shortened and altered the Isaiah text considerably. The word
translated **beautiful** by the NIV is in Greek *hōraios*, originally meaning "the right season" or "the ripe moment." Just as long years of
captivity prepared Israel for the good news of release, so the
proclamation of the gospel came at the most opportune moment
for its reception by the Jews. This too heightened their culpability
for not believing it. The messengers to Israel doubtlessly include
the prophets and Jesus (Mark 12:1–12), and later Paul himself.

Above all, the quotation underscores the idea of *sending*.
The gospel is not a philosophy or an idea. It is not a logical
inference or a conclusion drawn from the laws of nature. The
gospel comes through the proclamation of the *word*, at moments
ordained by God, and through chosen persons. The gospel is always and everywhere "incarnational," i.e., it is God's word communicated through persons. Where the gospel is not personal, it
is not the gospel. The incarnation of Jesus Christ was, of course,
the perfect and consummate example of God's revelation of himself in history. Apostles, prophets, and witnesses of all sorts are

not simply individuals who have had "religious experiences" or who have "studied theology," but individuals who by God's gracious will have been called to the person of Jesus Christ, endowed with his authority, and commissioned in his service. And if they are called, commissioned, and empowered by Christ, then their word is Christ's word (v. 17).

Yes, Israel had heard the message. It had been proclaimed, but **not all the Israelites accepted the good news** (v. 16). There is a word play in the original Greek on **accepted** (which is a derivative of the word for "hearing"): Jews heard the gospel (*ēkousan*, v. 14), but they did not obey it (*hypēkousan*, v. 16). Paul quotes a passage from the fourth servant song of Isaiah (53:1), attesting that the message had been delivered but not believed: **"Lord, who has believed our message?"** For Jews *hearing* was the indispensable prerequisite of religion, because learning depends on hearing. Paul agrees that **faith comes from hearing the message** (v. 17).

But, *had* Jews heard the gospel? Throughout verses 14–21 the driving concern is whether or not the Jews have *heard* of salvation in Christ. Paul asks point-blank in verse 18, **But I ask, Did they not hear?** His answer, coming from Psalm 19:4, is unequivocal: **Of course they did: "Their voice has gone out into all the earth, their words to the ends of the world."** Psalm 19, which refers to the heavenly bodies that "declare the glory of God" (Ps. 19:1), is applied by Paul to the evangelization of Jews. It could, of course, be objected that not all *had* heard the gospel. Surely Paul must have become aware of the endless task of evangelizing Jews (and Gentiles) the further he pressed into Asia and Europe. His goal of preaching in Spain (15:24) was itself evidence of this concern. The quotation, therefore, seems to be employed to the effect that the gospel had already been preached widely in Jewish regions (due in no small measure to Paul's tireless activity), and that its sparse acceptance there was typical of what could be expected in the future.

Israel may indeed have heard, but perhaps it did not **understand**. Perhaps, like Pharaoh, Israel had been hardened so it *could not* understand. Or, perhaps, as one not uncommonly hears today, the gospel is valid only for Gentiles (and Torah for Jews). To this final question Paul quotes three passages from the OT. He again speaks of **Israel** rather than "Jews," indicating his concern with a people as opposed to individuals.

The first quotation (v. 19) comes from Deuteronomy 32:21. The verse might be paraphrased: If Israel had made God jealous by worshipping non-gods, then God will make Israel jealous by raising up a non-people. Israel may not understand, implies Paul, but "a nation that has no understanding" will! The non-people, of course, are the Gentiles, and the verse anticipates the argument of chapter 11 that the inclusion of the Gentiles in salvation will provoke Jews to jealousy so that they also will accept the gospel.

Neither could Israel complain that the message was obscure, for Isaiah (65:1), with greater boldness than Moses, asserted that the Gentiles who never sought it or asked for it have indeed found it. That is the gist of the second quotation in verse 20. Like a true rabbi, Paul follows a quotation from the Law with one from the Prophets. If untutored Gentiles received the gift of righteousness, how much more should favored Israel have received it?

The bare truth is that Israel is without excuse. **"All day long I have held out my hands to a disobedient and obstinate people"** (Isa. 65:2). The only thing more astonishing than the Gentiles' faith is Israel's lack of it. "The more I called Israel," said the Lord, "the further they went from me" (Hos. 11:2). With outstretched hands God offered Israel the gift of life, but Israel's hands were full of its own works.

Throughout the discussion of Israel's guilt Paul steers clear of the rhetoric we have come to associate with anti-Semitism. Governments (and more shamefully, churches) have justified their persecutions of Jews on the basis of race or blood or clannishness or historical destiny or economics or treachery or a thousand other slanders. All these so-called offenses against humanity are categorically rejected by the apostle. His sole and abiding concern is the *theological* mystery of Israel's disobedience to God (9:3). Israel, of course, means unbelieving Jews, but we may not be wrong to see in the expression the symbol of a danger inherent in all religious peoples, including Christians. The existence of Israel is a reminder to the church of what can happen when a chosen people grows deaf to the Spirit, when it is more desirous of accommodating itself and the gospel to the world than of proclaiming the victory of Christ over the world, and when it thinks more of fulfilling its own will than of honoring God's will. Israel, complacent and disobedient, is in varying degrees present in our churches and in ourselves.

Additional Notes   §24

10:5–8 / Calvin's note on v. 6 reads: "This passage is such as may not a little disturb the reader, and for two reasons—for it seems to be improperly applied by Paul—and the words are also turned to a different meaning" (*Romans*, p. 388).

Dunn cites interpretations of Deuteronomy 30:11–14 in 2 Apoc. Bar. 3:29–30, Tg. Neof. on Deut. 30, and Philo, *On the Posterity and Exile of Cain* 84–85 as evidence of its varied interpretations in Judaism; see *Romans 9–16*, pp. 604–5.

For Barth's impressive exposition of this passage, see *Romans*, pp. 377–79.

10:9–10 / For Augustine's pertinent story of belief and confession, see Additional Notes §14 (6:3–4).

10:11–13 / Luther applies verse 12 to prayer: "God is rich as he hears our prayers, but we are poor as we call upon him. He is strong when he fulfills our prayers, but we are hesitant and weak when we pray. For we do not pray for as much as he can and wants to give to us; in other words: we do not pray in proportion to his power, but far below his power in proportion to our weakness. But he cannot give except according to his power" (*Lectures on Romans*, p. 295).

Undoubtedly the single greatest achievement of the Protestant Reformation was the reclamation of preaching for faith and worship. The apostle would unquestionably have hailed this achievement, but he would have put equal responsibility on the *hearing* of the word! If preachers are accountable for their faithfulness to the report, then the world is equally accountable for its hearing of the report.

10:14–21 / On the necessity of proper hearing of the good news, see Str-B, vol. 3, pp. 283–84.

On Israel's warning to the church, see Gaugler, *Der Römerbrief*, vol. 2, pp. 138–39; and Barth, *Dogmatics in Outline*, ch. 11.

Israel's rejection of Jesus Christ was a denial of its own calling and redemption. It was as though an infant in the womb could somehow decide not to be born, and thus frustrate the rightful goal of its life. But contrary to expectation, Israel's denial of its destiny does not frustrate God's purpose. We saw in Romans 9 that God was prepared to make sovereign choices in history, even wrathful choices, in order to extend his mercy. The present section is closely tied to that argument. Verses 1–6 are a defense of God's grace in the establishment of a believing remnant in Israel, while verses 7–10 are a polemical description of God's hardening of greater Israel. But Israel's hardening is neither total nor final. It is not total because God's grace has preserved a remnant of Israel which has confessed Christ (v. 5); and it is not final because it is Paul's understanding that all Israel will be saved (11:26). In the following section (11:11–24) Paul will argue that Israel's unwillingness to enter the promise allowed room for the Gentiles to precede Israel. Israel's loss is the Gentiles' gain (11:12), but it will not be a permanent loss (11:11, 23), according to Paul, for once the Gentiles have fully entered into salvation, Israel will be aroused to jealousy and will return to its saving heritage (11:25–32).

11:1–4 / It is true, as Paul established in 10:21, that Israel rejected God. But God is sovereign, which means that God's will is not determined by something outside itself; and God is love, which means that God, unlike humanity, does not have to reject those who reject him. **Did God reject his people?** (v. 1). Paul counters with the strongest possible negation, **By no means!** The idea of the chosen people (Gk. *laos*) is controlled by two understandings in the OT. On the one hand, it separates Israel from the "nations" and assures its election as God's "treasured possession" (Exod. 19:4–6). On the other hand, both the prophets and Paul warn Israel against complacency over that fact. Being God's treasured possession does not entitle Israel—or the church—to an exemption from faithful obedience; rather, it *heightens* their responsibility to God.

Paul argues for God's abiding purpose for Israel not by a theological argument, but by personal experience. **I am an Israelite myself, a descendant of Abraham, from the tribe of Benjamin.** Paul is "Exhibit A" that God has not rejected his people. There can be no doubt of the central role which Paul's conversion experience played in his subsequent understanding of the gospel. Would God have chosen a Jew to be his special envoy to the Gentiles if he were finished with the Jews? As Luther notes, "if God had cast away his people, then above all he would have cast away the apostle Paul who fought against him with all his strength" (*Lectures on Romans*, p. 305). The Damascus road experience was, of course, a demonstration of grace to Paul personally. But it was more than that. Paul saw it also as an example of grace to his people, believing that his conversion was but a foreshadowing of the conversion of all Israel.

Paul emphatically denies his own question, **God did not reject his people** (v. 2). The OT assured him of this (cf. 1 Sam. 12:22; Ps. 94:14). The existence of a remnant of Jews who had believed in Jesus Christ was a further sign. From the time of Elijah onward had not God provided for a righteous minority within greater Israel? At a particularly bleak passage in Israel's history, when worship of the true God seemed to hang by a thread, Elijah, overcome by discouragement, cried out, **"Lord, they have killed your prophets and torn down your altars; I am the only one left, and they are trying to kill me"** (v. 3; loosely quoted [from Paul's memory?] from 1 Kings 19:10–14). But God's perspective differed greatly from Elijah's. **And what was God's answer to him? "I have reserved for myself seven thousand who have not bowed the knee to Baal"** (v. 4; again loosely quoted from 1 Kings 19:18). The Greek original does not exactly say **God's answer**. A word occurring only once in all the NT, *ho chrēmatismos*, and meaning, "a divine statement or answer," appears here. The choice of expression heightens the contrast between Elijah's opinion and the divine authority: Elijah may figure he is the only true believer left, but in actuality there were **seven thousand who have not bowed the knee to Baal. Seven thousand** is not to be understood as 6,999 + 1; in Hebrew thinking it means completion or totality, i.e., "more people than you can count." Baal was a fertility god of the Canaanites whose influence the prophets, in particular, dreaded in Israel. Despite Baal's cancerous growth in Zion, God still preserved a faithful remnant. It was not given to Elijah to know precisely who the true believers were. Nevertheless, a faithful minority survived, and not by chance, but by God's grace. "There is a remnant chosen by grace" (v. 5). Elijah presumed to number the elect but failed to get beyond himself; God had preserved the elect beyond number *for* himself.

11:5–6 / Verse 5 contemporizes the Elijah story and shifts the focus to the present. This is less apparent, however, in the NIV than in the Greek. As God had preserved a faithful minority in Elijah's day, so he had preserved a minority of Jews who believed in Jesus Christ as **a remnant chosen by grace** (v. 5). This is the only place in the NT where the word **remnant** (Gk. *leimma*) occurs, although it is quite close in meaning to the word "chosen" (Gk. *eklogē*, vv. 5, 7). The idea of the remnant was first presented in 9:27, though in different terminology. The word for **remnant** (*leimma*, v. 5) may have been suggested in Paul's mind by the word for "reserved" (Gk. *kataleipō*) in verse 4 above, of which it is a cognate. It is not a remnant of virtue or good works or merit, but a **remnant chosen by grace**. Israel *and* the church rightly understand their election only when they understand it as an action of God's free grace, not as an achievement of their works. Had the Jewish Christians become a remnant because of their works, they would have had no significance for greater Israel, for Israel itself "pursued a law of righteousness" (9:31). But since the remnant had been preserved by grace, it became a pledge of God's continuing favor towards Israel as a whole. The remnant of grace, in other words, affirms that Israel was called into existence by grace (9:8–11) and awaits a future consummation of grace (11:28–32).

11:7–10 / Paul now repeats and amplifies the thought of 9:31 ("Israel, who pursued a law of righteousness, has not attained it"). A portion of Israel, the elect or "remnant" of Jewish Christians, has attained righteousness (see 9:6). But the larger part of unbelieving Israel, holding fast to its righteousness by the law, was **hardened** (v. 7). The idea of hardening recalls the thought of 9:18, though in different terminology. The Greek word here, *pōroō*, a medical term, can refer to a (gall or kidney) stone, or the collar of bone which grows around a fracture. The passive voice, **were hardened**, is clearly a "divine passive," meaning God's hardening of Israel. The quotations of verses 8–10 were gathered by the early church to explain why Jews failed to receive Jesus as Messiah. As we saw earlier (e.g., 1:24ff.), God hands people over to the sins they desire. Human resistance and disobedience are of course present and working concurrently with God's will, but the final result is more than human failure. The outcome is a hardening from God so that they cannot see what they will not see, or hear what they will not hear. From this perspective hardening is not an obstacle to Israel, but God's *judgment* on Israel.

The bulk of the supporting quotation from Deuteronomy 29:4 in verse 8 recalls Israel's resistance to God in the wilderness. The phrase, **spirit of stupor**, however, is adopted from Isaiah 29:10 as part of Isaiah's scathing attack against the city of David for its faithlessness. The word for **stupor** is a rare word in Greek literature and means "torpor" or "spiritual insensitivity." Coupled with the references to blindness and deafness, the quotation signifies Israel's utter inability to recognize or respond to righteousness.

The second quotation in verses 9–10, taken from Psalm 69:22–23, is equally direct. Psalm 69 played a central role in the formation of the passion narratives of Jesus (Matt. 27:34, 48; Mark 15:23, 36). Paul quotes the passage where the suffering righteous man, having been subjected to every form of abuse, reproaches his tormentors. Since the early church identified the lament of Psalm 69 with Jesus' fate, it is worth considering whether in this instance Paul employs the reproach of the righteous sufferer as Jesus' reproach to Israel.

The reference to **their table** becoming **a snare and a trap** (v. 9) might derive, according to some commentators, from a blanket on which a bedouin would lie to eat or sleep. Should he be surprised by an enemy and try to jump to his feet, it might catch his feet and trip him. A cultic interpretation, however, would regard it as a reference to the table of showbread or perhaps the altar of the temple, which, when maintained apart from its reference to Christ, became **a snare and a trap**. A more general (and perhaps preferable) interpretation sees in the **table** a simple but profound irony of table fellowship: when the hospitality of eating together, so honored in the ancient Near East, is broken by treachery (recalling Judas at the Last Supper?), then the table becomes **a snare and a trap**. Whatever the precise meaning, all three quotations underscore Israel's blindness and obstinacy in the face of God's grace. The fact that the three quotations come from the three major divisions of the Hebrew Bible—Law, Prophets, and Writings—amounts to a comprehensive condemnation of Israel from its own scriptures. This returns the reader to the conclusion of 3:20ff., that condemnation is the necessary and inevitable prelude to grace.

Additional Notes   §25

11:1–4 /   Several Greek manuscripts substitute "inheritance" for **people** in v. 1, but this is probably an assimilation to Ps. 94:14 ("For the Lord will not reject his people; he will never forsake his inheritance"), the first part of which is quoted in v. 2. See Metzger, *TCGNT*, p. 526.

The significance of Paul's claim to be a Benjaminite (**a descendant ... from the tribe of Benjamin** [v. 1]) owes to several beliefs from Scripture and tradition. Gen. 35:16–20 records that Benjamin was the only patriarch born *in* the Promised Land. According to rabbinic tradition, the tribe of Benjamin was the first to cross the Red Sea on dry land. Tradition also attested that the Shekinah (the presence of God) dwelled in the region assigned to Benjamin. On the prominence of this small tribe in Israel, see Str-B, vol. 3, pp. 286–87.

For discussions of Baal, see "Gods, Pagan," *NIBD*, pp. 433–35; and D.F. Payne, "Baal," *NBD*, p. 115. Curiously, Paul supplies **Baal** (a masculine word) with a feminine article here. This may be due to the Hebrew custom of substituting "shame" (feminine) for the names of foreign gods (see *Baal*, BAGD, p. 129) or of supplying "image of" (also feminine) before **Baal** as a term of contempt (so Bengel, *Gnomon*, vol. 3, p. 147).

11:5–6 /   The NIV notes that some manuscripts append a longer ending to verse 6 (see NIV footnote). But there seems to be no reason why the words should have been deleted if they were original. Moreover, the various forms of the addition throw the whole of it into question. The shorter reading is thus preferable. See Metzger, *TCGNT*, p. 526.

§26 Salvation to the Ends of the Earth (Rom. 11:11–24)

A skeletal outline of the history of salvation can be found in the call to Abraham in Genesis 12:1–3. It ends with the promise that "all peoples on earth will be blessed through you." The fulfillment of that promise lay conspicuously fallow throughout the OT. Only in Jonah and Second Isaiah is the blessing to the Gentiles again taken up. In Isaiah 49:1–6 the servant is told, "it is too small a thing for you to . . . restore the tribes of Jacob. . . . I will make you a light for the Gentiles, that you may bring my salvation to the ends of the earth." The early church saw that design supremely fulfilled in Jesus of Nazareth. Salvation had come from the Jews (John 4:22), but it was not limited to them. "First for the Jew, then for the Gentile," said Paul (1:16). In Paul's day the final and oft-forgotten promise to Abraham that "all peoples on earth will be blessed through you" had reached fruition in the enormously successful Gentile mission. But ironically, the earlier and seemingly secure parts of the promise—land, nation, name, and blessing—had miscarried, for Jews on the whole had rejected Christ and the gospel.

The present section is devoted to this dilemma. Paul speaks throughout to Gentiles in the second person, whereas Jews are spoken of in the third person. The tone is no longer polemical, but apologetic toward Jews and admonitory toward Gentiles. For the first time since the beginning of Romans 9 Paul quotes nothing in this section from the OT. The passage is dominated by the illustration of the olive tree, which may have been inspired by Isaiah 56:3–8. Nevertheless, more than anywhere else in Romans 9–11, the script here is written by the apostle himself, and in it we come closer to an answer about the place of Jews in salvation history.

11:11–12 / **Did** the Jews **stumble so as to fall beyond recovery?** asks Paul (v. 11). His concern is no longer with the

remnant of Jewish Christians, but with "the others [who] were
hardened" (11:7), i.e., the majority of Jews who rejected the gospel. Were the "spirit of stupor" (11:7) to prevail, it would spell
doom for the Jews. As a whole Israel indeed "stumbled over the
'stumbling stone' [of Christ]" (9:32; also 11:9), but their **stumbling**
and **fall** had resulted in a remarkable paradox. **Because of their
transgression, salvation has come to the Gentiles to make Israel
envious** (v. 11). The failure of Jews to enter the kingdom brought
by Christ made room for the Gentiles to enter (cf. Acts 18:6).
Moreover, Paul understands that the Gentiles' participation in
salvation will create envy in unbelieving Israel and awaken Israel
to salvation. Both Jews and Gentiles, in other words, benefit each
other, although in quite unexpected ways. Jewish rejection of
Christ caused the gospel to be spread with great success among
the Gentiles, whereas Gentile acceptance of the gospel would
arouse jealousy in Israel and ultimately bring Israel to faith.

Thus, what initially seemed to be a fatal misfire in the divine plan turned out to be the secret of its fulfillment. Verse 12
witnesses to both the irony and the majesty of sovereign grace by
a contrast of superlatives. The Jews' **transgression** leads not to
disaster but to **riches for the world; their loss** results not in bankruptcy but in **riches for the Gentiles**; they who are now but a
"remnant" (11:5) will become a **fullness**! The Spirit of God is
again hovering over the face of the deep and creating life from
chaos.

11:13–16 / In Romans 9–11 Paul speaks to Gentiles *about*
Jews. Here he addresses Gentiles directly in the second person,
I am talking to you Gentiles (v. 13). The tone also changes from
analysis to exhortation and admonition. As we noted in the Introduction, surely one reason that Paul wrote Romans was to heal
the breach between Gentiles and Jews after the latter returned to
Rome following their expulsion under Claudius. Verses 13ff. quite
probably were penned with this in mind, although the message
was certainly not limited to Gentiles in Rome, for the issue was
larger than whatever might have been happening in the capital.

Jewish society as a rule regarded Gentiles with condescension and scorn, likening them to tax collectors (Matt. 18:17) or
dogs (Mark 7:27). But far from begrudging his apostleship to the
Gentiles (Gal. 2:7, 9), Paul gloried in it and highlighted his unique
calling. Verse 13 might be translated, "*I am the Gentile apostle*"

(see 1:5, 13). Interestingly, in a passage addressed to Gentile readers Paul accents his mission to the Jews: **I make much of my ministry in the hope that I may somehow arouse my own people to envy and save some of them** (v. 14). By **my own people** and **some of them** Paul means unbelieving Israel and the faithful remnant, respectively. Thus, Paul's ministry to the Gentiles could scarcely be regarded as a betrayal of his people. On the contrary, his tireless mission to the Gentiles had as one intent the salvation of some of the *Jews*. Herein lay a great paradox: the success of the Gentile mission was essential for the success of the Jewish mission and was part of the fulfillment of God's purpose for Jews. Gentile Christians, as the illustration of the olive tree will evince, have not replaced Jews; neither can they boast against them. Rather, in addition to procuring their own salvation, their faith and discipleship serve for the eventual salvation of Israel. This is why Paul writes of his hopes for the Jews in a passage addressed to Gentiles. For the present his best service to the Jews is to preach the gospel to the Gentiles.

Verses 15–16 repeat and expand the idea that Israel's loss is the Gentiles' gain (v. 12). The idea of verse 15—that the eventual Jewish acceptance of Christ will be **life from the dead**—is a matter of some debate. One possibility is to regard **life from the dead** eschatologically, i.e., when all Israel is saved (11:26), then the final consummation and the resurrection of the dead will be at hand. Another possibility is to take the phrase metaphorically (so John 5:24; Luke 15:32) as a reference to salvation: when Jews accept Christ, then their restoration to the purpose of God will transfer them from death to life. The majority of modern commentators follows the first view, seeing in **life from the dead** a fixed eschatological expression, that when Israel converts *en masse* to the gospel, the Parousia, the return of Christ, would be imminent. I am inclined, on the other hand, to see it as a reference to the salvation just noted in verses 11 and 14, and thus take it to be more figurative than eschatological. Paul's topic, after all, is not the end of history and the final judgment, but rather Israel's enduring place in God's purpose and Israel's eventual salvation.

Two metaphors in verse 16—the dough and the root—show that what God has already done with the remnant he will one day do with greater Israel. They are proleptic metaphors pointing to the future. The present numbers of Jewish converts, though small, are the **firstfruits** of Israel as a whole. The second metaphor of the root introduces and governs the discussion of the olive tree, to which we now turn.

11:17–24 / The analogy of the olive tree is given in full in verse 17: **some of the branches have been broken off, and you, though a wild olive shoot, have been grafted in among the others and now share in the nourishing sap from the olive root**. Paul's horticulture runs counter to normal procedure, for it is the good scion implanted into the wild stock (and not the reverse) which determines a successful graft. The apostle acknowledges that his analogy is "contrary to nature" (v. 24), but it witnesses to the theological truth he intends, that it was as unnatural for God to include Gentiles in salvation promised to Israel as it would be for a farmer to graft useless shoots into a cultured tree.

Some of the elements in the analogy are readily apparent. Both Jews and Gentiles are considered **branches**. This is stated explicitly in verses 23–24. Gentiles are branches of a wild olive tree engrafted into a cultured olive tree, and disbelieving Jews are natural branches of the cultured olive tree which have been broken off. The passive voice of the verb, **have been broken off** (v. 17), is doubtlessly a "divine passive," and, like its counterpart in 11:7 (they **were hardened**), it means that this has happened according to God's will. But, as we have noted, Israel is also responsible for its excision from **the nourishing sap of the olive root** (v. 17), for **they were broken off because of unbelief** (v. 20). This accords with Paul's teaching especially in 9:30–10:4 that Israel's present alienation is due to its rejection of the gospel. As evidence he speaks of the Jews' "transgression" (v. 11), "loss" (v. 12), and "rejection" (v. 15). But behind the Jewish rejection of Jesus as Messiah is a profound mystery (11:25) which was foreseen and willed by God. The most apparent effect of Israel's hardening and disbelief is, of course, the inclusion of Gentiles in salvation. Nevertheless, Jewish rejection of Jesus is not the final word, for "God did not reject his people, whom he foreknew" (11:2).

What, then, is the **root**? One thing is clear: it cannot be the Jewish people, for, according to the analogy, Jews, like Gentiles, are branches. A majority of commentators would identify the root with Abraham, an understanding which has the advantage of having been grounded in the pre-Pauline tradition (1 Enoch 93:2, 8; Jub. 16:26; T. Jud. 24:1, 5; Isa. 11:1; 53:2; Sir. 47:22) and is clearly presupposed in 11:28, "as far as the gospel is concerned, they (unbelieving Jews) are enemies on your account; but as far as election is concerned, they are loved on account of the patriarchs (Abraham)." Barth, on the other hand, would identify the **root** with Christ, but his view has the disadvantage of omitting the work of salvation already begun in Abraham (ch. 4; 11:28). For my part, I am inclined to see the **root** as a reference to the history of salvation extending from Abraham to Christ, into which both Gentiles and Jews must be engrafted. This is supported by the argument of chapter 4, where Abraham is seen as the bearer of the promise of salvation in Jesus Christ, a promise which can be received only by faith.

It is not physical descent from Abraham, therefore, but participation in the covenant of faith which extends from Abraham to Christ, which characterizes the true Israel. This was essentially the argument of 2:28–29 where Paul distinguished between the outward Jew of circumcision and the inward Jew of the spirit, or of 9:6ff., where he distinguishes between two Israels, one of election and faith in Abraham, and one of mere physical descent from Abraham. The illustration of the olive tree, therefore, is preeminently one of *grace*. **You do not support the root, but the root supports you** (v. 18).

There are other offshoots of the illustration worth considering too. Most importantly, the root and branches show how completely Paul identified the Christian church with Israel. The church is not a new plan, but the "Israel of God" (Gal. 6:16) which grows from and completes the root of Abraham. There is no salvation apart from the **root**! Whoever desires to be included in God's saving plan must be grafted into *that* stock. God did not cut down the tree and plant a new one. He grafted other shoots into the true and eternal **root** (Eph. 2:1ff.; 1 Cor. 10:1–13)—although not into the place of the former branches! Thus, the church does not replace the synagogue, but is joined to the historic root of Israel extending from Abraham to Christ. This shows that there remains room on the stock for Jews to be grafted again into their former place.

The illustration thus excludes any hint of anti-Semitism. How keenly Karl Barth saw this when he wrote during the Nazi years, "The attack on Judah means the attack on the rock of the work and revelation of God, beside which work and which revelation there is no other" (*Dogmatics in Outline*, p. 76). To deny that

Christianity grows from Israel or that Jesus was a Jew is to lay an ax at the root of the *Christian* religion. When Gentile Christians deny their OT heritage, they are, according to Paul's illustration, sawing off the branch on which they sit. Anti-Semitism is a boomerang which will return to lop off the heads of Christians!

Moreover, if Christians are grafted into the **root** of the history of salvation leading from Abraham to Christ, then any pride on their part is excluded. An express purpose of the illustration is to admonish Gentile believers against arrogance toward not-(*yet*)-believing Jews. **Do not boast over those branches. If you do, consider this: You do not support the root, but the root supports you** (v. 18). The power of life is in the root, not in the branches. There is no salvation apart from Jesus the Jew, there is no church which is not an engrafting into and a continuance of God's work in Israel. There is but *one* tree, *one* people of God.

Another offshoot of the illustration pertains to the theme of judgment. **Consider . . . the kindness and sternness** of God, says Paul (v. 22). **Do not be arrogant, but be afraid. For if God did not spare the natural branches, he will not spare you either** (vv. 20–21). The fear to which Paul appeals is the OT fear of God which, in the words of James Dunn, prevents "faith from deteriorating into presumption" (*Romans 9–16*, p. 663). Gentile Christians experience the **kindness** of God because of faith, whereas unrepentant Israel experiences the **sternness** of God because of disbelief (see Wisd. of Sol. 5:20; 12:19). The analogy of the olive tree brings to fruition the themes of grace and faith which have governed Romans throughout. Gentiles have not been grafted into the **root** because they are preferred, but simply because of their response of faith to God's grace. If Gentiles recognize that fact and Jews do not, it is not to the Gentiles' credit. In their temptation to denigrate Jews Paul sees the danger of spiritual pride, and he warns against it: if God did not spare the natural branches (Jews), is there any reason to suppose that he will spare the wild branches (Gentiles)?

Finally, the olive tree is an illustration of hope. Lest anyone suppose that Jews are condemned and that God's sternness against them is irrevocable, Paul concludes that **God is able to graft them in again** (v. 23). He adds, **if they do not persist in unbelief**, which implies that human free will is also operative in the accomplishment of God's eternal purpose. But his point stands: it is easier to graft natural branches back into the tree from which they came than to graft wild branches into a different tree. A host organism will more readily accept an organ transplanted from itself (or from a blood relative) than from a stranger. How much more readily will these, the natural branches, **be grafted into their own olive tree** (v. 24)?

Paul may have been unrealistic to expect in his lifetime what 2,000 years of history have yet to witness, for Jews as a whole have still not turned to the gospel (although the growing number of messianic Jews is very significant). Nevertheless, the church which is truly Christian will continue to pray to that end. Humanly speaking, the prospect of Jews converting to Christianity does not look hopeful, especially in the wake of the church's shameful record of anti-Semitism over the centuries, and not excluding by and large its record during the ghastly spectre of the Holocaust. Perhaps the hopeful prospect of the olive tree illustration is best viewed from a historical perspective. When compared with the course of humanity on earth, Christianity is a relatively young religion. In contrast to the vast reaches of time which preceded Christ, 2,000 years since his birth are relatively short. If God waited for the fulness of time to send his Son (Gal. 4:4), we must not doubt that he continues to achieve his purpose in history between the first and second advents of his Son. This is the certain hope of Romans 9–11. As Luther noted, just as the sons of Jacob (Israel!) rejected Joseph and sold him into slavery, only years later to reencounter and acknowledge their brother in the most unexpected way, so "it will happen that the Jews who expelled Christ to the Gentiles, where he now reigns, will come to him in the end" (*Lectures on Romans*, pp. 315–16).

Additional Notes   §26

11:11–12 / Writing several centuries after Paul, at least one rabbi echoed the apostle's teaching on the role of jealousy in conversion. In the fourth century A.D. Rabbi Papa said, "If the ox runs and falls one has to replace it in the stall with a horse, something which one would not have done before the accident because of his preference for the ox. When the ox recovers, however, it is difficult to send the horse away after one has become used to it. So it is with God: when he saw the fall of Israel he gave her greatness to the peoples of the world, and when the Israelites turn and repent God finds it difficult to destroy the peoples of the world on account of the Israelites" (Str-B, vol. 3, p. 289 [my translation]).

11:13–16 / There are no exact parallels in the OT to the metaphors of verse 16, but similarities to the **dough** and **whole batch** may perhaps be found in Num. 15:17–21, Neh. 10:37, and Ezek. 44:30, and to Israel as a planting of God in Isa. 5:1ff., Jer. 11:17, and Lev. 19:23–24(?). See Str-B, vol. 3, p. 291. Whether Paul was indebted to either set of images is a matter of question.

11:17–24 / For Barth's view of Christ as the **root**, see *Church Dogmatics* (II/2), trans. and ed. G. Bromiley and T. Torrance (Edinburgh: T. & T. Clark, 1967), p. 286. For an understanding of salvation history extending from Abraham to Christ, see C. Maurer, *"rhiza," TDNT*, vol. 6, p. 988–89, and Dunn, *Romans 9–16*, pp. 659–60. Thorough discussions of the whole issue are presented in Cranfield, *Romans*, vol. 2, pp. 515–20, and especially in O. Hofius, "Das Evangelium und Israel: Erwägungen zu Römer 9–11," *ZTK* 83 (1986), pp. 297–324.

For an extended treatment of the significance of vv. 17–24 for the Jews' place in salvation history, see J. Edwards, "A Response to 'A Theological Understanding of the Relationship Between Christians and Jews,' " in *Christians and Jews Together. Voices from the Conversation,* ed. D. Dawe and A. Fule (Louisville: Presbyterian Publishing House, 1991), pp. 72–83.

For a reminder of the relative lateness of Christianity on the historical scene and its achievements since its arrival, see K. S. Latourette, *A History of Christianity* (New York: Harper and Brothers, 1953), pp. 3ff.

§27 The Salvation of Israel and the Glory of God (Rom. 11:25–36)

So far in chapters 9–11 Paul has advanced his argument with care and deliberation. He has shown that from all peoples on earth God separated one people to receive his promise by faith. When the chosen people refused to believe and held fast to righteousness by law, God extended the promise to the Gentiles who received it by faith. But Israel's rejection of God did not force God to a countermove of rejecting Israel. "God's gifts and his call are irrevocable," says Paul (v. 29). From unbelieving Israel God produced a remnant of faith, and this remnant became a firstfruits of the salvation of Israel as a whole. The inclusion of Gentiles in salvation would arouse hardened Israel to faith, "and so all Israel will be saved" (v. 26).

That final triumph of Israel's salvation is celebrated in 11:25–36. In reaching the crest of his argument Paul himself is borne by its wondrous force. The previously guarded development of his argument gives way to a summary of the themes in chapters 9–11. The place of Israel in the plan of salvation is anchored to two points—mystery and mercy. This is revealed by reviewing Paul's original sequence of salvation, "first for the Jew, then for the Gentile" (1:16). Now, however, the order is reversed. The "full number of the Gentiles" must first enter salvation, and then "all Israel will be saved" (vv. 25–26). This is not something strictly discernible to the mind. It is a mystery which can be known only through revelation and apprehended only by faith. Paul's faith soars to a hymnic doxology in verses 33–36, not unlike the end of chapter 8. But there the doxology was a hymn to God's love in Christ; here it is a hymn to God's wisdom in salvation.

11:25–27 / **I do not want you to be ignorant of this mystery, brothers,** begins Paul. At critical junctures of thought the apostle often employs solemn avowals like this one to underscore the importance of his argument (1:13; 10:1; 2 Cor. 1:8; 1 Thess. 4:13). The governing word in this section is **mystery** (v. 25). In the NT "mystery" generally means the purpose of God for salvation in Jesus Christ (Mark 4:11; Eph. 1:9). It is a mystery not because God desires to keep it hidden, but because if it is to be apprehended it must be made known by God. Contrary to all reasonable expectations, God loves this world and commits himself sacrificially to its redemption. This mystery is personified and supremely knowable in Jesus Christ, the "visible expression of the invisible God" (Col. 1:15, Phillips).

Mystery means all this and more in verse 25. Its specific reference is to the salvation of Israel. The **hardening** of Israel belongs to the plan of salvation **until the full number of Gentiles has come in. And so all Israel will be saved** (vv. 25–26). It may seem an odd way of redeeming Israel, but it leaves no doubt about God's mercy and omnipotence. God accomplishes his purposes in uncommon ways. It is, quite literally, a **mystery** which cannot be penetrated by human observation or by the most enlightened reason, but is received only as a revelation from God himself. Who would have supposed that God would include Gentiles in salvation and, moreover, that their salvation would *precede* that of the chosen people? This accounts for Paul's warning **that you** Gentiles **may not be conceited** (v. 25). The salvation of Gentiles is entirely a matter of God's grace, not of their merits—and the same will be true for Jews.

The reference to Israel's **hardening in part** (v. 25) probably does not mean a temporal hardening of limited duration, since Paul nowhere else uses the expression in this way. Rather, it should be understood quantitatively as that part of Israel (albeit the larger) which remains outside salvation **until the full number of Gentiles has come in**. Not the least remarkable aspect of Romans 9–11 is Paul's refusal to write off unbelieving Israel. He remains confident that God has not rejected unbelieving Israel (11:1), and therefore he continues to consider it as a unified whole. Israel's (mis)fortunes may be perplexing, but they are not a nightmare of the absurd or a betrayal by God. They are the result of God's plan. The **so** in verse 26 is a little word with great force: in this way—and only in this way—will Israel be saved. The progression of events is clear: Israel's hardness, the Gentiles' inclusion, Israel's jealousy, and finally Israel's acceptance of Christ and salvation. Paul does not elaborate *why* God ordains this so, but the result is that **all Israel**, like the Gentiles, **will be saved** by grace alone (cf. v. 26).

The assertion that **all Israel will be saved** (v. 26) is no less problematic in our day than in Paul's. The various interpretations which have been suggested fall into two camps. One camp attempts a figurative interpretation. Augustine and Luther understand it as a reference to "spiritual Israel" (so Gal. 6:16) or the church. Similarly, Calvin and Barth take **Israel** to refer to the elect portion of both Gentiles and Jews (9:11; 11:5, 7), whereas Bengel understands it to refer to the Jewish Christian remnant (11:5). In one way or another, however, all these views surrender the one thing in Romans 9–11 that Paul refuses to surrender—unbelieving Israel. Such views may accord with the historical facts that greater Israel has not responded to the gospel, but they cancel the offense of unbelieving Israel (9:2ff.; 11:25–26) and discount the clear context of verse 26 that **all Israel** consists of the believing remnant *plus* those Jews who were hardened (11:7, 25).

The second camp attempts a literal interpretation, understanding **all Israel** to include every Israelite, the numerical total of Jews. This might appear to be the sense of the Mishnah, "All Israelites have a share in the world to come" (m. *Sanh.* 10.1; elsewhere, T. Benj. 10.11). Even the Mishnah, however, does not mean that every single Jew would be saved, for it proceeds to enumerate a considerable list of exceptions (e.g., deniers of the resurrection, deniers of the law, readers of heretical books, magicians, certain kings of Israel [Jeroboam, Ahab, Manasseh], the generation of the flood, the generation of the wilderness, inhabitants of an apostate city, and so on). "All Israelites" here, as elsewhere in Jewish literature, means Israel as a people, a collective unit, without specifying that every Jew will be saved.

This is surely Paul's meaning in verse 26. Throughout chapters 9–11 the apostle has been thinking less of individual salvation than of Jews and Gentiles as a whole. He does not say that every Jew will be saved anymore than he says that every Gentile will be saved. Indeed, were Paul to assert that Jews would be saved simply *because* they were Jews, he would assert the very position which he earlier combatted, that circumcision alone (2:28–29), or descent from Abraham (4:1ff.), qualified one for salvation. That would compromise the meaning and necessity of faith ("and if they [Jews] do not persist in unbelief, they will be grafted in," 11:23). Paul's thought rather is of salvation of the

Gentile world *as a whole* (**the full number of Gentiles**, v. 25, also
Acts 13:48), and of Israel *as a whole* (i.e., **all Israel**, v. 26). The
apostle thus envisions a point in the future when by grace greater
Israel will embrace the gospel by faith, as have Gentiles in the
past.

This is supported by a quotation in verses 26–27, whose
first three lines come from Isaiah 59:20–21, and the fourth from
Isaiah 27:9. Whether or not "**The deliverer** who **will come from
Zion**" was understood messianically in Paul's day (see Cranfield,
Romans, vol. 2, p. 578), Paul applies the quotation to Christ Jesus
as a reminder that the messianic hope is fulfilled in him. Paul is
silent about when and how this will happen, but it is clear that
he does not link it to the reestablishment of the Jewish nation (or
state of Israel). Neither does the apostle suggest that there are two
ways of salvation, one for Gentiles through Jesus Christ, and one
for Jews through Torah. Paul teaches that there can be no deliverance for Israel (as there could be none for Gentiles) apart from
Christ. For both Jews and Gentiles, salvation is wholly dependent
on a common faith in their common savior (1:16–17; 3:21–24).

Furthermore, the opening line of the quotation in verse 26
reveals a change from the original. Both the Hebrew and Greek
texts of Isaiah 59:20 read that a deliverer will come *to* Zion,
whereas Paul says the **deliverer will come** *from* Zion. How this
change occurred is anyone's guess, but it is worth considering
that Paul altered the text to emphasize that the savior *to* Israel
would come *from* Israel, thus persuading Jews that Jesus was *their*
savior foretold in the OT.

11:28–32 /   C. K. Barrett sees the following two parallel-
isms in this passage:

> A—**Enemies on your account** (v. 28)
> B—**Loved on account of the patriarchs** (v. 28)
> C—**For God's gifts . . .** (v. 29)
> A′—**You were at one time . . . have now** (v. 30)
> B′—**They too have now . . . that they too may now** (v. 31)
> C′—**For God has bound . . .** (v. 32; Barrett, *Romans*, pp. 224–25).

These balanced statements give the passage a definite rhetorical structure and reveal the finesse with which Paul concludes
chapters 9–11. The passage repeats and culminates two contrasts
already mentioned: "objects of wrath" and "objects of mercy"
(9:22–23), and "the kindness and sternness of God" (11:22).

Israel is both God's enemy and God's friend. Israel is an enemy **as far as the gospel is concerned**, but **loved on account of the patriarchs** (v. 28; so Jub. 15:30; 22:9; 4 Ezra 3:13; 5:27). Gentiles once were objects of wrath (1:18ff.), but they are now objects of mercy because of their faith in the gospel. For Jews the issue is exactly the opposite: they once were objects of mercy because of their election and knowledge of the law, but they are now objects of wrath because of their disbelief in the gospel. Thus, God comes to his people in only one of two ways, in wrath or mercy. There is no third way. If we will not receive the mercy of God then we must face the wrath of God which would drive us to his mercy (Isa. 63:10—14). God's mercy is the final word, **for God's gifts and his call are irrevocable** (v. 29).

As we come to the end of Romans 9–11 we realize how clearly this verse has charted Paul's course all along. Israel's calling was discussed at length in 9:6–29, but even Israel's antagonism to that calling could not cancel the purpose of God. God does not pull down the olive tree and plant another because its branches are worthless. He cuts off the fruitless branches, grafts others onto the tree, and eventually regrafts the faithless branches back onto the tree as well. The end result? An unpromising sowing yields an unimaginable harvest, "thirty, sixty, or even a hundred times," according to the parable of the sower (Mark 4:1–9).

What has lain beneath the surface of Romans looms inescapably before us in verses 31–32. Disobedience leads to obedience; disbelief to faith, wrath to mercy. Human disobedience—in whatever form, from whatever people—does not jeopardize sovereign grace. The Gentiles cannot boast in their blessing, nor can Jews despair in their hardness. The blessing of the former results from grace, the judgment of the latter leads to grace. In both cases, grace triumphs.

The second parallelism is concluded, and with it the argument of Romans 9–11, in verse 32, **For God has bound all men over to disobedience so that he may have mercy on them all. All** does not imply universalism, but, with reference to verses 25–26, it suggests that God's salvation is offered to and appropriated by Jews and Gentiles alike. The Greek term for **bound over**, *synkleiō*, means to "shut up" or "imprison" and is a close parallel of Galatians 3:22. Gaugler likens verse 32 to a master key which opens all the doors to Paul's gospel (*Der Römerbrief*, vol. 2, pp. 209–13).

That may be an overstatement, but it certainly is the master key to Romans 9–11. What a breathtaking conclusion: God goes so far as to hand over *all* peoples to disobedience—Jews to pride in the law and Gentiles to rebellion against the law—in order to show mercy to both. At long last comes the answer to the dreary rehearsal of sin in Romans 1–3. "There is no difference, for all have sinned and fall short of the glory of God" (3:22–23). God has locked sinners in their own rebellion and barred and bolted the doors, eliminating any way of escape except through his mercy.

It is now apparent that Paul applies the same lines of argument to world history which he applied to the justification of sinners in chapters 3–5. For the sinful world as well as for the sinful individual, the only access to mercy is from condemnation. This is assuredly a great mystery (v. 25), which apart from revelation would be sheer folly. God does not work with merely unserviceable material, he works with *enemies*. In 5:10 the enemies were individuals, here (v. 28) they are entire peoples. Before they can be justified they must all be condemned. God creates *and* redeems out of nothing.

11:33–36 / Eastern Orthodoxy has always taught that worship begins where theology ends. Where the legs of reason grow weary, the heart may yet soar on wings like eagles. Verse 33 marks the frontier between theological argumentation and sublime worship. Paul's long and difficult philosophy of history now yields to a doxology to God's wisdom. A lesser soul than Paul, having plunged into the labyrinth of divine sovereignty and human sin, might, like Job, have emerged shaking his head in despair. Not so the apostle. The severity of the problem *magnifies* the greatness of God. **Oh, the depth of the riches of the wisdom and knowledge of God!** (v. 33). What the mind cannot know, the heart, as Pascal recognized, may know by other reasons. The limits of reason lead not to defeat and despair but to the threshold of faith.

The doxology at 11:33ff. does not follow the normal pattern of Jewish doxologies. It is patterned rather after the end of chapter 8, though here the doxology exalts God's wisdom rather than his love. This doxology is not the result of Paul's argument in chapters 9–11, but the assumption which underlies it. Paul begins with God's **unsearchable judgments** (v. 33), just as he began chapter 9 with God's sovereign judgments in Israel. He concludes with God's inscrutable ways (v. 33), just as he concludes chapter 11 with the mystery of God's redemption of Israel. Unfathomable love governed God's work of redemption at the end of chapter 8; unspeakable wisdom directs God's course in history at the end of chapter 11. Where the mind cannot know God's thoughts (v. 34), the heart may yet trust his character. If God's love spelled salvation by surprise, his wisdom results in sovereign acts in history leading to mercy. **All things,** says Paul, are **from him and through him and to him** (v. 36). This verse finds a close parallel in 1 Corinthians 8:6, though whereas the prepositions there refer to Christ, here they refer to God, who is at once creator, sustainer, and goal of creation. **To him be the glory forever! Amen.**

Additional Notes   §27

11:25–27 / "Let us remember of this word *mystery*," says Calvin, "that [the Jews'] conversion will neither be common nor usual. . . . It is called a mystery because it will be incomprehensible until the time of its revelation" (*Romans*, p. 435). Note also Paul Achtemeier's discussion of **mystery:**

> Clearly, Israel's rejection of Christ is open to a variety of interpretations. One interpretation: They rejected Christ because when Christ came, God was through with them, and so their call proved to be only temporary. Another interpretation: Israel's call never was valid, and their claims of a special relationship to God the Creator were self-serving illusions. Yet another: In the end God rejected them because of their rejection of his Son. All are possible, indeed even plausible—and all are wrong. The reason for Israel's being hardened in its rebellion against God's Son? Grace! Grace for gentiles, and finally grace for Israel as well! God's plan, says Paul, runs from God choosing Israel, to his hardening Israel to save gentiles, and then to his saving gentiles in order finally to save Israel (*Romans*, p. 188).

Ernst Käsemann (*Romans*, p. 324) and Otfried Hofius ("Das Evangelium und Israel," *ZTK* 83 [1986], pp. 318–19) argue that whereas Gentiles come to faith through proclamation of the gospel, Jews will come to faith only through the word of Christ himself at his second coming. It is an intriguing thesis, but does it not run counter to passages like 9:2ff. and 11:23, where Paul struggles with the Jews' disbelief? Must the future tense of **the deliverer will come from Zion** (which is, after all, an OT quotation) refer unconditionally to the Parousia, or could it not possibly refer to Christ's first coming and the **covenant** (v. 27) of the cross? Moreover, does not 10:14–21 imply that Jews, like Gentiles, come to faith through the preaching of the gospel?

11:28–32 / A footnote in the NIV draws attention to the second **now** in verse 31. Some ancient manuscripts either omit the word or substitute "later" in its place (which better agrees with Paul's sense). The meaning would then be, Jews are *now* disobedient but *later* will receive mercy. On the other hand, the inclusion of **now** is the more difficult reading, which might argue for its originality since scribes tended to render difficult readings easier. Evidence is nearly divided on this reading (see Metzger, *TCGNT*, p. 527). I would suggest that **now** was added to agree with verse 30 and to enhance the parallelism of verse 31. On the other hand, if **now** is original, Paul is perhaps telescoping the future mercy of God into the present, since he regards the time between the cross of Christ and the return of Christ as a unity (e.g., "Now is the time of God's favor, now is the day of salvation," 2 Cor. 6:2).

11:33–36 / A beautiful Jewish doxology is found in 2 Apoc. Bar.: "O Lord, my Lord, who can understand your judgment? Or who can explore the depth of your way? Or who can discern the majesty of your path? Or who can discern your incomprehensible counsel? Or who of those who are born has ever discovered the beginning and the end of your wisdom?" (14:8–9).

The person who is justified by faith shall live (1:17). That is the theme of the epistle. In chapters 5–8 Paul began to discuss the characteristics of the "new life" (6:4), but not until chapter 12 does he devote himself to the ethical and ecclesiastical shape of it. Justification by faith produces neither moral passivity nor permissiveness. Rather, the indicative of chapters 1–11 leads to the imperative of chapters 12–16. The faith which saves is a faith which can and must be lived, and only the faith which is lived is a faith which saves. The righteousness which comes *to* us in Christ must become rooted *within* us in the Spirit. If by justification we were born to a "living hope" (1 Pet. 1:3), then in sanctification we must become a "living sacrifice" (12:1). Being and becoming—these are but renditions of the idea already broached in chapter 6 that our old self has been crucified with Christ so that we may live to God (6:5–10; also Gal. 2:19–20). The ethical exhortations of chapter 12 are not an epilogue to the gospel. Neither are they ends in themselves; rather, they flow out of righteousness by faith and are demanded by it. Good works are not a prelude to salvation, but a consequence of it. We do not try to be good in order to be saved, but we must be saved in order to be "pleasing to God" (12:1).

Chapter 12 brings us to a promontory from which we can see the end of the epistle, and it may be helpful to provide an overview of the terrain still before us. Romans 12:1–2 is a magnetic pole for everything Paul will teach about the church and Christian life in the end of the letter. Verses 3–8 begin by discussing the nature and order of the body of Christ in light of Paul's appeal to be a "living sacrifice" (12:1). He then outlines the manifestations of love within the church and social relations (12:9–21), which he follows by discussing attitudes toward the state and government (13:1–14). He concludes in 14:1–15:21 by addressing the issue of judging others. Chapter 15 highlights Paul's travel plans for Rome and Spain, and chapter 16 concludes with a lengthy list of personal greetings. The purpose throughout is to show that grace is not an abstraction, but a gift of God which shapes and structures Christian life both corporately and personally.

12:1–2 / **Therefore, I urge you, brothers, in view of God's mercy, to offer your bodies as living sacrifices** (v. 1). So begins the most aesthetic formulation of Christian ethics in Scripture. Earlier buds of ethics (6:12–23; 8:12–13) now come to full flower. The issue concerns not religious renewal or increased spiritual consciousness, but the transformation of bodily existence as an expression of spiritual worship.

Usually when Paul begins with the words, **Therefore, I urge you, brothers,** he asserts his apostolic authority as the basis for an appeal to follow. But here he appeals to a higher authority. The sacrifice of obedience is evoked not by Paul's authority but by *God's mercy*. All ethical systems make some appeal to moral law and rules. For example, Kant's Categorical Imperative ("Act only on that maxim whereby you at the same time would wish that it should become a universal law") appeals to an "oughtness" of moral behavior. Paul, however, makes no appeal to moral principles. He appeals solely to God's mercy. If Christian morality were simply a deterrence of divine wrath, then it would not be morality at all, for it would not be free. It would simply be some sort of moral ransom rooted in fear. If it were done in hopes of receiving something from God, then it would be manipulative and egocentric. True Christian ethics, on the other hand, are ethics of gratitude. The obedience pleasing to God is characterized by free and willing submission because of God's prior sacrifice of his Son on our behalf (8:32; 9:16).

In 8:29 Paul made the remarkable claim that God predestined believers "to be conformed to the likeness of his Son." It is that shaping or remaking of the believer in the whole of his bodily existence according to the image of Christ that Paul appeals to here. It is one thing to give *things* to God (money, time, talents, services, sacrifices, etc.) but quite another to give *oneself*. God sent his Son not to enlighten our minds, raise our emotional level, cultivate our talents, or improve our morals, but to redeem the whole person, and beyond that the world itself. As creator of the universe, sustainer of all things, and eternal judge, God is Lord of all things. If God loves the whole person, then the only fitting response is to return the whole person to that love, **to offer** our **bodies as living sacrifices** (v. 1). This sacrifice is **holy and pleasing to God** and our **spiritual ... worship**. If "God is for us" (8:31) then God is free from the charge of being arbitrary or even vindictive. We may be assured that, as our compassionate and merciful Father, God has our eternal good ever before him. The finality of Paul's appeal, therefore, rests entirely in God's mercy.

The imagery here—**offer, holy, pleasing, sacrifice**—stems from animal sacrifice in Israel. The gift which was brought to the altar became consecrated to God and no longer belonged to the one who offered it, but to God. So it is in the Christian faith. Christians no longer belong to themselves but to God who redeemed them. Their lives are countersigned in faith to God's account. A **living sacrifice** is, of course, an oxymoron. The effectiveness of an animal sacrifice in the OT was precisely in its *death* (**sacrifice** [Gk. *thysia*], comes from a root meaning "to kill" [*thyō*]). But through faith believers have died and been raised with Christ, and the worship pleasing to God is not the final devotion of a victim's death, but the total devotion of a believer's life. Since Christ "died for all, . . . therefore all died" (2 Cor. 5:14). "Now if we died with Christ, we believe that we will also live with him" (6:8). The hope of life eternal *with* Christ begins by living *for* Christ in bodily existence.

Holy in both its Greek and Hebrew originals does not mean "perfection" so much as "set apart," i.e., the separation of something from its former allegiances and its devotion to God. No one is a person without a body and the things which pertain to it. Likewise, the body, or the whole person, is the visible and practical expression of faith. Similarly, in the old covenant the word for **pleasing** (*euarestos*) frequently referred to the pleasing odor of a burnt sacrifice. But in the new covenant, since believers have been "crucified with Christ" (Gal. 2:20) who is the perfect sacrifice, the "fragrance" of *life* is now more pleasing than the odor of death.

The presentation of our bodies is a **spiritual act of worship** (v. 1; see Deut. 11:13). The Greek word for **spiritual**, *logikos*, has no exact English equivalent, although the word "logic" (which derives from the term) carries the sense that the presentation of our bodies is a *logical* or reasonable form of worship. At a deeper level the word concerns the inner integrity of a sacrifice as opposed to its external form. Both Jews and pagans made a practice of placing the bodies of animals on altars to propitiate God, but whether the sacrifice actually expressed a sacrificial *attitude* was another question. **Spiritual** narrows the distance between sacrificer and sacrificed. The sacrifice acceptable to God cannot be something apart from believers, but it must be believers themselves! This thought finds a parallel in Hebrews 10:19–22 where Christ appears both as high priest and sacrificial victim.

All persons, Christians included, live within a network of relationships. Recognizing this fact, Paul continues, **Do not conform any longer to the pattern of this world, but be transformed** (v. 2). His concern is with *form*: the form or **pattern of this world** versus the **transformation** of faith. Paul does not say not to conform; that would be a utopian dream. What, after all, does it mean to be human if not to choose patterns and models which provide meaning in life? The question was not *whether* one should conform, but *to what* one should conform. He urges his readers to cooperate with the work of God in their lives by being "conformed to the likeness of his Son" (8:29; also Eph. 4:13).

Conformity, then, must be patterned after Jesus Christ. Modern society beams a collage of intense images at believers and non-believers alike through the media, advertising, polls, style, social and materialistic pressure, and ideologies. These images are often most effective when they are least recognized. The Christian life is an ongoing discipline of learning to be transformed by the lordship of Christ rather than being conformed to social, moral, and even spiritual images. When the church accommodates itself uncritically to this age, the Christian must resist that conformity as well, not only out of obedience to Christ, but for the purpose of reforming the church to its rightful calling.

The wording of the NIV, **do not conform . . . be transformed** (v. 2) renders the verbs as a summons to the divine will and purpose out of the free obedience which is evoked by God's mercies in verse 1. The rendering thus conveys the necessary assent and cooperation of human free will with the work of grace. It is equally possible, however, to render the verbs as imperative passive (rather than middle), "do not *be* conformed . . . but *be* transformed," thus connoting that free will is aided by the divine will. This age indeed works on us, but so does the Holy Spirit. It is not we who cause the gospel to have this transforming power, but the gospel itself which transforms us. The surrender of life is the believer's responsibility, but the transformation of life is

God's. Sanctification, like justification, is equally the work of God in the believer's life. Thus the apostle summons believers to *be* transformed (v. 2), to *be* led by the Spirit (8:14), to become his "workmanship" (Eph. 2:10).

Transformation by God begins by the **renewing of your mind**. Among much of Christianity there is, if not a skepticism about the intellect, an uncertainty about it. A greater premium is placed on right actions than on right thought, on proper behavior than on the reasons and motives for it.

The renewed mind must be understood against the "depraved mind" of 1:28. A depraved mind, of course, does not regard itself as depraved any more than a hypochondriac regards his or her illnesses as imagined. Consequently, what "seems" right to such a mind may not be at all right in God's eyes. Likewise, the new management of life by the Spirit may call for changes that at first do not seem right. After the resurrection, for example, Jesus told Peter that in the future "someone [will] lead you where you do not want to go" (John 21:18). The very sign of God's lordship, in other words, was that God would require of Peter something he would not will of his own accord. Discipleship, which means "to learn" in Greek, consists of *un*learning as well as learning. On another occasion it was assuredly a reasonable thing in Peter's mind to try to dissuade Jesus from the cross, but a sharp rebuke exposed the error of his thinking (Mark 8:33). Or again, it seemed logical that if the chosen people rejected their Messiah then God would reject them, but Paul passionately disagrees (11:1–2). Only a spiritual "mind transplant" will produce an ability **to test and approve what God's will is**. The **renewed mind** is the gift of grace to see ourselves, others, and the world from the perspective of the cross of Jesus Christ, which alone produces a hatred for our sins instead of delight in them, and a love for sinners instead of rejection of them. "Oh, the depth of the riches of the wisdom and knowledge of God!" (11:33).

The renewal of the mind **approves what God's will is—his good, pleasing and perfect will** (v. 2). If Christian conduct were simply adhering to a legal code or moral principle, then there would be no need **to test and approve what God's will is**. But Christian conduct grows only from discipleship, and discipleship from learning and following Christ. The renewed mind is thus the discipled mind, and the discipled mind must be a discerning mind which approves what is **good, pleasing and perfect**. The will of God is **good** because it is morally right, it is **pleasing** because it is acceptable and agreeable to his character, and it is **perfect** because it promotes his saving will for humanity.

12:3 / In a somewhat abrupt transition Paul now reminds believers on the basis of his apostolic authority (**by the grace given me**) that the first rule of the new life, both personally and socially, is a sober self-estimate. This can be derived only from the acknowledgement that one is a forgiven sinner. The Greek reflects a fourfold play on the word "think" (*phronein*). **Do not think of yourself more highly** (*hyperphronein*) **than you ought** to think (*phronein*), **but rather think** (*phronein*) **of yourself with sober judgment** (*sōphronein*). It is not coincidental that an admonition to think rightly follows a verse about "the renewing of your mind." It is precisely those who take their calling most seriously who are most prone to overestimating or misjudging it (Gal. 2:6). "Know thyself" is a difficult imperative, but it is necessary for the health of the fellowship.

Self-understanding must be based on **the measure of faith God has given you** (also Eph. 4:7). The outward proclamation of the gospel in preaching and Scripture and the inward testimony of the Holy Spirit (8:16) remain the two standards, or **the measure of faith**, by which believers must judge themselves and their gifts. Measurement by our own standards tends to result in a superiority complex, while measurement by the standards of others leads to an inferiority complex. Faith, on the other hand, always holds two things before believers: *simul justus et peccator*—we are sinners, but we are being redeemed by grace. Faith teaches that we are not who we think we are. We are not indispensable, but neither are we useless. Faith holds fast to the promise that despite ourselves the Holy Spirit can and does use us as instruments of God.

12:4–5 / The first consequence of being "transformed by the renewing of your mind" (v. 2) is a new self-understanding. This self-understanding is not achieved in a vacuum of individualism, however. It comes only through the body of Christ. The ancients were much taken with the idea of the one and the many, or the sum and its parts, and Paul finds this a serviceable construct for the church. The metaphor of the body argues not for a pattern of uniformity and sameness, but for a unity of faith and diversity of gifts. The human body is not a unity *despite* its diversity, but a unity *because of* it. So it is with the church. In God's economy, self-understanding comes only through the "inner"-connectedness of believers, where the **many members** (v. 4) are freed from competing with one another and freed for complementing one another. Christians—all Christians—are members of an orchestra; not one of them is a soloist. The believer must first know who *we* are before he or she can know who *I* am. Faith, in other words, is corporate before it is individual.

Paul does not say that Christians are *like* a body but that they *are* the body of Christ. Moreover, it is not they who constitute Christ's body, but, in the same way that the root constituted the branches (11:17ff.), it is Christ who constitutes them. The church, then, is the vessel of Christ's revelation and saving work, but it is *not* identical with Christ. Where the church sets itself in place of Christ, there it makes the mistake of "outward" (2:28) or "natural" (9:8) Israel. Only where the church exists *in* Christ, and not in place of Christ, where **each member belongs to all the others**, is the church the body of Christ.

12:6–8 / In verse 6 Paul turns abruptly from the whole (the body) to its parts (the gifts). Grace not only saves and sanctifies sinners, it also equips them with gifts for ministry in the body. The word for **gift** (*charisma*, v. 6), in fact, is but a different form in Greek of the word for "grace" (*charis*). *Charisma* (**gifts**) is rare in Greek literature outside and prior to the writings of Paul, but it is especially characteristic of Paul in the NT. Spiritual gifts are the enactments or *event*ualizing of grace through human agency. Paul draws a corollary between faith and spiritual gifts. According to verse 1 faith must express itself concretely through our bodies; here in verses 6ff. grace expresses itself concretely in the church. Like parts of the human body, the gifts of the Spirit differ, though more according to purpose than value. In addition to discussing the various gifts, the following verses suggest a structure to administer such gifts through church order and government.

The gifts mentioned here, as well as in 1 Corinthians 12:27–31, are representative rather than exhaustive. Some gifts appear to be natural talents strengthened by the Spirit, whereas others are unique abilities following conversion. They are and remain gifts, however. True to their name, they are spiritual endowments for ministry within Christ's body; they are not *our* possessions or status-builders.

Prophecy stands at the head of the list. Paul devoted an entire chapter to prophecy in 1 Corinthians 14 and regards it as a decisive gift because of its close relationship to the proclamation of the word. Prophecy may suggest to our ears the predicting of future events, and it often entailed this element, but it primarily concerns offering guidance from the Spirit or God's word for the church in particular circumstances. Seven examples of early Christian prophecy can be found in Revelation 2–3. Its decisive element is that of spiritual or supernatural insight into the meaning of God's will. Genuine prophecy naturally corresponds to other manifestations of the Spirit. That seems to be the force of the corollary, **let him use** prophecy **in proportion to his faith** (v. 6). The Greek actually reads, "in proportion to *the* faith"—the idea being that spiritual gifts (in this case spiritual utterances) must correspond to the rule of faith as proclaimed by the apostles and believed, confessed, and taught in the churches.

The second gift, **serving**, is in Greek *diakonia* (from which "deacon" is derived). Literally meaning "to wait on tables," *diakonia* encompasses a wide variety of common labors, though "indicating very personally the service rendered to another" (Beyer, *TDNT*, vol. 2, p. 81). How interesting that this gift would precede the prestigious gift of teaching. It is not often that table waiters are ranked above theology professors! This undoubtedly is due to the remembrance of Jesus himself who exalted service of others over self; "the Son of Man did not come to be served, but to serve, and to give his life as a ransom for many" (Mark 10:42–45; also John 13:1–20). From the beginning Jesus' example of humility challenged the church to "consider others better than yourselves" (Phil. 2:1–11). The gospel thus consists of an indivisible unity of word and deed, faith and life, a unity which finds expression in the first two gifts, **prophecy** and **serving**.

A third gift is **teaching**. The prophet interprets the gospel according to the Spirit's direction in given circumstances, but the teacher, through knowledge of and reflection on the revelation of God, instructs the church in "the whole counsel of God" (Acts 20:27, RSV). Dunn notes, "That Paul recognizes the importance of *both* [prophecy and teaching], but prizes prophecy the more highly, needs to be remembered: teaching preserves continuity, but prophecy gives life; with teaching a community will not die, but without prophecy it will not live" (*Romans 9–16*, p. 729).

A further gift includes **encouraging** or exhortation (v. 8). This term literally depicts someone who is called alongside another as a helping companion. It should not be overlooked, and it is not coincidental, that the Gospel of John later calls the Holy Spirit, Paraclete (Gk. *paraklētos*), which picks up on this image. "I will ask the Father, and he will give you another Counselor to be with you forever—the Spirit of truth" (John 14:16–17, 26; 15:26; 16:7).

Verse 8 concludes with virtues rather than offices. The gift of giving is to be practiced **generously**, by which Paul intends the spirit of giving rather than the thing given. The Greek word for **generously** carries the idea of freedom and "single-mindedness," without second thoughts, ulterior motives, or divided allegiances. Likewise, leaders are to **govern diligently**. The Greek word might be translated "with haste," i.e., not begrudgingly, but readily and eagerly. By ministering **cheerfully** the servant of God liberates those whom he or she serves.

Four of the seven gifts in verses 6–8 relate to what the church traditionally has called the diaconate. Faced with burgeoning social ills and suffering, with a gospel which is increasingly marginalized, ministries of the diaconate afford the church numerous opportunities to reach "the least of these," i.e., those who for whatever reason no longer hear the gospel from the church. In so doing the church bears witness to the world that Jesus "did not come to be served, but to serve, and to give his life as a ransom for many."

Additional Notes §28

12:1–2 / Luther saw more clearly than many the occasional ill-fit of being transformed to God's will. "Every Christian should rejoice most, precisely when something is done against his will and intention, and he should be very apprehensive when he has his own way. I say this not only with respect to the desires of the flesh, but also with respect to the great achievements of righteousness" (*Lectures on Romans*, p. 328).

It is noteworthy how perfectly the prayer of St. Francis captures the essence of Romans 12:1–2.

12:3 / The metaphor of the body of Christ (which is related more fully in 1 Corinthians 12:12ff.) warns against both superiority and inferiority complexes. A superiority complex frustrates the participation of other members ("If the whole body were an eye, where would the sense of hearing be? If the whole body were an ear, where would the sense of smell be?" 1 Cor. 12:17), while an inferiority complex deprives the body of one's own contribution ("If the foot should say, 'Because I am not a hand, I do not belong to the body,' it would not for that reason cease to be part of the body," 1 Cor. 12:15).

The word for **sober judgment** (Gk. *sōphronein*, see Acts 26:25; 1 Tim. 2:9, 15; 2 Tim. 1:7; Titus 2:4) occurs in various contexts in the NT. The same word played an important role in Greek philosophy and ethics as one of the four cardinal virtues, promoting moderation and self-control (see Aristotle, *Nicomachean Ethics*, 1117b.13). Paul may employ the word here to defend against ecstatic or charismatic tendencies, but more probably to admonish Jews and Gentiles in Rome to be understanding and to act in moderation toward one another.

12:4–5 / Dunn's discussion of the body of Christ brings many essential points to light (*Romans 9–16*, pp. 722–25).

12:6–8 / Ernst Käsemann distinguishes between *pneumatika* and *charismata* here and in 1 Corinthians. Both terms refer to spiritual gifts, but the former means "charismatic" experiences and miracles, whereas the latter are more specialized gifts for ministry. In Käsemann's judgment both are important for Paul, but especially the latter are ordered for the benefit of Christian fellowship. "*Charisma* is the *pneumatika* taken into the service of Christ" (*Romans*, pp. 333–34).

Early Christian rules of faith can be found in 1:3–4; 1 Cor. 11:23–26; 15:3–5; Col. 1:15–20; 1 Tim. 3:16. Such rules of faith provided then, as they do now, a necessary balance to ecstatic prophecy, guarding the church from becoming a cult of sincere but misguided visionaries. For further instructions about traveling teachers, apostles, and prophets in early Christianity, see Did. 11–13.

A. Weisner distinguishes **serving** from slavery in the following manner: "The [slave] words express a relationship of dependence and the subordination of the [slave] to the [master]. [Serving] and its cognates, on the other hand, express much more strongly the idea of *service* on behalf of someone" (*EDNT*, vol. 1, p. 302).

§29 The Marks of a Christian (Rom. 12:9–21)

In his famous hymn to love in 1 Corinthians 13 Paul says, "if . . . I have not love, I am nothing" (v. 2). In Romans 13 he says that "love is the fulfillment of the law" (v. 10), and he enjoins Christians to owe no one anything except the debt of love (v. 8). In the latter half of Romans 12 Paul provides insight and guidance concerning the nature of love. Love is defined at the outset (v. 9), middle (v. 17), and end (v. 21) as a commitment to *good*, and especially the victory of good over evil. This section is something of a manual on the fruit of the Spirit, for nearly every virtue listed in Galatians 5:22 is expounded here. The examples are loosely joined together, although Paul directs them first to love within the Christian community (vv. 9–13), and then to love toward the world at large (vv. 14–21). The exhortations are seasoned throughout with OT wisdom, especially Proverbs, and the whole echoes the teachings of Jesus in the Sermon on the Mount (Matt. 5–7). In their teachings on love both Jesus and Paul reveal the chasm between the ethics of egoism and the "most excellent way" of *agapē* (1 Cor. 12:31). Christian love is shaped neither by the standards of the world nor by the promptings of self, but by the power of the Holy Spirit bearing witness within believers to the character of God.

12:9 / Paul first appeals for sincere or genuine love, since love is the primary fruit of the Spirit (Gal. 5:22). An examination of the Greek text reveals several important features not readily apparent in a translation. First, the opening sentence contains no verb and might be correctly translated "love (is) sincere" (cf. NIV, **Love must be sincere**). It may, in other words, be a statement about the nature of love and not merely a summons to love. Again, the word for **love**, *agapē*, has the definite article, indicating that Paul is not thinking of love in general, but of *the* (Christian) love. Finally, the word for **sincere** in Greek means "without hypocrisy" or "unstaged." In Greek drama a single actor (*hypokritēs*)

normally played several roles, with corresponding masks for each
character he played. But true love, says Paul, is *anypokritos*, "un-
hypocritical," because it does not play different roles. Love is not
a counterfeit, a mask of pretense, but a sincere expression of one's
intentions. It is, of course, possible to be kind or good from motives which are neither kind nor good. Indeed, there is great
temptation for religious people to render obligatory love. Jesus
criticized the scribes and Pharisees as *hypokritai*; they are, he said,
"whitewashed tombs, which look beautiful on the outside but on
the inside are full of dead men's bones and everything unclean"
(Matt. 23:27). Sincere love, Christian love, cannot be measured,
calculated, or staged. It must be honest, genuine, and true to the
motive of the giver.

Paul characterizes *agapē* as that which **hates what is evil;
clings to what is good**. In modern society love is used for a host
of things which have little, if anything, to do with *agapē*. If love is
not twisted by its ubiquitous associations with lust and sex, then
it is reduced to a sentiment. Sentimentality is a particular danger
because it grounds behavior in feelings of emotional idealism and
divorces itself from a world of imperfect choices. *Agapē*, on the
other hand, commits itself to the good of the other regardless of
cost to self. It is discriminating, for it distinguishes truth from
falsity. "Love does not delight in evil but rejoices with the truth"
(1 Cor. 13:6). *Agapē* is not a nice or pleasing disposition, and it is
not complacent in the face of wrong. It **hates evil**. The word
for **evil**, *ponēros*, is the strongest word for evil or wickedness in
Greek, and this is its only occurrence in Romans. The Christian
response to it must be equally strong. The Greek word *apostygein*
means to "detest" or "abhor." Whoever does not hate evil does
not love good. Refusing to condemn evil in whatever form it
takes (though not the people who do it), or tolerating evil for
whatever reason when there is within our power the ability to do
something about it, is no longer love. The prayer for social justice
in the *Book of Common Prayer* says that love "makes no peace with
oppression."

12:10–13 / Ten poignant examples of *agapē* comprise this
section, all of which are cast in parallel form. Each begins in Greek
with a substantive in the dative case which is followed by a
response in the participial mood; i.e., first a virtue, then an action
with respect to it. The sequence is enclosed between two homo-

phones in Greek, *philadelphia* (**brotherly love**, v. 10) and *philoxenia* (**hospitality**, v. 13). The following attempts to reproduce the flavor of the original:

> In brotherly love, being devoted to one another;
> in honor, outdoing one another;
> in zeal, never flagging;
> in the Spirit, being aglow;
> to the Lord, serving;
> in hope, rejoicing;
> in tribulation, being patient;
> in prayer, being constant;
> to the needs of the saints, sharing generously;
> in hospitality, being diligent.

The sequence begins with Christian fellowship: **be devoted to one another in brotherly love** (v. 10). Two words define the love of verse 9 in terms of the family. The first, *philadelphia* (**brotherly love**), refers to sibling love, while *philostorgos* (**devoted**) refers to the love of parents for children. Intimate affection among family members thus becomes a fitting model for the church. In reality, of course, families are not always charitable, and neither are churches. Nevertheless, with this term at the head of the sequence, Paul establishes familial love as the ideal characteristic of Christian fellowship.

The second word is to **honor one another above yourselves**. The Greek is somewhat obscure, but it seems to mean "prefer one another with honor" (cf. Phil 2:3, "consider others better than yourselves"). If our neighbor is one for whom Christ died, and if, as Matthew 25:31–46 makes abundantly clear, the Son of Man is mysteriously present in our neighbor (and especially in the *needy* neighbor), then our neighbor represents Christ to us and is worthy of greater honor than we show ourselves. This essential virtue became the masthead of the Rule of St. Benedict, namely, to receive all strangers as Christ.

The third word is, **never be lacking in zeal** (v. 11). True love, like any meaningful experience, wants to express itself, and it is no different with Christian love. Christians are constantly confronted by new challenges in life, in the face of which they cannot remain spectators. When such challenges represent the call of God and present opportunities for serving Christ, idleness is disobedience. The word translated **never be lacking** (Gk. *oknēros*), means the indolence or laziness of a slave as opposed to the eager motivation of a free citizen. The real enemy of zeal is not opposition but complacency, being "neither cold nor hot" (Rev. 3:15).

In conjunction with zeal Paul says to **keep your spiritual fervor** (v. 11). The Greek word for **fervor**, meaning to "boil or bubble," is used to describe the ardent spirit of Apollos in Acts 18:25. Is there a more attractive model of faith or a more worthy vessel of love than the glowing spirit of a Christian? The very image of ardor, however, warns against zealotry or false enthusiasm. Therefore, lest zealous Christians think themselves more deserving of God than others, let them recall the words of Jesus, "So that you also, when you have done everything you were told to do, should say, 'We are unworthy servants; we have only done our duty' " (Luke 17:10).

To **zeal** and **spiritual fervor** Paul adds, **serving the Lord** (v. 11). A few ancient manuscripts read "time" here rather than **Lord**, but the NIV, following the majority of manuscripts, is doubtlessly correct in its rendering. Paul is not thinking of seizing or savoring the moment (e.g., the classical idea of *carpe diem*), but of serving Christ. And lest anyone were to confuse **zeal** and **spiritual fervor** with mere spiritual effervescence, the apostle interjects the sanguine note of **serving**. The ardor of the Spirit does not dissipate in emotionalism but produces the constructive energy of service.

The sixth word is, **be joyful in hope** (v. 12). There is a slight oxymoron in the combination of hope and joy. Joy normally stems from favorable circumstances in the present, whereas hope looks to the good of the future. Consequently, joy may be shortsighted regarding the future, and hope oblivious of the present. Paul, however, says to **be joyful in hope**. Christian joy finds its source not in the present (whether favorable or not), for that is a hope which "disappoint[s] us" (5:5). Christian joy consists in the hope of "our adoption as sons [and] the redemption of our bodies" (8:23–25).

Not coincidentally, Paul follows being **joyful in hope** with being **patient in affliction** (v. 12). Earlier he said that suffering produces perseverance, character, and hope (5:3–4). Afflictions are not illusions as some religions maintain, nor are they necessarily the result of human or even religious failure. If the world hates Christ (Matt. 10:22; John 15:18), then **affliction** is one of the inevitable consequences for the follower of Christ. James says to "consider it pure joy, my brothers, whenever you face trials" (1:2). Where affliction cannot be accepted with joy, then it must be endured with patience. Endurance (5:3; Col. 3:13, "putting up with") is itself a Christian virtue. If one cannot overcome one's enemies, one may still hope to outlive them! Since the present world is not the final state of affairs, Christians hold on and hold out for the hope to come (John 16:33). For the present, enduring troubles prepares the soul for "an eternal glory that far outweighs them all" (2 Cor. 4:17).

There is a logical connection between being **patient in affliction** and **faithful in prayer** (v. 12). Prayer makes endurance possible. The verb rendered **faithful** carries the sense in Greek of "holding fast to" or "persisting in," and is frequently associated with prayer (Luke 18:1; Acts 1:14; 2:42; 6:4; Eph. 6:18; Col. 4:2; 1 Thess. 5:17). There is nothing either in the OT or in Judaism corresponding to the early Christian ideal of constant prayer. Here again constancy in prayer prepares the soul for its future glory. With the possible exception of faith, nothing in the Christian life requires more effort than prayer. It is a battle between flesh and Spirit, the world and God (Gal. 5:16ff.). Christians pray, and rightly so, for deliverance from harm and adversity on their earthly pilgrimage. But if their prayer is not answered accordingly they must not conclude that God is punishing them or give up their faith. The gospel is indeed a hospice of heaven in this life, but it is more often, and more importantly, a training camp for the life to come. The Spirit does not exempt Christians from hardship, but he promises to support them in it. The NT lays great emphasis on the virtue of endurance (Mark 13:13), and on patience, faithfulness, and self-control (Gal. 5:22–23) as signs of genuine faith.

The ninth admonition is to **share with God's people who are in need** (v. 13). Hospitality and generosity were hallmarks of early Christianity, and sharing was an important way by which Christians identified themselves (Acts 2:43ff.; 4:32ff.; James 2:14ff.). **Sharing** (Gk. *koinōnein*) is a concrete expression of "brotherly love" (v. 10) and defines the ideal of the church as a *koinōnia*, a sharing community of believers. Sharing was an appropriate reminder for Roman Christians who, because they lived in the capital city, received many visitors. In at least some quarters local inns were places of ill-repute. When this was the case, principle was augmented by necessity to provide lodging for the community's needy, and particularly for itinerant missionaries and preachers. In light of the probable conflicts between Jewish and Gentile Christians in Rome following the edict of Claudius (see Introduction), verse 13 may have been more than a general platitude. Paul clearly envisioned practical acts of giving as a way of overcoming the estrangement between Gentiles and Jews (15:26ff.). Given the fact that Western Christians today enjoy a standard of living considerably higher than the majority of people in the world, the relevance of this particular injunction would appear to surpass mere historical interest.

Paul concludes with **hospitality** (v. 13). This was a matter of practical necessity in a period when there were no church buildings or social agencies. The Greek word for **hospitality**, *philoxenia*, literally means "kindness to strangers" and complements *philadelphia*, "kindness to the brotherhood," at the head of the list (v. 10). The word for **practice** (Gk. *diōkein*) actually means "to press or pursue." **Practice hospitality**, therefore, carries the sense of intentionally striving to embrace strangers and needy individuals. Again, in the modern West where jobs are increasingly characterized by bureaucracy and depersonalization, and where cities contain entire districts inhabited by ethnic and racial minorities, it would seem incumbent on the church to consider anew the implication of this imperative for the present day.

12:14–16 / This world is not utopia, whether of a classless society or limitless prosperity. Like everyone else, Christians live in a world twisted by disparities between ideals and double standards, success and failure, friend and foe, life and death. Faced with the sometimes hostile, sometimes hospitable, but usually indifferent nature of this world, believers are not presented with the alternative of withdrawing in Stoic detachment or impassivity. Christians are *human* believers, and they cannot be more or less than that. But because their minds are being renewed (12:2), they are called to have a significantly different response to the world than they would have apart from the influence of the Spirit. Verses 14–21 cluster around that response and particularly around the problem of retaliation in the face of opposition and persecution.

The first command is to bless and not curse enemies (v. 14). There is no essential contradiction between this command and the earlier command to hate evil (v. 9), for Christians are commanded both in their own person and in others to hate *sin* but not to curse *sinners*. The difficulty of this commandment is com-

pounded by the fact that the urge to retaliate against adversaries is not only natural but seemingly justified. No one finds it easy to bless persecutors. The difficulty of the command to love one's enemies (Matt. 5:44) is evidence, however, that it is the will of God that is commanded here. And where the will of God is revealed, the Spirit of God enables those who receive it with faith and prayerfulness to obey it.

Nearly as difficult is the command to **rejoice with those who rejoice; mourn with those who mourn** (v. 15). Ancient Judaism as a rule did not extend *agapē* to this degree, although Sirach 7:34 is close, "Do not fail those who weep, but mourn with those who mourn." Christians often rejoice and grieve for reasons which are unchristian. Our joy and sorrow are too easily measured by *personal* gain or loss rather than by the cause of Christ. To rejoice with others (even when we are deprived of their joy) and to weep with others (even when we have not suffered their loss) requires a selflessness which only the power of *agapē* can bestow. Apart from the renewing of our minds, such commandments make no sense; and apart from the indwelling of the Holy Spirit, they are impossible to realize. The converted heart agrees that this is the perfect love of Christ, but the flesh rebels, reminding us of the unfinished progress in our lives before we approximate the "likeness of [God's] Son" (8:29).

Live in harmony. . . . do not be proud . . . associate with people of low position. . . . do not be conceited (v. 16). Although it is not apparent in the NIV, Paul stresses again (see verse 3) the intentionality of Christian behavior. The Greek word for "thinking" (*phronein*) appears three times in verse 16 and might be rendered, "Have this mind (*phronein*) among yourselves, do not think (*phronein*) inflated things. . . . do not be wise (*phronimos*) in yourselves." The final clause echoes Proverbs 3:7 and repeats Romans 11:25. Paul again reminds us that *agapē* begins with a renewed understanding.

The Greek of verse 16 is unclear whether association with lowly *things* is meant (a warning against haughtiness and ambitiousness) or lowly *people*. On the one hand, the neuter gender of the preceding phrase, "do not think inflated things" (NIV, **Do not be proud**), would appear to argue for "lowly things." On the other hand, the Greek word **low** (*tapeinos*) is used in the NT only of persons, and not things. Moreover, **associate** seems to suit persons better than objects. **People of low position** (so NIV) is therefore the preferable rendering (see 1 Cor. 1:27–29). This accords with the posture and parables of Jesus. "The King will reply, 'I tell you the truth, whatever you did for one of the least of these brothers of mine, you did for me' " (Matt. 25:40). Paul thus urges Roman Christians to show solidarity with the poor and oppressed, as he himself did (Gal. 2:10).

12:17–21 / The apostle now tackles the problem of retaliation, **Do not repay anyone evil for evil**. Retaliation is a response of the natural person (i.e., "flesh") to exact justice for a wrong incurred. The Christian, however, is not bound to a natural reflex, no matter how just it may seem, but to a considered response (Gk. *pronoein*, v. 17), which reflects the renewing of the mind and God's "good, pleasing and perfect will" (12:2). It is probably not coincidental that this command follows on the heels of associating with the humble and needy, for when Christians take their stand with the oppressed they often become the objects of persecution. That early Christians were often in such positions is well known, and that they were tempted to retaliate against their oppressors cannot be doubted. This teaching appears to have been standard throughout early Christianity (Matt. 5:38–42; 1 Thess. 5:15; 1 Pet. 3:9).

The NT is equally clear about **peace** (v. 18). Christians are commanded to be not only peace *keepers* (i.e., maintain peace, so Mark 9:50), but peace *makers* (promote peace, so Matt. 5:9). Like love, peace is a fruit of the Spirit (Gal. 5:22; see also 2 Cor. 13:11; 1 Thess. 5:13). **If it is possible** (v. 18) implies that peace is not a compromise of good and cannot be purchased at any price. Christians must do all they can to promote peace and tolerance without betraying the will of God. When the good is at stake, however, believers have no alternative but to choose it, even at the risk of jeopardizing peace. For modern Christians, serenaded by the subtle influences of peer pressure to be liked and popular above everything else, there is no negligible caution here.

God is not complacent in the face of evil, but his just wrath is of a wholly different character from human vengeance, which often and easily is fueled by self-interest, excess, and vindictiveness. The early church broke new ground at this point, for in Judaism revenge was permissible against non-Israelites or in cases of personal injury. Paul categorically excludes revenge: **Do not take revenge, my friends, but leave room for God's wrath** (v. 19). "The anger of man does not work the righteousness of God"

(James 1:20, RSV). This is particularly true where vengeance is unleashed because of personal injury. The reading of the Greek text, "Do not avenge *yourselves*," is instructive at this point. Certainly, nowhere is revenge *less* likely to express divine justice than where it is pressed into the service of self.

Paul quotes Proverbs 25:21–22 in support of peaceableness over vengeance (v. 20). It is as unnatural as it is difficult to forego revenge apart from God's help. While it may not be impossible to refrain from revenge in a given circumstance (v. 19), it is quite another matter to *do good* to the wicked (v. 20). Here, as elsewhere, the flame of *agapē* purges the dross of selfish ambition and tempers believers to conform to the image of God's Son.

At first reading verse 20 suggests that the reason for doing good to enemies is to cause them severer punishment, **"In doing this, you will heap burning coals on his head."** But considering the importance of *motive* in NT ethics (above all in the Sermon on the Mount, Matt. 5–7), it is quite impossible to reconcile a malicious intent with the *agapē* of God, who demonstrated his love by sending his Son to die for sinners (5:8). Rather, **heap**ing **burning coals on his head** intends to bring shame on wrongdoers so that they will repent of their evil. In this way evil will be overcome with good (v. 21).

Verse 21 consummates everything Paul has said of *agapē*. **Do not be overcome by evil, but overcome evil with good**. *Agapē* corresponds to God's nature (1 John 4:16) and his way of acting toward enemies (5:10). Since Christians are being transformed by God's will (12:2), love must also become their nature and manner of behavior. Pelagius said, "The enemy has overcome us when he makes us like himself" (quoted from Cranfield, *Romans*, vol. 2, p. 650). To repay evil for evil is to become like Satan. But to repay good for evil is to become like God. The essential victory over evil is the work of love. And this is no imaginary victory. Overcoming evil with good is the most revolutionary force in the world. Love cannot fail because it represents the sovereign will of God (1 Cor. 13).

Additional Notes §29

12:9 / In the history of creedalism there is a tendency not only to define what the church stands *for*, but also what it is *against*. This may be a doctrinal echo of **hating what is evil; clinging to what is good**, for the love of pure doctrine demands a condemnation of false doctrine. A modern theory of truth verification propounded by Anthony Flew, who maintains that the criterion for truth necessitates the establishing of the falsity of its opposite, would appear to corroborate Paul's idea here. "If there is nothing which an assertion denies then there is nothing which it asserts either." See John Hick, ed., *Classical and Contemporary Readings in the Philosophy of Religion*, 2d ed. (Englewood Cliffs, N.J.: Prentice-Hall, Inc., 1970), p. 466.

12:10–13 /   For the Benedictine Rule and its many echoes of Rom. 12:9–21, see *The Rule of St. Benedict*, ed. T. Fry, O.S.B. (Collegeville, Minn.: Liturgical Press, 1981).

On the textual variant in v. 11, Metzger notes that a scribe could have easily misread the Greek abbreviation for "Lord" for that of "time" (see *TCGNT*, p. 528). For full discussions of the variant, see Cranfield, *Romans*, vol. 2, pp. 634–36, and Dunn, *Romans 9–16*, p. 737.

On hospitality in v. 13, see V. H. Kooy, "Hospitality," *IDB*, vol. 2, p. 654. Especially in the nomadic, Mediterranean world, hospitality was regarded as an unspoken duty independent of written codes. In the Judeo-Christian tradition Abraham was venerated as a model of hospitality (Gen. 18), and more especially Jesus, because of his dependence on hospitality (e.g., Mark 1:29–31) and his teaching about it (e.g., Mark 2:15–17; Luke 14:1–24). Regarding the unreliability of inns in the ancient world, Plato warns of the unseemliness of tavernkeepers and the dishonorableness of the trade (*Laws*, 11.918).

12:14–16 /   The starting point for the NT understanding of *agapē* is in the OT. Exodus 23:4ff. commanded Israelites to render assistance to their enemies (including non-Israelites) in various emergencies. The fruit of such charity would be peace and friendship among peoples, with the hope that one's enemies might becomes one's friends. But ancient Judaism never succeeded in formulating the *love* for enemies as Jesus taught his disciples. The apex of its formulation was the negative principle not to rejoice over the misfortune of one's enemies, and not to repay evil for evil. See Str-B, vol. 1, p. 368.

12:17–21 /   On Jewish attitudes toward revenge, see Str-B, vol. 3, p. 300. On the same topic, Bengel offers something of a corollary to Pascal's "wager": Suppose that your adversary is not better, and that you are not worse, than you think. He will either obtain divine grace at the end, or not. If he obtains grace he will in so doing repent of the wrong he did to you, and you will not desire to press your case to deny him the grace God wills to give him. If he does not obtain grace, the supreme Judge will justly punish him for the wrong. Either way, judgment belongs to God. See Bengel, *Gnomon*, vol. 3, p. 167.

The metaphor of heaping burning coals on someone's head may have derived from Egypt where penitents carried burning coals on their head as a sign of contrition. See the material presented in Michel, *Der Brief an die Römer*, p. 311, footnote 1. This metaphor, and the theology behind it, is the root of the ethics of non-violence as personified by Gandhi and Martin Luther King, Jr. In accepting violence without retaliation, and in repaying hatred with kindness, the victim reveals the extent of the persecutor's crime, thereby hoping to shame him or her into repentance.

In Galatians 6:2 Paul speaks of fulfilling "the law of Christ," by which he means the spirit and manner of "loving your neighbor as yourself" (13:9). It is this which is the subject of Romans 12 and 13. If grace is the gospel reduced to one word, then *agapē* is the law reduced to a word (13:9). In chapter 12 Paul spoke of "the law of Christ" as sincere and practical expressions of *agapē* both inside and outside the church. Another expression of *agapē* is an affirmation of and submission to governments (13:1–7). Some commentators, noting the abrupt transition at 13:1 and the switch from the second to third person in 13:1–7, regard this section as a departure from Paul's teaching on *agapē* and an independent unit of thought. But, in fact, the instruction here is very much a part of the design since chapter 12. In agreement with 12:2 Paul appeals for a considered response "to approve what God's will is" with respect to rulers. "Those who do what is right" (v. 3) in civil duties also accomplish the good (the word for "right" is in Greek the same word for "good" in 12:9–21) and thus fulfill the rule of *agapē*. Calvin was surely correct that obedience to magistrates is not the least important way by which to cherish peace and preserve love of others (*Romans*, pp. 484–85).

13:1–5 / The question under consideration is a practical one: what ought to be the attitude of believers toward **governing authorities**? At the outset we must note the obvious: the apostle was not writing for Americans nurtured by the Declaration of Independence and modern ideas of civil rights, or for any constitutional and participatory democracies. Paul was addressing first-century Christians who were a quite powerless minority under a Roman oligarchy. Willi Marxsen's observation that Paul was not writing a dissertation on the relation of church and state, but rather making a pragmatic appeal "for loyal conduct in order to avoid a fresh edict" has much to recommend it (*Introduction to the NT*, p. 100).

Marxsen further warns that it is inadvisable to consult this passage as a timeless theology of church and state. Rather, he continues, Paul is admonishing the Romans not to pull the roof of Nero's wrath down on their heads as they had under Claudius. On both points Marxsen is doubtlessly correct. Nevertheless, both the context and structure of 13:1–7 reveal that this is not the sum of the matter. Paul's purpose is more than a note of political expediency, and this becomes apparent when we consider the circumstances in which he wrote.

We may be reasonably certain that on the whole many of Paul's Jewish Christian readers would have been less hospitable toward Roman rule than he was. This was due to the fact that Israel regarded submission to a heathen nation as a fundamental violation of its status as the chosen people. "Do not place a foreigner over you, one who is not a brother Israelite," warned Deuteronomy (17:15). After the fall of the monarchy in 586 B.C., Jews tolerated Persian and Egyptian rule, but the outrageous affront of Antiochus IV in sacrificing a sow on the altar of the Jerusalem temple in 168 B.C. swept them into revolt against the Seleucids. Their stunning success under the Maccabees reminded Jews ever after that it was possible to depose Gentile overlords and establish a rule more faithful to the old Israelite ideal (cf. 1 Macc.; m. *'Abot* 1.10; 2.3; 3.5). These sentiments reached their zenith in the Zealot movement of Paul's day, which combined the orthodox theology of the Pharisees with the militant nationalism of the Maccabees. Within a decade of the writing of Romans, in fact, the Zealots would plunge the nation into a disastrous revolt against Rome in A.D. 66.

Nor were such sentiments confined to the Zealot party. They surfaced in a long litany of protests in the first century, including large segments of Jews refusing to pay taxes, riots in Rome and Alexandria, Jewish defiance in the face of Pontius Pilate's blunders (governor of Palestine from A.D. 26–36), a near-disastrous Jewish revolt when Emperor Caligula threatened to erect—and demand worship of—his statue in Palestine in A.D. 39, and in Claudius' expulsion of Jews from Rome a decade later. The fledgling church was not unaffected by these movements and the sentiments which provoked them. Had not the disciples put a question to Jesus freighted with political expectations, "Lord, are you at this time going to restore the kingdom to Israel?" (Acts 1:6)? In Thessalonica some years earlier Paul had been accused of "defying Caesar's decrees, saying that there is another king, one called Jesus" (Acts 17:7), and shortly after writing Romans he would be mistaken for an Egyptian terrorist (Acts 21:38; see also Acts 5:37).

Within this politically charged atmosphere, both Jesus and Paul took a remarkably conciliatory attitude toward Rome and instructed their followers likewise. When asked, "[Is] it right to pay taxes to Caesar or not?" Jesus replied, "Give to Caesar what is Caesar's, and to God what is God's" (Matt. 22:15–22). Paul was proud of his Roman citizenship and may have considered Roman rule the power which "holds back" the outbreak of the anti-Christ (2 Thess. 2:7). It is often supposed that Romans 13 depicts Caesar in a positive light because at the time of writing (ca. A.D. 57) Christians had not yet suffered at the hands of the empire. This is only partially true, at best. Paul had not forgotten that Jesus had died at the hands of a corrupt Roman overlord; neither had he forgotten his own humiliation from a Roman governor in Corinth (Acts 18:12–17). Moreover, writings attributed to Paul (1 Tim. 2:1–2; Titus 3:1) and Peter (1 Pet. 2:13–17) preserve substantially the same teaching on government at a period when Rome was openly hostile to Christians.

How then is Romans 13 to be understood? The question has been long and intensely debated in the church. The foregoing historical review would suggest that Paul desired to instruct his Roman readers on the place of government in God's economy, including the responsibilities of rulers to execute justice and of citizens to submit themselves to government rule. His purpose in so doing was both to demonstrate that civic responsibility was a legitimate and necessary expression of discipleship, indeed of *agapē*, and to thwart any separatist or antinomian political sentiments in the minds of Roman Christians. His overall purpose was therefore more comprehensive and evangelical than Marxsen's suggestion that he was trying to avoid further recriminations from Rome, although that short-term goal cannot have escaped his attention. Moreover, Paul had to accomplish this within the social and political exigencies which prevailed in the first-century Mediterranean world, which I have briefly reviewed. From the foregoing, then, we may draw the following conclusions.

First, Paul is speaking of human government in terms of an ideal. This is apparent from the general terminology of the passage. By "ideal" we need not imagine a state of perfection, but simply what government *ought* to be, which, according to Paul, is an ordered civil structure ordained by God to reward good and punish evil. At the same time, Paul's failure to raise the question of resistance to governments which violate the ideal cannot be interpreted to mean that he foresaw no circumstances where resistance might be justified. In writing to the capital Paul quite wisely chose to discuss the subject from the ideal rather than from its possible exceptions. This not only showed political savvy on his part (Rome was, after all, a totalitarian state), but it suited his purpose, which was to assert that government is ordained of God and thereby within the scope of Christian discipleship.

Second, the political problem in Paul's mind was not at all the problem in the minds of modern Christians. Nearly all governments today *claim* to represent the interests of their constituents, a claim usually reflected in their names (whether or not they are democratic in reality). This is true even (or especially) of repressive governments. It is precisely this democratic ideal which creates the modern political dilemma, i.e., what are the legitimate means of redress for citizens to take against states which claim to be democratic, but which exhibit undemocratic policies?

This is a justifiable concern of modern peoples, including Christians. But it was not Paul's concern. The Roman Republic was not a democracy; it was, politically speaking, an aristocratic oligarchy, but in practice it was a totalitarian state. The democratic ideals which we hold dearly lay a millennium and a half in the future when Paul wrote Romans 13. Neither Paul nor the nucleus of believers he represented had the right, much less the power, to challenge an iota of an imperial decree.

Paul's question was simply this: given Rome's supremacy, what should be expected of Christians with regard to it? On the one hand, he had to combat a naive antinomianism which thought itself exempt from all forms of restraint, including government control. This error might have suggested itself thus: If believers are no longer of this world (John 17:13–16), if they are "aliens and strangers on earth" (Heb. 11:13) and their "citizenship is in heaven" (Phil. 3:20), and above all, if Christ has overcome this world (John 16:33), why should they obey earthly authorities, much less pagan Romans? On the other hand, Paul had to face the fact that the tremors of Zealotism, which were shaking the foundations of Jewish synagogues around the Mediterranean, might also split Christian congregations. To parties of both per-

suasions—the one threatening anarchy, the other insurrection—
Paul argues that the kingdom of Christ has not yet displaced the
kingdom of Caesar, but even now operates through it. These two
lines of thought—or something close to them—were the bound-
aries between which Paul was forced to operate, and any modern
interpretation of Romans 13 which fails to take them into consideration will scarcely do justice to his teaching on church and
state.

We must add, however, that neither Paul nor the NT teaches
that when a government forsakes its God-ordained function of
honoring good and punishing evil that a Christian is obligated to
serve it. Paul, after all, calls the powers **governing authorities**, not
supreme authorities. He nowhere discusses what would constitute such a departure from God-ordained authority, for to have
raised the question in his day would have been tantamount to
treason. An answer, were he to offer one, would again have to be
found in 12:2 where the renewed mind of believers "test[s] and
approve[s] what God's will is." That Christians throughout history have found themselves in such dilemmas is no secret. They
have sometimes disagreed about what constitutes the legitimate
limits of government, but on one point they concur: when the
claims of earthly authorities conflict with divine authority over
faith and conscience (v. 5), Christians are obliged to confess, "we
must obey God rather than men" (Acts 5:29). Obedience to rulers
apart from (or against) conscience is idolatry. If all authority is
indeed from God, then the claims of God rest on governments as
well as on their subjects. Christians know better than the ruling
authorities themselves whence their power comes, and they are
obliged in their submission to such authorities to remind them
that they are **God's servants for good** (v. 4).

This lengthy prolegomenon now permits us to move rap-
idly through the details of verses 1–5. The fundamental principle
of verses 1–2 is that God is the source of all rightful authority, of
which civil authority is one expression. This is axiomatic in Hebrew literature, in fact. Paul again draws on a family of Greek
words (*hypotassein* [**submit**, v. 1], *antitassesthai* [**rebels**, v. 2], *diatagē*
[**instituted**, v. 2], and *tassein* [**established**, v. 1]), all of which are
derivatives of the last word and emphasize God-ordained *order*.
Reinhold Niebuhr rightly noted the paradox in divine order: it
is God's goodness in creation which makes civil order possible,
but it is the corruption of sin which makes civil order necessary

(quoted from Achtemeier, *Romans*, p. 204). When the authorities exercise their power for **right** (v. 3) they faithfully represent the source of their authority and fulfill their duty. Paul does not say that a government must be "Christian" to do this. Nero, who was emperor when Paul wrote, was certainly not a Christian and did not recognize the source of his authority. Nor need government be perfect. But it must reflect the divine order of honoring good and punishing evil.

When Paul writes, **Everyone must submit himself to the governing authorities** (v. 1), the **everyone** (literally in Greek, "every soul"), which is a Hebraic expression meaning the whole person, emphasizes individual responsibility. The admonition to **submit** characterizes a wide range of Christian social relations, including government, Christian fellowship (1 Cor. 16:16), marriage (Eph. 5:21), and the church's relationship to Christ (Eph. 5:24). Christian submission, however, is not slavish or blind obedience without regard to moral responsibility. Always in the NT submission carries the sense of that which would honor Christ, or as Paul says in Colossians 3:18, "as is fitting in the Lord."

Having established the duty of believers to submit *to* government in verses 1–2, Paul establishes the responsibilities of government in verses 3–4. Three times he calls rulers **God's servants** to honor right and punish wrong (vv. 4, 6). In stating the issue thus Paul establishes the essential and constructive purpose of government. But his formulation implies an unmistakable if unspoken corollary: when a state wholly perverts the ideal (by promoting evil and persecuting good, for example) it can no longer be regarded as **God's servant,** and it cannot take the submission of its citizens for granted. The Christian's higher allegiance to God and good releases him or her from the claims of an idolatrous regime. Martin Luther mistakenly overlooked this corollary when he made the idea of two kingdoms—one sacred, one secular—into a theological doctrine. Some 30 years after Paul wrote Romans, when the Emperor Domitian (A.D. 81–96) aspired to usurp the place of God, the author of the Revelation saw that both the purpose and limits of government had been exceeded and that the state had become "a great prostitute" (Rev. 14:8, 17–18). Obedience to God in such circumstances meant resistance, not submission. This is essentially the message of Exodus, Daniel, and the early disciples' refusal to obey the Sanhedrin in Acts. Finally, the importance of verse 5 for Paul's argument ought not be overlooked. He counsels submission on the basis of **possible punishment** and **conscience**. Franz Leenhardt draws an important conclusion from this:

> It is significant that Paul has brought out in this connection the positive character of obedience, because such a point of view at the same time implies the limits of obedience. If obedience is a matter of conscience, then it is no longer servile; when conscience is introduced as the motive of obedience, the latter can no longer be counted on! It becomes possible to object to authority on the grounds of conscience (*Romans*, p. 335).

Paul thus approached the relation of church and state not as a Sadducee who lived from the advantages of the state, nor as a Zealot who lived to overthrow the state, nor as a Pharisee who divorced religion from the state, nor as a Roman citizen for whom the state was an end in itself. Paul wrote as a free man in Christ, and he appeals to the church to be equally free in obedience to the state, but not conformed to it.

13:6–7 / Because authority is ordained by God, submission entails the practical duties of the paying of **taxes**, **revenue**, **respect**, and **honor** (v. 7). For Jews, census enrollments and taxation were two of the most onerous effects of foreign rule. In Roman-occupied Palestine, where tax collectors unscrupulously overcharged Jews, the populace was tempted to underpay (or withhold) taxes without compunction. Bitterness over taxes was not confined to Palestine, however. The Roman historian Tacitus reports mounting unrest over taxes in Rome in A.D. 58—only a year after Paul wrote (*Ann.* 13.50; *OCD*, "Publicani," pp. 898–99). But Paul does not lend his voice to this protest. The payment of taxes is also an expression of *agapē*, **for the authorities are God's servants**. The Greek word rendered **taxes** normally refers to direct taxes or tribute, whereas that rendered **revenue** refers to indirect taxes, customs duties, etc.

One further duty of the state, according to verse 4, is the use of the "sword." In the present context the sword is directed to civil disorders rather than military engagements, although in ancient Rome, where soldiers comprised both the police force and the army, there was admittedly less distinction between the two than there is in most modern democracies. At any rate, the metaphor is too general to be conscripted as justification for war. But it does seem to denote the right of capital punishment, for a sword (as opposed to a whip, for instance) was an instrument of death. In the present context, however, it is "God's servant" who bears the sword, and this excludes all arbitrary and indiscriminate uses of power apart from the cause of justice.

Additional Notes   §30

13:1–5 / The Greek word which Paul uses for **governing authorities** (*exousia*) is nowhere used in this manner in extrabiblical Greek. Some commentators have therefore suggested that Paul is thinking of supernatural angelic powers (1 Cor. 15:24; Col. 1:15ff.; Eph. 3:10) which manifest themselves in political agencies. This explains, according to the argument, Paul's surprisingly positive attitude toward Roman rule. In disagreement with this position, it must be said that Paul nowhere calls for submission to powers which in the main oppose Christ (8:37–39; Gal. 4:8–11; Col. 2:15). Moreover, the designation of **governing authorities** is quite similar to nomenclature for rulers in 1 Timothy 2:2 and 1 Peter 2:13. Above all, the subject here is not supernatural powers (that would belong at the end of ch. 8), but civil authorities and taxation (vv. 6ff.). Full discussions are given in Gaugler, *Der Römerbrief*, vol. 2, pp. 275–79; and Dunn, *Romans 9–16*, p. 760.

Similar to Marxsen, Schlatter suggests that word of Paul's clashes with Roman officials on the missionary field had reached Rome. In response to this, continues Schlatter, Paul wrote 13:1–7 to assure Christians in the capital that he had no intention of challenging authorities in Rome, thus precluding any precautionary measures against him. See *Gottes Gerechtigkeit*, pp. 350–51.

On Jewish-Roman relations in the first century A.D., see the following: for the Jewish revolt of A.D. 66–70, consult the account of Josephus in *Jewish War*; for Jewish refusal to pay taxes, Josephus, *Ant.* 17.355; 18.1–10; for Jewish riots in Alexandria, London Papyri 1912 (quoted in Barrett, *New Testament Background*, pp. 44–47; for Pilate's blunders, Josephus, *Ant.* 18.55ff.; for Caligula's megalomania, Josephus, *War* 2.184–87; 192–203; for Claudius' expulsion of the Jews, Suetonius, *Claudius* 25.

Among the many passages in Hebrew literature which witness to God as the source of political power, see Ps. 2:2; Prov. 8:15–16; Isa. 45:1–2; Jer. 27:5ff.; Dan. 2:21, 37; Wisd. of Sol. 6:1ff.; and in the NT, John 19:10–11. For rabbinic sources, see Str-B, vol. 3, pp. 303–34.

Luther's introduction of the idea of two kingdoms entails a separation of the sacred and secular, and this is seemingly foreign to Paul.

> In the preceding chapter, [Paul] taught that one must not disturb the order of the church; in this chapter, he teaches that also the secular order must be maintained. For both are of God: it is the purpose of the former to give guidance and peace to the inner man

and what concerns him, and it is the purpose of the latter to give guidance to the outer man in his concerns. For, in this life, the inner man cannot be without the outer one.

From this Luther derives the alarming conclusion, "Christians should not refuse, under the pretext of religion, to obey men, especially evil ones." See *Lectures on Romans*, p. 358. It must not be forgotten that Luther courageously challenged corrupt papal authority, but he nevertheless discounted the right to challenge secular authority. Calvin, on the other hand, although he affirmed the right and necessity of governments to rule, did not extend this to include tyrannies, which "are full of disorder [and] are not an ordained government" (*Romans*, p. 479).

§31 Love is the Sum of the Law
(Rom. 13:8–10)

Paul now returns expressly to the theme of love which dominates chapters 12–13, although more noticeably at some points (12:9–21; 13:8–10) than others (12:1–8; 13:1–7, 11–14). The idea of owing taxes (Gk. *opheilē*) in verse 7 reminds him that there is one debt (Gk. *opheilō*, v. 8) which can never be paid. The debt of love always remains outstanding. It is the only mortgage which can never be burned. In returning to the personal ethics of *agapē* in verses 8–10 Paul recalls that good citizenship (13:1–7) is neither the sum of nor a substitute for true Christianity. Beneath civic duties and good causes, even beneath personal world-views and life-styles, lies the essential and indispensable characteristic of Christian faith, love for others.

13:8–10 / Verse 8 begins with an emphatic double-negative in Greek, which might be rendered, "Owe nothing to anyone," **except the continuing debt to love one another**. The debt of love is categorical and admits of no exceptions. In Buddhism love is a rather dispassionate feeling of benevolence toward humanity in general, though much less is said of its expression toward particular individuals. Not so in Christianity. *Agapē* is not an abstract concept; it is a will in search of an object. Four times Paul identifies that object as **one another** (v. 8), **fellowman** (v. 8), and **neighbor** (twice in vv. 9–10). The other person represents God's claim on our love. We normally think of our neighbor as a person who is like us, but in the parables of the Good Samaritan (Luke 10:25–37) and Final Judgment (Matt. 25:31–46) the neighbor is very much *un*like us. Others are our neighbors not because they are like us, not even because they are chosen by us, but because they are given to us by God with a need which we can meet. Indeed, Christ himself meets us in that need (Matt. 25:40, 45).

Whereas in the foregoing section Paul anchored love to civic responsibility, here he defends against conceiving of love as a euphoric high. Love is not a world apart, but the transformation of this world. It is not above the law but it **fulfills the law** (v. 8), and keeping the commandments is an expression of *agapē*. In verse 9 Paul quotes not from the first part of the Decalogue, which honors God, but from the latter, which honors our **fellowman**. This is an explicit confirmation of the thesis we argued earlier, that keeping the law is not a prerequisite to saving faith, but saving faith is a prerequisite to keeping the law (3:31). Love is the visible side of faith in relation and responsibility to others. The law is **fulfilled** and **summed up** in love, for love penetrates to the intent of the law and thereby exceeds the outward minimum prescribed by the commandments.

Verse 10 recapitulates the whole idea in the negative, **Love does no harm to its neighbor**. We noted earlier that a positive assertion is verified by the denial of its opposite. Verse 10 performs that function: the positive principle is given in verse 9 (**Love your neighbor as yourself**), and the negative follows in verse 10 (**Love does no harm to its neighbor**). On the one hand, the latter safeguards against reducing *agapē* to the principle of utility (e.g., "the greatest good for the greatest number"). Great evils have been visited on minorities in the name of helping the masses. This was in fact Caiaphas' justification for handing over Jesus for crucifixion, "It is better . . . that one man die for the people than that the whole nation perish" (John 11:50). On the other hand, verse 10 prevents *agapē* from being reduced to the principle of expediency (e.g., the attempt to justify evil means for ostensibly good ends). Love does good, and the doing of good rules out the doing of evil.

Additional Notes   §31

13:8–10 / The Christian love-command stems from the OT, which Paul quotes in v. 9 (Lev. 19:18). But Jesus' *agapē* is free from two limitations normally imposed on love by the Jewish synagogue. In rabbinic writings the **neighbor** was normally restricted to fellow Israelites and did not include Gentiles. Moreover, rabbinic interpretations of Leviticus 19:18

were phrased in the negative, as the following story indicates. A Gentile approached Rabbi Hillel (ca. 70 B.C.–ca. A.D. 10) and promised to become a proselyte if the famous teacher could summarize the Torah while he (the Gentile) stood on one foot. Hillel said, "What you would not want done to you, do not do to someone else" (Str-B, vol. 1, p. 357). *Agapē*, however, includes outsiders and even enemies (12:17–21; Matt. 5:44), and involves not merely refraining from negative actions (i.e., harming others), but doing positive ones as well (i.e., that which is good).

The order of the commandments in v. 9 differs from that in Exod. 20:13–17 and Deut. 5:17–21. Paul's order follows the LXX of the latter passage, which was used in the Greek-speaking diaspora.

"Love your neighbor as yourself" (v. 9) is sometimes interpreted as a command to self-love, i.e., one cannot love others until one loves self. This interpretation owes more to self-help psychology than to biblical theology. In all the Bible there is no command to love self, but there are countless commands to love God and others. The text which is quoted (Lev. 19:18) ends with "I am the Lord," which directs attention away from self and toward God. Leviticus 19:18, therefore, is not a command to self-love but to the love of God through love of others. Self-love and happiness come as a by-product of love of God and others (e.g., "Whoever loses his life for me will find it," Matt. 16:25). All people do, in fact, show love for themselves in various ways by providing for their needs and desires. Few people need be taught how to promote their own good. Paul (and Jesus, cf. Mark 12:31) simply commands believers to promote the good of others in like manner! That is the meaning of **"love your neighbor as yourself."**

§32   The Future Is Retroactive (Rom. 13:11–14)

Christians sometimes make contradictory claims about their faith, for faith, like life, cannot be reduced to purely logical categories. A parent, for example, can love and hate a child at the same moment, or so it seems. Christians likewise assert one thing about God and then another thing quite different—but also quite true. Early in Romans Paul spoke of justification as though it were entirely of God. "When we were God's enemies, we were reconciled to him through the death of his Son" (5:10). It sounds as though we had nothing to do with it (which, in fact, we did not). That is the forensic or juridical meaning of justification. But in chapter 12 Paul began speaking of human involvement in the salvation process. "Offer your bodies as living sacrifices" (12:1), and "put aside the deeds of darkness and put on the armor of light" (13:12). The emphasis shifted from righteousness before God to righteousness in human relationships, from being accounted right with God to becoming right with ourselves and others. Salvation thus has an *already* and a *not yet* aspect. Christians are already justified by faith, but not yet conformed to the image of God's Son.

The present section bears similarities in theme and vocabulary to Ephesians 5:6–20. Paul again (cf. 12:9–15) rises to poetic felicity with his careful balance between day and night, darkness and light, with the three couplets in verse 13, and especially with the imagery of putting on Christ.

In chapters 12–13 Paul rooted Christian behavior in *agapē*. He now adds that the final day of salvation is an equally important stimulus to Christian transformation. The admonition of 12:2 not to be conformed to this age is here completed in the transformation of life by the age to come. The model of the resurrected Jesus is even now the pattern for Christians. The teaching of the final consummation of salvation is no outmoded appendage to Christianity. It is, in fact, the eschatological perspective of the gospel which prevents Christianity from being reduced to a philosophy or moral code. The expectation of the return of Christ preserves the central truth of the faith. Christianity is a relationship with the person of Christ which begins in "cloth[ing] yourselves with the Lord Jesus Christ" (13:14) and ends in glory by being fully "conformed to the likeness of [God's] Son" (8:29).

13:11–14 / **The present time** of verse 11 is not clock-time, but the unique moment of time which began in God's sending his Son (Mark 1:15; Gal. 4:4–6) and which concludes at the final revelation of Jesus Christ as Lord of all. It is the eschatological moment which transforms the otherwise monotony of time into an opportunity for decision and salvation. Paul utilizes imagery common to other NT writers in verses 11–14 (the **hour** [v. 11], **wak**ing **from slumber** [v. 11], **night** and **day** [v. 12]) to admonish believers to faithfulness before the coming Day of the Lord.

The present is a time of **night** and **slumber,** when the mind (see 12:2) is weak and inactive, and when ignorance, confusion, and wickedness prevail. But **the night is nearly over** (v. 12), and the **day** of salvation is **nearer now than when we first believed** (cf. Heb. 10:25; 2 Apoc. Bar. 23:7; 1 Enoch 51:2). Note the imagery. Paul does not say that people are getting better, or that the world is improving, or that humanity will find a way to overcome its problems and usher in the kingdom of God. Not even believers determine the nearness of salvation, but the nearness of salvation determines them. The present is a time of crisis not because of anything we do, but because of what God will do in the future. Even now the light of the coming age shines into the darkness of the present. With Abraham, believers see deadness in their bodies and the world around them (4:19); but because of the resurrection of Jesus and the beginnings of new life in them, they know that the deadness is not the final reality. The sharp antithesis between present and future is conveyed even by the consistent use of the aorist tense in this section. This sets before readers a summons to decisive action and recalls the vocabulary of conversion, or perhaps even the liturgy of baptism.

Believers can walk in the light because they are properly clothed in **armor of light** (v. 12), indeed in the **Lord Jesus Christ** (v. 14). They are to be done with shameful acts, with **orgies and drunkenness, sexual immorality and debauchery, dissension and jealousy** (v. 13). The word translated **orgies** (Gk. *kōmoi*), which originated in the Bacchus cult, means carousing and revelry to excess. In Greek the first four terms are plural, connoting frequency or habitual behavior. These are the properties of the flesh or **sinful nature** (v. 14).

Christians are summoned to cater no longer to the flesh, but to **clothe yourselves with the Lord Jesus Christ** (v. 14). The concrete imagery (getting up in the morning and getting dressed) is an unusually common metaphor for such a profound spiritual reality, and it reminds believers that the life of faith is not an esoteric or mystical experience, but a life of discipleship, intentionally following Jesus in the most common and practical matters. Discipleship is following Jesus step by step in the direction he leads, as opposed to any other, and, as the Greek says in verse 13, "walking honorably." The idea that "the clothes make the person" is a theological truism in this instance, for in "putting on Christ" believers discover that Christ's character and behavior become their own. This far exceeds mere morality, important as that is. It means claiming Christ's identity as our identity, his way in the world as our way, and his promise of the future as our path in the present.

Additional Notes   §32

13:11–14   /   The stark antithesis between light and darkness, and particularly the idea of **the armor of light**, recalls similar imagery from "The War of the Sons of Light and the Sons of Darkness" in the Dead Sea Scrolls. Such imagery was common not only to Qumran, but to intertestamental Jewish literature in general, and apocalyptic literature in particular.

On a historical note, Augustine, in his deep turmoil, credits verses 13-14 with his conversion. "I had no wish to read more and no need to do so. For in an instant as I came to the end of the sentence, it was as though the light of confidence flooded into my heart and all the darkness of doubt was dispelled" (*Confessions*, bk. 8, ch. 12).

§33   The Strong and the Weak (Rom. 14:1–12)

The general exhortation on *agapē* in chapters 12–13 proceeds now to a specific discussion of the "strong" and "weak" in 14:1–15:13. Paul divides the entire unit into three subsections. In the present section he argues that self-righteous judgments are divisive in the body of Christ; in 14:13–23 he teaches that responsibility for the other takes priority over individual rights; and he concludes in 15:1–13 with the servant role of Christ as the example for behavior within the Christian fellowship.

Although Paul was addressing a particular problem (or set of problems) in Rome, he frames the discussion in a general way, perhaps because he does not have firsthand knowledge of the situation in Rome and does not wish to appear presumptuous, but more likely because the problem was clear enough to all concerned and needed no rehearsing. Even though Paul had yet to set foot in the capital, he cannot have been uninformed about events there. He had recently worked in Corinth with Aquila and Priscilla who, along with all Jews, had been expelled from Rome by Claudius not long before (Acts 18:1–2). The lengthy list of names in chapter 16 testifies that he had many acquaintances in Rome from his contacts on the mission field. On another occasion Paul had received direct inquiries from his followers in Corinth (1 Cor. 1:11), and his advice here may be the result of something similar on the part of the Romans.

Paul frames the discussion in terms of the "strong" and "weak," terms which refer not to character or conviction, but to *faith*, and thus faith determines the discussion. It is clear that dietary regulations played a large part in the problem. One person's faith allowed the consumption of anything, another's restricted the diet to vegetables (vv. 2–3). The same seems to have been true with regard to drinking wine (14:21) and to the observance of holidays and festivals (vv. 5–6). The general impression is that persons of weaker faith rather scrupulously observed these matters, whereas those of stronger faith felt themselves free from such observances.

Who were the "strong" and "weak"? We cannot know for certain, but it appears that the weak refer to Jewish converts who continued to accept the yoke of the law, whereas the strong were largely Gentile Christians whose faith freed them from the law. This identification has been challenged by some recent interpreters who note that first-century Jews were not forbidden from eating meat and drinking wine. While this is true, we know from 1 Corinthians 8 and 10 that many Jews and Jewish Christians living in the Diaspora avoided eating meat for fear that it had been sacrificed to idols, which would violate the first commandment (" 'You shall have no other gods before me,' " Deut. 5:7). They also may have avoided wine for the same reason, since it may have been used in libations to pagan deities. Or it may have been a practical way of separating themselves from the excessive drinking, carousing, and orgies common in Gentile regions. Moreover, despite what some commentators say, Paul's advice in 1 Corinthians and Romans is quite similar on this matter. In both instances he appeals to the motive of *agapē* (Rom. 14:15; 1 Cor. 8:1) and warns not to offend the conscience of the weak (Rom. 14:13; 1 Cor. 8:9). Although the discussion of 14:1–15:13 is couched in general terms, it still bears a close resemblance to Jewish-Gentile tensions familiar in the NT as a whole (Acts 15:1–21; Gal. 4:10; 1 Cor. 8:1–13; 10:1–22; Col. 2:16–23?). Immediately following the crux of the argument in 15:7 Paul explicitly identifies Jews and Gentiles (15:8–9), whose relationship, of course, is one of the overarching themes in Romans.

The presumption that Paul is thinking of Jewish-Gentile tensions beneath the language of the strong and weak is reinforced by our reconstruction of the origin of the epistle (see Introduction). In A.D. 49 the Emperor Claudius expelled all Jews from Rome (Acts 18:2) due to troubles that were aroused by a certain "Chrestus," according to Suetonius (*Claudius* 25.4). Whether "Chrestus" was a reference to Christ (Latin: "Christus") cannot be certain, but it is not improbable that it was. If so, the troubles among Jews may have been related to the preaching of Jesus as Messiah in the Roman synagogues. Expulsion of Jews also would have included Jewish Christians, leaving Christian congregations in Rome under the auspices of Gentile Christians who were free to develop their understanding of the gospel apart from Torah. When Claudius died in A.D. 54 and the edict was rescinded, Jewish Christians would have returned to Rome with their more legalistic understanding of faith. It is not difficult to imagine the strains which their reintegration must have placed on congregations that had been under Gentile leadership for several years, and which, even under the best of circumstances, found understanding and tolerance of Jewish cultic laws in short supply.

These circumstances (or something similar) appear to lie beneath the surface of 14:1–15:13. Some doubt, of course, necessarily remains about the exact conditions which Paul is addressing, but there is no doubt about his advice. To be sure, Paul counts himself among the strong (15:1), but he does not commend the strong as the ideal or demean the weakness of believers whose faith does not permit them certain freedoms which the gospel allows. There is a greater issue at stake than strength or weakness in faith, and that is the danger of judgments *from both sides* regarding matters that are not essential for salvation. The weak judge the strong for what they believe to be illicit uses of freedom; the strong despise the weak for their lack of freedom. Each side judges the other from its own conscience in an attempt to compel the other to its opinion. Thus a great pitfall imperils the unity of Christ's body. The issue, in Ernst Gaugler's words, is the lack of "reverence for the conscience of the other" (*Der Römerbrief*, vol. 2, p. 317). The Reformers called these non-essentials *adiaphora*, or matters about which Christians may differ without endangering their salvation. There are, of course, far more *adiaphora* than there are *diapheronta* (2:18), or essentials of faith. Understanding this, Paul makes no attempt to take sides. Rather, in the irenic spirit of Second Isaiah (cf. 40:11), he exhorts his readers not to judge fellow Christians on points which from God's perspective are not of ultimate importance. "Accept one another, then, just as Christ accepted you, in order to bring praise to God" (15:7).

14:1 / Paul begins with a word to the strong: **Accept him whose faith is weak, without passing judgment on disputable matters**. J. D. G. Dunn suggests that Paul's use of the singular may refer to Jewish Christians who were trickling back to Rome in ones or twos after Claudius' death (*Romans 9–16*, p. 798). Paul admonishes the strong not to gang up against weaker believers or to treat them condescendingly. The key issue, after all, is **faith**. Weak in faith does not mean lack of faith, but rather, as the following examples show, a lack of "knowledge" (as Paul says in 1 Cor. 8:10). The weak, who have not (yet) thought through the full implications of the faith, attempt to impose their doubts on the strong to prevent them from a full exercise of the Christian liberty that their faith allows them. The strong are enjoined to welcome the weak not for purposes of settling accounts with them or of trying to show them the folly of their beliefs. They are charged to accept them genuinely for what they are—as fellow Christians.

An acceptance that is predicated on converting another to one's own opinion in such matters is coercive. It is an unlovely love rather than Christian love, for *agapē* "is not self-seeking" (1 Cor. 13:5). The middle voice of the Greek verb translated as **accept** suggests a genuine embracing of the weak, not a reluctant toleration. Had not Jesus taught that his Father would clothe those "of little faith" (Matt. 6:30), and, in speaking of little children, that "the kingdom of God belongs to such as these" (Mark 10:14)? This is no less true of the weak in Rome. **Passing judgment on disputable matters** simply exalts the strong and humiliates the weak. It is an exercise of knowledge (1 Cor. 8:1) rather than of faith. Knowledge creates gulfs; faith and love build bridges. To accept the weak is to accept Christ, for Christ comes to us *incognito*, as one despised and rejected, as one from whom men turn their faces (Isa. 53:3), as one who "was rich, yet for your sakes . . . became poor, so that you through his poverty might become rich" (2 Cor. 8:9).

14:2–3 / Clean and unclean foods were an issue of contention in the early years of Christianity when the church was comprised of both Jewish and Gentile Christians. **One man's faith allows him to eat everything, but another man, whose faith is weak, eats only vegetables** (v. 2). It was common knowledge that in dietary customs, as in morals, Jews were far more scrupulous than were Gentiles (Acts 15:20ff.). The gulf between them, in fact, widened in the post-Maccabean period and in the Diaspora, where kosher observance became an important means of maintaining and asserting Jewish identity. But what one ate was of less concern to Paul than the judgments that arose from eating—pride and contempt from the "strong," censure and condemnation from the "weak." To both sides Paul applies the principle that God has accepted the person whom you condemn (v. 3). How then can believers presume to pass judgment on one whom God has already accepted?

The NT warns of the damaging consequences of human judgments, and as a rule it commands believers not to judge others (Matt. 7:1ff.; 1 Cor. 4:5; James 4:11). This ought not be construed as moral indifference, however. The universal and persistent cry of the prophets for justice (e.g., Amos 5:24), the Baptist's judgment against Antipas' adultery (Mark 6:17), Jesus' judgments of Pharisaic abuses (Matt. 23), and Paul's judgment against sexual immorality in Corinth (1 Cor. 5:1ff.) are clear evidence that biblical faith decisively rejects injustice and immorality wherever they occur. The church is obliged to be rigorous with itself and discerning toward the world in the interest of both personal and social righteousness. But in making such judgments Christians must be aware that they too stand under God's judgment. This is the meaning of verse 12. An attitude of superiority stems from blindness toward one's own faults, and results in hardness toward the faults of others. When Christians must judge, they judge only as *fellow* sinners. To think that they are anything other than that, or that they are exempt from the faults (or similar ones) which they see in others, is to fall victim to self-righteousness, which is what Paul condemns in 2:1ff. and here. Such judgments, to be sure, play a role only in the realm of the *diapheronta*, i.e., where moral and theological truths are at stake. At points of *adiaphora*, or nonessentials, where no such issues are at stake, Paul has but one word: when God's acceptance of the other is not in question, then human judgments have no place.

14:4 / Paul intensifies his appeal by shifting to the second person singular, **Who are you to judge someone else's servant?** If he is consistent in his word usage, he is speaking here of the weak judging the strong. In 14:1–12 two different words occur for the judgments of the strong and weak. The problem with the strong is that they "look down on" the weak (vv. 3, 10). The Greek word behind this translation (*exouthenein*) means "to despise or disdain." The problem with the weak, on the other hand, is that of "judging" (Gk. *krinein*, vv. 3, 4, 5, 10). The predominance of the latter verb in 14:1–12 suggests that Paul is primarily concerned with the problem of the weak. We might add that this is the same verb (*krinein*) which appeared in 2:1ff. Paul, therefore, sees a parallel tendency among his Jewish kinsfolk in their judgments of Gentiles in society and their judgments of Gentile-Christians in the church.

In an effort to expose the error of such judgments Paul turns to a master-slave analogy. Its purpose is to remind the scrupulous weaker believer of the proper lines of authority. It is not the weaker believer's (or anyone's) conscience to which the fellow believer is obliged, but to God. A slave is accountable to his or her master, not to a fellow slave. **And he will stand**, regardless of what the fellow slave may think or say, **for the Lord is able to make him stand**. A Christian is defined not by what others think, but by what God thinks. God does not desire sameness and uniformity within the body. God frees believers from the consciences of others (even of other believers) and enables them to be transformed to the image of Christ. "It is for freedom that Christ has set us free. Stand firm, then, and do not let yourselves be burdened again by a yoke of slavery" (Gal. 5:1). There are, of course, limits to Christian freedom (e.g., Gal. 5:16–21), but the matters under discussion fall well within those limits.

14:5–6 / To say that the *adiaphora* are not essential for salvation is not to say that they are of no importance at all. All circumstances in life, the ordinary no less than the extraordinary, provide tests and opportunities of faith. The observance of days is a case in point. **One man considers one day more sacred than another; another man considers every day alike** (v. 5). This verse presents a twofold problem for the interpreter not only because the reference to **days** is vague, but because the entire verse is less clear in Greek than in the NIV. The sensitive nature of the judgments under consideration, coupled with its evident familiarity to the Romans, dictated that a tactful allusion to it (as opposed to an explicit reference) was the better part of judgment on Paul's part. This being the case, we are probably correct in assuming that Paul is referring to Jewish calendric observations, perhaps the regular Monday and Thursday fast days, perhaps the Sabbath and various feast days, or perhaps even, as Schlatter suggests, the debate over the shift from Saturday to Sunday as the day of worship in Christian churches (*Gottes Gerechtigkeit*, p. 371).

Again, without taking sides on the matter, Paul employs a ruling principle as he did on dietary matters above (v. 3). **Each one should be fully convinced in his own mind** (v. 5). Each must act with a clear conscience in everything. In matters where there is no specific guidance, each person must be persuaded that the manner in which he or she acts is in accordance with God's will. The Christian can know if a given action is pleasing in God's sight by committing it to the Lord with *thanksgiving*. Bengel is right: "thanksgiving sanctifies all actions, however outwardly different" (*Gnomon*, vol. 3, p. 176). Even the simplest of deeds must be dedicated to God, indeed every thought taken captive in obedience to Christ (2 Cor. 10:5). Whoever eats or refrains from eating, or observes special days or does not observe them for the sake of conscience alone, attests that conscience is the final arbiter in such matters. But in relinquishing a given action to God in thanksgiving, the believer is granted peace and freedom, for one cannot dedicate a course of action thankfully to God about which one is in doubt. The rule in life's exciting (if sometimes perplexing) drama, therefore, is to be united in things essential for faith, tolerant in things non-essential, and wise in knowing the difference between them. All things are to be committed thankfully to God.

14:7–9 / In vintage Pauline fashion, the apostle now rises above the mundane issues which launched the discussion in the first place and soars poetically on a thermal current of praise to the all-sufficient lordship of Christ. William Ernest Henley may have been convinced of his "unconquerable soul," and that his head, though bloody, remained unbowed, that he was the "master of his fate and the captain of his soul" (see "Invictus"), but Paul is convinced of the all-sufficiency of Jesus Christ, and of his possession by Christ, in both life and death. We are not, as Henley boasts, autonomous beings, for **none of us lives to himself alone and none of us dies to himself alone** (v. 7). Our culture may teach that individualism and self-fulfillment are the sole guarantors of happiness, but Paul exults not in *who* we are, but in *whose* we are, for **we belong to the Lord** (v. 8).

Since our lives belong to him, we are not our own (see also 1 Cor. 6:19). We cannot (and do not, in fact) live to ourselves. We are to live for the one to whom we belong. This simple truth forms the bedrock of all Christian ethics, for ethics constitutes the visible side of our relationship with Christ, in which his lordship is manifested (e.g., Eph. 4:1). The one who gave his life without reserve for us is worthy of our lives without reserve for him. In life and death we are his. Not only in physical life and death are we his, but in *all* life.

14:10–12 / In light of this Paul returns to the issue at hand, the weak who **judge** and the strong who **look down on**. **You, then, why do you judge your brother? Or why do you look down on your brother?** (v. 10). In the original Greek the **you** is again singular, and thus direct and emphatic. Since we all must stand before God's judgment seat (v. 10), it is only there (and not in individual conscience or preference) where judgment takes place. This idea is repeated in the three final verses of this section. God alone is judge (cf. Matt. 12:36).

We are what we are only as we stand before God. Before the almighty Judge we shall be revealed for what we always have been. **"Every knee will bow before me; every tongue will confess to God"** (v. 11; see Isa. 49:18; 45:23; Phil. 2:10–11). This quotation was a standard proof text of the rabbis for the inevitability of the last judgment, and no less so for the rabbi from Tarsus. On that day all pretense will be dispelled, all moral judgments and altruistic pronouncements will be exploded as self-serving masks of pride, all gifts and sacrifices will be seen in the light of their real motives, all strivings and hopes and goals will be judged only from the perspective of whatever faith and love inspired them. **Each of us will give an account of himself to God** (v. 12). How stark and final is this word **each**! Before God each individual must give an **account**—not of his credits and achievements, but of **himself**!

There will be no one to vouch for us—except Jesus Christ! There we shall be like Peter who, having betrayed his Lord and deceived his friends, prayed the simplest of all prayers, " 'Lord, you know all things' " (John 21:17). We cannot know all things about ourselves, much less about others. The fact that we must all stand naked before the judgment seat of God is a bracing reminder not to take the judgment seat against another person. We relinquish the cause of judgment to Christ the merciful, for he is the incarnation of the God who causes us—and our fellow believers—to stand.

Additional Notes §33

Gaugler entitles 14:1–15:13, "Reverence for the Conscience of the Other." See his sensitive discussion of this matter in *Der Römerbrief*, vol. 2, pp. 317–31.

The identification of the target groups in 14:1–15:13 has been the focus of a specialized study by Paul Minear, *The Obedience of Faith* (London: SCM Press, 1971). Minear, who regards this part of the epistle as the key to the whole, seeks to identify five different groups within this section. My reconstruction of the strong and weak corresponds roughly to his first two groups. Groups 3–5 in Minear's scheme are much less evident, however. Their descriptions appear to me to correspond in one form or another to the only two groups Paul specifies, the strong and weak. Ernst Käsemann (*Romans*, pp. 364–68) offers a reasonable alternative on this matter.

§34 Rights and Responsibilities (Rom. 14:13–23)

Continuing with the subject of the "strong" and the "weak," Paul now turns to the proper relationship of freedom to love and faith. The strong in faith are free from observance of days and food regulations, but if they express their freedom at the expense of weaker believers, they violate love. The weak in faith are constrained to observe both days and food regulations, but if they abandon these constraints in the name of freedom, they violate their faith. Each side's judgment of the other is a subtle infraction of the order of creation by attempting to make others in one's own image instead of in the image of God.

The issue at hand is the proper use of freedom: freedom in service of love, love expressing itself through freedom, but not freedom as an end in itself or freedom at the expense of others. Freedom is an important characteristic of the Christian faith (cf. Gal. 5:1), but in contrast to the understanding of freedom in the modern West, Christian freedom is not an end in itself, but a means to a greater end. Freedom is not the foundation on which Paul builds Christian ethics; that foundation is reserved for the deeper and more permanent force of love. Writing to the Corinthians on a related matter, the apostle said that "knowledge puffs up, but love builds up" (1 Cor. 8:1). Whether Christians are free to do something does not settle the matter; the point is whether they *ought* to do it in light of *agapē*. On this issue Paul is thoroughly indebted to the teaching of Jesus. "Things that cause people to sin are bound to come, but woe to that person through whom they come. It would be better for him to be thrown into the sea with a millstone tied around his neck than for him to cause one of these little ones to sin. So watch yourselves" (Luke 17:1–3). Paul Achtemeier is right, "The question at issue in this passage is the relationship between the *right* of Christians to use their freedom and their commensurate *responsibility* to use that undoubted freedom in a way that is constructive rather than destructive of Christian fellowship" (*Romans*, p. 219).

In addressing primarily the "strong" in this section, Paul anchors his argument to the mooring points of freedom and love. Freedom is asserted in verse 14 ("no food is unclean in itself") and love in verse 20 ("do not destroy the work of God for the sake of food"). The whole section falls into three parts, each initiated by "therefore" (in Greek). The first shows how the principle of freedom in service of others affects weaker believers (vv. 13–15); the second concerns its effect on others in general (vv. 16–18); and the last shows how it builds up the church (vv. 19–23).

14:13 / The opening line, **Therefore let us stop passing judgment on one another**, summarizes the train of thought in 14:1–12. The word for "judging" (Gk. *krinein*) is no longer limited to the "weak" as it was in 14:1–12, but is now used generally of both parties. What follows, however, is addressed largely to the "strong." In Greek there is an effective word play on "judge," although it is difficult to reproduce in English. Bengel's free translation comes close to the gist: "Let us no longer judge one another. But if we must judge, let this be our judgment, not to put a stumbling block or obstacle in a brother's way" (*Gnomon*, vol. 3, p. 178). This exhortation echoes the teaching of Jesus (Matt. 7:1–5; 17:27; Mark 9:42), as well as the apostle himself (9:30–32; 1 Cor. 8:9–13), and it may have been influenced by an oft-quoted passage in Judaism, "Do not put a stumbling block in front of the blind" (Lev. 19:14). A *proskomma* (**stumbling block**) is a static metaphor of a stone in the road which causes one to stumble, whereas *skandalon* (**obstacle**) is a more dynamic metaphor, meaning an allurement or enticement to sin, and hence a temptation or entrapment. The words are close synonyms, but there is this difference: a *proskomma* is something that happens by chance, whereas a *skandalon* is intentional and thereby more serious. The meaning, obviously, is that believers are to avoid those circumstances in which, either unknowingly or intentionally, they might injure fellow Christians. The issue is again that of freedom and love. Barth's warning is worth recalling:

> No triumphant freedom of conscience, no triumphant *faith to eat all things* justifies me, if, at the moment of my triumph, I have seated myself upon the throne of God and am myself preparing

stumbling blocks and occasions of falling instead of making room for God's action. Gone then are my faith and my freedom; and all my knowledge is as though I knew nothing (*Romans*, p. 519).

14:14 / In this verse Paul clearly asserts his apostolic authority (**As one who is in the Lord Jesus**) and personal conviction (**I am fully convinced**) in order to justify **that no food is unclean in itself**. Paul rarely refers to our Lord simply as **Jesus** (normally, "Christ" or "Christ Jesus"); his doing so here may indicate that he is recalling the authority of Jesus on this matter (Mark 7:15–23 and parallels). The grounding of his authority in both Christ and conscience spares him from Hamlet's subjectivism, "there is nothing either good or bad, but thinking makes it so" (Act 2, Scene 2, lines 255ff.).

The issue here is not one of morality, but of things in their created state. In themselves they are neutral, although they *become* clean or unclean according to the attitudes which believers bring to them and the purposes for which they ordain them, whether that be the service of others or the gratification of self (cf. 1 Tim. 4:3–5). Jesus taught similarly, "Nothing outside a man can make him 'unclean' by going into him. Rather, it is what comes out of a man that makes him 'unclean' " (Mark 7:15). To a Jew who had been raised within the framework of the law such understandings may have seemed rather subjective. Both Jesus and Paul, however, were literally removing "the dividing wall" (Eph. 2:14) that, as was also true in Hamlet's case, had become a prison rather than a rampart of righteousness. "If the heart is pure," says Leenhardt, "everything is pure, and in consequence everything is permitted; [one] is then free to use the works of God in conscience, and it is a matter of no importance whether [one] abstains or not from such and such a thing" (*Romans*, p. 352).

14:15 / To cinch the argument Paul shifts to the second person. Far from being a matter of general importance, the argument is inexorably pressing. If **you** use your freedom, says Paul, so as to cause someone to stumble or fall, then love has been forfeited to (self-serving) freedom, and your fellow believer's salvation is imperiled. There is a telling parallel to this verse in 5:6 that speaks of Christ dying for the "powerless." The word for "powerless" (Gk. *asthenos*) is the same word employed throughout 14:1–15:13 for the weak! The fact that Paul introduces the cross of Christ at the point of **eating** reveals that this is not an incidental issue but a matter of salvation. Even "right" theology becomes very wrong when it violates love! (So Gaugler, *Der Römerbrief*, vol. 2, p. 347). Absurd, says Barth. "Christ died for him, and I—eat against him!" (*Romans*, p. 519). Or as Bengel said, "Do not value thy food more than Christ valued his life" (*Gnomon*, vol. 3, p. 179). The problem is compounded by the fact that the greater one's conscience has been violated, the more difficult it is to induce repentance. In an impassioned judgment Luther calls such a Christian "a cruel murderer, because . . . you despise, in your brother, the death of Christ, for he died certainly also for him" (*Lectures on Romans*, p. 398). Lest it seem that Luther overstates the case, it may be noted that the Greek word for **destroy**, *apollynai*, suggests, among other things, spiritual ruin and loss of eternal life.

14:16 / Continuing with direct, second-person address, Paul enjoins, **Do not allow what you consider good to be spoken of as evil**. The original Greek has greater voltage, "Do not allow your good to be *blasphemed*." Why might the apostle use such incendiary language here? Several commentators suggest that **good** is the spiritual freedom of the strong, and that Paul admonishes them not to bring it into disrepute. This is quite possible in light of the fact that Paul appears to have been addressing the strong since 13b. But in conjunction with the latter half of verse 15 where he speaks of spiritual ruin, and with the mention of blasphemy in this verse, it is more likely that **good** refers not to Christian freedom, but to the gospel of salvation itself. If that is so, then he here addresses both the strong and weak. If Christian freedom is employed to the detriment of a believer's salvation, then the work of God in the life of the believer is itself **spoken of as evil** and blasphemed. The weak may thereby attribute to Satan what is actually of God, and this borders on the sin against the Holy Spirit (Mark 3:23–30).

14:17–18 / The direct admonition of the foregoing verses now yields to a positive formulation of the gospel. **For the kingdom of God is not a matter of eating and drinking, but of righteousness, peace and joy in the Holy Spirit** (v. 17). The **kingdom of God** is a rare expression in Paul (occurring some 10 times), which is somewhat surprising when we recall that it was the *main* theme of Jesus' teaching. Paul normally employs it eschatologically to mean the kingdom of God which will follow the return of Christ. Here, however, it denotes a present reality, and this may again argue for Paul's dependence on the teaching of Jesus at this point. **Righteousness, peace and joy in the Holy Spirit** are characteristics of the reign of Jesus Christ in the lives of believers. This is the last appearance of the towering concept of **righteousness** in Romans. **Peace** is the health and harmony which results from righteousness in believers' lives (5:1). The consequence of righteousness and peace is **joy**, which is introduced here for the first time in Romans.

The reduction of the **kingdom of God** to **eating and drinking** is like playing a Mozart piano concerto with one finger. The reign of God confounds all attempts to reduce it to caricatures and formulas. These are human contrivances designed to serve human ends, but the gospel is a matter of serving **Christ** (v. 18). The idea of serving is doubly appropriate in this context because it corresponds to the larger issue of humility and the surrendering of rights out of love. God is not made in the human image, but humanity is made in God's image and exists to glorify him. **Righteousness, peace and joy** are the essential characteristics of the life transformed by Christ. The individual who subordinates his or her life to Christ receives them freely and is thereby **pleasing to God and approved by men**. The language here clearly echoes the thesis in 12:2. **Approved** doubtlessly stands in contrast to "blasphemed" above (v. 16). Whoever desires God's purposes rather than personal freedom will be so recognized **by men**.

14:19–21 / Having concluded the discussion of freedom and love, Paul proceeds to the third theme of this section in verse 19: the "reverent use of freedom" (*The Book of Common Prayer*) and the upbuilding of the church in love. **Peace** and **edification** (v. 19) are not conceived of passively, but actively and positively. Paul advocates not merely keeping the peace, but pursuing (Gk. *diōkein* [see Additional Note]) peace and growth, thus bringing into reality something which does not yet exist.

The pursuit of peace is an important vocation of the believer (12:18). The NT understands peace not simply as "peaceful coexistence," i.e., an absence of hostility and tolerance of differences and difficulties. It is rather an active participation in wholeness and well-being that results from God's pronouncement of righteousness in Christ (5:1). Paul expressly prefaces **edi-**

fication with **mutual**, thus repeating the theme of 12:3ff. that the transformed life is a life in relationship with others and in community (also 1 Thess. 5:11). Individual godliness cannot be conceived of without corporate godliness, in the same way that healthy lungs and kidneys, for example, presuppose a functional circulatory system.

Verse 20 returns to the thought of verse 14, but the change to the second person intensifies it, **Do not destroy the work of God for the sake of food**. **Destroy** obviously stands in contrast to **edification** in verse 19. Food, of course, cannot destroy God's work, but people's attitudes toward food may. The **work of God** may refer to the edification of the church that Paul just alluded to, but it more likely refers to the work of God on the cross for the salvation of weaker believers (v. 15b). The strong may mistakenly think that their freedom is the final word, in which case they violate love. Or again, they may reckon that the constraint of weaker believers means that God is less active in their lives, in which case the strong violate the faith of the weak.

In certain circumstances, therefore, a Christian will be willing to refrain from doing something that is permissible in faith because it is not responsible in love (also 1 Cor. 10:31–33). Paul himself practiced such behavior on several occasions, often to the surprise of his contemporaries (Acts 16:3; 21:20–26; 1 Cor. 9:20). His rationale was not simply that he did not want to offend a weaker believer; rather, he did not want the behavior of the strong to encourage the weak to do something which in the latter's eyes was wrong; or worse yet, he did not want to carry his new-found liberty to excessive and destructive lengths.

14:22–23 / Paul concludes with an appeal to act in nothing apart from that unconditional trust and reliance on God which is known as faith. Greater faith will, of course, permit a wider range of activities than will weaker faith, but the range of activities is finally irrelevant. The point is not to transgress the field, regardless of its size, which faith creates for the believer. **Whatever you believe about these things keep between yourself and God**, says the apostle (v. 22). This is far from an apology for a private faith. "Private faith" is as foreign to Christianity as is a private virus to medicine. This statement, along with the following beatitude, **Blessed is the man who does not condemn himself by what he approves**, is an appeal for integrity or consistency between belief and behavior. In the matter of food regulations and observance of days one may know an inner freedom, even if love counsels a more prudent course.

The strong can accommodate their faith to the weak without harming their faith, but the weak cannot accommodate their faith to the strong without harming theirs. That is the point of verse 23, **the man who has doubts is condemned if he eats, because his eating is not from faith**. The weaker believer has acted "beyond" his faith, so to speak, in doing something for which he does not possess the inner freedom. The admonition is again laid at the doorstep of the strong. Their very freedom in dietary matters must not inflate them to overconfidence, but should induce the cautionary note of love as the final arbiter of action. Throughout this discussion, of course, the issue remains one of *adiaphora*, or things not essential for salvation. The apostle has no intention of advocating moral subjectivism.

A contemporary of Paul, Rabbi Johanan ben Zakkai, once asked the meaning of the verse, "Righteousness exalts a nation, but sin is a disgrace to any people" (Prov. 14:34). The answers he received from various quarters of Judaism agreed that even the good deeds and merciful acts of heathen peoples were accounted as sin because they were done (or so it was supposed) from pride, ambition, and the like (see Str-B, vol. 1, pp. 204–5). Paul's bold declaration, **everything that does not come from faith is sin** (v. 23b) has been the subject of similar misunderstanding, as evidenced by Augustine's pronouncement, for example, that pagan virtues were but "splendid vices" (*Contra Julianum* 4.32; see Cranfield, *Romans*, vol. 2, p. 728). The assumption behind such interpretations seems to be that unless one is a Christian one's virtues are only apparent and not genuine.

This is a gross misreading of verse 23, however, as well as an infraction against charity. It not only contradicts what Paul said in 2:14–15, for example, but it also wrenches the statement from its context. **Everything that does not come from faith is sin** is controlled by the issues of eating, drinking, and observance of days. In a larger respect it may be true that whatever is not of faith is ultimately idolatrous, as Paul taught in 1:18ff. But this larger issue of faith versus disbelief (e.g., Christianity versus paganism or other religions) is not under consideration here. The present issue is the way Christians, both "strong" and "weak," practice their faith *among one another*. Verse 23b is thus a negative rendering of the thought of verse 18, "anyone who serves Christ in this way is pleasing to God." Verse 23 awakens the reader to the conviction that freedom is true freedom only where it embodies faith. Where it stands independently of faith, or exceeds faith, it is sin. Ethically speaking, Christian faith is freedom in the service of love. "For everything God created is good, and nothing is to be rejected if it is received with thanksgiving, because it is consecrated by the word of God and prayer" (1 Tim. 4:4–5).

Additional Notes   §34

14:13 / On the use of the Lev. 19:14 quotation in Judaism, see Str-B, vol. 3, pp. 310–12.

On the meanings of *proskomma* and *skandalon*, see BAGD, pp. 716 and 753, respectively.

Note Schlatter's insight on v. 13: "[The strong] should waive their rights not because they do not have freedom, but precisely because they have it; and they should honor the right of the other not because they doubt their own rights, but because they desire to guarantee the same rights to others that they claim for themselves" (*Gottes Gerechtigkeit*, p. 375 [my translation]).

14:15 / The Mishnah preserves the following teaching on the inestimable worth of the individual soul: "Therefore . . . to teach that if any man has caused a single soul to perish from Israel Scripture imputes it to him as though he has caused the whole world to perish" (m. *Sanh.* 4.5).

14:19–21 / A significant textual variant occurs in the Greek text of v. 19 (**make every effort** [Gk. *diōkein*, "pursue"]). The oldest and best manuscripts report the indicative mood (Gk. *diōkomen*), which would mean that since we are members of God's kingdom we do in fact make every effort for peace and edification. In terms of manuscript evidence this reading has the stronger support and is therefore preferred by many commentators. A minority reading gives the hortatory subjunctive (Gk. *diōkōmen*), which means that we *ought* to pursue peace and edification. The latter view is represented by the NIV (**Let us therefore make every effort**) and may have the stronger argument in its favor (despite its weaker external support), for if the Romans were already pursuing peace and edification, why would Paul have warned them against divisive judgments? Context seems to call for the latter reading. On the whole question, see Metzger, *TCGNT*, p. 532.

As we noted in §33 (Rom. 14:1–12), neither eating meat nor drinking wine was forbidden to Jews, but abstinence from either or both could have arisen if meat were not properly drained of blood (Gen. 9:4; Deut. 12:15–16); if it were unclean (Lev. 11:8; Deut. 14:8) or sacrificed to idols (1 Cor. 8:13), or, in the case of wine, if it were offered in libation to gods. See Dunn, *Romans 9–16*, pp. 826–27.

§35 Christ: The Point of Convergence (Rom. 15:1–13)

The first 13 verses of chapter 15 continue and conclude Paul's discussion of the "strong" and "weak." The discussion which began in 14:1 with the "weak *in faith*" broadens to the strong and weak in the most general sense. Verses 8–9 reveal that the conflict between the strong and weak basically reflects the differences between Jews and Gentiles which have occupied Paul throughout the epistle. He demonstrates that unity between the two groups can be achieved in Jesus Christ, whose striving was not to please himself but to build up others (vv. 2–3), and who provided a model for true acceptance of others, particularly those different from ourselves (v. 7). Christ is thus the focal point of faith, which Paul noted in 14:23, and both the object of the church's worship and the model of its life. From this focal point three themes radiate outward. The first, which is keyed off the word "to please" (vv. 1, 2, 3), argues that reconciliation between strong and weak occurs where believers forego self-serving interests in favor of "Christ [who] did not please himself" (vv. 1–3). Second, Christ has come to fulfill the promises made to the patriarchs for the inclusion of Gentiles in salvation (vv. 8–12). And finally, Christ is the ground of hope for all believers (vv. 4, 12, 13). Twice in the argument Paul rises to the height of joyful doxologies or benedictions (vv. 5–6, 13); the latter thematically concludes the epistle, the remainder of which will be devoted to Paul's travel plans and personal greetings.

15:1 / For the first time since 14:1 Paul designates the **strong** by name, and his use of the first person plural indicates that he considers himself as one of them. The **strong**, however, are not the ideal. Rather, strength is a privilege which carries *responsibility*. **We who are strong ought to bear with the failings**

of the weak. Implicit in the word **ought** is a moral claim that follows as a result of the love of neighbor (cf. 13:8–10; 15:27). In Greek the term for **strong** is literally "those who are able," i.e., those who have the power and means of dominating others; it stands in direct antithesis to the **weak** (Gk. "those who are unable"). But if Paul does not establish strength as the ideal, neither does he argue against it. He argues instead for a redirection of its potential, advocating power *for* others rather than power *over* them.

This thought is reinforced by a word (**bear**; Gk. *bastazein*) that is used both of Isaiah's suffering servant and of Jesus: " 'He took up our infirmities and carried (*bastazein*) our diseases' " (Isa. 53:4; Matt. 8:17; also Gal. 6:2). Adolf Schlatter was right in saying that Paul argues for more than tacit toleration. 'Toleration is never quite free from disdain and puts the weaker person in danger of being overpowered. Whoever is merely tolerated is not really accepted in his weakness, but is treated in such a way that he is expected to be what he cannot be" (*Gottes Gerechtigkeit*, p. 379 [my translation]). *Agapē* is always more than tolerance, and also more than condescension. Christians must *accept* others (v. 7) and help bear their burdens, just as Christ took our burdens upon himself. Acceptance of the weak, however, is not the same as living for them, much less saving them. That only God can do. The parameters of the present admonition are defined by an earthy realism, namely, *as we are able* to take the burdens of others upon ourselves and provide what help we can. The accent, however, falls on accepting the weak, not changing them.

15:2 / **Each of us should please his neighbor for his good, to build him up**. This is not to say that personal pleasure is bad. Radical asceticism always forgets that God made the world good and for the purpose of human delight (Gen. 1–2). Paul's imperative says nothing either for or against self-gratification, but concerns pleasing *others* (which in the present context means the weak); and under no circumstances should the self be pleased at the expense of others. *Agapē* seeks to please the neighbor **for his good, to build him up** (cf. Phil. 2:3–4). Furthermore, this protects the virtue of forbearance from being reduced to "niceness." We may, for example, be nice when we should be just, or be agreeable when we should be truthful, or be flattering when honesty and integrity are demanded. The good, as any physician will tell you, is not always what the patient wants to hear, and a Christian, as well as a physician, is worthy of the name only where the *good of the other* prevails over any other interest.

15:3 / Accepting and bearing the weak are not presented as moral ends, but as extensions of the ministry of Christ, **For even Christ did not please himself**. Paul, of course, could have supported the principle on the basis of Christ's teachings (e.g., Matt. 5:43–46; Acts 20:35), but he grounds it instead in Christ's *example*. There is thus a historical reality beneath Paul's ethical principle. Christians are called to act in like manner not simply because it might be shown from ethical canons that this is a proper course of behavior, but because *it is the way of Christ*. The echo of Christ's humbling himself and making himself nothing in Philippians 2:5–11 is unmistakable here (see also Mark 10:45; 1 Cor. 11:1; 2 Cor. 8:9).

Nevertheless, there is more here than a general appeal for humility and other-centeredness (e.g., 1 Cor. 10:33). The quotation which Paul appends in verse 3 (**"The insults of those who insult you have fallen on me"** [Ps. 69:9]) indicates the lengths to which Jesus went *not* to please himself. More precisely, in his association with sinners Jesus became the most despised of human beings, and this was necessary if he was to be the Messiah of God. In like manner, Christians, through their association with the weak and needy, expose themselves to the reproach and derision of the world, and this too is God's will for them. If the Son of God willingly forsook claims of privilege and prestige, giving himself up for the weak and needy, how much more should his followers renounce self-gratification and "bear with the failings of the weak" (v. 1).

15:4 / For the early Christians the holy Scriptures (**everything that was written in the past**) were what we today call the Old Testament. In the modern world the Hebrew Scriptures are read from many different perspectives. "Bible as Literature" courses read the OT as a repository of Hebrew saga, poetry, and narrative. Some theologians are interested in the OT's layers of oral and written traditions, and others read it as a record of Hebrew social history. Some Christians see it as a book of law analogous to a moral counterpart of the gospel, and others relegate it to a book of preparation and prediction, now superseded by Christ. And, of course, there have always been Christians who have sought to reject the OT (and its God) as inferior and vengeful.

Whatever the merits (or lack thereof) of these various approaches, none of them aptly describe Paul's approach to the Hebrew Scriptures, for he did not read them as a source book for a particular theory or ideology. The Scriptures were not something he referred to, but something he lived from, for what **was written in the past was written to teach us.** The Scriptures were, of course, ancient, but not in the sense of being "dated." In his day, what was oldest was normally thought to be truest because it had survived the most difficult of all tests—time! We do not know what external interests (if any) Scripture held for Paul. We know only that he considered it a living, dynamic tradition which was breaking into his own time, through which God was acting and revealing himself in Christ. Scripture was an unfolding drama wherein what God communicated to one generation became valid for another, for "Jesus Christ is the same yesterday and today and forever" (Heb. 13:8). Of all contemporary approaches, Dietrich Bonhoeffer's question, "Who is Jesus Christ for us *today*?" would have found perhaps greatest resonance from Paul. This question does not exclude historical and literary questions, although it limits them to a secondary status. The validity of such questions would depend on their leading to a renewed understanding of the meaning of the Scriptures for each generation. Bengel's saying might also speak for Paul, "Apply yourself wholly to the text, and apply the text wholly to yourself."

Through endurance and the encouragement of the Scriptures we might have hope. In these words Paul introduces the theme of hope with which he will conclude the epistle (v. 13). We might have expected that Scripture would impart knowledge or salvation, but the apostle views its essential message as one of **hope.** Hope is the claiming of Christ's coming triumph and reign by saving faith (8:24–25). Of course, Paul speaks of hope that comes not from the Scriptures per se but from the "God of hope" (v. 13), to whom the Scriptures bear witness.

15:5–6 / In verses 4–6 we discover a continuum from right authority (= Scripture, v. 4), to right thinking (= theology, v. 5), to right glorification (= worship, v. 6). The two benefits of Scripture in verse 4 are steadfastness or constancy ("endurance") and promise ("encouragement"). These same benefits describe

God's attributes in verse 5, about which believers are (literally in Greek) "to think the same." This produces right thinking, which culminates in right worship **with one heart** in verse 6. Right thinking about God and unity among believers are not exactly products of the church. They are gifts from God (v. 5; see also 12:16; Eph. 4:3), the first the gift of revelation, and the second the work of the Spirit. Earlier in Romans we spoke of "alien righteousness" as a righteousness not intrinsic to humanity but as a gift of God. The expression **with one heart** (v. 6) might also be considered "alien unity." The Greek word behind it, *homothymadon*, means a unity that comes from outside ourselves rather than from any denominator common to ourselves. Demosthenes once used the term to describe the sort of oneness that results when a group of soldiers is attacked by an enemy; whatever their differences, the threat of destruction welds them into a fighting unit. So it is that grace draws us into a new relation with God and one another, making the church into something that it was not before, namely, a family of Jews and Gentiles *in Christ* (so Eph. 3:14–15).

The unity of believers is related inseparably to the purpose of God in redemption, both quantitatively and qualitatively. At the quantitative level Paul will assert in verses 8–9 that redemption radiates outward like ripples in a pool to include Gentiles within the household of faith. At the qualitative level he has just shown how division between the strong and weak (v. 1) has resulted in a unity **with one heart** in Christ (v. 6). On both levels it is abundantly clear that disruption of the unity of believers also disrupts the work of redemption.

15:7 / Verses 7–13 summarize and conclude what Paul has said since 14:1. Verse 7 especially captures the spirit of the argument, **Accept one another, then, just as Christ accepted you, in order to bring praise to God**. Addressed to both the strong and weak, this injunction calls for unconditional affirmation and acceptance of each by the other. Paul moves from the historical indicative of Christ's death for us to the present imperative of acceptance of others. Again, it is not moral principles in themselves but the person of Jesus who provides both rationale and empowerment for such acceptance. There are many ways to give glory to God, among them truth (3:7) and faith (4:20). Not least among them, however, is acceptance of those different from ourselves. How

strange, said Luther, is the glory of God, for God is glorified when
believers of differing persuasions accept one another and when the
strong bear the burdens of the weak! (*Lectures on Romans*, p. 411).

15:8–9 / In a solemn summary of the thrust of the epistle, Paul affirms, **For I tell you that Christ has become a servant
of the Jews on behalf of God's truth, to confirm the promises
made to the patriarchs so that the Gentiles may glorify God for
his mercy** (cf. 1:16–17). **Truth** and **mercy** are, as Otto Michel notes,
frequent attributes of God in the OT (*Der Brief an die Römer*, pp.
358–59). But whereas they were once thought to be restricted to
Jews, they now are seen to include Gentiles. This passage offers
rather compelling evidence that the "strong" and "weak" of chapters 14–15 generally correspond in Paul's thinking to Gentiles and
Jews. If the phrasing of verses 8–9 is somewhat rough, it is, as
Käsemann reminds us, because Paul has a double purpose in
mind. He wants to establish that the saving grace of Christ is
available to Jews and Gentiles alike, but that priority was given
(at least historically) to the Jews (*Romans*, p. 385). Gentiles, on the
one hand, must understand that their salvation comes through
the Hebrew patriarchs. Jews, on the other hand, must understand
that God's promise to the patriarchs was from the beginning
inclusive of Gentiles (e.g., Gen. 12:3). Christ is the **servant** of both,
of Jews by **confirm**ing **the promises made to the patriarchs**, of
Gentiles by fulfilling the original purpose of the covenant with
Israel. In both instances God's glory is served.

15:10–13 / The conclusion of verses 8–9 finds support
from all three divisions of the Hebrew Scriptures (Torah, Prophets, Writings), thus enhancing its effect. All four quotations (v. 9
= Ps. 18:49 / 2 Sam. 22:50; v. 10 = Deut. 32:43; v. 11 = Ps. 117:1;
v. 12 = Isa. 11:10) follow the LXX faithfully. They share a common
theme of praise of God by a joint chorus of Jew *and Gentile*. Praise
is expressly emphasized by no fewer than six terms in Greek, most
of which survive in translation—**praise, sing hymns, rejoice, sing
praises**, and **hope**. The final quotation in verse 12 culminates with
that humblest of messianic metaphors—**the root of Jesse**—which,
in the present context, is entirely in character with a Messiah who
"did not please himself" (v. 3). This Christ is the Gentiles' ruler
and hope. Thus, the salvation of the Gentiles, as Paul argued
resolutely in chapters 9–11, is anything but a scissors-and-paste
act on God's part. Their salvation was inherent in God's promise

to Israel from the beginning! There should of course be nothing very surprising in this. The God who once defended the cause of an abandoned slave people in Egypt, and later defended the cause of the sojourner, widow, and orphan in its midst, now advocates the cause of the distant Gentiles (Eph. 2:11–13). And the same Lord who draws them into salvation builds bridges between them in the community which bears his name. The weak must not condemn the strong, but rather permit them their freedom of conscience; and the strong must not press for victory, but rather convert their power into advocacy for the weak.

The discussion of the strong and weak is concluded with a rich and festive benediction of hope in verse 13. Christian hope is not merely a sentiment of good fortune or a vague wish that "things will turn out all right in the end." Hope is an affirmation of the nature of God. **The God of hope** enables those who put their faith in him to **overflow with hope**. Gone are the things of the flesh: law, sin, wrath, and death. The benediction sums up the new life in Christ: **joy, peace, trust, hope,** and **power of the Holy Spirit**. True, these are not yet present in full measure, but the work and promise of God in Christ are a surety of their ultimate triumph. "Now we see but a poor reflection . . . then we shall see face to face. Now I know in part; then I shall know fully, even as I am fully known" (1 Cor. 13:12).

Additional Notes   §35

15:1 / Paul's admonition **to bear with the failings of the weak and not to please ourselves** cuts across the grain of dominance, success, and identity by association which runs through our society. The highest good in a consumer society is usually to please oneself and "do it my way" (if not at all costs, then at least first). It may seem odd (and equally as difficult) for people inculcated with such values to attempt to break them and seek the good of others above self, for the person to whom *agapē* calls me may neither please me nor enhance my reputation. Moreover, **bearing with the failings of the weak** means that in some sense we become like the weak. "You know the grace of our Lord Jesus Christ, that though he was rich, yet for your sakes he became poor, so that you through his poverty might become rich" (2 Cor. 8:9).

15:3 / Paul's appeal to the *example* of Christ finds a strong echo in the ethics of Albert Schweitzer, the theologian-physician of Lambarene

(W. Africa). When it comes to influencing behavior, said Schweitzer, example is not simply the most important thing, it is the *only* thing that matters! See *Everyone Needs a Philosophy of Life. Albert Schweitzer's Philosophy of Reverence for Life*, ed. and arr. by M. O'Hara (Great Barrington, Mass.: Albert Schweitzer Friendship House, 1978). Ernst Käsemann offers a clear exposition of this verse in *Romans*, p. 382.

15:4 / Among the works where Bonhoeffer poses the question, Who is Jesus Christ for us today?, see his *Christologie* (Munich: Kaiser Verlag, 1981).

The Bengel quotation is from his 1734 edition of the Greek New Testament, quoted in Nestle's *Novum Testamentum Graece*, 25th ed. (London: United Bible Societies, 1963), p. 3.

15:5–6 / On the meaning of **with one heart**, and for the Demosthenes references, see H. Heidland, "*homothymadon*," *TDNT*, vol. 5, pp. 185–86.

§36 Rome and Beyond: The Missionary Calling of the Apostle Paul (Rom. 15:14–33)

In the present section Paul returns to matters of personal interest which he broached at the beginning of the epistle (1:8–15). Romans 1:8–15 and 15:14–33 are the only two sections of the epistle which might be called autobiographical. Although they fall outside Paul's main argument, they provide vital information about his reasons for writing. Both sections attest to the apostle's longstanding desire to visit Rome (1:10, 13; 15:22–24, 28, 32) and to bring his readers a spiritual blessing (1:11–13; 15:29). Both bear witness to his commission as apostle to the Gentiles and to his desire to present them obedient in faith to God (1:5, 14; 15:15–17). And in both he presents himself united with and dependent on the prayers of believers in Rome (1:9–10; 15:30–31).

What stands before us is an eloquent testimony to the missionary impulse of Paul's life, and to his sense of being apprehended by Christ in order to bring the redemptive message of the gospel to distant and disinherited Gentiles. Nevertheless, Paul must walk something of a tightrope at this point in the epistle. Considering that he has yet to set foot in Rome, has he been presumptuous in giving advice to the strong and weak in 14:1–15:13? Might his self-understanding as apostle to the Gentiles be viewed by the Romans as pretentious and ambitious? His upcoming trip to Rome—how should he explain it? If, as he states, he wanted "to preach the gospel where Christ was not known so that [he] would not be building on someone else's foundation" (v. 20), why was he planning to visit Rome, which had already been evangelized? Might his epistle, in fact, be seen as an attempt to build on someone else's foundation? In an opposite vein, might the Romans feel slighted if his road led not *to* Rome, but *through* it to Spain? And what contribution could Rome make to his Spanish mission, or might Paul be thought of as using Rome (financially, for example) for ulterior purposes? The waters of 15:14–33 may at first reading seem trouble free, but a closer look reveals a number of reefs and shoals lurking below the surface. Here as elsewhere Paul needed to interpret his mission pastorally in order to enlist understanding and support from those to whom it was addressed.

15:14 / The apostle Paul is commonly thought of as a theologian—perhaps a rather forbidding one. A theologian he was, but his first calling was to be a missionary pastor to the churches he founded. Both his missionary passion and pastoral devotion surface in an opening statement laden with emphasis, **I myself am convinced, my brothers, that *you yourselves* are full of goodness, complete in knowledge and competent to instruct one another.** By **goodness** Paul is probably thinking not of ethics in general, but of a specific moral commitment to heal the breech between strong and weak, with **knowledge** of the gospel (e.g., 15:3) undergirding it. Considering the tensions that existed between Jews and Gentiles (e.g., chs. 9–11; 14–15), some readers may suspect Paul of being unduly optimistic in verse 14. Others may suspect him of flattery, and perhaps even of insincerity. Granted, Paul was a master of social propriety when he needed to be (see his appearance before Agrippa in Acts 26, his appeal to Philemon [Philem.], or his impression on captain and crew in Acts 27). The declaration of verse 14, however, is more than social decorum. It is quite literally a testimony to the priesthood of all believers and to the **goodness** and **knowledge** on which that priesthood depends.

15:15–16 / The apostle concedes that he has **written . . . quite boldly on some points**, by which he means his advice to the strong and weak in the foregoing section. Well might the Romans consider his words an intrusion into their affairs were such words not a result **of the grace God gave** him. Giving advice to others on what they should do in specific situations is a serious responsibility (if not a heady presumption). Paul would not have offered his advice were it not a consequence of God's grace to him. If advice is nothing more than one person speaking to another, then well ought restraint or silence be observed; but where advice is prompted by grace and is thus more than human speech, there it has a higher responsibility to God and can be spoken **quite boldly**. If in his advice Paul treads on the limits of propriety, he quickly adds that it is only **to remind you . . . again** (v. 15) of that which the church everywhere teaches and takes for granted.

Verse 16 provides a window into the consciousness of Paul. God's grace has enabled him **to be a minister of Christ Jesus to the Gentiles with the priestly duty of proclaiming the gospel of God, so that the Gentiles might become an offering acceptable to God, sanctified by the Holy Spirit**. Remarkably, Paul describes his commission to non-Jews in emphatically Jewish terms! **Minister . . . priestly duty . . . an offering acceptable to God . . . sanctified**—the language of temple sacrifice is applied to those excluded from the temple. This indicates rather indisputably that Paul considered his ministry to the Gentiles as fulfilling the commission of *Israel*. The promise that God would "bring all your brothers, from all the nations, to my holy mountain in Jerusalem as an offering to the Lord" (Isa. 66:20) had broken into the present. Eschatology was being realized in salvation history. Paul saw himself as a priest through whom the offering of the Gentiles was being brought before the Lord. This offering consisted not in holy *things*, such as cereal offerings, drink offerings, or animal sacrifice, but in holy *persons* "who were at one time disobedient to God" (11:30), but who now have been led "to obey God by what I have said and done" (v. 18).

15:17–19a / Paul could not have been unaware that such a calling posed a danger to his ego. It would have been tempting to seize the calling in Promethean fashion and pit himself against the God who gave it. It cannot be coincidental that Paul uses the word *kauchēsis*, "boasting" (NIV, **glory**) at this point, a word that often (e.g., 3:27) denotes arrogant pride against God. The apostle, however, refuses to arrogate glory to himself, but chooses rather **to glory in Christ Jesus in my service to God** (v. 17). Paul harbors no illusions of himself being the demiurge of salvation. He is simply its "minister" (v. 16) and its steward on Christ's behalf. He **will not venture to speak of anything except what Christ has accomplished through** him **in leading the Gentiles to obey God**. He himself is not the source and power **of signs and miracles** but rather their vessel **through the power of the Spirit**. None of which is to belittle Paul's role. He was awed by his commission to convert the Gentiles and by what God had done through him, but he would not cross the Rubicon that separates faith from megalomania. Dedicated to God's mission, Paul sidestepped delusions of self-importance. His emphasis was always on **what Christ has accomplished through me**. Both his usefulness to God and his greatness in history are due to the fact that he did not confuse the servant of the mission with the Lord of the mission.

15:19b–21 / When the apostle stood before Agrippa with no defense but his faith and his chains, he recounted the Damascus road experience in these words: "So then, King Agrippa, I was not disobedient to the vision from heaven" (Acts 26:19). Verse 19 discloses the geographical extent to which Paul was obedient to that vision. **So from Jerusalem all the way around to Illyricum, I have fully proclaimed the gospel of Christ**. As a statement of fact this verse raises rather considerable questions, for there is no reference in Acts (or anywhere else in Christian literature) to a Pauline mission to Illyricum (modern Serbia, Croatia, Albania). If the reference is meant to be inclusive, it may be, as one scholar suggests, that Paul evangelized the region from neighboring Macedonia when he revisited that province after his Ephesian ministry (Acts 20:1). But since by his own admission Paul did not evangelize in Judea (Gal. 1:18f.), it is possible, as Käsemann suggests, that he did not evangelize in Illyricum either, but that **Jerusalem** and **Illyricum** refer to the *limits* of Paul's missionary activity, though not including them (*Romans*, pp. 394–95). But we cannot say for sure.

Equally curious is the impression that Paul has worked himself out of a job in those regions. **All the way around . . . I have fully proclaimed the gospel of Christ**. Again, "There is no more place for me to work in these regions" (v. 23). This quite obviously cannot mean that Paul had preached everywhere and to everyone in those places. The ignorance of and opposition to his mission as recorded in Acts, let alone the physical impossibility of one person's saturating several nations with the gospel, exclude a literal interpretation here. The key to these statements must be found in the apostle's *missionary* consciousness. As a pioneer evangelist who desired to preach **the gospel where Christ was not known**, Paul determined his strategy, which was to establish Christianity in urban centers and to allow his converts to evangelize outlying areas. A classic example of this was his ministry in Ephesus, from which converts moved up the Lycus valley to plant churches in Laodicea, Hierapolis, and Colossae (Acts 19:8–10; Col. 1:7; 4:12–16). A nineteenth- and twentieth-century missionary aspiration which hopes for every soul to hear the gospel in our generation will misunderstand Paul here. In comparison to the global dimensions of modern missions Paul's vision must have seemed rather provincial. The expectation of the imminent return of Christ, which Paul shared (so far as we can tell) with most Christians of the time, forged his strategy, which was the maximum spread of the gospel in the minimum time allotted.

What emerges is a missionary ardor **to preach the gospel where Christ was not known, so that I would not be building on someone else's foundation**. At a practical level this resulted in a policy that avoided rivalry with other missionaries (cf. 1 Cor. 3:10). Some souls, perhaps, may have objected that in the epistle to Rome Paul was violating his own principle on both counts, since the gospel had already been preached there by others. Paul assures his readers, however, that he has no intention of ministering in Rome (v. 24), but only of passing through it to the west **where Christ was not known**. In the fourth servant hymn of Isaiah (52:15) Paul found a witness to his mission, which he quotes in verse 21. **Him** and **hearing** refer to the servant of Yahweh and his report, which Paul sees fulfilled in Jesus Christ and the gospel. It is this impulse, i.e., Christ and his gospel, which is the source and power of Paul's commitment to proclaim the gospel to the least likely and farthest removed—the Gentiles.

15:22–23 / For years Paul had desired to visit Rome, but had been **hindered from coming** because of his labors in the eastern Mediterranean. **But now that there is no more place for me to work in these regions**, says Paul, the way is clear for the long-awaited visit. On the face of it, that is an astounding claim. As we noted at verse 19, the claim **that there is no more place for me to work** is surely tempered by the prospect of the imminent return of Christ. The nail of Christianity had been set in the east due to his missionary efforts, but it remained for others to drive home.

15:24 / Paul's last frontier was Spain, the western-most limit of the Roman Empire. Exactly why he chose to evangelize Spain (as opposed to Gaul, for instance) we are not told. We know that Spain had an established Jewish population at the time, although how much of an attraction that would have been for the apostle to the Gentiles is a matter of debate. Spain's network of roads promised an itinerant missionary access to the entire peninsula, but Paul can scarcely have chosen Spain simply because of its roads. Perhaps the word "around" (Gk. *kyklō*, v. 19) provides a clue. If we draw an arc from Jerusalem to Illyricum and extend it westward, it reaches Spain. If such an arc represented Paul's missionary design, it may suggest that he hoped to cover the northern hemisphere of the Mediterranean, trusting that others would cover the southern hemisphere, and thus complete a full circle. A passing reference in 1 Clement 5:6 that Paul "was a herald both in the east and in the *west*" may lend credence to this view. Whatever the reason(s), Rome lay en route to his proposed Spanish mission, and Paul hoped to be received and assisted by believers in the capital as he reached westward.

Paul does not specify what form of assistance he hopes for. If his insistence that representatives from Gentile churches accompany him to deliver the Jerusalem collection is any indication, we might suppose that he hoped for representative missionaries (proficient in Latin?), rather than simply for financial assistance. But, in fact, Paul leaves his plans decidedly ambiguous, stating only that he hopes to **have enjoyed your company for a while.** At the very least, this is a tender admission of his need for spiritual nurture from Rome. Paul does not write as one who has arrived (Phil. 3:12). He too is part of the body of Christ, which means that his life is incomplete apart from other members of that body. He pays the Romans a great compliment in conveying that he stands in need of their company.

15:25–29 / Ironically, in the same breath in which he mentions Spain, he says he must first go to Jerusalem. Consider for a moment the range of Paul's plans: he writes from Corinth to Rome, about a visit to Spain, with a trip to Jerusalem first. His plans reflect the tension between his allegiance to the mother church in the Jewish east and his missionary call to the Gentile west. The gospel did not present Paul with the option of serene detachment from the world. It made him increasingly vulnerable to the far-flung forces of his world. He had, in the words of Robert Frost, "promises to keep, and miles to go before I sleep."

The purpose of the Jerusalem interlude was **to make a contribution for the poor among the saints in Jerusalem** (v. 26). This enterprise had occupied Paul greatly during the latter years of his third missionary journey. He made frequent reference to it in his letters to churches in Galatia, Macedonia, and Achaia (1 Cor. 16:1; 2 Cor. 8:1ff.; 9:2, 12; also Acts 19:21; 20:22). Exactly why the believers in Jerusalem were poor we cannot say, although C. H. Dodd's suggestion (*Romans*, p. 230) that their early experiment in economic communism (see Acts 2:44–45; 4:32–5:11) so divested the church of capital that when hard times hit it had nothing on which to fall back (e.g., Acts 11:27–30) is worth a second thought. Whatever the causes, Paul shows no interest in rehearsing them. His response was one of ministry, not analysis, endeavoring to unite the church in charity (lit., *koinōnia*), **for the poor among the saints in Jerusalem** (v. 26).

Many reasons have been advanced for Paul's intentness on the contribution, but none is as compelling as his own explanation. If Gentiles have become the beneficiaries of **the Jews' spiritual blessings**, then it is only proper, especially in time of need, that Gentiles **share with them their material blessings**. Paul speaks of a *debt* which Gentiles owe to Jews (v. 27). The financial contribution from the Gentiles is a vital installment in the making good of that debt, a tangible expression of both the unity and equality of Gentiles and Jews in the body of Christ. The church consists of Jews and Gentiles, as Paul has argued from the beginning, and both belong to it not because of their strengths but because of their *indebtedness*. Gentiles are indebted to the spiritual blessings of Israel, Israel is indebted to the material blessings of the Gentiles. The church consists of both the spiritual and the material, and both are in equal measure a ministry (Gk. *leitourgein*, v. 27) and **service of the saints** (v. 25). The contribution was, in fact, an object lesson of the strong bearing the weak, for which Paul argued in 14:1–15:13. Finally, we cannot discount the idea that in taking the offering to Jerusalem Paul saw himself as fulfilling his "priestly duty" of bringing the Gentiles as "an offering acceptable to God" (v. 16). His presentation of the financial offering in Jerusalem symbolized his much greater presentation of the Gentiles to God.

15:30–33 / After completing the relief offering, Paul hopes at last to be free to pursue his Spanish mission, stopping in Rome en route "in the full measure of the blessing of Christ" (vv. 28–29). Paul was under no illusions about latent hostility awaiting him in Jerusalem. Neither (apparently) was anyone else. He had already escaped one plot on his life there (Acts 9:29–30), and omens of yet another awaited him (Acts 20:22–25; 21:10–11). It is for good reason that Paul hopes to be **rescued from the unbelievers in Judea** (v. 31). In no uncertain terms he reckons with the possibility of losing his life at the hands of Jews who were opposed to the messiahship of Jesus. So ominous were impending events that in this, the only direct personal appeal to his readers in the epistle, he solicits their aid in his **struggle by praying to God for me** (v. 30). In going to Jerusalem Paul was quite literally risking his life for the unity and equality of Gentiles and Jews. In this too he needed prayer, not only that his life would be spared, but that **my service in Jerusalem may be acceptable to the saints there**.

Events in Jerusalem, of course, transpired quite differently from the hopes of verse 28. Paul fell victim to a misconceived plot and was nearly beaten to death in the temple precincts by an angry mob of Jews (Acts 21:17ff.). After an anxious rescue by Roman soldiers, he languished two years under as many governors in jail in Caesarea. Paul eventually reached Rome, but not as a pioneer missionary. He arrived as a prisoner in chains, and our chief source for these matters, the book of Acts, closes with his awaiting trial under Caesar in Rome.

Whether Paul ever made it to Spain we do not know. The NT leaves no record that he did. The traditional view is that Paul died at the hands of Nero shortly after the end of the narrative of Acts (ca. A.D. 62). There is, however, at least one brief though tantalizing piece of evidence that Paul may have fulfilled his goal of reaching Spain. The early record of 1 Clement (ca. A.D. 95) that Paul "taught righteousness to *all* the world" and gave his testimony "when he had reached the limits of the west" (5:7) is no negligible witness. It is, of course, possible to take "limits of the west" to mean Rome, but that is rendered less likely considering the fact that Clement wrote *from* Rome, which was the western limit of neither the empire nor Europe. What 1 Clement says implicitly, the Muratorian Canon (also from Rome, though a century later and of less value) says explicitly: "from the city (of Rome) [Paul] proceeded to Spain." Whether Paul actually reached Spain is, in the final analysis, of no material consequence for our understanding of Romans. It is largely a point of historical curiosity. Nevertheless, 1 Clement and the Muratorian Canon caution us against foreclosing the question too hastily. Even if Paul fulfilled his goal of preaching "the gospel where Christ was not known" (in Spain), however, he must have been arrested again a few years later and executed in Rome, for tradition is unanimous that he died there sometime during the latter years of Nero's reign (ca. A.D. 64–68).

Additional Notes   §36

15:19-21 / On references to Illyricum in Christian literature, see BAGD, p. 376. The suggestion of a mission outreach to Illyricum after Paul's visit to Macedonia is from B. F. C. Atkinson, *NBD*, pp. 555–56. In agreement with this (and in disagreement with Käsemann's view), F. F. Bruce suggests that the use of the Latin form *Illyricum* (as opposed to the Gk. *Illyria*) may indicate that Paul entered the Latin environment of Illyricum in order to prepare himself for his proposed Spanish mission (*Apostle of the Heart Set Free*, pp. 316-17). The view that v. 19 is a reference to early Christian expansion as a whole rather than to Paul's personal missionary endeavors (entertained by Dunn, *Romans 9–16*, pp. 863–64) is surely mistaken. Paul is not writing a history of missions but describing his own missionary theory and activity (**I have fully proclaimed**, v. 19). Moreover, Illyricum scarcely represented the high-water mark of Christian expansion at the time of writing.

15:24 / We are mistaken if we consider Spain the "wild west" of the Roman Empire. It had been for two and one-half centuries an established part of the Empire. An excellent system of Roman roads and bridges crisscrossed the peninsula, of which a bridge at Alcantara and an aqueduct at Segovia remain to this day. Spain had made no negligible contribution to Roman culture and politics: the writers Seneca, Martial, and Quintilian hailed from there, as did the emperors Trajan, Hadrian, and Theodosius I. See J. Finegan, "Spain," *IDB*, vol. 4, pp. 429–30.

The arc-theory of Paul's missionary vision from Jerusalem through Illyricum to Spain is suggested by Dunn, *Romans 9–16*, p. 872.

15:25-29 / Dodd's mention of early Christian communism ought not be confused with Marxism. As an economic theory Marxism is determined by the compulsory ideal of common ownership of capital, whereas the early Christians were motivated by *agapē*, of which (at least in Jerusalem) the voluntary sharing of property was one expression.

On the reason for Paul's contribution to the saints I am indebted to Achtemeier, *Romans*, pp. 230–31.

15:30-33 / The reference to the Muratorian Canon is from *New Testament Apocrypha*, vol. 1, ed. E. Hennecke and W. Schneemelcher (Philadelphia: Westminster, 1963), p. 44. There is a further reference to Paul's journey to Spain (though quite legendary) in the apocryphal *Acts of Peter* 2.6. Witnesses to the existence of Christianity in Spain in the second century can be found in Irenaeus and Tertullian, but with no mention of Paul in relation to it. On the whole question, see Sanday and Headlam, *Romans*, pp. 413–14.

§37 Names and Faces of the Gospel (Rom. 16:1–27)

At first glance the final chapter of Romans offers little more than a list of names, of interest to Paul and his readers perhaps, but of doubtful consequence for modern readers. Of what significance after all, is a list of unidentified names? Is not a name about which we know nothing really no name at all? Is not our commentary reduced to an exercise in historical trivia at this point? Does not the strangeness of the names remind us how foreign and remote Paul's world really is from ours, lessening the likelihood of this epistle's speaking to us today?

The sixteenth chapter has a checkered history in the interpretation of the epistle. According to the testimony of Origen, already in the second century Marcion eliminated it (and chapter 15) from his edition of Romans (*Commentary on Romans*, 7.453; cited in Metzger, *TCGNT*, p. 533). Luther also struck it from his commentary on the premise that Paul would scarcely have concluded such a powerful epistle with a roster of names (*Lectures on Romans*, p. 419). Nearly two centuries ago David Schulz began in earnest the historical-critical assault on the final chapter, postulating that Romans 16 is actually a cover letter attached to a second copy of Romans originally ending at 15:33 which Paul sent also to Ephesus, and which introduces Phoebe (16:1–2) as the letter carrier. According to this theory, Romans circulated in at least two versions—a shorter original (chs. 1–15) which was destined for Rome, and a longer copy (chs. 1–15, plus 16) which was destined for Ephesus. During the course of time, the theory continues, the two copies (and their copies) became confused, thus accounting for the fragmentary ending of the epistle, and especially the doxology (16:25–27). This accounts for the fact that among various manuscripts the doxology occurs at the close of chapters 14 or 16 (or both 14 and 16), in one manuscript at the end of chapter 15, and in others not at all. Among recent interpreters T. W. Manson has given classic proportions to the Ephesian theory.

Whatever the merits of the theory, it appears destined to play only a minor part in the exegetical history of Romans. The evidence which can be orchestrated against it (see Additional Notes) makes it virtually certain that chapter 16 belonged to the autograph hand of the epistle (though there is more doubt about the doxology). Throughout our commentary we have considered the likelihood that the problems which resulted from the return of Jewish Christians to Gentile Christian churches in Rome after the lapse of the edict of Claudius played a discernible role in both the themes and the method of the epistle. If Romans were originally intended for another destination, or, at the very least, equally applicable to another destination (both of which the Ephesian theory suggests), then its historical context is essentially lost—not to mention the questions which such a theory would raise about the pastoral integrity of Paul. But if, as we have argued, the epistle was written by Paul in order to commend his gospel and himself *to Rome* and to enlist Roman support in his proposed Spanish mission, then the greetings in chapter 16 are quite in harmony with the missionary purpose set forth in 15:14–33. The persons greeted are colleagues (and acquaintances of colleagues) from the eastern mission field, whom the apostle mentions in order to marshall support in Rome for his proposed trip to Spain. What could be more natural given his pastoral and missionary interests? One reason why Paul was the successful missionary he was is that he did not act in accordance with some of the theories which scholars have since attributed to him.

16:1–2 / At the head of the list of greetings stands a woman, Phoebe. Paul calls her **our sister**, which means she was a Christian, and judging from her name, she must have been a Gentile Christian, since Jewish parents would scarcely have named a daughter after the Titaness of Greek mythology (the daughter of Heaven and Earth, Hesiod, *Theogony*, 136). She is a **servant of the church** (v. 1) at Cenchrea, a port town adjacent to Corinth to the southeast. The Greek word for **servant** is *diakonos*, more commonly rendered "deacon." Whether by "deacon(ess)" he means a church official or a general helper is disputed, though the former is more likely. Paul's word choice in Greek suggests a formal office (*ousan diakonon*), whereas general help would more naturally

have been expressed either by the verb *diakonein* ("to serve"), or
by the abstract noun *diakonia* ("service"). We know that the offices
of bishop and deacon were established at the time (or not much
later), and there is reasonable evidence that women were entitled
at least to the latter office.

Phoebe was evidently a person of means (or influence, or
both), because the Greek term translated **a great help** (v. 2; Gk.
prostatis) means a "protectress or patroness." She is mentioned
first, however, not because she was a benefactor, but because she
was in all likelihood the bearer of the epistle from Corinth to
Rome. The term for **commend** (v. 1), *synistēmi*, was roughly the
Greek equivalent to a letter of recommendation today. In antiquity inns and hotels were not only sparse but of dubious reputation, and persons who travelled to foreign parts needed such
recommendations as protection against all sorts of liabilities, especially if they were unknown women. Paul asks the church to
receive her, as was the custom throughout early Christianity (e.g.,
15:7; Matt. 25:31–46), **in a way worthy of the saints**.

16:3–4 / Phoebe's name is followed by the names of two
fellow workers (v. 3) who had **risked their lives for** Paul (v. 4),
and who had a remarkable missionary record of their own. Having
been expelled from Rome by Claudius in A.D. 49 (Acts 18:2), Prisc(ill)a
and Aquila worked with Paul in Corinth and Ephesus, but at the
time of writing they were back in Rome. Given Paul's adventurous
missionary career, there were several places where they could have
risked their lives for him, but no place has better claim than at the
riot at Ephesus (Acts 19:23–40; but see also 2 Cor. 6:5; 11:23). This
Jewish married couple played a critical role in Paul's missionary
enterprise and receives unqualified praise from him. Like Phoebe,
they appear to have been people of means. More importantly, they
were dedicated to community, for five of the six references to them
in the NT include a note of either companionship with or influence
on fellow believers. In Ephesus (1 Cor. 16:19) and Rome (v. 5) they
had founded house churches. In their conduct they exemplified the
nature of the body of Christ, and it is perhaps for this reason that
they were so endeared to Paul. In four of the six references to them
Prisc(ill)a is mentioned before Aquila, which suggests that she im-
pressed her contemporaries as the more dominant partner.

Two of the three names which head the list, then, are of
women, one of whom, probably a deaconess, is entrusted with

carrying the epistle to Rome, the other being a church developer and mentor to missionaries (Acts 18:24–28). No other persons listed receive credits equal to those of Phoebe and Prisc(ill)a. Nor is this the sum of the matter. Four of the first seven names in the list belong to women, one of whom lays good claim to being an apostle. Of the 29 names in the total list, fully one-third are women's. Suffice it to say that Paul is not the despiser of women, nor the advocate of a male-dominated ministry, that he is often portrayed as being.

16:5–16 / There now follows a rapid-fire review of names, about which much spadework has produced, for the most part, only modest gains. But what commentators have lacked in hard evidence they have made up for in a gold mine of guesswork, some of it quite intriguing.

Epenetus (v. 5) is a name found frequently in inscriptions, but otherwise unknown in biblical Greek. Epenetus, a male Gentile, was distinguished as the first convert **in the province of Asia** (= modern western Turkey).

Mary (v. 6), a woman, was most probably a Jewess (though a variant spelling of the same name was not uncommon among Gentiles).

Andronicus and Junias (v. 7), both Greek names, were doubtlessly Jewish since Paul calls them **my relatives** (literally in Greek, "fellow-countrymen"). Depending on the Greek accenting of *Iounian* (a form of the name which unfortunately obscures its gender), the name could be either male (Junias) or female (Junia). The name is normally presumed male (so NIV), but a recent study reveals over 250 examples of it in Greek literature, not one of which is masculine! This seems to be nearly incontrovertible evidence that the name is feminine (Junia), which would make the pair husband and wife (or perhaps brother and sister). If the name is feminine, then Paul's referring to Andronicus and Junia as **outstanding among the apostles,** who **were in Christ before I was**, is very significant. It would indicate that (1) **apostles** refers to a group larger than the original Twelve, (2) among whom was to be counted a woman, (3) and probably a wife, (4) who had been an apostle before Paul was! In saying this we are still holding to the high ground of probability. Now to plunge to more speculative depths: that Andronicus and Junia were Christians before Paul, and indeed were **outstanding among the apostles**, raises the question whether they might have been among the Roman visitors to Jerusalem converted at Pentecost (Acts 2:10), who then returned to evangelize the capital. And to speculate further, if Paul greets those **outstanding among the apostles**, would this not imply that the most outstanding among them—Peter—is *not* in Rome (see Schlatter, *Gottes Gerechtigkeit*, p. 400)? This may be a small piece of evidence in the mosaic that Roman Christianity was not founded by Peter.

Ampliatus (v. 8) and **Urbanus** (v. 9), both men, were common Roman slave names. **Ampliatus** is found frequently in inscriptions, one of which dates from the first century in the catacomb of Domitilla in Rome.

Stachys (v. 9) is a common Greek name for a slave.

Apelles (v. 10), also a common Greek name, was known among the imperial household.

Aristobulus (v. 10), a Greek name, was common among the Herodian dynasty. There is a possibility (but only that) that the Aristobulus here mentioned was the grandson of Herod I and brother of Agrippa I, who lived in Rome and was a friend of the Emperor Claudius. That Paul refers to **those who belong to the** *household of* **Aristobulus** implies that Aristobulus either was not a Christian or was deceased.

Herodion (v. 11), a Jewish name, is also probably to be associated with the family of Herod. The mention of a Herodian immediately after verse 10 adds weight to the conjecture that Aristobulus was the famous member of the same family.

Narcissus (v. 11), a Greek name, may also have been either a non-believer or deceased since Paul mentions only his household. F. F. Bruce asks whether this Narcissus was the wealthy freedman of Emperor Tiberius and confidant of Claudius who was later executed at the insistence of Agrippina under Nero's reign, and whose retainers and slaves would have then passed into the imperial household. Might they have been "those who belong to Caesar's household" whom Paul greeted in Philippians 4:22 (see Bruce, *Apostle of the Heart Set Free*, p. 386)? But this too is a finely spun web of conjecture.

Tryphena and Tryphosa (v. 12), both feminine Greek names, were perhaps sisters.

Persis (v. 12), also a feminine Greek name, was common to the slave class.

Rufus (v. 13) was a common slave name. We can guess the color of his hair (or complexion) from his name (Lat., *rufus* = "red"). There is a better than even chance that this was the son of the man who carried Jesus' cross, Simon of Cyrene, "the father of Alexander and Rufus" (Mark 15:21). The mother of Rufus had greatly served or endeared herself to Paul, for he calls her his **mother**.

Asyncritus, Phlegon, Hermes, Patrobas, Hermas (v. 14) are all either Latin or Greek slave names. **Phlegon** was the name of a dog in Xenophon; we would hope the name did not represent his owner's opinion of him. The groups of names in this and the following verse suggest members of two house churches.

Philologus, Julia, Nereus and his sister, and Olympas (v. 15) are likewise slave names, among which Julia was common in the imperial household.

Paul directs the group to **Greet one another with a holy kiss** (v. 16). Kissing as a form of social respect was widespread throughout the orient. Rabbinic Judaism permitted it on the occasions of greeting honored guests, after long separations, or good-byes (See Str-B, vol. 1, pp. 995–96). The kiss is already a sign of Christian fellowship in the NT (1 Cor. 16:20; 2 Cor. 13:12; 1 Thess. 5:26; 1 Pet. 5:14), deriving perhaps from the celebration of the Lord's Supper where, more than any other sign, the kiss exemplified the intimacy and forgiveness characteristic of the extreme sacrifice of Christ. Whether the reference to kissing means that Paul expected the epistle to be read at the Lord's Supper is anyone's guess, but he can scarcely have wished its reading to be limited to that occasion.

We began the discussion of 16:1–27 by questioning the value of examining a list of names. Of what consequence are they? A summary review leads to three important insights. First, despite the uncertainty about many of them, the names reveal a remarkable diversity in early Christianity. Paul mentions 29 persons, 27 of them by name, a full third of whom are women. There are Jewish, Greek, and Latin names. A few stem from the nobility and ruling classes, but the majority are names of slaves or freedpersons. The Roman churches appear to have been cross-class churches, with membership predominantly from the lower strata of society. This motley list is evidence of a veritable social revolution! Where but in the church could there be found such social and ethnic diversity; and yet, more importantly, where were social and ethnic distinctions of less significance than in the church, where *persons* counted more than gender or class or ethnicity or nationality or color? The list bears unassuming though eloquent witness to Galatians 3:28, "There is neither Jew nor Greek, slave nor free, male nor female, for you are all one in Christ Jesus."

Second, the list testifies to the uniqueness of each member of the community. This is no roster of faceless names (much less numbers), but a naming of persons who were known and valued. Paul calls them **dear friend . . . relatives who have been in prison with me . . . tested and approved . . . hard worker . . . chosen**. Each is important not so much for his or her own sake, *but in relationship to the gospel*. Each epithet witnesses in some way to a labor of obedience to plant and perpetuate the faith which has been passed down to the present day. If the adjectives are anything to judge by, we should conclude that the early church was characterized above all by hard work (Gk. *kopian*) and affection (Gk. *agapētos*)—two not insignificant traits for a healthy church in any age. While there is ignorance about the specific contributions of some of them, the church is nevertheless indebted to their witness.

Finally, this list is a reminder that Romans was not conceived as a bloodless theological tract. It was written to *persons*, and judging from their names, to a very average cross section of persons in first-century Rome. The names of Epenetus, Persis, and Tryphena—whoever they were—remind us that Paul penned Romans with individuals in mind, confident that its contents would be both understandable and meaningful for their *lives*. It was quite literally "good news" to its first readers, and it is no less so today.

16:17–20 / The tone changes abruptly in verses 17–20. Heretofore Paul has approached the matter of advice-giving with absolute discretion, doubtlessly because he was personally unknown to the churches. The sudden mood change accounts for the quite predictable doubt in some scholars' minds about the originality of verses 17–20. But the mood change can also be accounted for on other grounds. That Paul was capable of such pendulum swings is no surprise, especially when a pressing danger came to mind that had escaped his attention earlier (e.g., see 1 Cor. 16:22; Gal. 6:11–15; Phil. 3:12–21; 1 Thess. 2:15–16). The fact that Paul has majored on the problems of Jews and Gentiles may have detained him until now from addressing other problems that, though of less magnitude, were not unimportant. The familiarity of the preceding list of names may have induced him to drop his reserve and indulge in the pastoral urgency for which he was known.

This compact admonition sums up not only the foregoing ethical injunctions (chs. 12–15), but the theme of the unity in faith of Jews and Gentiles that runs through the entire epistle. Regarding the polemical thrust of this section, suffice it to say that where critical issues were involved—and the **teaching** of the faith was a critical issue for Paul—he did not enter the fray unarmed. The use of **teaching** (v. 17) with reference to the gospel (also 6:17) is evidence that already the Christian faith was regarded as a content of belief as well as a personal experience of trust, and that something approximating a catechetical office (e.g., **you have learned**) was the means by which it was taught. And, as we have noted before, where truth was at issue, the *proposition* of that truth was but half the battle; the other half was its *opposition* to error and falsehood. The Christian community cannot afford to be naive about evil; evil must be named and opposed if it is to be defeated.

Who the troublemakers were we can only guess. Paul describes them as causing **divisions** and putting **obstacles in your way**, which suggests Judaizers (Gal. 1:6–9; 3:1ff.; 5:3ff.). If so, he might be warning against the (re)imposing of Jewish legalism, which was doubtlessly a problem with the return of Jews to Rome following the edict of Claudius. But Paul had also had his fill of **divisions and obstacles** in Corinth (1 Cor. 1:10–17; 3:4–9), and probably from non-Jewish elements. In verse 18 he says that such people serve **their own appetites** and **deceive the minds of naive people . . . by smooth talk and flattery**. Mention of **appetites**, suggesting unbridled impulses, recalls the whole concept of "flesh" in Paul, more specifically in fact the libertine and permissive factions which wracked the church at Corinth (2 Cor. 10–13). There thus appear to be dangers from the right (legalism) and dangers from the left (libertinism) in verses 17–20. We cannot identify either side further, and is it perhaps unnecessary to do so, for the same two dangers (in various forms) plague the church to the present day. Curiously Paul does not mention expelling the troublemakers from their midst. He must have known (and where would this have been truer than in Rome?) that where the church cannot live apart from error, it, nevertheless, must not succumb to error.

The distinctive Christian response to antagonism and heresy is **obedience** to the gospel (v. 19; cf. 1:5). The advice of verse 19, **I want you to be wise about what is good and innocent about what is evil** must have been guided by Matthew 10:16. This may strike the reader (especially the modern reader who is attuned to social injustice) as a rather complacent response. **Obedience**, however, is not complacency. True, there is no hint of retaliation against opposition here, and it is that which may appear naive to modern readers. But of what use is physical force against spiritual powers? They must be met on their own terms, i.e., by truth, justice, love, and above all, prayer. Hence, Paul appeals to an unmitigated trust in divine sovereignty in such matters. "Do not take revenge, my friends, but leave room for God's wrath" (12:19). **The God of peace will soon crush Satan under your feet** (v. 20). Obvious here is the allusion to Genesis 3:15 as well as to the thought which arose during the intertestamental period that the Messiah would endue his followers with power over evil forces (e.g., T. Levi 18.12).

16:21–24 / The brief benediction in verse 20b (which can also be found in some manuscripts as verse 24) would be a fitting conclusion to Romans. But Paul gives the impression of not wanting to draw the epistle to a close. In verse 21 he sends greetings to Rome from several associates. It has been suggested that these associates comprised the delegation carrying the collection for Jerusalem (cf. 15:25ff.), but the fact that Paul calls them *syngeneis* ("fellow-countrymen"; NIV, **my relatives**) lessens the likelihood of this. In 9:3 *syngeneis* refers to fellow Jews, and it is hard to imagine that Paul would have enlisted Jews to carry a Gentile offering to Jerusalem.

First named, and deservedly so, comes Timothy, Paul's companion on the second and third missionary journeys. No colleague had been a comrade-in-arms over the years as had Timothy, who is mentioned in the salutations of several epistles. Whether the **Lucius** mentioned here is identical with the Lucius of Acts 13:1 is impossible to say. At any rate, the name is not to be confused with Luke, a one-time traveling companion of Paul and traditional author of the Third Gospel (see Col. 4:14; 2 Tim. 4:11; Philem. 24). The correlation of **Jason** and **Sosipater** with their possible counterparts in Acts 17:5 and 20:4, respectively, is also uncertain. More endearing is the note on **Tertius**, Paul's amanu-

ensis who transcribed the epistle, who interjects a personal greeting in the first person in verse 22. It was common in rabbinic
literature to mention the name of an amanuensis, but one can
sense Tertius' special pride in being the transcriber of such a
monumental work. Since Paul is writing from Corinth, the **Gaius**
of verse 23 is probably the same Gaius of 1 Corinthians 1:14 who
was baptized by Paul. An inscription to an Erastus, commissioner
of public works, which was unearthed in Corinth in 1929, very
likely concerns the **Erastus** of verse 23 (see Introduction, p. 21,
note 2), although nothing is known of his brother **Quartus**.

16:25–27 / The benediction with which Paul brings his
magnum opus to a close is baroque and powerful. Apart from the
full benediction in Ephesians 3:20–21, the other epistles ascribed
to Paul end more simply (as in v. 20b). Many scholars have supposed
that the present benediction derives from later editors who produced a grand finale befitting of Romans. The occurrence of the
benediction in at least three different places in surviving manuscripts of Romans suggests a secondary origin to some scholars. But
the fact that the benediction sums up several key themes of the
epistle (e.g., **mystery** [v. 25; cf. 11:25] and "obedience of faith" [v. 26,
cf. 1:5]) may tip the scales in favor of its originality.

Whatever its pedigree, the benediction is a majestic conclusion to Romans. Anyone who thinks that the early Christians
breathed only the rarefied air of Shaker-like simplicity has yet to
come to terms with the theological sophistication of Romans. Nor
has such an individual breathed the liturgical incense of this
doxology. It gives eloquent testimony to the rich and formulaic
blood which circulated in the veins of earliest Christianity. Struc-
turally it reviews the history of salvation by scanning the major
summits of the epistle. From all eternity God, in his eternal purpose, ordained to save the nations in Jesus Christ. The mystery
which had been hidden for interminable ages has *now* been
revealed through Jesus Christ, as foretold by the Law and the
Prophets, **so that all nations might believe and obey him**.

That all nations might believe and obey him. That is the
will of God and the abiding commission of the church. It was the
seed which gave birth to this epistle nearly two millennia ago as
a visionary apostle paced to and fro in his quarters on the Pelo-
ponnesus and recited the immortal words of Romans to a quite
overwhelmed amanuensis. **That all nations might believe and**

obey is the goal to which the Holy Spirit bears witness in every age, and it is the prayer which the church must forever hold in its heart and pursue in its life. **To the only wise God be glory forever through Jesus Christ! Amen.**

Additional Notes §37

The reference to David Schulz's 1829 article is from Manson's article, "St. Paul's Letter to the Romans—and Others," in *Romans Debate— Revised*, p. 10. Manson argues for an Ephesian destination of Romans 16 on the grounds that (1) it is unlikely that Paul had so many (close) friends in Rome, which he had not visited; (2) those in the list who are known are connected with Ephesus or Asia; (3) the admonitions in 16:17–20 are out of place if they are addressed to Rome where Paul was a stranger, but they fit well with Ephesus (cf. Acts 20:25–31); and (4) the discovery of papyrus P^{46} in 1935 placed the doxology (16:25–27) at the end of ch. 15 (just as the theory suggests).

These reasons, however, are far from conclusive. Regarding 1, it is not at all surprising that Paul would know (or know of) many people in Rome, which was the hub of the empire (cf. Tacitus' comment, "[in Rome] all things hideous and shameful from every part of the world find their centre and become popular" [*Ann.* 15.44]). Given the gravitational pull of Rome we should be surprised if Paul did *not* know a considerable number of people there. Regarding 2, only three names in the list (Priscilla and Aquila, v. 3 / Acts 18:24–26, and Epenetus, "the first convert to Christ in the province of Asia" v. 5) can be connected for certain with Asia Minor: it does not place undue strain on one's imagination to suppose that three of Paul's associates from Asia had since made their way to Rome. Manson's first two arguments fail to take into account the mobility of first-century peoples (and especially missionaries). Regarding 3, the long list of names in chapter 16 is evidence that Paul was not such a stranger to the Romans after all. Moreover, it should be noted that Paul ventures on the admonitions of 16:17–20 only *after* establishing his credibility in the list of acquaintances in verses 1–16. Regarding 4, the witness of P^{46} is far from persuasive, since its text of Romans is both fragmentary and idiosyncratic (see B. Metzger, *The Text of the New Testament: Its Transmission, Corruption and Restoration* [New York: Oxford, 1974], pp. 37–38; 252). Furthermore, P^{46} remains the *only* papyrus which places the doxology after ch. 15 (but, as A. Wedderburn notes [*The Reasons for Romans*, (Edinburgh: T. & T. Clark, 1988), p. 17], it also follows the doxology at the end of ch. 15 with 16:1–23).

Two further comments might be added. Hans Lietzmann made an insightful (though acidic) comment against the Ephesian destination of chapter 16: "A letter consisting almost entirely of nothing but greetings . . . is a monstrosity" (*An die Römer*, 3d ed., *HBNT* [Tübingen: Siebeck,

1933], p. 129). Finally, Lietzmann's and T. Zahn's observation made years
ago remains a critical argument in favor of an original Roman destination
for ch. 16. The evidence from Paul's epistles, they noted, shows that the
apostle did not send greetings in letters to congregations he had founded
(since he could not greet them all, and to greet some and not others might
cause discord). He does greet people by name, however, in letters to
congregations he had *not* visited, in order to establish rapport with them
(e.g., Colossians and Romans). This observation lays an ax at the root of
Manson's thesis, for if Rom. 16 were originally destined for Ephesus (i.e.,
to a congregation he had founded) we should *not* expect greetings in it!
Thus, the above evidence argues that ch. 16 was originally part of the
epistle to Rome, and not a cover letter of a copy to Ephesus. For further
arguments against the tenability of reading ch. 16 with reference to Ephesus, see Schlatter, *Gottes Gerechtigkeit*, pp. 393–407. For complete discussions of the problem, see H. Gamble, *The Textual History of the Letter to the
Romans*, Studies and Documents 42 (Grand Rapids: Eerdmans, 1977);
Cranfield, *Romans*, vol. 1, pp. 5–11; Dodd, *Romans*, pp. xvii–xxiv; and
Metzger, *TCGNT*, pp. 533–36.

16:1–2 / On the question of women deacons, see 1 Tim. 3:11,
which (despite the NIV rendering) almost certainly lists women deacons
alongside men deacons (so RSV, "The women likewise must be serious
. . . "). Writing some 60 years after Paul, Pliny the Younger spoke of tor-
turing two Christian maidservants who were deaconesses (Epistle 96;
cited in H. C. Kee, *The New Testament in Context: Sources and Documents*
[Englewood Cliffs: Prentice-Hall, 1984], p. 44). Thereafter, no certain literary evidence of deaconesses is found until the Greek Fathers recognized them in the third century. On the whole question, see Dunn,
Romans 9–16, pp. 886–87; and A. F. Walls, "Deaconess," *NBD*, p. 298.

16:3–4 / The six references to Prisc(ill)a and Aquila in the NT are
Acts 18:2, 18, 26; Rom. 16:3–4; 1 Cor. 16:19; 2 Tim. 4:19.

16:5–16 / The study of the gender of Junia/Junias is by P. Lampe,
entitled "Iunia/Iunias: Sklavenherkunft im Kreise der vorpaulinischen
Apostel (Röm 16:7)," *ZNW* 76 (1985), pp. 139–47 (cited in Dunn, *Romans
9–16*, p. 894). See in English, P. Lampe, "The Roman Christians of Romans
16," in *Romans Debate—Revised*, pp. 216–30.
        For references to Aristobulus, the grandson of Herod I and brother
of Agrippa I, see Josephus, *War* 1.552; 2.221; and *Ant*. 18.133, 135; but we
cannot be certain that this individual is the same as the Aristobulus of
v. 10.
        For further possible identifications of the names in verses 14–15,
see again Bruce, *Paul*, pp. 387–88.

16:21–23 / On the Erastus inscription, see V. Furnish, "Corinth
in Paul's Time," *BAR* 15 (3, 1988), p. 20. There is an Erastus associated with
Corinth also in Acts 19:22 and 2 Tim. 4:20. It should be noted, however,
that the Greek of v. 23 calls Erastus "the city treasurer" (*hō oikonomos tēs
poleōs*), and not exactly **director of public works** (NIV).

For Further Reading

Achtemeier, P. *Romans*. Interpretation. Atlanta: John Knox, 1985.

Barrett, C. K. *A Commentary on the Epistle to the Romans*. HNTC. New York: Harper & Row, 1957.

Barth, K. *The Epistle to the Romans*. 6th ed. Trans. E. Hoskyns. London: Oxford, 1976.

Barth, K. *Dogmatics in Outline*. Trans. G. Thomson, New York: Harper & Row, 1959.

Beker, J. C. *Paul the Apostle*. Philadelphia: Fortress, 1980.

Bengel, J. A. *Gnomon of the New Testament*. 7th ed. Vol. 3. Ed. M. E. Bengel, rev. J. Steudel. Edinburgh: T. & T. Clark, 1873.

Black, M. *Romans*. NCBC. Greenwood, S.C.: Attic Press, 1973.

Bruce, F. F. *Apostle of the Heart Set Free*. Grand Rapids: Eerdmans, 1977.

Calvin, John. *The Epistle of Paul the Apostle to the Romans*. Trans. and ed. J. Owen. Grand Rapids: Eerdmans, 1948.

Cranfield, C. E. B. *The Epistle to the Romans*. 2 vols. ICC. Edinburgh: T. & T. Clark, 1975–79.

Dodd, C. H. *The Epistle of Paul to the Romans*. MNTC. New York and London: Harper and Brothers, 1932.

Donfried, K., ed. *The Romans Debate—Revised and Expanded Edition*. Peabody, Mass.: Hendrickson, 1991.

Dunn, J. D. G. *Romans 1–8*. WBC. Vol. 38A. Dallas: Word, 1988.
_____. *Romans 9–16*. WBC. Vol. 38B. Dallas: Word, 1988.

Gaugler, E. *Der Römerbrief*. 2 vols. Zürich: Zwingli-Verlag, 1952–58.

Harrisville, R. *Romans*. Minneapolis: Augsburg, 1980.

Käsemann, E. *Commentary on Romans*. Trans. and ed. G. Bromiley. Grand Rapids: Eerdmans, 1980.

Kaylor, R. *Paul's Covenant Community. Jew and Gentile in Romans*. Atlanta: John Knox, 1988.

Leenhardt, F. *The Epistle to the Romans*. Trans. H. Knight. Cleveland and New York: World Publishing, 1961.

Luther, Martin. *Commentary on the Epistle to the Romans*. Trans. J. Mueller. Grand Rapids: Zondervan, 1954.
_____. *Lectures on Romans*. Trans. and ed. W. Pauck. LCC. Vol. 15. Philadelphia: Westminster, 1961.

Manson, T. W. "Romans." PCB. London: Thomas Nelson, 1962.

Michel, O. *Der Brief an die Römer*. 4th ed. MeyerK. Göttingen: Vandenhoeck & Ruprecht, 1966.

Nygren, A. *Commentary on Romans*. Trans. C. Rasmussen. Philadelphia: Muhlenberg Press, 1949.

Sanday, W., and Headlam, A. *A Critical and Exegetical Commentary on the Epistle to the Romans*. 5th ed. ICC. Edinburgh: T. & T. Clark, 1895.

Schlatter, A. *Der Brief an die Römer*. Erläuterungen zum Neuen Testament. Vol. 5. Stuttgart: Calwer Verlag, 1987.

_____. *Gottes Gerechtigkeit. Ein Kommentar zum Römerbrief*, 3d ed. Stuttgart: Calwer Verlag, 1959.

Wedderburn, A. J. M. *The Reasons for Romans*. SNTW. Edinburgh: T. & T. Clark, 1988.

Subject Index

Aaron, 91

Abba, 128, 207, 208, 210, 222, 246

Abraham: cenotaph, 112; circumcision, 79; credentials, 112, 113; history of salvation, 27, 29, 62, 119, 146, 230–37, 239, 245, 261, 265, 268–70, 272, 275; hope of glory, 211; hospitality, 300; love of God, 222; righteousness by faith, 3, 16, 19, 42, 80, 99

Abram, 122

Achaia, 6, 348

Achtemeier, P., 38, 54, 71, 84, 85, 96, 109, 120, 155, 176, 195, 243, 251, 279, 307, 326, 351

Acquittal, 50, 63, 100

Adam: creation subject to corruption, 211–13, 220; disobedience produces death, 145–55, 158, 160, 162, 163, 170, 171, 176, 179–81; general references, 16, 102, 242; indwelling sin, 185, 186, 188, 190; sinful nature, 199, 202, 204, 207

Adam-Christ typology, 146, 150, 151, 207

Adiaphora, 76, 319, 321, 322, 332

Adikia, 48, 50, 56, 69

Adokimon, 56, 137

Adoption, 30, 122, 208, 211, 215, 220, 230, 294

Adultery, 74, 77, 78, 86, 124, 179, 182, 321

Advent: of Christ, 107, 178, 203, 210, 220, 231, 271; of law, 18

Aedile(ship), 21

Affliction, 69, 135, 136, 220, 248, 294, 295

Agapē, 138, 217, 223, 291, 292, 297, 299, 300, 302, 304, 308, 311–14, 317, 318, 320, 326, 336, 341, 351

Agapētos, 358

Agrippa, 104, 344, 346, 356, 363

Agrippina, 356

Ahab, 54, 275

Akiba, Rabbi, 65, 217

Alexander the Great, 71, 357

Alexandria, 303, 309

Allegory, 96, 146, 179

Altar, 105, 135, 250, 263, 283, 303

Amanuensis, 140, 361

Ambrosiaster, 8

Amen, 279, 362

Ampliatus, 356

Anathema, 230

Andronicus, 355

Angel, 50, 59, 171, 226, 244, 309

Anger, 49, 59, 69, 298, 350

Antinomianism, 10, 19, 23, 157, 169, 304, 305

Antiochus, 303

Antipas, 321

Antitassesthai, 306

Anti-Christ, 304

Anti-docetic, 180

Anti-Semitism, 24, 187, 250, 258, 269, 270, 271

Anypokritos, 292

Aparchē, 215

Apelles, 356

Aphorismenos, 28

Aphormē, 188

Apistein, 85

Apocalypse, 242, 316

Apocrypha, 351

Apodoses, 207

Apodosis, 77, 206

Apokaradokia, 212

Apollos, 294

Apollynai, 329

Apolytrōsis, 103

Apostellein, 27

Apostle, 3, 8, 11, 15, 22, 23, 26, 27, 29, 31, 34–37, 39, 56, 58, 62, 68, 80, 83, 89, 90, 97, 136, 143, 157, 163, 169, 173, 183, 186, 190, 193, 212, 218, 226, 229, 230, 239, 256, 258, 261, 265, 266, 268, 271, 273, 275, 276, 278, 282, 285, 286, 288, 290, 294, 298, 302, 323,

326–29, 331, 332, 338, 343–47, 351, 353, 355, 356, 361

Apostleship, 25, 30, 266

Apostolos, 27

Apostygein, 292

Apuleius, 166

Aquila, 9, 10, 13, 317, 354, 362, 363

Ara oun, 151

Ara nyn, 198

Archelaus, 8

Areopagus, 51

Aries, P., 32

Aristobulus, 356, 363

Aristotle, 72, 172, 176, 290

Ark, 104, 109, 110, 230

Armor, 314, 315, 316

Asceticism, 159, 171, 336

Asebeia, 50, 116

Asia, 6, 60, 257, 355, 362

Assarion, 256

Asthenos, 328

Asyncritus, 357

Asynetous, 57

Asynthetous, 57

Athanasius, 154

Atkinson, B. F. C., 351

Atonement, 3, 97, 101, 104, 105, 106, 108, 110, 111, 115, 117, 138, 205, 209, 223

Augustine, 1, 21, 71, 80, 147, 148, 155, 166, 185, 188, 195, 200, 203, 259, 275, 316, 332

Augustus, 7, 22

Aulen, G., 110

Authority: advocacy of Spirit, 200, 204, 210, 211, 226; Christians as living sacrifices, 282, 286; church and state, 302, 305–10; death through Adam and life through Christ, 147, 148, 151, 165, 172, 176; general references, 37, 59, 71, 322, 328, 338; indwelling sin, 185, 189, 195; married to Christ, 178–80, 182; relationship of Israel to gospel, 229, 257, 261

Aphelein, 79

Baal, 154, 261, 262, 264

Babylon, 41, 103, 248, 256; Babylonian captivity, 256

Bacchus, 316

Bainton, R., 21

Balkans, 14

Balthasar, H. V. U., 119

Baptism, 9, 159–61, 164, 166, 168, 173, 174, 254, 315, 361

Barrett, C. K., 22, 38, 65, 79, 140, 173, 251, 276, 309

Barth, K., 2, 21, 23, 32, 38, 44, 72, 82, 85, 88, 95, 102, 106, 126, 130, 154, 157, 259, 269, 272, 275, 327, 329

Bastazein, 336

Bathsheba, 74, 86

Baur, F. C., 11

Beck, L., 73

Beker, J., 220

Beethoven, 106, 198

Belief, 31, 42–44, 56, 59, 76, 109, 123, 128, 199, 209, 255, 259, 264, 320, 332, 359

Believers: consequences of new life for the church, 282–87, 291, 295, 296, 298, 299, 302, 305, 306, 313, 315, 316, 319, 321–24, 326–28, 330, 331, 335, 339, 340, 343, 344, 348, 354; divine righteousness, 34–38, 42, 43, 66, 80, 98, 105, 109; faith, 114, 118, 119, 129, 132–34, 136–38, 141, 142, 151, 157, 159–66, 170, 172–74, 178, 179, 182, 183, 185–88, 191, 194, 195, 197–200, 204–9, 211–13, 215–220, 224, 225; introduction, 3, 4, 12, 13, 15, 19, 20; relationship of Israel to gospel, 230, 233, 248, 252–54, 261–62, 270

Benedict, Rule of, 293, 300, 341, 360, 361

Benediction, 335, 341, 360, 361

Benevolence, 30, 66, 122, 172, 218, 222, 226, 253, 255, 311

Bengel, J. A., 57, 77, 82, 98, 106, 115, 143, 147, 152, 155, 167, 172, 176, 182, 200, 210, 221, 226, 252, 264, 275, 300, 323, 327–29, 342

Benjamin, 59, 91, 261, 264

Beyer, H. W., 288

Bible, 1, 2, 4, 5, 36, 44, 60, 66, 67, 97, 127, 132, 134, 139, 148, 152, 183, 187, 212, 222, 248, 264, 313, 321, 337, 342, 355

Billerbeck, P., 248. *See also* Strack-Billerbeck.

Blasphemy, 186, 329, 330

Ecstasy, 193, 197, 290
Eden, 171, 188
Edification, 330, 331, 333
Edokimasan, 56
Edom, 232, 234
Edwards, J., 44
Egypt, 9, 40, 54, 103, 201, 300, 303, 304, 341
Eiper, 205
Eirēn, 134
Eis, 105
Ek, 172
Ekchein, 137
Eklogē, 262
Ēkousan, 257
Elder, 7, 22, 181
Elect, 40, 67, 121, 224, 230, 232, 236, 244, 262, 275
Election, 20, 27, 62, 70, 106, 228, 229, 232–36, 238, 241, 243, 245, 260, 262, 269, 277
Eleusis, 104
Eliezer, 114
Elijah, 91, 154, 261, 262
Ellogeitai, 149
Ellul, J., 95
Emperor, 7, 8, 71, 198, 303, 307, 318, 351, 356
Encouragement, 36, 289, 337, 338
Endtime, 65, 161
Endurance, 38, 68, 136, 143, 216, 228, 267, 295, 332, 338
Enlightenment, 51, 59, 95
Envy, 57, 266, 267
Epaischynō, 137
Epenetus, 355, 358, 362
Ephesus, 6, 12, 346, 352–54, 362, 363
Eph' hō, 148
Erastus, 21, 361, 363
Eritheia, 69
Esau, 96, 232–34, 237, 245, 246
Eschatology, 132, 138, 140, 142, 155, 233, 239, 241, 244, 267, 314, 315, 329, 345
Esther, 75, 217
Eternal, 18, 26, 29, 41, 68, 69, 104, 106, 143, 154, 163, 164, 168, 175, 176, 178, 195, 211, 218, 219, 224, 229–34, 236, 241, 269, 270, 282, 283, 295, 329, 361
Ethics, 1, 19, 43, 59, 63, 72, 73, 81, 100, 105, 121, 159, 164, 172, 183, 198, 202,

204, 240, 281, 282, 290, 291, 299, 301, 311, 323, 326, 333, 337, 341, 344, 359
Euarestos, 283
Euphrates River, 112
Europe, 39, 74, 257, 350
Evangelization, 9, 67, 257, 304, 343, 346, 347, 356
Eve, 53, 60, 147, 170, 171, 176, 188, 189, 212
Evil, 47, 49, 50, 54, 56, 58, 59, 63, 64, 68, 69, 85–88, 91, 92, 95, 146, 147, 154, 157, 165, 167, 169, 171, 174, 180, 184, 187, 188, 192, 194, 195, 200, 201, 210, 212–14, 218, 222, 227, 291, 292, 296, 298–300, 305–7, 310, 312, 329, 359, 360
Evolution, 48, 102, 198, 242
Exile, 10, 20, 41, 103, 259
Exousia, 309
Expiation, 97, 104–6, 234

Faith: introduction, 1–4, 6, 8, 11, 13, 16, 17, 19, 21, 24; Paul and gospel, 25, 30, 31, 33–36, 38; righteousness by faith, 42–45; human guilt, 46, 49, 59; righteous judgment of God, 63, 67, 68, 75, 76, 79, 81, 82, 85, 86, 91, 94; righteousness by faith, 97–131, 133–38, 143, 156, 157, 159, 160, 163, 164, 166, 169, 172, 174, 177, 180, 185, 188, 193, 194, 200, 203, 205, 206, 214–18, 222, 225, 226; relationship of Israel and gospel, 229, 232, 235, 237, 245–50, 252–55, 257–59, 262, 266, 267, 269, 270, 273, 275–80; Christian duties, 281, 283, 284, 286–88, 290, 294, 295, 297, 306, 311, 312, 314–16; strong and weak, 317–29, 331–33; unity in Christ, 335, 338, 339, 341; Paul's mission, 343–46, 358, 359, 361
Faithlessness, 48, 57, 83, 85, 86, 100, 277
Fall, 1, 21, 25, 41, 46, 47, 52, 59, 69, 75, 84, 91, 102, 110, 122, 146, 149, 151, 152, 162, 170, 180, 188, 190, 195, 201, 202, 206, 209, 213, 215, 265, 266, 271, 275, 278, 303, 321, 322, 328, 337, 343, 349, 350
Fate, 47, 48, 53, 136, 143, 153, 161, 188, 213, 233, 240, 243, 244, 263, 323

Father, 16, 18, 31, 32, 35, 52, 62, 82, 95,
  111, 112, 118–21, 125, 128, 135, 137,
  142, 185, 187, 188, 201, 207, 208, 210,
  222, 231, 246, 248, 250, 254, 283, 289,
  320, 357, 363
Fatherhood, 119, 125
Fear, 60, 66, 92, 94, 136, 207, 208, 210,
  213, 214, 238, 270, 282, 318
Fellowship, 15, 38, 102, 161, 198, 207,
  263, 286, 290, 293, 307, 317, 327, 357
Feuerbach, L., 52
Finegan, J., 351
Firstborn, 214, 218, 219
Firstfruits, 20, 211, 215, 267, 273
Flesh, 29, 32, 39, 81, 93, 99, 112, 139,
  155, 162, 180–82, 186, 187, 190, 191,
  197, 198, 200–202, 204, 205, 207, 209,
  289, 295, 297, 298, 316, 341, 359
Flew, A., 300
Follower, 138, 208, 294, 304, 317, 337,
  360
Foreknowledge, 218, 219, 233, 268
Forgiveness, 49, 78, 94, 100, 104, 116,
  117, 129, 141, 152, 169, 176, 183, 185,
  230, 246, 250, 286, 357
Forum, Roman, 7
Francis, St., 289
Franklin, B., 59
Freedom: advocacy of Spirit, 197, 200,
  204, 207; alive in Christ, 157, 158,
  164; general references, 40, 95, 109,
  135, 152; hope of glory, 213, 214,
  219; indwelling sin, 184, 186, 189;
  married to Christ, 179, 181; salvation of Jews and Gentiles, 229, 238,
  241, 289; slaves of righteousness,
  170–75; strong and weak, 319, 322,
  323, 326–33, 341
Freedpersons, 103, 356, 357
Frerichs, E., 251
Freud, S., 95, 192
Friend(ship), 63, 96, 112, 142, 174, 277,
  296, 298, 300, 342, 324, 356, 358, 360,
  362
Fruit, 31, 43, 53, 67, 129, 152, 161, 175,
  180, 182, 188, 189, 195, 291, 298, 300
Fruitfulness, 161, 179, 180, 219, 220,
  265, 270
Fry, T., 300
Fulfillment, 19, 29, 31, 43, 58, 93, 99,
  114, 142, 250, 253, 265, 267, 291

Fulvia, 8, 78, 82
Future: day of salvation, 314–16;
  hope of glory, 211, 213–16, 218, 219,
  226; salvation of Jews and Gentiles,
  257, 262, 267, 276, 279, 280

Gager, J., 24
Gaius, 361
Galatia, 10, 16, 348
Galilee, 39
Gallio, 6, 22
Gamaliel, 18
Gamble, H., 363
Gandhi, 301
Gaston, L., 24
Gaugler, E., 46, 59, 143, 166, 195, 196,
  227, 249, 251, 259, 277, 309, 319, 325,
  329
Gaul, 347
Gehenna, 79, 95
Gemara, 181
Genomenou, 32
Gentiles: Christian duties, 290, 295,
  296, 303, 312, 313; God's righteous
  judgment, 46, 48, 51, 52, 59, 61–63,
  65, 66, 70–72; guilty under the law
  of conscience, 74, 75, 77, 78, 80, 82,
  83, 84, 89, 90, 92, 95; history of
  Christianity in Rome, 10, 11; introduction, 3, 4, 6; Paul and gospel, 25,
  27, 28, 30, 31, 34, 36, 37; Paul and
  law, 17, 20; Paul's mission, 343–45,
  347–49, 350, 353, 355, 358, 359, 360;
  purpose of epistle, 12–16; relationship of Israel to gospel, 228, 229,
  233, 234, 236, 238, 239, 241–47, 252,
  255, 257, 258, 260, 261, 265–71, 273–
  80; righteousness by faith, 97, 101,
  107–9, 111, 116–19, 121, 122, 125,
  129, 146, 153, 154, 178, 209; strong
  and weak, 318–20, 322; unity with
  Jews in Christ, 335, 339–41; universality of salvation, 39, 41, 44
Gentile-Christians, 322
Gentile-Jewish, 16
Gethsemane, 50, 152, 212
Gift, 3, 4, 14, 15, 17–19, 36, 66, 67, 78,
  84, 100, 101, 113, 115, 121–23, 130,
  141, 142, 150, 151, 155, 168, 170, 175,
  176, 186, 195, 212, 215, 217, 237, 245,

Rollins, W. G., 32
Romans: authorship, 5, 6; debate over purpose, 12, 13, 15, 23; general references, 25, 26, 31, 32, 34, 35, 39, 43, 46, 47, 52, 64, 70, 97, 103, 111, 132, 156, 158, 169, 184, 185, 194, 211, 222, 225, 228, 230, 235, 240, 281, 318, 325, 335, 338, 340, 343, 347, 350, 352–55, 357, 359, 360, 361, 363; history and provenance, 8–11; outline, 1–5; place and date of composition, 6
Rome: beginnings of Christianity, 7–11; consequences of new life from God, 282, 290, 296, 303–5, 308, 309, 317–20; God's righteous judgment, 57, 78, 96, 101; introduction, 1, 6; faith, 166, 169, 176, 178, 182, 193, 206, 221, 225, 247, 266; Paul and gospel, 35–37, 39, 40, 44; Paul and law, 22, 23; Paul's mission, 343, 347–50, 352–56, 358–60, 362, 363; purpose of epistle, 12–16; salutation, 25–27, 31–34
Rufus, 357
Russell, J. C., 22

Sabbath, 20, 187, 322
Sabine hills, 7
Sacraments, 79, 80, 159, 160, 180
Sacred, 75, 173, 216, 307, 309, 322
Sacrifice: of Christ, 97, 101, 103–6, 108; Christians as living sacrifices, 281–84; faith of Abraham, 111, 114, 115, 126, 127; general references, 1, 4, 49, 135, 140, 202, 205, 215, 219, 222, 223, 230, 274, 284, 303, 314, 318, 324, 334, 345, 357
Sadducee, 62, 308
Saint, 31, 64, 191, 293, 348, 349, 350, 351, 354
Salutation, 25, 26, 31, 360
Salvation: consequences of new life from God, 281, 314, 315, 319, 322, 328–32, 335, 338, 340, 341, 345, 361; definition, 41; divine righteousness, 27–29, 39–42, 44, 47, 49–51, 59, 66, 70, 72, 79, 83, 84, 88–90, 93, 96, 98, 99, 102, 103, 108, 110; and faith, 111, 112, 114, 116, 118, 119, 124, 125, 129, 132–46, 152, 153, 157, 158, 163, 172, 174, 177, 179, 185, 194, 198, 201,

204, 206, 207, 211–15, 218, 224–26, 228–36, 239, 242–58, 260, 265–80; introduction, 1–3, 17, 19, 20; strong and weak, 317–34
Samaritan, 311
Sanctification, 43, 55, 124, 156, 157, 159, 164, 166, 174–76, 186, 207, 220, 281, 285, 287, 323, 345
Sanday, W., 44, 351
Sanders, E. P., 24
Sanhedrin, 307
Sarah, 114, 126, 129, 232
Sarkinos, 190
Sarx, 93, 180, 204
Satan, 37, 40, 41, 52, 154, 189, 213, 224, 299, 329, 360
Savior, 4, 19, 39, 40, 44, 108, 177, 178, 198, 202, 234, 250, 276
Sōphronein, 286, 290
Sōtēria, 40, 41
Sōzō, 40
Schlatter, A., 59, 72, 82, 95, 110, 130, 155, 309, 322, 333, 336, 363
Schneemelcher, W., 351
Schnider, F., 32
Schulz, D., 352, 362
Schweitzer, A., 341, 342
Scribe, 280, 292, 300, 339
Scripture, 28, 41, 84, 91–93, 97, 102, 105, 111, 130, 133, 139, 152, 205, 233, 237, 243, 251, 253, 264, 282, 286, 333, 337, 338, 340
Seal, 93, 118, 128, 129, 229
Seed, 30, 32, 122, 160, 163, 231, 361
Seleucids, 303
Selfishness, 69, 207, 299
Self-control, 290, 295
Self-righteousness, 50, 62, 66, 96, 317, 321
Seneca, 351
Septuagint, 92
Sermon on the Mount, 19, 108, 291, 299
Serpent, 147, 189
Servant, 26, 27, 29, 30, 103, 114, 129, 136, 168, 170, 172, 201, 217, 223, 224, 257, 265, 289, 294, 306–9, 317, 321, 336, 340, 346, 347, 353
Service, 8, 72, 102, 122, 171, 172, 175, 181, 206, 257, 267, 288, 290, 294, 299, 326, 327, 328, 333, 345, 349, 350, 354

Shakespeare, William, 18

Shame, 39, 175, 176, 195, 222, 247, 255, 258, 264, 271, 299, 301, 315, 362

Shekinah, 264

Silvanus, 26

Simeon, 107

Simlai, Rabbi, 45

Simon: of Cyrene, 357; the Magician, 125

Simplicianus, 166

Sin: advocacy of Spirit, 197–209; consequences of new life from God, 285, 296, 306, 316, 326, 327, 329, 332, 333, 337, 341; dead to sin, 157–60, 162, 164–82; divine righteousness, 29, 41, 42, 44, 46, 47, 49–51, 53–58, 60–62, 65, 66, 68, 69, 74, 78, 82, 84, 86, 89–97, 99, 101, 102, 104–8; and faith, 110, 112, 115–17, 123, 124, 127, 129, 133, 134, 136, 140, 141, 145–55; hope of glory, 220–25; indwelling sin, 184–96; introduction, 1–4, 6, 11, 16, 18, 19, 21; relationship of Israel to gospel, 230, 236, 250, 263, 278

Sinai, 20, 53, 110, 130, 230

Sinner: advocacy of Spirit, 198, 200, 223, 224; Christian duties, 285–87, 296, 299; dead to sin but alive in Christ, 157–59, 169, 174, 177, 194; God's righteous judgment, 54, 61, 63, 62, 66, 89, 100, 101, 103, 105–7, 109; justification by faith, 118, 121, 129, 133–35, 139–41, 142, 144, 152, 153; Paul and gospel, 30, 41, 44; relationship of Israel to gospel, 229, 237, 239, 246, 278; strong and weak, 321, 337

Sister, 141, 353, 355–57

Skandalon, 327, 333

Skepticism, 98, 285

Sklērotēs, 66

Slander, 157, 258

Slave(ry), 4, 6, 9, 22, 26, 32, 52, 97, 103, 155, 162, 168–76, 181, 182, 184–86, 190–93, 204, 207, 208, 211, 218, 271, 290, 293, 322, 341, 356–58

Smith, D. M., 95

Sobriety, 92, 286, 290

Sodom, 114, 243

Sola gratia, 108

Soldier, 165, 175, 308, 339, 350

Solomon, 46, 47, 48, 61, 62, 63, 74

Solus deus, 108

Son: of Abraham, 114, 118, 126; of God, 16, 28–30, 32, 35, 40, 44, 50, 52, 99, 103, 105, 133, 141, 142, 147, 148, 159, 188, 197, 201, 202, 209, 214, 218–20, 222–24, 232–34, 237, 243, 271, 279, 282, 284, 288, 293, 297, 299, 314, 315, 337, 357

Sonship of believers, 207, 208, 211, 214

Sosipater, 360

Sosthenes, 25

Soteriology, 241

Soul, 1, 41, 91, 107, 126, 180, 182, 213, 220, 278, 295, 307, 323, 333, 347

Sovereignty, 6, 26, 40, 88, 115, 204, 218, 220, 231, 278, 360

Spain, 5, 6, 11, 14, 15, 35–37, 257, 282, 343, 347–51, 353

Sparta, 145

Spivey, R., 95

Stalin, 58, 61

State: and church, 302–8; general references, 28, 29, 40, 49, 102, 130, 136, 141, 145, 160, 171, 179, 206, 214, 276, 281, 295, 328

Stenger, W., 32

Steward(ship), 83, 345

Stewart, J. S., 166, 203

Stoicism, 56. 57, 60–62, 182, 296

Stone, 58, 62, 110, 182, 233, 247, 262, 266, 327

Strack–Billerbeck, 45, 59, 71, 72, 81, 82, 88, 95, 96, 107, 109, 110, 119, 130, 143, 176, 192, 195, 209, 210, 217, 220, 227, 234, 239, 242, 243, 248, 251, 259, 264, 272, 300, 309, 313, 332, 333, 357

Submission: church and state, 302–4, 306–9; general references, 114, 151, 152, 154, 216, 245, 249, 282

Substitution, 104, 152, 253

Suetonius, 9, 22, 309, 318

Suffer, 30, 39, 52, 96, 112, 129, 134, 136, 152, 180, 186, 194, 202, 209, 211–14, 215, 216, 220, 223, 225, 226, 234, 263, 289, 294, 297, 304, 336

Supernatural, 40, 160, 191, 203, 226, 231, 288, 309

Symparakalesthai, 36

Symphytos, 161

Scripture Index

Cicero, *Pro Flacco* **28.66**, 22

Juvenal **3.188–202**, 22

Martial **1.117**, 22; **7.95**, 22; **8.23**, 22; **12.57**, 22

Pliny the Elder, *Natural History* **3.5.66**, 22

Pliny the Younger, *Epistle*, **96**, 363

Suetonius, *Claudius* **25**, 309; **25.4**, 318; *Tiberius* **36**, 22

Tacitus, *Annals* **2.85.4**, 22; **13**, 23; **13.50**, 308; **15.44**, 362; **17.355**, 309; **18.1–10**, 309; **18.133**, 363; **18:135**, 363

GREEK AUTHORS

Aristotle, *Nicomachean Ethics* **4.8.10**, 73; **1117b.13**, 290

Dio Cassius, *History* **60.6**, 22; **68.7**, 22; **57.18.5a**, 22; **60.6**, 22

Hesiod, *Theogony* **136**, 353

Plato, *Republic* **10.613**, 217